ODEON - SOUTHEN

General Manager: A. G. Levenson | ON THE STAGE | Telephone:

Monday, 24th February at 6.30 & 8.45

ROBERT STIGWOOD ASSOCIATES LTD.

Presents **ALL STARS '64**

JOHN LEYTON — **MIKE SARNE**

SPECIAL GUEST STARS

The SWINGING BLUE JEANS

DON *FIREBALL* **SPENCER** | **BILLY BOYLE**

SPECIAL GUEST STARS

THE ROLLING STONES

MIKE BERRY *and the* **INNOCENTS** | **BILLIE DAVIS** *and the* LEROYS

... And the return of **JET HARRIS**

"MONEY" **BERN ELLIOTT** *and the* **FENMEN**

	CIRCLE	
8/6	6/-	4/6
	STALLS	
10/6	7/6	6/-

POSTAL BOOKING FORM

To.. **ALL STARS '64 SHOW**

Please forward ....seats at ... . for the 6.30/8.45 performance on Monday 24th February

I enclose stamped addressed envelope and P.O./cheque value.........................

NAME ....

ADDRESS ....

Hastings Printing Company, Portland Place, Hastings.   Phone 2450

TERRY RAWLINGS • KEITH BADMAN

WITH ANDREW NEILL

ACKNOWLEDGMENTS

For their kind assistance and patience (especially the latter):-

Tom Keylock - for ripping yarns and priceless pictures.

Reg Pippett - for the use of an extensive written archive and assistance beyond the call of duty.

Pat Bodell - for access to his collection of jaw-dropping memorabilia.

Dawn Malloy and Kathy Etchingham - for the use of irreplaceable momentos.

Doug McLauchlan, Ted Tuksa and Roz Fleetwood - for the use of their "fan's eye" shots.

Paul McEvoy and all at MC80.

Jaap Hoeksma - "Shattered!" Magazine, P.O Box 3723, London SE15 1HW. (The last word on the Rolling Stones!)

Mark Paytress, Andy Davis, John Reed and all at "Record Collector" Magazine.

David Wedgbury for his invaluable help.

Tony Gale and all at Pictorial Press.

Redfern's photo library.

Neil Sommerville (BBC), Bill Parker (Thames), Len Brown and John Piper (Granada TV), Jon Keeble (Polygram/ITC)

Indy Saha - J. Walter Thompson (Kellogg's Media) and Dick Fiddy, Veronica Taylor and Sue Bobbermein at the B.F.I.

Film and Audio Libraries:

U.K (and all regions) - BBC, ITN, Movietone, Pathé, Granada, LWT, BVL Enterprises.

USA/Europe - CBS TV, NBC TV, ABC TV, WEWS TV, Radio Bremen ("Beat Club"), French/Belgium media stations.

Harold Bronson (at Rhino).

Design and Layout - Terry Rawlings and Jonathan Graham.

Silk Screen and Design - Paul McEvoy and Terry Rawlings.

Special Personal Thanks to:-

Simon Benson, Henry Scott-Irvine, Tim Derbyshire, Ali Zayeri, Alan Collins, Dave Williams, Dave Godin, Jason Reilly, John Bloomfield, Steve Holmes, Jason Hobbs, Paul Bird, Robert Batchelor, Stephen Rouse, Kathleen (for her wonderful patience), Sheila (for her memories), Bill Graham, Eric Aernodt, Mark Waine, Paul Hallam, John Hellier, Lesley Benson, Art Wood, Pat Andrews, Beatrice Mathy, Dave Clark, Jude Carr, Dave Hogan, Adrian Croasdale, Adrian T'Vell ("Mangled Mind"), Miles, Paul Jones, Dermott O'Hara, John Baker "Social End Product", "Big" Dave, Dave "laugh", Mike Dalton, Mark Saunders, Lieselotte, Jenny Gaylor, Peter, Finella, Gary, Nicky, Micheal, Pauline, Anne Damone, Paul Waine and to anyone else we've missed, a big "Thank You" to all!!

CONTENTS

As Keith Richards is often fond of pointing out, there are people who "haven't known a world without the Rolling Stones", and he has a point. Some 34 years on, from their struggling (and starving) days as crusading Chicago Rhythm 'n' Blues zealots, to the mega-buck grossing stadium globetrotter's of today, the Rolling Stones have been so fully assimilated into popular culture, that it's hard to imagine a world without them. Having withstood pressures and disasters that would have destroyed lesser bands, the group show no signs of flagging until (in Keith's words), "they roll over dead"! Whether they really are the "World's Greatest Rock 'N' Roll Band" (or the "World's Oldest"!), it's a mantle they shrewdly neither confirm nor deny. For many, the group's formative and successful years, (back in that place they call "The Sixties"!), continue to hold the most interest and fascination, even for ex-bassist Bill Wyman, whose 1989 autobiography, "Stone Alone", concentrated almost solely on this period. It is also the focus of this book. Back in 1981, after the publication of the Beatles day-by-day chronology, "A Day In The Life" (Simon & Schuster), the idea of a similar book on the Rolling Stones first germinated in our minds. Over the ensuing fifteen years, facts and figures were gathered and information double-checked from various sources, including the plethora of Rolling Stones-related books that flooded the marketplace (many, unfortunately, riddled with inaccuracies). It is the fruit of these endeavours that is presented to you, the casual or discriminating Rolling Stones reader, together with photographs and memorabilia from those heady years (much previously unseen or unpublished). Although we justly feel it ranks as the most comprehensive (and accurate) listing to date, we're at great pains to stress nobody is infallible, and sometimes even we had to give in! The Rolling Stones, unlike their closest '60's rivals, The Beatles, cannot boast an intricately logged well of information, waiting to be tapped. This is particularly true in respect of the group's recording sessions. The Stones never felt contractually or geographically bound to record in just one locale. Important documentation relating to the group's early English sessions at long defunct studios, such as Kingsway in Holborn and Regent Sound, in Denmark Street, the more experimental sessions at Chess in Chicago and RCA in Hollywood, together with their nocturnal habits at Olympic Studios, in Barnes, remain frustratingly elusive; if in fact, they still exist. Aside from this one grey area, nothing was considered too trivial to be excluded. (Right to the eleventh hour, queries as to whether Brian Jones wore a Nehru jacket to some long-forgotten film premiere, were treated with the utmost urgency, to the disgruntlement of certain parties!) Corrections or additions, with documentary evidence, are openly encouraged and sought, for an addendum, to be included in a future reprint of this book. Please write to:- "G.T.B.T", P.O Box 290, Slough, Berks. SL3 7UL. Lastly, rather than being just a list of dates, it is hoped this tome reveals a sense of the personalities and outside influences behind an incredible work rate, that may surprise some and shame others!

Present throughout many of the events described (from 1965 onward), was well respected driver/minder, Tom Keylock (whose previous charges included Shirley Maclaine and Yul Brynner). He began his tenure with those " 'orrible Rolling Stones", as one of the group's drivers, before being promoted to the role of Tour Manager. Contained in the book's last chapter is an appendix of notes he made, illustrated with personal "snaps", while on the job, which have remained a well-kept secret until now. Keylock was in a position to witness first hand the Stones' personal triumphs and tragedies, Number One records and sell-out concerts, drug busts, inter-group power plays and relationships, immense wealth, births, marriages and ultimately, a tragic death. Highs and lows...Good Times And Bad... Enjoy!

TERRY RAWLINGS   **KEITH BADMAN**   **ANDREW NEILL**

Below: Co-author, Terry Rawlings, aged 6 (bottom right with mother Maureen and brother Mick) in 1968 at Redlands, Sussex. Tom Keylock lurks in the background, eerily predating this books collaboration by 29 years

Below: Tom Keylock, driving his beloved Austin Princess limo en-route to Scotland, as photographed by Brian Jones.

MICK JAGGER
Born: Michael Philip Jagger. July 26th, 1943.
Parents: Basil Fanshawe ("Joe") and Eva Mary.
Place: Dartford, Kent.
Schools Attended:-Maypole County Primary, Wentworth County Primary, Dartford Grammar School
Later studied at the London School of Economics (LSE) and worked briefly as a physical education
counsellor, games and sports instructor on a US service base in 1961.

KEITH RICHARDS
Born: December 18th, 1943.
Parents: Herbert William and Doris Maud Lydia.
Place: Dartford, Kent.
Schools Attended:-Westhills Infant School, Wentworth County Primary, Dartford Technical College
(expelled at the age of 16, due to truancy). Later did three years at Sidcup School of Art.

BRIAN JONES
Born: Lewis Brian Hopkin-Jones. February 28th, 1942.
Parents: Lewis Blount and Louisa Beatrice.
Place: Cheltenham, Gloucestershire.
Schools Attended:-Dean Close Public School and Cheltenham Grammar School.

BILL WYMAN
Born: William George Perks. October 24th, 1936.
Parents: William and Kathleen May.
Place: Lewisham, South London.
Schools Attended:-Oakfield Road Junior School, Beckenham and Penge Grammar School.

CHARLIE WATTS
Born: Charles Robert Watts. June 2nd, 1941.
Parents: Charles Richard and Lillian Charlotte.
Place: Islington, North London.
Schools Attended:-Tyler`s Croft Secondary Modern School, three years at the Harrow School of Art

MICK TAYLOR
Born: Michael Taylor. January 17th, 1948.
Parents: Lionel and Marilyn.
Place: Welwyn Garden City, Hertfordshire.
Schools Attended:-Onslow Secondary Modern School.

MICK JAGGER:

Met Keith in 1949, living on the same block, but neither exchanged words as such, until Mick sold him an ice-cream during a holiday job, outside Dartford Library. Both shared the same school (Wentworth County Primary) and would often walk home together, as they lived in nearby streets. (Mick in Denver Road, Keith in Chastillian Road). Mick lost touch with Keith when the Richards family moved to 6 Spielman Road, on the new Temple Hill Council Estate, situated on the other side of Dartford. A 16-year old "Mike" made his television debut on the educational "Seeing Sport" programme, scaling a rock face, at High Rocks, Tunbridge Wells, Kent. This "Rockclimbing" edition, presented by Peter Lloyd, was broadcast on the ATV/ITV network between 5 - 5:25 pm on Monday, September 14th 1959. Mick formed a skiffle group in 1958, but switched his allegiance to R & B, ordering rare and obscure discs from record companies in the States.

KEITH RICHARDS:

Sang as a school choirboy, including a christmas public recital before the Queen, at Westminster Abbey, when he was 13. During his time at Dartford Tech, he went through a brief Teddy Boy phase, wearing drainpipe trousers and pink socks. At 15, his mother bought him a £7 guitar, on which his grandfather, Gus Dupree, taught him his first chords. His first public performance was playing guitar with a Country & Western group made up of fellow art students. During the Christmas period of 1962, he worked four days as a postman.

BRIAN JONES:

His mother, Louisa, encouraged his early musical inclinations by giving him piano lessons from the age of six. Lewis (Brian) became the organist and a choirboy at the local parish church. At twelve, he joined the school orchestra learning clarinet. During his time at Cheltenham Grammar School (even though he was expelled for encouraging rebellion against the prefects), he passed nine 'O' levels, and two 'A' level GCE`s; way above average for that age (16). He talked of becoming a dentist. In 1958, his interest in music led him to become membership secretary of the local jazz "66 Club". During this time, he learnt guitar and played saxophone in many local groups such as Bill Nile's Delta Jazz Band and The Ramrods, who played at local dances and art school get-togethers. Lewis would often be remembered in Cheltenham for his promiscuity. In 1958, he fathered his first illegitimate child, the mother only being 14 years of age, which resulted in him being forced to leave school early. Instead of his expected future at university, he found himself an odd assortment of jobs, including training in the Borough Architect's office of Cheltenham Council. Later, after moving to London, he worked temporarily on the buses (as both conductor and driver), in a record shop, as an assistant in the electrical department of Whiteley's department store, and even finding employment as a coal man!

BILL WYMAN:

One of Bill's earliest memories was of being evacuated from London to escape the Blitz, during World War II. The eldest of five children, he sang in the local church choir and by the age of 14, was an accomplished player of the piano, organ and clarinet. After leaving school he joined the firm, City Tote, as a bookmaker's clerk, in London's West End, before doing two years national service in the Royal Air Force. Much of this had him stationed in West Germany, where he became friendly with a fellow serviceman, Lee Wyman, whose surname appealed to him. Returning to England, he worked at an engineering firm in Lewisham, before going on to become an "under manager". Bill met his first wife, Diane Cory, at the Royston Ballroom, Penge. They married on October 24th, 1959 (his 23rd birthday). A year later, he bought a £52 Burns guitar on hire purchase. His first group, The Cliftons, played semi-professionally at engagements in, and around the London area. In 1961, after witnessing a concert by novelty group, The Barron Knights. Bill made the decision to switch to bass, buying a secondhand £8 model. On March 29th, 1962, Diane gave birth to their first and only child, Stephen Paul.

CHARLIE WATTS:

At the age of 14, Charles was given his first drum kit; a Christmas present from his parents (costing £12). He practiced by playing along with jazz records. After leaving school, with several prizes in Art and English, he attended Harrow Art School before working for a Regent Street advertising agency, Charles Hobson and Gray. His first public performance was with the group Blues By Six, at the Troubadour Club, Chelsea.

MICK TAYLOR:

After leaving Onslow Secondary Modern School at 15, he worked for three months as a commercial artist engraver, then as a labourer in a paint factory. Taylor, a self-taught guitarist, joined The Gods, a local group in Welwyn Garden City. When Eric Clapton missed a gig with John Mayall's Bluesbreakers, Mick deputised for him, and later, when Peter Green left the Bluesbreakers, Taylor was asked to replace him. (He would stay with the group two years and appeared on the albums "Crusade", "Bare Wires" and "Blues From Laurel Canyon").

"Top Of The Pops" rehearsals, October 5th, 1966

NINETEEN SIXTY-SIXTY-SIXTY-SIXTY TWO

TUESDAY OCTOBER 25th 1960

At 7:32am, whilst waiting to take the train from Dartford Station to the L.S.E. (London School of Economics), 17-year old Mick Jagger encountered 16-year old Keith Richards on the platform, who was on his way to Sidcup Art College. Keith, recognising him from years earlier, was further drawn to the four or five albums (imported directly from Chess Records in Chicago) Mick was clutching under his arm, including Chuck Berry, Little Walter, and Muddy Waters. "You're into Chuck Berry, really? That's a coincidence."

Also by chance, the two had a mutual friend, Dick Taylor, whose group, Little Boy Blue and The Blue Boys (with Bob Beckwith and Allen Etherington), Mick was currently singing for. Following their chance meeting at the station, Keith was invited by Mick (on Thursday, October 27th during their by-now regular Dartford train rendezvous) to join the band. The early rehearsals, from Saturday, October 29th (with Keith playing a semi-solid Hofner cut away guitar), were held at the Jagger household, but, following noise complaints from neighbours, were moved shortly afterwards to Keith's, then again to Dick Taylor's house in Bexleyheath, for the same reason. A 31-minute tape, featuring an early rehearsal of Little Boy Blue and The Blue Boys survives from this period. The songs performed were:-"Around And Around" / "Little Queenie" / "Beautiful Delilah" (all Chuck Berry)/ "La Bamba" (trad. arrangement, based on Ritchie Valens' version)/ "On Your Way To School" / "I Ain't Got You" (Billy Boy Arnold)/ "You're Right, I'm Left, She's Gone" (Elvis Presley)/ "Down The Road Apiece" (Bobby Troup via Chuck Berry's version) / "Don't Want No Woman" (unknown) / "I Ain't Got You" (take 2) / "Johnny B. Goode" / "Little Queenie" (take 2) / "Beautiful Delilah" (take 2)(all Chuck Berry). (The tape is now in the possession of Mick Jagger, after being bought at Christie's auction house, on May 25th,1995.)

In 1960, Brian met the "Father of British Blues", Alexis Korner during a concert by Chris Barber's Jazz Band, in Brian's home town of Cheltenham. Already a drifter and father-of-two, Jones was bored and travelled to Scandinavia, where he earned money playing guitar and harmonica with local bands and then hitch-hiked around Europe. Upon returning to Cheltenham in 1961, he joined local group, The Ramrods, playing alto-saxophone. (Their short-lived local fame came to an abrupt end when their lead singer, choked to death on a chip, during his honeymoon!)

On 22nd October,1961, Jones became a father again, when Patricia Andrews (whom Brian had met at the Aztec Coffee Bar, during another spell of unemployment) gave birth to his third child, Mark Julian. After promising to marry her, Brian took up Korner's advice, moving to London with friend Dick Hattrell, where he rented a small flat in Weech Road, West Hampstead. Pat arrived with the baby, in Easter,1962. Soon after, Jones took a job in Whiteley's department store, but his abiding passion was to form his own band, which prompted him to place an advert in the trade paper, "Jazz News". Pianist Ian "Stu" Stewart replied to the advert, bringing with him singer Andy Wren and guitarist Geoff Bradford.

Early 1962

Brian accepted an offer to play guitar with Paul Jones' group, Thunder Odin's Big Secret, during their residency in Oxford.

SATURDAY MARCH 17th

The first British "blues band", Blues Incorporated, founded by Alexis Korner at the end of 1961, played the first of a Saturday night residency at the Ealing Jazz Club in West London (situated below the ABC bakery, opposite Ealing Broadway tube station). The line-up featured:- Alexis on guitar, Charles Watts on drums, Dave Stevens on piano, Dick Heckstall-Smith on tenor sax, Cyril Davies on harmonica and Andy Hoogenboom on bass. Amongst the audience that night were Little Boy Blue and The Blue Boys, arriving in the Pathfinder car belonging to Allen Etherington.

SUNDAY MARCH 18th

Inspired by what the group had witnessed at the Ealing Jazz Club, Little Boy Blue and The Blue Boys (Mick, Keith, Dick Taylor, Allen Etherington and Bob Beckwith) recorded a tape including "Reelin and Rockin" / "Bright Lights, Big City" and "Around And Around", to be sent to Alexis Korner. With it, a letter solicited his opinions and queried the possibility of some gigs.

TUESDAY MARCH 20th

Alexis received the tape and letter from Mick. Korner remembered his opinion of the tape as "absolutely terrible". (The tape was subsequently lost.)

SATURDAY MARCH 24th

Brian joined in on guitar with Blues Incorporated for the first time during their weekly residency at the Ealing Jazz Club (the first time that Brian played with Charlie Watts). The session began at 7:30pm, with admission being 5 shillings.

SATURDAY MARCH 31st

Brian joined in on harmonica (and occasional guitar) for a few numbers with Alexis Korner's Blues Incorporated (with Charlie) at the Ealing Jazz Club. The session began at 7:30pm, with the standard admission of 5 shillings. Jack Bruce replaced Andy Hoogenboom on bass.

APRIL

During the month, following on from the tape Mick had sent the previous month, Alexis Korner recorded Little Boy Blue and The Blue Boys in Dartford (with the same line-up-see March 18th entry). Songs taped that afternoon included:-

"La Bamba" (trad. arrangement, based on Ritchie Valens version)

"Around And Around" (Chuck Berry)

"Reelin' And Rockin' "(Chuck Berry)

"Bright Lights, Big City"(Jimmy Reed)

Alexis, in stark contrast to the first recordings he'd heard of the group (see March 18th & 20th entries), was now most impressed with Mick's vocals, and invited him to sing with Blues Incorporated, during their residency at the Marquee Club, in Oxford Street.

SATURDAY APRIL 7th

At the Ealing Jazz Club, the evening's entertainment consisted of "Blues Incorporated featuring Elmo Lewis" (Brian's pseudonym in view of his obsession with slide bluesman, Elmore James). Jones was, by now, a regular at the club, where he played Muddy Waters and Elmore James numbers with P.P. Pond (Paul Jones, later of Manfred Mann), pianist Ian "Stu" Stewart and guitarists Brian Knight and Geoff Bradford. During the evening, Alexis announced to the audience: "We got a guest to play some guitar. He comes from Cheltenham. All the way up from Cheltenham just to play for ya!" Brian arrived on stage to play slide guitar on Elmore James' "Dust My Broom", which greatly impressed Mick and Keith, who were in the audience. Later, the three chatted for the first time, discovering that they all shared the belief that they were the "only cats in the world who was doin' it!" During the session that night, Mick and Keith along with Dick Taylor joined up with Charlie Watts and Cyril Davies (a harp player, who doubled as a panel beater!), to perform "Around And Around" (the first time the pair played with Charlie). Before leaving, Brian invited Keith to come and listen to his group again, during their upcoming gigs at various Soho pubs and clubs.

APRIL (late in month)

A nervous Mick Jagger (on vocals) joined Blues Incorporated at the Marquee International Jazz Club, 165 Oxford Street. Their set included:-

"Bad Boy" (Eddie Taylor)

"Ride 'Em On Down" (Muddy Waters)

"Don't Stay Out All Night" (Billy Boy Arnold)

"I Put A Tiger In Your Tank" (Muddy Waters)

"Got My Mojo Working" (Muddy Waters)

Note: The latter song featured Paul Jones and Long John Baldry trading vocals with Mick.

Meanwhile, Mick, Keith and Brian, spent Mondays and Wednesdays, rehearsing their embryonic group at the Bricklayer's Arms in Broadwick Street, Soho. Geoff Bradford, a blues purist, was the first to leave after a personality clash with Keith, over the latter's Chuck Berry tendencies.

MAY (during month)

In an attempt to obtain more work, Mick, Keith and Brian joined the National Jazz Federation, while Mick sang with Blues Incorporated, during residencies at both the Marquee and the Ealing Jazz Club. (This continued until mid-June).

The fledgling group moved to the Wetherby Arms in Chelsea for rehearsals. (The venue being near to the Edith Grove flat that Mick, Keith and Brian would rent in August).

JUNE

Rehearsing, while Mick continued his studies at the L.S.E. and Keith, unemployed, spent his days fanatically practising guitar, by listening to records at Brian's flat in Beckenham. During this period, the name of "The Rollin' Stones" was suggested for the group by Brian, inspired by a line from the Muddy Waters song, "Mannish Boy" (not "Rollin' Stone Blues", as always thought). Ian Stewart strongly objected to it: "It sounded like the name of an Irish show band, or something that ought to be playing at the Savoy".

SATURDAY JULY 7th

Page 10 of the "Melody Maker" carried an advert for an up-coming gig on July 12th at the Marquee, featuring Long John Baldry's Blues Band and "The Rollin' Stones".

WEDNESDAY JULY 11th

"Jazz News" reported:- "Mick Jagger, R & B vocalist, is taking a rhythm and blues group into the Marquee tomorrow (Thursday), while Blues Inc. is doing it's Jazz Club gig. "I hope they don't think we're a rock 'n' roll outfit" says Mick.

THURSDAY JULY 12th

The BBC booked Blues Incorporated for a session on the Light Programme radio show "Jazz Club", but Mick did not participate. The band's explanation was that due to a BBC restriction which only allowed payment for 5 group members (Blues Incorporated featured 6), Mick kindly offered to step down. The BBC meanwhile, told another story, by saying (after listening to a set at the Marquee the previous week) "the BBC did not consider Mick a jazz vocalist". Ironically, things turned out for the better. Being that the radio show co-incided with Blues Incorporated's regular Thursday night gig at the Marquee, a replacement was required. Long John Baldry's Blues Band was substituted as the main act. For the intermission, Harold Pendleton, the manager of the Marquee, reluctantly gave a break to the group, who he knew had been rehearsing at the Bricklayer's Arms nearby.

The line-up featured the nucleus of Mick on vocals, Keith and Brian (billed as Elmo Lewis) on guitars, with Stu on piano, Dick Taylor on bass and future member of The Kinks, Mick Avory (billed as Mike Avery) on drums. Songs performed that night, at their debut (written on a page of Ian Stewart's pocket diary) included:-

"Kansas City" (Little Richard)
"Baby What's Wrong" (Jimmy Reed)
"Dust My Broom" (Elmore James)
"Down The Road Apiece" (Chuck Berry)
"Confessin' The Blues" (Chuck Berry)
"Hush Hush" (Jimmy Reed)
"Bright Lights, Big City" (Jimmy Reed)
"I Want To Love You" (Jimmy Reed)
"Ride' Em On Down" (Muddy Waters)
"Bad Boy" (Eddie Taylor)
"I Ain't Got You" (Billy Boy Arnold)
"Back In The USA" (Chuck Berry)
"Big Boss Man" (Jimmy Reed)
"Happy Home" (Elmore James)
"Blues Before Sunrise" (Elmore James)
"Kind Of Lonesome" (Jimmy Reed)
"Don't Stay Out All Night" (Billy Boy Arnold)
"Tell Me That You Love Me" (Jimmy Reed)
"Up All Night" (unknown)

For the booking, the group were paid a sum of £20. Alexis Korner would also book them for further performances at both the Ealing Jazz Club and again at the Marquee.

JULY - SEPTEMBER

Further residencies for the Stones at the Marquee International Jazz Club. Drummer Mick Avery (Avory) left the band. Keith: "He was terrible. Couldn't find the off-beat". He was replaced by Tony Chapman, of South London group, The Cliftons, who had answered an ad placed in "Melody Maker". The group were still keeping tabs on Charlie Watts, but due to his well paid, weekday job in a central London advertising agency, he was interested in doing only weekend gigs. Besides Blues Incorporated, Watts had played (without a fee) for The Don Byas Band, whilst in Denmark on business in late 1961 (returning to London in February 1962) and had sat in at sessions at the Troubadour Club, Chelsea.

Mick, Keith and Brian (the latter, now out of work, after losing his job at Whiteley's when caught with his hand in the till) were low in money.

In an attempt to save the little they had, the three moved into a two-room flat at 102 Edith Grove, Chelsea, at the rate of £16 per week. Food and money were supplied by Keith's and Stu's parents, while Keith's mother Doris regularly called round to collect (and deliver) their laundry. The group continued to play further gigs at the Ealing Jazz Club and the Marquee Jazz Club. During September, Dick Taylor left to continue his studies at the Royal College of Art.(He later formed The Pretty Things, with fellow Sidcup art student, Phil May).

FRIDAY OCTOBER 5th

"The Rollin' Stones" gigged at the Woodstock Hotel, North Cheam, Surrey.

SATURDAY OCTOBER 27th

The group went to the Curly Clayton Sound Studios in Highbury, North London, for what was to become their first recording session. During the afternoon period, the line-up of Mick (vocals), Keith (guitar), Brian (guitar), Stu (piano) and Tony Chapman (drums) recorded:-

"Soon Forgotten" (Muddy Waters)
"Close Together" (Jimmy Reed)
"You Can't Judge A Book (By Looking At The Cover)" (Bo Diddley)

The tape was subsequently sent to an unimpressed Neville Skrimshire at EMI Records. The sessions, produced by Curly Clayton, remain unreleased.

WEDNESDAY OCTOBER 31st

A letter from Brian Jones was published in "Jazz News". In the piece, Jones attempted to explain exactly what form of music the term "Rhythm & Blues" applied to. The letter was signed "Brian Jones, London SW10", with a footnote:- "(Brian Jones plays guitar with The Rollin' Stones)".

NOVEMBER

During the month, Blues Incorporated played two further shows at the Ealing Jazz Club, two concerts at the Flamingo Jazz Club and their first performance at the Red Lion Public House in Sutton, Surrey. Tony Chapman, due to his daytime job as a travelling salesman, continued to miss rehearsals and gigs with the Stones. A drummer named Steve Harris sat in on these occasions.

FRIDAY NOVEMBER 30th

Piccadilly Jazz Club (with Blues Incorporated and Dave Hunts R&B Band).

TUESDAY DECEMBER 4th

Ealing Jazz Club.

WEDNESDAY DECEMBER 5th

Tony Chapman introduced Bill Wyman to Ian Stewart, at the Red Lion, Sutton, who suggested he audition for the vacant bass role in "The Rollin' Stones".

FRIDAY DECEMBER 7th

Bill auditioned for the band, in the backroom of the Wetherby Arms Public House, Worlds End, Chelsea. He and Tony Chapman had arrived

Above: The embryonic Rollin' Stones perform at the Marquee, 1962

in Tony's father's car. Bill was introduced firstly to Mick by Ian Stewart, who was friendly, but Keith and Brian, drinking at the bar, were aloof. Things changed when Bill brought in his equipment. "We all turned up for rehearsals and in walks Bill with a huge speaker and a spare Vox AC30 amp, which was the biggest amp we'd seen in our lives!" Keith remembered. "That's spare" Bill told them, "you can put one of your guitars through there". (This, plus his generous rationing of food and cigarettes, were instrumental in him eventually getting the gig!)

WEDNESDAY DECEMBER 12th
Sidcup Art College Xmas dance.

SATURDAY DECEMBER 15th
St. Mary`s Parish Church Hall Youth Club, Hotheley Road, Richmond
(Bill Wyman on bass).

DECEMBER
The Red Lion, Sutton and South Oxey, North Watford.

FRIDAY DECEMBER 21st
Piccadilly Jazz Club.

SATURDAY DECEMBER 22nd
Ealing Jazz Club.

102, Edith Grove,
London S.W.10.

Dear Dave,

Herewith the tape on which you very kindly agreed to stick some Reed gear. I couldn't put the blank side on the outside, as I didn't have a spare reel. The one side has Bo Diddley on most of it, — it is an Extra Play tape, so you should easily be able to stick "Rockin' with Reed", "I Can't Hold Out" and flip (Elmore) and your Reed singles (only ones which aren't duplicated on LPs) on it.

Also, Dave, if you possibly could grab hold of one, could you tape "Just Jimmy", the latest Reed L.P. over Bo Diddley. But please don't record over Bo when it is "Just Jimmy".

This is really very good of you mate — if there's anything we can do for you — let us know.

Cheers,

Brian Jones.

P.S. Was it you who wrote to "Disc" some time ago about R+B and mentioning the Garages + us? We never saw it, but we were talking to Ricky Fenson and Carlo Little the other night and they told us about it. We can't think who can have wrote it. Incidentally, Carlo and Rick should be doing quite a few dates with us in the near future. We can do with a solid rockin' rhythm section. — Hope you had a good Christmas.

The original Rolling Stones six-man line-up, with Ian "Stu" Stewart (centre), April 1963

Introduction by
THE ROLLING STONES

mick

HI, THERE!
    We've got something that we've just got to say ! It's simply that we're knocked out to have this book all about ourselves—and to add that it's one of the biggest thrills we've had in what's certainly been a fantastic year.

People keep asking us what we think about the fans. You know the sort of thing—"Do you boys ever get fed up with being asked for autographs ? " or "Do you ever want to be left alone ? " Well, we'd like to tell you that we love the life and we love the fans. And if that sounds corny . . . well, it's none the less true.

But seriously, the music business is a great business to be in. Once or twice, we've been a bit frightened . . . like when about a thousand people rushed the rostrum at the Empire Pool, Wembley. Keith was upended and nearly lost his guitar. Charlie was pulled away from his drums. But it was the warmth, the enthusiasm, of everybody that got through to us. Even if we did think we were going to be torn to pieces, we still loved every minute of it—because it showed that we had a lot of people who were behind us all the way.

In this book, you'll read about how our show business career developed. You'll read about how some people in particular have helped us a great deal. You'll read the INSIDE story of all of us individually . . . though, of course, we'd have a lot more to say about each other if only the censor would let us !

Honestly, it's a wonderful feeling !

But it's rhythm 'n' blues that's responsible. Like on our LP—well, we enjoyed every minute of making it. It wasn't work to us . . . it was a session of sheer pleasure ! We knew the sort of sound we wanted to achieve and built up everything from there. Sometimes we don't like the records we make . . . and it does us a power of good to know that the fans DO dig !

keith

Sometimes it IS hard work. But we love it all. Hey . . . hang on, a minute ! The way we're talking now, it looks like we should be paying YOU for listening to us.

Seriously, all of us hope that you enjoy the book. We've enjoyed helping collaborate so that we've got the facts and the figures just right. Incidentally, we're also writing regularly in our own Monthly Magazine, where we try and answer your queries as fully as possible.

We've had an almost unbelievable year in which so much has happened we just can't even now let it all register properly. We're glad you've joined us in our efforts to get our sort of music across. And we're not kidding ourselves that any of it would have been possible without your support.

Sometimes we look into the future and we get scared all over again. But then we remember the wonderful fans we've found during the past year.

Best of luck to all of you . . .

charlie

brian

bill

NINETEEN SIXTY THREE

WEDNESDAY JANUARY 2nd

Brian wrote to BBC Radio, requesting an audition for the weekly show, "Jazz Club", saying he was the "leader" of the group that played authentic Chicago Rhythm and Blues music.

SATURDAY JANUARY 5th

Ealing Jazz Club. The group's repertoire from this period included:- "Talkin' Bout You" / "Bye Bye Johnny" / "Memphis Tennessee" / "Roll Over Beethoven" / "Jaguar And The Thunderbird" / "Our Little Rendezvous"(all Chuck Berry) / "Bo Diddley" / "Bring It To Jerome" / "Cops and Robbers" / "Hey Bo Diddley" / "Pretty Thing" / "Mona" / "Nursery Rhyme" / "Road Runner" / "Crawdad" / "Diddley Daddy"(all Bo Diddley), as well as covers of Elmore James, Muddy Waters, Jimmy Reed, Willie Dixon, John Lee Hooker and Slim Harpo. (An approximation of about 80 songs in total).

MONDAY JANUARY 7th

The group's debut at the Flamingo Jazz Club, Wardour Street, to an indifferent audience of jazz snobs.

WEDNESDAY JANUARY 9th

The Red Lion, Sutton, with The Presidents (featuring future record producer, Glyn Johns, on vocals). Charlie who was still not playing with anyone on a permanent basis, was asked by Mick, Keith and Brian to join the Stones. Charlie watched the group perform again and was knocked out. "You're great, man" he told Keith after their set, "but you need a fucking good drummer!" Keith: So we said "Charlie, we can't afford you, man, because Charlie used to love playing, but he always had to do it for economic reasons". Charlie later told Blues By Six (in Keith's words) to "fuck off, I'm going to play with these guys!" Later, questioning the wisdom of his decision, he asked Alexis Korner's wife, Bobbie, for advice. "Well, if you're not doing anything else, why don't you? What have you got to lose?!"

THURSDAY JANUARY 10th

The Marquee International Jazz Club, supporting Cyril Davies All-Star R&B Group.

FRIDAY JANUARY 11th

Ricky Tick Club, Star and Garter, Windsor. Tony Chapman was sacked after the gig. Keith (on Chapman's prowess as a skinsman): "Terrible. One of the worst. He would start a number and end up either three times as fast as he started it, or four times as slow!" A fuming Chapman approached his mate, Bill Wyman: "Well that's it! We can form a group of our own now!" Wyman, despite slowly adapting to the Stones music, cannily sensed this band could offer more than he'd experienced in The Cliftons. "No, I think I'm all right where I am!" Bill, according to Keith, "didn't want to play in those shitty rock bands anymore!"

MONDAY JANUARY 14th

The Flamingo Jazz Club (with Charlie Watts on drums).

THURSDAY JANUARY 17th

The Marquee International Jazz Club, supporting Cyril Davies All-Star R&B Group.

SATURDAY JANUARY 19th

Ealing Jazz Club.

MONDAY JANUARY 21st.

Flamingo Jazz Club. Brian received a BBC application form regarding a radio audition, in response to his letter dated January 2nd (see entry).

TUESDAY JANUARY 22nd

Brian wasted no time in filling out and sending the application back to the BBC. Under personnel, he listed: "Brian Jones (guitar/harmonica), Keith Richard (guitar), Mick Jagger (vocal/harmonica), Ian Stewart (piano), Bill Perks(bass) and Charles Watts (drums)". He described the group as a "Rhythm and Blues Band".

WEDNESDAY JANUARY 23rd

The Red Lion, Sutton.

THURSDAY JANUARY 24th

The Marquee International Jazz Club, supporting Cyril Davies All-Star R&B Group.

FRIDAY JANUARY 25th.

Ricky Tick Club, Star and Garter, Windsor. After receiving Brian's application, the BBC filed it under "Audition Warranted".

SATURDAY JANUARY 26th

Ealing Jazz Club.

MONDAY JANUARY 28th

Flamingo Jazz Club (supporting the Graham Bond Trio).

THURSDAY JANUARY 31st

Marquee International Jazz Club, supporting Cyril Davies All-Star R&B Group. After asking Davies for more money, they were fired on the spot.

FRIDAY FEBRUARY 1st

Ricky Tick Club, Star and Garter, Windsor.

SATURDAY FEBRUARY 2nd and TUESDAY FEBRUARY 5th

Two gigs, one each night, at the Ealing Jazz Club.

WEDNESDAY FEBRUARY 6th

Red Lion, Sutton.

THURSDAY FEBRUARY 7th

The group, sharing equal billing with Blues By Six (featuring Brian Knight), made their debut at the "Gala Opening Night" of the Haringey Jazz Club in the Manor House Pub, opposite Manor House tube station.

FRIDAY FEBRUARY 8th

Ricky Tick Club, Star and Garter, Windsor.

SATURDAY FEBRUARY 9th and TUESDAY FEBRUARY 12th

Ealing Jazz Club.

THURSDAY FEBRUARY 14th

Haringey Jazz Club, Manor House.

SATURDAY FEBRUARY 16th and TUESDAY FEBRUARY19th

The group performed a gig each night, at the Ealing Jazz Club.

WEDNESDAY FEBRUARY 20th

Red Lion, Sutton.

FRIDAY FEBRUARY 22nd

Ricky Tick Club, Star and Garter, Windsor.

SATURDAY FEBRUARY 23rd

Ealing Jazz Club.

SUNDAY FEBRUARY 24th

The group made their debut at the Station Hotel (directly opposite Richmond tube station), run by flamboyant Russian emigre' filmmaker, Giorgio Gomelsky. Brian had approached him at the Red Lion (on February 6th), with the idea of filling the Sunday afternoon slot, which Gomelsky had already promised to Dave Hunt's Blues Band. When Hunt's band failed to appear, Gomelsky rang Ian Stewart, telling him to inform the others of the booking, with the promise of £1- per man. They actually ended up receiving £7 -10s between them, after 150 people showed up. The building response was so great, that they landed themselves a regular Sunday afternoon residency. (By Easter, the club was being packed to it's 400 capacity, with queues forming for the doors to open, many being turned away).

THURSDAY FEBRUARY 28th

Haringey Jazz Club.

SATURDAY MARCH 2nd

Ealing Jazz Club.

SUNDAY MARCH 3rd

The group made their debut (and what was to become a six-month residency) at Ken Colyer's Club, "Studio 51" at 10/11 Great Newport Street (between 4 and 6:30pm), then travelled across London, to perform at the Station Hotel, Richmond.

WEDNESDAY MARCH 6th

Red Lion, Sutton.

THURSDAY MARCH 7th

Haringey Jazz Club.

FRIDAY MARCH 8th

Ricky Tick Club, Star and Garter, Windsor.

SATURDAY MARCH 9th

Wooden Bridge Hotel, Guildford.

SUNDAY MARCH 10th

Studio 51, followed by the Station Hotel.

MONDAY MARCH 11th

Recording sessions at IBC Studios, Portland Place, London.

These demo sessions were produced by Glyn Johns, and featured:-

"Diddley Daddy" (Bo Diddley)

"Road Runner"(Bo Diddley)

"Bright Lights, Big City"(Jimmy Reed)

"I Want To Be Loved" (first version)(Willie Dixon)

"Baby, What's Wrong"(Jimmy Reed)

Again, the tracks remained unreleased and IBC retained ownership of the tapes. They would later charge a fee of £106 (studio & tape costs) before relinquishing the tapes, leaving the group free to sign to Decca Records. (see May 6th entry).

THURSDAY MARCH 14th

Haringey Jazz Club.

FRIDAY MARCH 15th

Ricky Tick Club, Star and Garter, Windsor.

SUNDAY MARCH 17th

Studio 51, followed by the Station Hotel.

WEDNESDAY MARCH 20th

Red Lion, Sutton, Surrey.

FRIDAY MARCH 22nd

Ricky Tick Club, Star and Garter, Windsor.

SUNDAY MARCH 24th

Studio 51, followed by the Station Hotel.

FRIDAY MARCH 29th

Ricky Tick Club, Star and Garter, Windsor.

SATURDAY MARCH 30th

Wooden Bridge Hotel, Guildford.

SUNDAY MARCH 31st

Studio 51/Station Hotel.

WEDNESDAY APRIL 3rd

Red Lion, Sutton.

SUNDAY APRIL 7th

Studio 51/Station Hotel.

SATURDAY APRIL 13th

A gig at the Antelope Hotel, Poole, Dorset was cancelled. The first ever newspaper report on The Rolling Stones appeared in "The Richmond

And Twickenham Times". The reporter, Barry May, had asked Gomelsky the name of the club (one still hadn't been appointed), to which he instantaneously responded, "The Crawdaddy" (in honour of Bo Diddley).

SUNDAY APRIL 14th

Afternoon (4 to 6:30pm) gig at Studio 51, followed by the Crawdaddy. Amongst the audience that night were The Beatles, who had been nearby at Teddington Studios, taping an appearance for the weekly ABC TV show "Thank Your Lucky Stars". Gomelsky: "At this time, I was still in documentary films and I was talking with Brian Epstein, about an hour-long, Goon-type musical, I wanted to do on The Beatles. I met them when they were rehearsing and recording "Thank Your Lucky Stars" and I invited them to come to the Richmond Club and see the Stones. They came and caught the last 20 minutes. Following the gig, both groups went back to Edith Grove, where they chatted about music until 4am. Brian asked The Beatles for an autographed picture, which he hung on a wall. Before The Beatles departed, they invited the group to be their guests at the Royal Albert Hall "Top Pop Proms" concert the following week.

THURSDAY APRIL 18th

Accepting the Beatles invitation, Mick, Keith, Brian and Giorgio went to the Royal Albert Hall, for the "Top Pop Proms" concert. Following the performance, Brian and Giorgio helped carry the Beatles gear out, during which, hysterical fans mistook Brian for one of the "Fab Four" and mobbed him. "That's what I want!" Brian enthused to Gomelsky.

FRIDAY APRIL 19th

Wooden Bridge Hotel, Guildford.

SATURDAY APRIL 20th

The group went to R.G. Jones Studios, in Morden, Surrey, to record the soundtrack to a projected twenty minute Giorgio Gomelsky film of the R & B scene in London. The two tracks recorded were:-
"Pretty Thing" (Bo Diddley)
"It's Alright, Babe" (unknown)
The sessions were mixed by R.G. Jones Jr. Ironically, Gomelsky took the finished tracks to Decca, who turned them down. Both tracks, as well as the film itself (shot the next day), remain unreleased.

SUNDAY APRIL 21st

The group were filmed arriving, setting up and miming "Pretty Thing" at the Crawdaddy Club (without an audience) to the recordings made the previous day. ("It's Alright, Babe" was used as background music.) The seven minute documentary, originally supposed to be 20 minutes in length, was never completed, due to the Stones signing with Andrew Oldham (see May 3rd entry). Gomelsky also requested music journalist, Peter Jones (of "Record Mirror") to be present.

TUESDAY APRIL 23rd

The group attended the BBC Studios, in Delaware Road, Maida Vale, to record an audition for BBC Radio. The rhythm section of Cyril Davies All Stars, Ricky Brown (aka Ricky Fenstone) and Carlo Little (from Screaming Lord Sutch's band) deputised for Bill and Charlie, who were forced to decline appearing, for fear of losing their current jobs (engineer & graphic artist respectively). Messrs Brown and Little, often replaced the two at gigs, when either of them needed a visit to the bar or toilet! In order to attend the session, Ian Stewart took time off from his job at ICI Chemicals.

WEDNESDAY APRIL 24th

Eel Pie Island, Twickenham.

FRIDAY APRIL 26th

Ricky Tick Club, Star and Garter, Windsor.

SUNDAY APRIL 28th

Studio 51/Crawdaddy Club. 19-year old ex-Beatles publicist, Andrew "Loog" Oldham and 36-year old theatre agent, Eric Easton, were in the audience at the Crawdaddy, acting on a tip-off from music journalist, Peter Jones (see April 21st entry).

WEDNESDAY MAY 1st

Eel Pie Island, Twickenham. While "acting" manager, Giorgio Gomelsky, was in Switzerland arranging his father's funeral, (who had died the previous month), Andrew Oldham, along with business partner, Eric Easton, acted quickly, with a three-year management contract being signed between themselves and Brian, on behalf of the rest of the group,

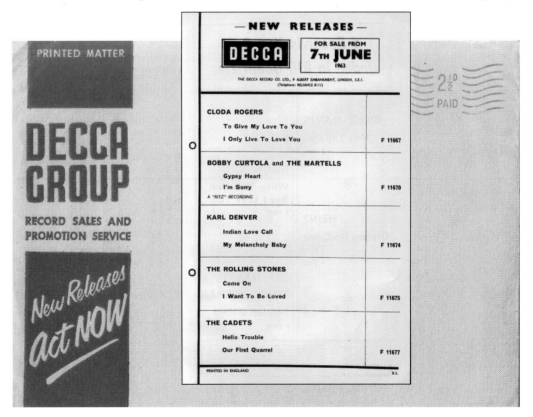

at their offices in Regent Street. Shortly afterward, Ian Stewart, who didn't fit into Oldham's grand image "master plan", was unceremoniously asked to step down, by Brian. With reluctance but graciousness, he accepted his position, being retained by the group as their road manager and session (and occasional stage) pianist. Eric Easton was also initially unsure as to Jagger's suitability as a singer (Brian apparently had Paul Jones on standby), but was eventually persuaded of his worth. Oldham pulled off another grand manoeuvre, by persuading Keith to drop the "s" from his surname. (His logic being that it would attract attention in it's similarity to U.K. pop singer, "Cliff Richard"!)

FRIDAY MAY 3rd

Ricky Tick Club, Windsor.

SATURDAY MAY 4th

Battersea Funfair Charity Concert, Battersea Park Pleasure Gardens, organised by the "News Of The World" newspaper.

SUNDAY MAY 5th

Studio 51/Crawdaddy Club.

MONDAY MAY 6th

Andrew Oldham secured a recording deal with A & R man, Dick Rowe, at Decca Records. After missing out on The Beatles (who had auditioned for the label on New Years Day, 1962), he was desperate not to miss out a second time, after the group were recommended to him by George Harrison (when both were judging a recent talent contest, in

Liverpool). Rowe caught the Stones, at the Crawdaddy (on the 5th) and was played the tapes recorded by the band at IBC Studios (see March 11th entry). Oldham and Easton formed "Impact Sound", a company solely managing the group's recordings, to lease to Decca.

TUESDAY MAY 7th

Gomelsky returned to London to discover the group had signed a contract with Oldham and Easton, from which he had been excluded.

WEDNESDAY MAY 8th

Eel Pie Island, Twickenham.

FRIDAY MAY 10th

After taking control of the group only a week earlier, Andrew Oldham arranged the group's first proper recording session, at Olympic Studios, Carton Street, near Marble Arch (featuring Oldham as producer and Roger Savage as sound engineer). Although Oldham gave himself credit as producer on the record, he had, in fact, never entered a studio before, let alone produced a recording! Legend has it, that when satisfied with the finished takes, Oldham went to leave the studio. "What about mixing it?!" Savage asked him. Oldham had no idea what he was talking about. When it was explained to him, Oldham retorted: "Look, I'm the producer and this is the first recording session that I've ever handled. I don't know a damn thing about recording. Or music for that matter!!" The session, which lasted from 10:00 am to 5:00 pm, yielded:-
"Come On" (Chuck Berry) (First aborted version)
"I Want To Be Loved" (Willie Dixon) (second released version).

SATURDAY MAY 11th

The group received their first article in a music paper, "Record Mirror". Gomelsky had called journalist Peter Jones in the second week of April, and suggested he came down to watch the Stones perform at the Crawdaddy on April 21st. Impressed, Jones returned on May 5th with fellow journalist Norman Jopling. In the article, Jopling wrote: "At the Station Hotel, Kew Road, the hip kids throw themselves about to the "jungle music" like they never did in the more restrained days of trad. And the combo they writhe and twist to, is called the Rolling Stones. The Rolling Stones are destined to be the biggest group in the R & B scene. Three months ago, only fifty people turned up to see the group. Now promoter Gomelsky has to close the doors at an early hour with over five hundred fans crowding the hall."

SUNDAY MAY 12th

Studio 51/ Crawdaddy Club.

MONDAY MAY 13th

David Dore (Assistant to BBC Light Entertainment Booking Manager) wrote to The Rolling Stones, regarding their radio audition on Tuesday, April 23rd (see entry):-"...after being played to our Production Panel with a view to General Broadcasting, the performance was not considered suitable for our purposes." (Legend has it that Mick's voice was considered "too black"!) The group were bitterly disappointed. Fans, angry at this rejection, started writing to the BBC, demanding another chance for the group.

WEDNESDAY MAY 15th

Eel Pie Island, Twickenham.

FRIDAY MAY 17th

Wooden Bridge Hotel, Guildford.

SUNDAY MAY 19th

Studio 51/Crawdaddy Club.

WEDNESDAY MAY 22nd

Eel Pie Island, Twickenham.

FRIDAY MAY 24th

Ricky Tick Club, Star and Garter, Windsor.

SUNDAY MAY 26th

Studio 51/Crawdaddy Club.

WEDNESDAY MAY 29th

Eel Pie Island, Twickenham.

FRIDAY MAY 31st

Ricky Tick Club, Star and Garter, Windsor.

SUNDAY JUNE 2nd

Studio 51/Crawdaddy Club.

MONDAY JUNE 3rd

Studio 51.

WEDNESDAY JUNE 5th

Eel Pie Island, Twickenham.

FRIDAY JUNE 7th

Wooden Bridge Hotel, Guildford. The groups first single "Come On" B/W "I Want To Be Loved", was released by Decca Records, who had paid for the A-side to be re-cut, at their own studios, in West Hampstead (Date unknown). The group were reluctant about releasing it, but bowed to pressure from Decca and from Oldham, who was furious that the group refused to plug the record, which they had little faith in, at their gigs.

SATURDAY JUNE 8th

Norman Jopling, in "Record Mirror":- "The disc doesn't sound like the Stones...It's good, catchy, punchy and commercial, but it's not the fanatical R&B sound that audiences wait hours to hear. It should make the charts in a smallish way."

SUNDAY JUNE 9th

Studio 51/Crawdaddy Club.

MONDAY JUNE 10th

Studio 51.

WEDNESDAY JUNE 12th

Eel Pie Island, Twickenham.

THURSDAY JUNE 13th

The group received their first mention in the national press with a full-page enthusiastic article by Pat Doncaster in the "Daily Mirror".

FRIDAY JUNE 14th

Ricky Tick Club, Star and Garter, Windsor.

SUNDAY JUNE 16th

Studio 51/Crawdaddy Club.

MONDAY JUNE 17th

Studio 51.

WEDNESDAY JUNE 19th

Eel Pie Island, Twickenham.

THURSDAY JUNE 20th

A gig at the Scene Club (formerly the Piccadilly Jazz Club) in Ham Yard, off Great Windmill Street, Soho.

FRIDAY JUNE 21st

Ricky Tick Club, Star and Garter, Windsor.

SATURDAY JUNE 22nd

Wooden Bridge Hotel, Guildford.

SUNDAY JUNE 23rd and MONDAY JUNE 24th

Studio 51.

WEDNESDAY JUNE 26th

Eel Pie Island, Twickenham.

THURSDAY JUNE 27th

Scene Club, Soho.

FRIDAY JUNE 28th

Ricky Tick Club, Star and Garter, Windsor. Meanwhile, David Dore (of the BBC), following a request from "Saturday Club" producer Bernie Andrews and numerous letters of protest from fans, made a phone call to Eric Easton, telling him the Stones were being re-considered for another radio audition.

SATURDAY JUNE 29th

On a rare night-off, the group visited the Mojo Club, Soho. The club was recently opened by their mentor, Alexis Korner.

SUNDAY JUNE 30th

Studio 51/Crawdaddy Club, the latter now moved to Richmond Athletic Ground for the rest of it's existence, as the brewery, after reading of the scenes at the Station Hotel, in the national press (see June 13th entry), closed it down.

MONDAY JULY 1st

Studio 51. David Dore informed Eric Easton, by letter, that The Rolling Stones had been placed on BBC Radio's waiting list for a future recording session.

TUESDAY JULY 3rd

Eel Pie Island, Twickenham.

THURSDAY JULY 4th

Scene Club, Soho. The Beatles, fresh from an Abbey Road recording session, watched the group.

FRIDAY JULY 5th

Ricky Tick Club, Star and Garter, Windsor.

SATURDAY JULY 6th

Kings Lynn. (cancelled)

SUNDAY JULY 7th

The Stones made their television debut when they were added to the bill of the Saturday night ABC/ITV pop show, "Lucky Stars Summer Spin" (a spin-off of the regular "Thank Your Lucky Stars" show). Co-manager, Eric Easton, was able to arrange this invaluable exposure, as he represented main presenter, D.J Brian Matthew. The show was pre-taped at the Alpha Television Studios, Aston, Birmingham. After nervous rehearsals in front of the cameras, the group mimed "Come On", dressed in matching houndstooth jackets, with black velvet collars, which Oldham insisted they wear, to smarten themselves up, ala' The Beatles. A horrified T.V. executive onlooker apparently advised Oldham to "get rid of the vile looking singer, with the tyre-tread lips!" The Stones performance, (for which they were paid £143.17s.6d) along with guests Helen Shapiro, Jimmy Henney, Patsy Ann Noble, Johnny Cymbal, Mickie Most, The Cadets, Gordon Mills and The Viscounts (also added to the bill) was included in the show, hosted by DJ Pete Murray,

transmitted July 13th, between 6:05 - 6:44pm across the ITV network.

MONDAY JULY 8th

Studio 51.

WEDNESDAY JULY 10th

Eel Pie Island, Twickenham.

THURSDAY JULY 11th

Scene Club, Soho.

FRIDAY JULY 12th

Twickenham Design College dance, Eel Pie Island, Twickenham.

SATURDAY JULY 13th

The group travelled to Middlesborough, for a booking at the Alcove Club (one of their first gigs outside the London area), supporting The Hollies.

SUNDAY JULY 14th

Studio 51/Crawdaddy Club.

MONDAY JULY 15th

Studio 51.

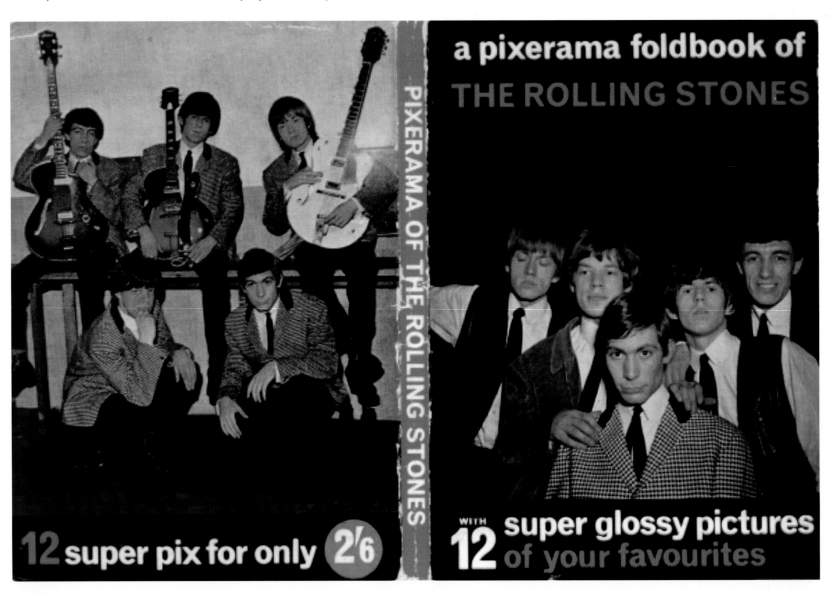

Have VOX...will travel

WEDNESDAY JULY 17th
Eel Pie Island, Twickenham.

FRIDAY JULY 19th
Morning photo sessions at Phillip Gotlop's and Dezo Hoffman's studios. The group attended a private deb "coming out" party, thrown by Lord and Lady Killerman for their daughter Roxanna, at St. Clements Hall, Hastings, but were unable to play, because Brian fell ill on the journey. "Disc" reported the group would be recording tracks for an L.P. including "Fortune Teller" and "What Kind Of Girl", to be completed by the end of the month.

SATURDAY JULY 20th
The Corn Exchange, Wisbech, Cambridgeshire.

SUNDAY JULY 21st
Studio 51/Crawdaddy Club.

MONDAY JULY 22nd
Studio 51.

WEDNESDAY JULY 24th
Eel Pie Island, Twickenham.

FRIDAY JULY 26th
Ricky Tick Club, Star and Garter, Windsor.

SATURDAY JULY 27th
California Ballroom, Dunstable.

SUNDAY JULY 28th
Studio 51/Crawdaddy Club.

MONDAY JULY 29th
Studio 51.

TUESDAY JULY 30th
Ricky Tick Club, Windsor. The venue had been moved half a mile to the

Thames Hotel, adjacent to the river.

WEDNESDAY JULY 31st
Eel Pie Island, Twickenham.

FRIDAY AUGUST 2nd
Wooden Bridge Hotel, Guildford. The NME reported that: "new chart entrants The Rolling Stones may be featured in a documentary pop musical, to be produced independently by Georgio Gomelsky, later this month, or early in September, with other guest stars."

SATURDAY AUGUST 3rd
St. Leonards Hall, Horsham, Kent.

SUNDAY AUGUST 4th
Studio 51/Crawdaddy Club.

MONDAY AUGUST 5th
Botwell House, Hayes, Middlesex.

TUESDAY AUGUST 6th
Ricky Tick Club, Thames Hotel, Windsor.

WEDNESDAY AUGUST 7th
Eel Pie Island, Twickenham.

FRIDAY AUGUST 9th
California Ballroom, Dunstable. During the morning, the group were photographed at Jenning's Music factory, Dartford, endorsing Vox amplifiers, in exchange for free equipment (an arrangement made by Eric Easton).

SATURDAY AUGUST 10th
The group travelled to Birmingham, for concerts at both the Plaza Theatre's in Handsworth and Oldhill.

SUNDAY AUGUST 11th
The group performed their regular afternoon session at Studio 51, then travelled to Richmond for an appearance at the 3rd National Jazz Festival, held in the grounds of the Richmond Athletic Association, between 2 and 11:30pm. Also on the bill were:- Acker Bilk, Terry

Lightfoot, Cyril Davies, Freddy Randall, Blue Notes, Long John Baldry and The Velvettes. Among the 1,500 crowd was 16-year old, Ronnie Wood, of The Birds.

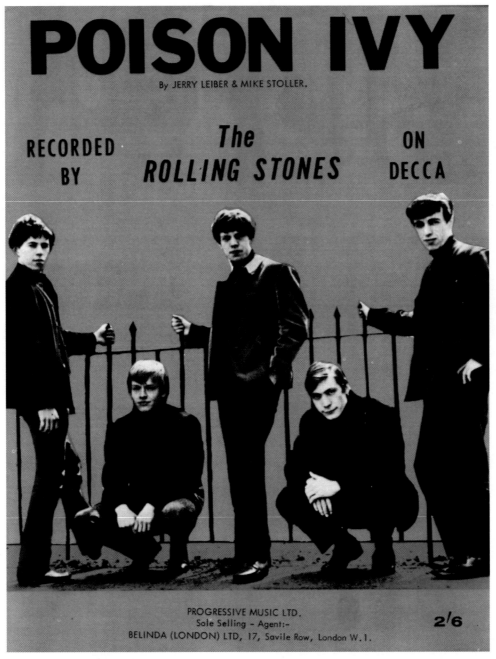

MONDAY AUGUST 12th
Studio 51.

TUESDAY AUGUST 13th
Town Hall, High Wycombe, Bucks.

WEDNESDAY AUGUST 14th
Eel Pie Island, Twickenham.

THURSDAY AUGUST 15th
Dreamland Ballroom, Margate, Kent (supported by The Barron Knights featuring Duke D'mond).

FRIDAY AUGUST 16th
Winter Gardens, Banbury, Oxfordshire.

SATURDAY AUGUST 17th
Memorial Hall, Norwich.

SUNDAY AUGUST 18th
Studio 51/Crawdaddy Club. The group visited Decca's London Studios, at West Hampstead, with staff producer Michael Barclay, to attempt to record their second single. It was a wasted session as the group disliked Barclay (and vice-versa). The morning session featured:- "Poison Ivy" (The Coasters) (two versions), "Fortune Teller" (Benny Spellman) Decca, although unimpressed with the results, were, nevertheless, eager for a quick follow-up to "Come On" (which had reached No.26 on the N.M.E chart). A catalogue number was allocated (F56117) and copies were pressed at Decca's factory, before Oldham persuaded them to withdraw it in favour of a better alternative (see Sept.10th entry).

MONDAY AUGUST 19th
Atlanta Ballroom, Woking. Chelsea Embankment morning photo session with Pictorial Press photographer, Tony Gale, on board H.M.S "Discovery".

TUESDAY AUGUST 20th

Ricky Tick Club, Thames Hotel, Windsor.

WEDNESDAY AUGUST 21st

Eel Pie Island, Twickenham.

FRIDAY AUGUST 23rd

Worplesdon Village Hall, Guildford. (cancelled). The group made their first ever appearance on Associated-Rediffusion's weekly T.V. pop show "Ready Steady Go!" miming "Come On". The show hosted by Keith Fordyce, included Jet Harris & Tony Meehan and Little Peggy Marsh and was transmitted between 7:00 - 7:29 pm, over the I.T.V network.

SATURDAY AUGUST 24th

Il Rondo Ballroom, Leicester.

SUNDAY AUGUST 25th

Studio 51/Crawdaddy Club.

MONDAY AUGUST 26th

Studio 51.

TUESDAY AUGUST 27th

The group performed as usual at the Ricky Tick, Thames Hotel, Windsor, but Brian missed the gig due to collapsing from nervous exhaustion. Stu sat in on piano.

WEDNESDAY AUGUST 28th

Eel Pie Island, Twickenham (without Brian. Stu, again, on piano).

THURSDAY AUGUST 29th

The group made their first appearance on Granada ITV's regional magazine programme "Scene At 6:30". Recorded in the afternoon in Studio 4, at the Granada Television Studios, Manchester, the group mimed "Come On", featured in the programme, broadcast later that night (in the Granada region only) between 6:30-6:59 pm.

FRIDAY AUGUST 30th

The group stayed in Manchester, to perform at the Oasis Club. An appearance at the New Brighton Tower, in Liverpool ("Southern Sounds '63", with Brian Poole and The Tremeloes) was cancelled after serious fire damage to the venue.

SATURDAY AUGUST 31st

The group travelled to Wales, for a gig at the Lido Ballroom, Prestatyn.

SUNDAY SEPTEMBER 1st

Studio 51/Crawdaddy Club.

MONDAY SEPTEMBER 2nd

Studio 51.

TUESDAY SEPTEMBER 3rd

Ricky Tick Club, Thames Hotel, Windsor.

WEDNESDAY SEPTEMBER 4th

Eel Pie Island, Twickenham. An ill Brian didn't appear after the interval.

THURSDAY SEPTEMBER 5th

Strand Palace Theatre, Walmer (with The Paramounts). Again, Brian was missing, not returning to the group until September 8th.

FRIDAY SEPTEMBER 6th

Grand Hotel Ballroom, Lowestoft.

SATURDAY SEPTEMBER 7th

A non-stop journey from Lowestoft to Wales, for a gig at the Kings Hall, Aberystwyth.

SUNDAY SEPTEMBER 8th

The group drove overnight from Aberstwyth to the Alpha Television Studios in Birmingham, to make another appearance on ABC TVs "Lucky Stars Summer Spin" (see July 7th entry). Brian was driven up from London, by Andrew Oldham. The show, also featuring Brian Poole and The Tremeloes, The Searchers, Craig Douglas, Patsy Ann Noble, Gregory Phillips and Heinz, was hosted by D.J's Pete Murray and Tony Hall and was broadcast September 14th, between 6:05 - 6:44 pm, over the ITV network.

Below: Tour programme for the Stones first English package tour which started September 29th

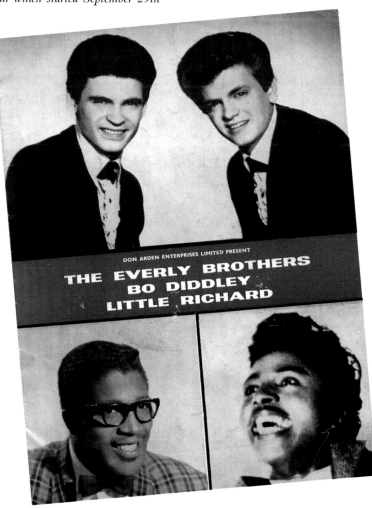

DON ARDEN ENTERPRISES LIMITED PRESENT

THE EVERLY BROTHERS
BO DIDDLEY
LITTLE RICHARD

MONDAY SEPTEMBER 9th

Studio 51.

TUESDAY SEPTEMBER 10th

Ricky Tick Club, Thames Hotel, Windsor. Andrew Oldham met John Lennon and Paul McCartney, in Jermyn Street, Mayfair. The pair were travelling in a cab from the Variety Club Awards, at the Savoy Hotel. Oldham told them of his problem finding a suitable follow-up to "Come On", for the Stones. John and Paul told him they may have "just the song". Oldham took them back to Studio 51, where the Stones were rehearsing. Lennon and McCartney borrowed their guitars, giving an impromptu rendition of "I Wanna Be Your Man" to the group, to which they gave their approval. The songsmiths then went off and huddled in a corner to finish writing it, which greatly impressed Mick and Keith, in particular.

WEDNESDAY SEPTEMBER 11th

Eel Pie Island, Twickenham.

THURSDAY SEPTEMBER 12th

The Cellar Club, Kingston-Upon-Thames.

FRIDAY SEPTEMBER 13th

California Ballroom, Dunstable.

SATURDAY SEPTEMBER 14th

The group returned to Birmingham, for two show's at the Plaza Theatre in Oldhill and the Ritz Ballroom in Kingsheath.

SUNDAY SEPTEMBER 15th

The Stones (who opened the show) performed on the "Great Pop Prom" at The Royal Albert Hall, organised by "Valentine", (a teen girl's magazine), in aid of the Printers Pension Corporation. Also on the bill were Susan Maughan, The Brook Brothers, Kenny Lynch, Shane Fenton

(later known as Alvin Stardust) and The Fentones, Clinton Ford, The Vernon Girls, The Lorne Gibson Trio, Arthur Greenslade and The Gee Men, The Viscounts and The Beatles (who closed the show). Compere:- DJ Alan Freeman. The usual evening gig at the Crawdaddy followed.

MONDAY SEPTEMBER 16th

Studio 51.

TUESDAY SEPTEMBER 17th

British Legion Hall, Harrow-on-the-Hill.

WEDNESDAY SEPTEMBER 18th

Eel Pie Island, Twickenham.

THURSDAY SEPTEMBER 19th

St. John's Hall, Watford.

FRIDAY SEPTEMBER 20th

Savoy Ballroom, Southsea.

SATURDAY SEPTEMBER 21st

Corn Exchange, Peterborough.

SUNDAY SEPTEMBER 22nd

Studio 51/Crawdaddy Club (end of the group's residency).

MONDAY SEPTEMBER 23rd

Studio 51 (the end of the group's residency). The Stones were invited back to the BBC studios at Delaware Road, Maida Vale, to record their first radio session. Proposed plans for a further audition were dropped by "Saturday Club" producer Bernie Andrews, an early admirer of the group, who made a fait accompli', by recording the group for a future edition of his BBC Light Programme show. The performance was first scheduled to appear in the edition broadcast on October 5th, but after a further bout of "cold feet" by BBC executives, it didn't see the light of day until October 26th (between 10:00-12:00 am, hosted by Brian Matthew). The group performed:-
"Talking About You" (sic)/ "Money" / "Come On" / "Memphis Tennessee" and "Roll Over Beethoven".
(Contrary to popular belief, a sixth song, Chuck Berry's "Beautiful Delilah" was not recorded.) The broadcast also featured The Caravelles, Eden Kane and resident house-band Arthur Greenslade and the Gee Men. Such was the impact the group had on Andrews and Jimmy Grant (a fellow joint "Saturday Club" producer) that Bill, Brian and Charlie were asked to remain, to back-up visiting R&B legend, Bo Diddley, later that afternoon in a separate BBC session. (Brian, inexplicably, failed to appear). The session produced the following:-
"Bo Diddley" / "Road Runner" / "Pretty Thing" and "Hey Bo Diddley".
(These were well known to Bill and Charlie, regularly forming a part of the group's repertoire - see Jan 5th entry). The session also featured in "Saturday Club", hosted by Brian Matthew, transmitted October 5th, between 10:00-12:00 am.

TUESDAY SEPTEMBER 24th

Ricky Tick Club, Thames Hotel, Windsor. (End of the group's residency.)

WEDNESDAY SEPTEMBER 25th

Eel Pie Island, Twickenham. (End of the group's residency.)

FRIDAY SEPTEMBER 27th

Floral Hall, Morecambe. The music press announced details of an impending Stones/Gerry & The Pacemakers tour for promoter John Smith, which would begin on December 5th.

SATURDAY SEPTEMBER 28th

Assembly Hall, Walthamstow.

SUNDAY SEPTEMBER 29th

The Stones began their first 36 date, six-week British tour, for promoter Don Arden, supporting The Everly Brothers, Bo Diddley, (with sister "The Duchess" & maraccas player, Jerome Green), Julie Grant, Mickie Most and The Flintstones. Compere: Bob Bain. The group were paid £21.5s per show. The first night opened with two performances (6:00 & 8:30pm) at the New Victoria Theatre, London. During the tour, the group's set was as follows:-
"Come On" / "Route 66" / "Poison Ivy" / "Fortune Teller" and "Money". As a mark of respect, the group dropped all Bo Diddley numbers from their act, later adding "I Wanna Be Your Man" to test audience reaction.

MONDAY SEPTEMBER 30th

Ballroom, Cambridge.

TUESDAY OCTOBER 1st

Odeon, Streatham. (Two shows.) (7:00 & 9:10pm.)

WEDNESDAY OCTOBER 2nd

Regal Theatre, Edmonton. (Two shows.) (6:45 & 9.00pm.) Due to regular compere, Bob Bain getting caught in traffic, Mickie Most became MC for the night.

THURSDAY OCTOBER 3rd

Odeon, Southend. (Two shows.) (6:45 & 9:00pm.) An altercation backstage, minutes before showtime, between Keith and Brian over a chicken dinner, resulted in a black eye for Brian. Ringo Starr caught the late show.

FRIDAY OCTOBER 4th

Odeon, Guildford. (Two shows.) (6:45 & 9:00pm.) The group spent their spare time backstage, jamming and getting "pointers" from Bo Diddley and The Everly's.

SATURDAY OCTOBER 5th

Gaumont Theatre, Watford. (Two shows.) (6:15 & 8:45pm.) To liven up ticket sales, Little Richard was flown in from America to join the bill.

SUNDAY OCTOBER 6th

The tour reached Wales, with two shows (5:45 & 8:00pm) at the Capitol Theatre, Cardiff. Dick Fontaine, a Granada TV producer and Gus Coral, a freelance photographer, took a series of informal stills to get an idea on how to present the group for a future television show. (Fontaine had been the first director to film The Beatles, at Liverpool's Cavern Club, in August 1962). Returning to London, the group's van broke down, at 2am, in Abergavenny. Luckily, an initially suspicious policeman, who happened to be passing, helped them push it to a nearby farm for repairs.

MONDAY OCTOBER 7th

A day-off from the tour. The group went to Kingsway Studios, Holborn, with Eric Easton producing. (Andrew Oldham was in France). During the five hour session (running from 10am to 3pm), the group recorded:-
"I Wanna Be Your Man" (as donated by Lennon & McCartney)
"Stoned" (a Booker T-type instrumental, with Stu on piano, credited to Nanker-Phelge, a pseudonym used for group compositions. A "Nanker" was a particularly grotesque face the band liked to pull, while Jimmy "Phelge" was a printer, with dubious personal habits, who had shared the squalor at 102 Edith Grove).

TUESDAY OCTOBER 8th

Two shows (7:00 & 9:10pm) at the Odeon Theatre, in Brian's home town of Cheltenham.

WEDNESDAY OCTOBER 9th

Gaumont Theatre, Worcester. (Two shows.) (6:45 & 9:00pm.)

THURSDAY OCTOBER 10th

Gaumont Theatre, Wolverhampton. (Two shows.) (6:30 & 8:40pm.)

FRIDAY OCTOBER 11th

Gaumont Theatre, Derby. (Two shows.) (6:30 & 8:45pm.)

SATURDAY OCTOBER 12th

Gaumont Theatre, Doncaster. (Two shows.) (6:15 & 8:30pm.)

SUNDAY OCTOBER 13th

Odeon Theatre, Liverpool. (Two shows.) (5:40 & 8:00pm.)

TUESDAY OCTOBER 15th

Majestic Ballroom, Kingston-upon-Hull (with Johnny Kidd and the Pirates).

WEDNESDAY OCTOBER 16th

Odeon Theatre, Manchester. (Two shows.) (6:20 & 8:45pm.) After the shows, the group rushed to Liverpool, to see The Big Three record their live E.P "At The Cavern". Mick: "We were really chuffed... we only went there to relax, not perform but as soon as the word got around that we were there, we were swamped with requests for autographs " (They also found time to demonstrate the "Nod", a bizarre dance that had originated on "Ready Steady Go!", to the Northerners.)

THURSDAY OCTOBER 17th

Odeon Theatre, Glasgow.(Two shows.) (6:45 & 9:00pm.)

FRIDAY OCTOBER 18th

Odeon Theatre, Newcastle. (Two shows.) (7:00 & 9:30pm.)The group went to the Club A-Go Go after the shows, watching and befriending The Alan Price Combo (who later renamed themselves The Animals).

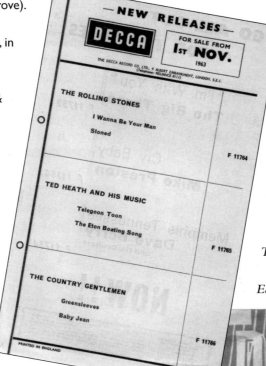

SATURDAY OCTOBER 19th

Gaumont Theatre, Bradford. (Two shows.) (6:20 & 8:45pm.)

SUNDAY OCTOBER 20th

Gaumont Theatre, Hanley. (Two shows.) (6:15 & 8:30pm.)

TUESDAY OCTOBER 22nd

Gaumont Theatre, Sheffield. (Two shows.) (6:30 & 8:45pm.)

WEDNESDAY OCTOBER 23rd

Odeon Theatre, Nottingham. (Two shows.) (6:15 & 8:30pm.)

THURSDAY OCTOBER 24th

Odeon Theatre, Birmingham. (Two shows.) (6:45 & 9:00pm.)

FRIDAY OCTOBER 25th

Gaumont Theatre, Taunton. (Two shows.) (7:00 & 9:20pm.)

SATURDAY OCTOBER 26th

Gaumont Theatre, Bournemouth. (Two shows.) (6:15 & 8:30pm.)

SUNDAY OCTOBER 27th

Gaumont, Salisbury. (Two shows.) (6:15 & 8:30pm).

TUESDAY OCTOBER 29th

Gaumont, Southampton.(Two shows.) (7:00 & 9:30pm.)

The Stones second (Lennon/McCartney-penned) single, "I Wanna Be Your Man".
Early copies had the B-side misspelt as "Stones"(Below)

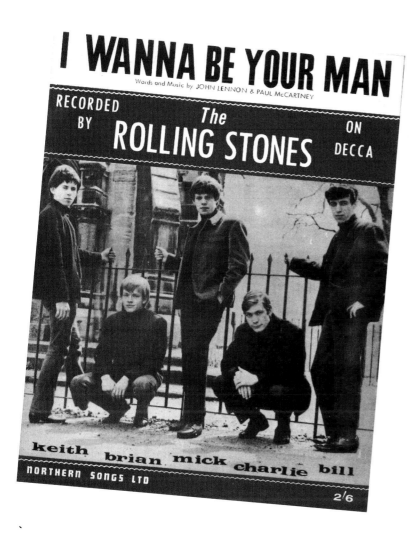

WEDNESDAY OCTOBER 30th

Odeon Theatre, St. Albans. (Two shows.) (6:45 & 9:00pm.)

THURSDAY OCTOBER 31st

Odeon Theatre, Lewisham. (Two shows.) (6:30 & 8:45pm.)

FRIDAY NOVEMBER 1st

The group's second single "I Wanna Be Your Man" B/W "Stoned" was released, entering the "Disc" chart at No.30, five days later, while that evening, the group performed two shows (6:45 & 9:00pm) at the Odeon Theatre, Rochester.

SATURDAY NOVEMBER 2nd

Gaumont Theatre, Ipswich. (Two shows.) (6:45 & 8:55pm.)

SUNDAY NOVEMBER 3rd

The tour ended with two shows (6:30 & 8:45pm) at London's Hammersmith Odeon. The group were annoyed at their fans disrespect to The Everly Brothers when, during their set, the Everlys were pelted with paper cups and had "We Want The Stones" chanted at them! A farewell backstage party continued at Mick and Keith's flat, at 33 Mapesbury Road, Hampstead (which they shared with Andrew Oldham).

MONDAY NOVEMBER 4th

Preston's Top Rank Ballroom.

TUESDAY NOVEMBER 5th

Liverpool, for a 45 minute set at the Cavern Club. Such was the demand to see the group, several hundred had to be turned away at the door. The group later followed club tradition by signing the cellar wall. It was here that the rest of the group learned to their dismay, of Brian's insistence on taking an extra commission for himself on bookings, as unacknowledged "leader" of the group. Meanwhile the press reported that the group had received a major film offer, with each playing dramatic roles as "dead end kids". Though still subject to their approval, the filming was scheduled to start next summer. Also, the group had turned down offers for a resident summer concert season.

WEDNESDAY NOVEMBER 6th

Queen's Hall, Leeds.

FRIDAY NOVEMBER 8th

Club A Go-Go, Newcastle-Upon-Tyne. The NME carried a review of the new single, by Derek Johnson, describing it as:- "...not one of Lennon and McCartney's best numbers, but there's an insidious and infectious beat which is ideal for The Rolling Stones".

SATURDAY NOVEMBER 9th

Club A Go-Go, Whitley Bay.

SUNDAY NOVEMBER 10th

Town Hall, Crewe.

MONDAY NOVEMBER 11th

Pavilion Ballroom, Bath.

TUESDAY NOVEMBER 12th

Town Hall, High Wycombe.

WEDNESDAY NOVEMBER 13th

"The Rhythm 'N' Blues Show", City Hall, Sheffield, promoted by the Stringfellow Brothers, with The Big Three, Wayne Fontana and the Mindbenders, The Sheffields, Johnny Tempest and the Cadillacs, Vince Arnold and the Avengers, The Vantennas, The Four Plus One and Karen Young.

THURSDAY NOVEMBER 14th

Seven hour session at Kingsway Studios, with Eric Easton producing. The tracks recorded would form their first E.P (see Jan.17th, 1964 entry):-

"Poison Ivy" (third version) (The Coasters)

"Money" (Barrett Strong)

"You Better Move On" (Arthur Alexander)

"Bye Bye Johnny" (Chuck Berry).

FRIDAY NOVEMBER 15th

Co-Op Ballroom, Nuneaton. (Two shows.)

SATURDAY NOVEMBER 16th

Matrix Ballroom, Coventry.

SUNDAY NOVEMBER 17th

The group recorded their third appearance on "Thank Your Lucky Stars" at the Alpha Television Studios, Birmingham. Following afternoon rehearsals, the group mimed to "I Wanna Be Your Man" in a show hosted by Brian Matthew, also featuring Cliff Richard and The Shadows, Bobby Rydell, Dave Curtiss and The Tremors, Ronnie Carroll, The Breakaways, Chris Sandford (of T.V. soap opera, "Coronation Street") and Gene Pitney. It was transmitted between 5:50 - 6:34 pm, on November 23rd, across the ITV network.

TUESDAY NOVEMBER 19th

Gaumont State Ballroom, Kilburn.

WEDNESDAY NOVEMBER 20th - SATURDAY DECEMBER 7th

The group joined Andrew Oldham at Regent Sound Studios in Denmark Street to record demos of early Jagger-Richard songs, intended for other artists, as well as playing with the Andrew Loog Oldham Orchestra (returning to the studio on odd occasions including December 7th). Working with sound engineer Bill Farley and musical directors Mike Leander and Chris Blackwell, these recordings included:-

"My Only Girl" (later to become "That Girl Belongs To Yesterday", a demo for Gene Pitney, after he had expressed interest in recording it, backstage at "Thank Your Lucky Stars", on the 17th.) "It Should Be You" / "Will You Be My Lover Tonight" (demos for George Bean)

"Shang-a-Doo-Lang" (demo for Adrienne Poster)

"I`ll Hold Your Hand"

"No One Knows"

"With A Song In My Heart"

"Funky and Fleopatra" (Charlie assisted with musical arranging!)

"365 Rolling Stones (One For Every Day Of The Year)" (Charlie -drums)

"Oh I Do Like To See Me On The B Side" (Charlie - drums, Keith - guitar and Bill - bass).

In the evening, the group played at the Chiswick Polytechnic Dance at The Crawdaddy, Richmond Athletic Club.

THURSDAY NOVEMBER 21st

McIlroys Ballroom, Swindon.

FRIDAY NOVEMBER 22nd

Town Hall, Greenwich. The group recorded another appearance on Associated-Rediffusion's "Ready Steady Go!", at Kingsway Television Studios. Following afternoon rehearsals, the group mimed "I Wanna Be Your Man", broadcast over the ITV network between 6:15 - 6:59 pm. The show, hosted by Keith Fordyce and Cathy McGowan, also featured Gerry and the Pacemakers, Freddie and the Dreamers, Kathy Kirby and Kenny Lynch.

SATURDAY NOVEMBER 23rd

The Baths, Leyton, followed by the Chez Don Club, Dalston.

SUNDAY NOVEMBER 24th

An afternoon session at Studio 51, followed by the Majestic Ballroom, Luton.

MONDAY NOVEMBER 25th

Ballroom, Warrington

TUESDAY NOVEMBER 26th

Ballroom, Altrincham.

WEDNESDAY NOVEMBER 27th

Wigan Ballroom, followed by the Memorial Hall, Northwich.

THURSDAY NOVEMBER 28th

The "Daily Mirror" carried a report on when Gene Pitney first met the Stones, at "Thank Your Lucky Stars" (see Nov. 17th entry):- "When I first saw them, I didn't know whether to say hello or bark!"

FRIDAY NOVEMBER 29th

The Baths, Urmston.

SATURDAY NOVEMBER 30th

King's Hall, Stoke-on-Trent.

DECEMBER

A curious chapter in the Stones legacy; namely recording the soundtrack to two television commercials for Kellogg's Rice Krispies breakfast cereal! During the month, the group entered Star Sound Studios, in London, to record an "I Wanna Be Your Man"-style soundtrack (with Brian on harmonica), over which, Mick sang:-

Wake up in the morning, there's a snap around the place,

Wake up in the morning, there's a crackle in your face,

Wake up in the morning, there's a pop that really says:

"Rice Krispies for you and you and you!"

Pour on the milk and listen to the snap that says "It's nice!"

Pour on the milk and listen to the crackle of that rice,

Get up in the morning to the pop that says:"It's rice!"

Hear them talking crisp. Rice Krispies!!"

This was used on two different 30 second advertisements. The first featured animated characters, (resembling the Stones), jumping out of a cereal box, with "Snap!", "Crackle!" and "Pop!" slogans. The second was a parody of the BBC's weekly record judging show, "Juke Box Jury", (see June 26th, 1964 entry), with three youngsters sampling the crackling delicacy, before triumphantly producing a "Hit!" sign of approval, hidden inside each bowl. The adverts were first premiered on the ITV network at approximately, 7:01 pm, on Wednesday, January 1st 1964, in an effort to catch viewers who had just watched the Stones open the inaugural edition of "Top Of The Pops", on the rival BBC-1 channel. (see entry). This unusual undertaking was unique in that future ventures of a similar nature were unanimously vetoed by the group and Andrew Oldham.

SUNDAY DECEMBER 1st

Oasis Club, Manchester.

MONDAY DECEMBER 2nd

Assembly Rooms, Tamworth.

TUESDAY DECEMBER 3rd

Floral Hall, Southport.

WEDNESDAY DECEMBER 4th

The Baths, Doncaster.

THURSDAY DECEMBER 5th
The group began a four date tour for promoter John Smith (supporting Gerry and The Pacemakers and Peter Jay and The Jaywalkers), at the Gaumont Theatre, Worcester.

FRIDAY DECEMBER 6th
Odeon Theatre, Romford, Essex.

SATURDAY DECEMBER 7th
Fairfield Halls, Croydon. The bill also featured The Original Checkmates, The Overlanders and Peter McLean and The Klan.

SUNDAY DECEMBER 8th
Olympia Ballroom, Reading, followed by two shows at the Gaumont Theatre, Watford. (Replacing Peter Jay and The Jaywalkers, at Watford, were The Searchers. The Stones and promoter John Smith reunited for concerts the following year).

TUESDAY DECEMBER 10th
Chester (cancelled).

WEDNESDAY DECEMBER 11th
Bradford Arts Ball, King and Queens Hall, Bradford. The group drove on to Liverpool for the night, staying at the Exchange Hotel.

THURSDAY DECEMBER 12th
Locarno Ballroom, Liverpool.

FRIDAY DECEMBER 13th
Ballroom, Hereford.

SATURDAY DECEMBER 14th
The Baths, Epsom, Surrey.

SUNDAY DECEMBER 15th
"A Concert In Rhythm 'N' Blues", Civic Hall, Guildford, with Georgie Fame and the Blue Flames, Carter Lewis and the Southerners, The Yardbirds and the Graham Bond Quartet. Introduced by the Flamingo Club's Johnny Gunnell.

TUESDAY DECEMBER 17th
Town Hall, High Wycombe.

WEDNESDAY DECEMBER 18th
Photo shoot for "Boyfriend" magazine, followed by a gig at the Corn Exchange, Bristol. The group drove especially back to London to attend a party at Decca PR-man, Tony Hall's, Mayfair flat.

The Rolling Stones

THURSDAY DECEMBER 19th
St. Michael's Youth Centre, in Sydenham Road, Sydenham, Kent, to appear in the "pilot" programme of a new BBC TV drama programme "Cops And Robbers" (with of all people, Australian entertainer Rolf Harris!). The group arrived at the Centre for rehearsals which began at 4pm, with the programme being recorded between 9:15 - 10:30 pm that evening. The Stones part of the programme featured them in brief acting roles as an "unknown pop group playing in the town's youth centre". The main storyline centred on the arguments which broke out between local thieves (having just robbed a jewellery shop) at the Centre, as the group played (albeit miming to playback) "Come On" and the results, after the local constabulary had been called. The group were paid a total sum of £52-10 shillings for appearing, with a further £17-10 shillings to be paid to the group if, and when, the programme was ever transmitted. Unfortunately, due to the "wooden" performances of the relatively unknown cast, (including the Stones), the show's producer Robin Scott, deemed the poor results unworthy and it was never screened. Thus, the group never received their additional payment, and the show (due to the closed circuit telerecording) was consigned to the BBC "junk" bin!

FRIDAY DECEMBER 20th
Lido Ballroom, Winchester. The group had been voted sixth in the "British Vocal Group" and fifth in the "British Small Group" categories in the N.M.E end-of-year poll.

SATURDAY DECEMBER 21st
Kayser Bondor Ballroom, Baldock.

SUNDAY DECEMBER 22nd
St. Mary's Hall, Putney (supported by The Detours, later changing their name to The High Numbers, before settling on The Who.)

Above: The group on the first ever edition of BBC's Top of the Pops, New Years Day, 1964
Right: Backstage, Harrow, January 6th, 1964

TUESDAY DECEMBER 24th
Town Hall, Leek.

THURSDAY DECEMBER 26th
Selby's Restaurant, London.

FRIDAY DECEMBER 27th
"Ready Steady Go!" taped live from the Kingsway studios of Associated-Rediffusion and transmitted live across the ITV network between 6:15 - 6:59 pm. (Star guest who had flown in from America was Little Stevie Wonder). Following the show, the group drove to Reading to appear at the Town Hall. Meanwhile, Richard Green, in the NME wrote: "The Rolling Stones create a sound so exciting and gripping, that few other groups can come within shouting distance of it."

SATURDAY DECEMBER 28th
Club Noreik at the corner of the Seven Sisters Road, Tottenham. The event was the "All Night Rave", which ran from midnight to 6am. (After performing two 30 minute sets, the group left around 3:45am).

MONDAY DECEMBER 30th
Studio 51 with Jimmy Powell and the Five Dimensions (featuring 18-year old singer, Rod Stewart). The show ran from 8:00 - 11:00 pm.

TUESDAY DECEMBER 31st
A gig at The Drill Hall, Lincoln, end-of-year party. The group stayed on to bring in 1964, all except for Brian and Stu, who went to the town cathedral (reputed to be haunted). The others returned to the White Hart Hotel, shortly after 1am.

NINETEEN SIXTY FOUR

WEDNESDAY JANUARY 1st.

The group performed "I Wanna Be Your Man" on the very first edition of the long running BBC TV show, "Top Of The Pops". Introduced by DJ, Jimmy Savile, it was recorded at the BBC TV studios, Dickenson Road, Manchester (a disused church). The group took a train from Lincoln to Manchester (paid for by the BBC at a cost of £4.12 shillings) and upon arrival, appeared with The Swinging Blue Jeans for a camera rehearsal at 2pm which ran for approximately one hour. (The North/South divide flared up, when Keith and Brian had a violent disagreement with the Liverpool group, in the BBC canteen). The Stones also took the honour of being the first artists to ever perform on the show, appearing after Jimmy Saville's introduction: "a swingin' disc from a real swingin' group". The live show, transmitted from 6:35 to 6:59 that evening, also featured Dusty Springfield, The Dave Clark Five, The Hollies and The Swinging Blue Jeans, who mimed to their records, while Cliff Richard and The Shadows, Freddie and The Dreamers and The Beatles all appeared by way of specially shot 35mm BBC film. For their performance (which was never recorded), the Stones were paid £73.10 shillings.

THURSDAY JANUARY 2nd.

The first of two days recording at Regent Sound Studios, with producer Andrew Oldham and musical director Mike Leander. The group performed as backing musicians, firstly for 18-year old female singer, Cleo Sylvester, on the Phil Spector song, "To Know Her Is To Love Her" ("To Know Him Is To Love Him"), while during the latter part of the sessions, the group recorded the backing track to "There Are But Five Rolling Stones" by the Andrew Oldham Orchestra. (The two songs would later form a Decca single, released on January 10th, with Cleo Sylvester as the A side).

FRIDAY JANUARY 3rd.

Glenlyn Ballroom, Forest Hill (again with The Detours - see Dec 22nd, 1963 entry.) At Regent Sound, three tracks were rehearsed and recorded (with Oldham and Bill Farley engineering):-
"Carol" (Chuck Berry)
"Route 66" (Bobby Troup via Chuck Berry)
"Mona" (Bo Diddley).

SATURDAY JANUARY 4th.

Town Hall, Oxford.

SUNDAY JANUARY 5th

Olympia Ballroom, Reading.

MONDAY JANUARY 6th

The group became involved with two different promoters, performing in concert tours running simultaneously. For promoter George Cooper, they co-headlined a package tour with The Ronettes, "Group Scene '64".

For these upcoming concerts, the group's repertoire featured:-
"Girls" (The Shirelles "Boys", as covered by The Beatles, in role reversal) / "Come On" / "Mona" / "You Better Move On" / "Roll Over Beethoven" and "I Wanna Be Your Man".

Other acts to feature in the package, included The Swinging Blue Jeans, The Cheynes, Dave Berry and the Cruisers and guest star Marty Wilde and His Wildcats. Compere: Al Paige. However, the group played two shows at the Granada Theatre, Harrow-on-the-Hill, for rival promoter, John Smith. (The Stones were due to start the "Group Scene '64" tour, the previous night at the Nottingham Empire, but the show was cancelled.)

TUESDAY JANUARY 7th

The first show on the "Group Scene" tour with two shows at the Adelphi Theatre, Bath Road, Slough, Buckinghamshire. Cyril Davies, who had originally inspired and encouraged the band, died of leukemia, aged 32.

WEDNESDAY JANUARY 8th

Another change of date on the Granada Theatre tour, with the proposed two "houses" in Mansfield swapped with two dates in Maidstone.

THURSDAY JANUARY 9th

Granada Theatre, Kettering. (Two shows.)

FRIDAY JANUARY 10th

Regent Sound Studios, (with Andrew Oldham), recording the first takes of the group's arrangement of Buddy Holly's "Not Fade Away". In the evening, two shows at the Granada Theatre in Walthamstow, with Bern Elliot and The Fenmen.

SATURDAY JANUARY 11th

More ballroom dates for John Smith, (announced to the press on November 1st, 1963), starting with a show at The Baths, Epsom.

SUNDAY JANUARY 12th

Granada Theatre, Tooting. (Two shows, with Johnny Kidd and The Pirates.)

MONDAY JANUARY 13th

While Andrew Oldham prepared the first mixes of the songs recorded earlier in the month at Regent Sound Studios, the group flew to Scotland for a gig at the Barrowlands Ballroom, Glasgow, for John Smith. After three numbers, they had to be taken off for their own safety.

TUESDAY JANUARY 14th

Granada Theatre, Mansfield (dates swopped with Maidstone on the 8th). (Two shows.)

WEDNESDAY JANUARY 15th

Granada Theatre, Bedford. (Two shows.) The windshield of the group's van shattered completely on the M1, on the way back to London.

THURSDAY JANUARY 16th

McGilroy's Ballroom, Swindon (for John Smith).

FRIDAY JANUARY 17th

City Hall, Salisbury (for John Smith). The group's first eponymous E.P, originally scheduled for Christmas 1963, was released, containing the tracks recorded at Kingsway (see Nov 14th, 1963 entry).

SATURDAY JANUARY 18th

Pier Ballroom, Hastings (for John Smith).

SUNDAY JANUARY 19th

Coventry Theatre (two shows), added to the John Smith tour itinerary. For these shows, The Ronettes made their only appearance for the promoter. Also as "special guests", Freddie and The Dreamers appeared.

MONDAY JANUARY 20th

Granada Theatre, Woolwich (Two shows). Johnny Kidd and The Pirates joined the bill for the remainder of the tour.

TUESDAY JANUARY 21st

An extra date added to the "Group Scene" tour with two shows at the Granada, Aylesbury. After an interview and photo session for "Fabulous" magazine, the group had journeyed up from London, without Brian, who was visiting his parents in Cheltenham. He managed to miss both shows, while driving hopelessly lost, in thick fog. The Ronettes were also absent for the same reason, arriving some five minutes before the end of the late "house".

WEDNESDAY JANUARY 22nd

Another extra date on the Ronettes tour, but this time the Stones did not appear. Their split loyalty between two promoters meant for the first time, they had to pull out of a show. They appeared instead at the Granada Theatre, Shrewsbury, Shropshire (two shows), while The Ronettes (with Johnny Kidd and The Pirates) played in Kingston.

THURSDAY JANUARY 23rd

Pavilion, Lowestoft.

FRIDAY JANUARY 24th

Palais, Wimbledon. The group returned to the BBC Studios at Maida Vale to record their second radio broadcast and their first for the programme, "Go Man Go!", as "Stars Of The Week", hosted by David Ede. During the session, they recorded:- "I Wanna Be Your Man" / "Pretty Thing" / "Bye Bye Johnny" / "You Better Move On" / "I Want To Be Loved" and "Roll Over Beethoven".

("Go Man, Go" would be replaced the following month with "The Joe Loss Pop Show" which the Stones would also appear on-see April 10th entry). This edition of the programme also featured The Rabin Band, Barbara Kay, Mike Taylor, Bill Suet and The Travellers. It was transmitted live between 12:31 - 1:30 pm.

SATURDAY JANUARY 25th

California Ballroom, Dunstable.

SUNDAY JANUARY 26th

An added date for John Smith at De Montfort Hall, Leicester with The Ronettes and Freddie and The Dreamers (Two shows).

MONDAY JANUARY 27th

The tour ended with an extra date, at the Colston Hall, Bristol. (Two shows.)

WEDNESDAY JANUARY 29th

After a day's rest from the previous 24-day touring schedule, the group made a brief appearance at Regent Sound where 10 days of recording began. (The tracks would tentatively form their first album). They then made their way, via train from London at a cost of £9.4 shillings each (return, paid for by the BBC), to the Dickenson Road Studios in Manchester for their second appearance on BBC TV's "Top Of The Pops". The group mimed to "You Better Move On". For this performance (and indeed for their next three TOTP studio appearances), they were paid a group sum total of £73.10 shillings. The song was included in the show, broadcast that night between 6:35-6:59 pm. The live show, again hosted by Jimmy Savile, featured The Searchers, The Fourmost, Manfred Mann and The Bachelors in the studio, while Brian Poole and The Tremeloes, Gerry and The Pacemakers, The Swinging Blue Jeans and Billy Fury appeared by way of filmed/Ampexed "inserts". Upon returning to London, the Stones re-joined Andrew Oldham and sound engineer Bill Farley at Regent Sound, to continue more "late night" recording:-

"I Just Wanna Make Love To You" (Willie Dixon)

"I`m A King Bee" (Slim Harpo)

"You Can Make It If You Try" (Wilson Pickett) (Stu on organ)

"Tell Me (You`re Coming Back)"

"Walking The Dog" (Rufus Thomas)

"Honest I Do" (Jimmy Reed).

THURSDAY JANUARY 30th

The group's next BBC-TV engagement, but in stark contrast to all their previous "Beeb" broadcasts, the group never actually appeared. The weekday magazine show, "Town and Around", (London and South East regions only) featured the song "You Better Move On" set against still pictures, which illustrated the songs lyrics. For this cheap exercise, the

Arthur Haynes Show, February 7th

group were paid £8.8 shillings, and it found its way into the show, transmitted on Tuesday, February 4th (between 6:10-6:29pm), along with poetry reading and an interview with Eileen Marshall, a woman stockbroker!

FRIDAY JANUARY 31st
Public Hall, Preston.

SATURDAY FEBRUARY 1st
"Valentine" Charity Pop Show, at the Royal Albert Hall, with Brian Poole and The Tremeloes, Dusty Springfield and The Echoes, The Swinging Blue Jeans, Alan Randall and The Heartbeats, The Original Checkmates, The Seekers and Terry Judge and The Barristers.

SUNDAY FEBRUARY 2ND
Country Club, Hampstead.

MONDAY FEBRUARY 3rd
The group recorded their second session for BBC Radio's "Saturday Club", hosted by Brian Matthew, broadcast 10:00 - 12:00 am, on February 8th. Other guests included Billy J Kramer and the Dakotas, Tommy Bruce and the Bruisers, Dev Douglas, Peter Harvey, The Velvettes, Lee Stirling and Arthur Greenslade and the Gee Men. The Stones performed:-

"Don't Lie To Me" / "You Better Move On" / " I Wanna Be Your Man" "Mona" / "Walking The Dog" and "Bye Bye Johnny."

With the calibre of groups like The Beatles and The Rolling Stones regularly appearing on the programme, the BBC announced that audience figures for each show, were now approaching 9 million! Decca, eager to cash in on this new found popularity, released an album "Saturday Club", the day before this show was transmitted. It contained "Fortune Teller" and "Poison Ivy", both sides of the aborted second Stones single (see August 18th, 1963 entry).

TUESDAY FEBRUARY 4th
Regent Sound. During this session, the following tracks were recorded (with Andrew Oldham and Bill Farley):-

"Can I Get A Witness" (Marvin Gaye)

"Little By Little" (a joint composition Phelge-Spector).

"Now I've Got A Witness (Like Uncle Phil And Uncle Gene)" (Nanker-Phelge)

"And Mr Spector And Mr Pitney Came Too"

"And The Rolling Stones Met Phil And Gene"

The last two remain unreleased, the former being an instrumental, similar to "Now I've Got A Witness", while the latter was a hilarious obscene jam (A/K/A "Andrew's Blues"), involving Phil Spector, Gene Pitney and Mick trading vocals, while Graham Nash and Allan Clarke, from The Hollies, added backing vocals. Pitney accompanied Stu on the

"Ready Steady Go!", February 14th

same piano, while Spector played maraccas and piano.

WEDNESDAY FEBRUARY 5th

Ballroom, Willenhall.

THURSDAY FEBRUARY 6th

Regent Sound, for additional work on the previous recordings.

FRIDAY FEBRUARY 7th

The group recorded an appearance on the ATV light entertainment show, "The Arthur Haynes Show" (a legendary British comedian), in place of Gerry and the Pacemakers. The group were two hours late for the rehearsals and missed the final run-through, arriving nonchalantly, back at the studio, some 90 minutes late, after shopping for clothes in Carnaby Street. They recorded, before a studio audience, "I Wanna Be Your Man" and "You Better Move On", in a set totalling 4 minutes 33 seconds. The performance was included in the show, transmitted across the ITV network the following night, between 8:25 - 8:59pm. The Stones were joined, along with host Arthur Haynes, by resident comic Nicholas Parsons and singer Dorothy Squires. The group's unprofessionalism was rewarded with an ATV ban, that was later (reluctantly) lifted due to the Stones swiftly ascending popularity.

SATURDAY FEBRUARY 8th

The group began another British tour, (their 3rd) opening with two shows at the Regal Theatre, Edmonton. For this tour, ("All Stars 64", working for the first time with promoter Robert Stigwood), as "Special Guests", the group's set featured:-

"Talkin 'Bout You" / "Road Runner" / "Roll Over Beethoven" / "Walking

The Dog "/ "You Better Move On" and " I Wanna Be Your Man".

Joining the package were joint bill-toppers John Leyton and Mike Sarne, (this tour replaced the proposed idea of the duo appearing together in a Christmas Show at a West End Theatre), along with Mike Berry, Billie Davis and the Le Roys, The Innocents, Jet Harris, Don Spencer and Billy Boyle. That night's guests were The Dowlands. Compere: Rod McLellan. Travelling with the group, on various dates, were five scriptwriters who were planning a film spotlighting each member of the group. Following the concerts, the group rushed to keep their next booking at a 12-6am show at Club Noreik, Tottenham.

SUNDAY FEBRUARY 9th

Leicester De Montfort Hall. (Two shows. The Swinging Blue Jeans joined the tour.)

MONDAY FEBRUARY 10th

Odeon Theatre, Cheltenham. (Two shows.)

TUESDAY FEBRUARY 11th

Granada Theatre, Rugby. (Two shows.)

WEDNESDAY FEBRUARY 12th

Odeon Theatre, Guildford. (Two shows.)

THURSDAY FEBRUARY 13th

Granada Theatre, Kingston-upon-Thames. (Two shows.)

FRIDAY FEBRUARY 14th

Gaumont Theatre, Watford. (Two shows.) The afternoon was spent in rehearsal at Television House, for a live performance on "Ready Steady Go!", transmitted across the ITV network that night between 6:15 - 6:59pm. The Stones mimed "You Better Move On" and "I Wanna Be Your Man", as well as being interviewed by Keith Fordyce. The show also included The Crystals, Dusty Springfield, Kenny Lynch, The Laurie Jay Combo and Dave Clark (minus his 5) playing that week's "Amateur DJ".

SATURDAY FEBRUARY 15th

Odeon Cinema, Rochester. (Two shows, with guests The Dowlands in place of The Swinging Blue Jeans.)

SUNDAY FEBRUARY 16th

Portsmouth Guildhall. (Two shows.)

MONDAY FEBRUARY 17th

Granada Theatre, Greenford. (Two shows).

TUESDAY FEBRUARY 18th

Before leaving London for the first of three consecutive dates at Rank Cinemas (substituted in place of the advertised Odeon venues), the group were interviewed by Keith Fordyce, on the BBC Light Programme, "Pop Inn", broadcast live between 1:00-1:44 pm. The Rank, Colchester (Two shows.)

WEDNESDAY FEBRUARY 19th

The Rank, Stockton-on-Tees. (Two shows.) The group stayed overnight at the Scotch Corner Hotel, Stockport.

THURSDAY FEBRUARY 20th

The Rank, Sunderland. (Two shows.)

FRIDAY FEBRUARY 21st

Gaumont Theatre, Hanley. (Two shows, with The Dowlands, in place of The Swinging Blue Jeans). "Not Fade Away" B/W "Little By Little" was released (eventually reaching No 3).

SATURDAY FEBRUARY 22nd

The package tour reached Bournemouth, for two shows at the Winter Gardens, with guests The Paramounts. In the afternoon, BBCTV cameras took silent footage of the group, with the idea to "dub" their latest release, onto the soundtrack, for inclusion in a future episode of "Top Of The Pops" (provisionally scheduled for March 4th).

The film featured the group at the beach in Weymouth, against a backdrop of rocks and rolling stones (pun intended!). Mick remembered the filming: "It was a freezing cold day. We were at the bottom of a cliff and they started throwing stones down on us. You see, Rolling Stones, a joke, while we mimed to "Not Fade Away". In fact, they never did mime to this song, or in fact, any song. The cameras made "wild shot" footage, so that the required track could be placed on later. For this, the group were paid a slightly less than standard fee of £73 exactly, but due to the group appearing personally on TOTP on March 4th (see entry) the film was never screened and was, unfortunately, later "junked" by the BBC.

The group stayed overnight at the White Hart Hotel, Bournemouth.

SUNDAY FEBRUARY 23rd

The group were requested to record another appearance on "Thank Your Lucky Stars", recorded in Aston, Birmingham. Due to their van breaking down, in Amesbury, Wiltshire, they arrived two and a half hours late for the appointment. The group mimed to "Not Fade Away". The show, hosted by DJ Alan Freeman, was transmitted across the ITV network, February 29th, between 5:50 - 6:34pm. Among the guests featured that week were The Hollies, Bobby Vee and Big Dee Irwin.

In the evening, the group played two shows at the Birmingham Hippodrome, with The Swinging Blue Jeans and Bern Elliott and The Fenmen.

MONDAY FEBRUARY 24th

Odeon Theatre, Southend. (Two shows 6:30 & 8:45pm, with The Swinging Blue Jeans and Bern Elliott and The Fenmen.)

TUESDAY FEBRUARY 25th

A session at Regent Sound, with Andrew Oldham, recording three tracks, including "Good Times, Bad Times". Odeon Theatre, Romford.(Two shows with The Swinging Blue Jeans and Bern Elliott and The Fenmen.)

WEDNESDAY FEBRUARY 26th

Rialto Theatre, York. (Two shows, with The Swinging Blue Jeans and Bern Elliott and The Fenmen.)

THURSDAY FEBRUARY 27th

City Hall, Sheffield. (Two shows, with The Swinging Blue Jeans and Bern Elliott and The Fenmen.)

FRIDAY FEBRUARY 28th

Sophia Gardens, Cardiff. (Two shows, with Bern Elliott and The Fenmen.)

SATURDAY FEBRUARY 29th

Hippodrome, Brighton, in place of a cancelled show at Stockport Essoldo. (Two shows, with The Dowlands.)

SUNDAY MARCH 1st

Liverpool Empire. (Two shows,with Bern Elliott and The Fenmen.)

MONDAY MARCH 2nd

Albert Hall, Nottingham. (Two shows, with Bern Elliott and The Fenmen and The Paramounts.) The group drove to Manchester for the night.

TUESDAY MARCH 3rd

Opera House, Blackpool. (Two shows, with Bern Elliott and The Fenmen and The Paramounts.)

WEDNESDAY MARCH 4th

The group took a train ride (again paid for by the BBC) to Manchester for the group's third studio appearance on "Top Of The Pops", to promote "Not Fade Away". After taking part in a brief camera rehearsal at 2pm, they recorded a videotape "insert" for inclusion in the show, that for tonight only, would be broadcast live from the BBC Studios in Glasgow. (6:35 to 6:59 pm). This edition, hosted by DJ Alan Freeman, featured only The Bachelors in the studio, while Dusty Springfield appeared by way of a specially shot 35mm film and The Hollies, Billy J. Kramer and the Dakotas, Brian Poole and the Tremeloes, Eden Kane, The Dave Clark 5 and Cilla Black all appeared by way of previously recorded inserts. The group also appeared live on Granada's "Scene At 6:30" (ITV 6:30 - 6:59 pm), miming "Not Fade Away". Leaving Manchester, they drove to Bradford for two shows at the Gaumont Theatre, with guests The Hollies and Bern Elliott and The Fenmen.

THURSDAY MARCH 5th

Odeon Theatre, Blackburn. (Two shows, with Bern Elliott and The Fenmen and The Paramounts.)

FRIDAY MARCH 6th

Gaumont Theatre, Wolverhampton. (Two shows, with Bern Elliott and The Fenmen.) Ray Coleman (of "Melody Maker"), interviewed the group backstage between shows. Amongst the topics covered were the group's verdicts on The Beatles latest single "Can't Buy Me Love" (they preferred the B-side, "You Can't Do That"). The finished article would become the infamous piece, "Would You Let Your Sister Go With A Rolling Stone?" After the shows, the group drove on to Manchester for the night.

SATURDAY MARCH 7th

The Winter Gardens, Morecambe. (Two shows, with guests Bern Elliott and The Fenmen.) Following the shows, the group took a week's holiday. Mick went to Paris, Brian to Scotland, Keith to Penzance, Charlie to Gibraltar, while Bill retired to a hotel in the New Forest.

SUNDAY MARCH 15th.

The group returned to the gig circuit, at the Invicta Ballrooms, Chatham. Charlie still hadn't returned from holiday, so his replacement, for a fee of £16, was Micky Waller (of Marty Wilde and the Wildcats, later of the

Camden Theatre, March 19th

Jeff Beck Group). Being free of the many support acts they had become accustomed to, the group played a longer set:-
"Talkin' About You" / " Poison Ivy" / "Walking The Dog" / "Pretty Thing" / "Cops And Robbers" / "Jaguar And The Thunderbirds" / "Don't Lie To Me" / "I Wanna Be Your Man" / "Roll Over Beethoven" / "You Better Move On" / "Road Runner" / "Route 66" and "Bye Bye Johnny".

TUESDAY MARCH 17th
Assembly Hall, Tunbridge Wells.

WEDNESDAY MARCH 18th
City Hall, Salisbury. (Two shows.) In the morning, the group went to Regent Sound Studios, to tape a slot for Radio Luxembourg's "Nestle's Top Swinging Groups" series, recording 14 tracks, including Jimmy Reed's "Ain't That Lovin' You Baby". The recordings formed four 15-minute slots on the station, the first being transmitted Friday, April 17th.
(The group were paid £240, taking over from The Dave Clark Five, in the series.)

THURSDAY MARCH 19th
Another BBC Radio performance, this time at the Corporation's Theatre in Camden, for a show titled "Blues In Rhythm", hosted by Long John Baldry, in front of a studio audience. The group began recording at an unusually early start, before 9am, performing:-
"Route 66" / (Bo Diddley's) "Cops And Robbers" / "You Better Move On" and "Mona".

The show was first broadcast on "Network 3", an experimental one hour "Stereophony" series, on BBC Light Radio, where listeners were invited to position themselves between their TV sets and radios to experience stereo-sound, marking the first time that "popular" music had been given such experimental treatment. The Stones, along with Georgie Fame and the Blue Flames and Long John Baldry, appeared in the first half of the broadcast (transmitted Saturday, May 9th, between 9:30 -10:30 am), with the second half of the programme being devoted to "Standard's From The Shows". A BBC sound engineer, known as "Bish", was reportedly "outraged" by Mick's "prancing around in a purple cat suit" (though Bill Wyman is quite certain that Mick never wore such a thing!).

SATURDAY MARCH 21st

Whitehall, East Grinstead.

SUNDAY MARCH 22nd

Isle of Wight Esplanade Pavilion, Ryde.

MONDAY MARCH 23rd

Guildhall, Southampton.

WEDNESDAY MARCH 25th

Town Hall, Birmingham. (Two shows.)

THURSDAY MARCH 26th

Town Hall, Kidderminster. (Two shows.)

FRIDAY MARCH 27th

Ex-Serviceman's Club, Windsor. Mick, Keith, Andrew Oldham and his business partner, Tony Calder attended a Decca press reception to launch the career of Oldham's latest protégé, 16-year old singer/actress Adrienne Posta. (Her first release, "Shang A Doo Lang", a Jagger-Richards comp., was released on today's date). 17-year old Reading convent schoolgirl, Marianne Faithfull attended the party, with her boyfriend, John Dunbar and was "discovered" by Oldham, who outlined a tentative arrangement to record her.

SATURDAY MARCH 28th

Wilton Halls, Bletchley, followed by Club Noreik, Tottenham, for another 12-6am "all-nighter". (The group played an hour-long set between 3-4am).

SUNDAY MARCH 29th

With Keith Relf ill, and unable to perform, Brian was asked to deputise on harmonica with The Yardbirds, for a gig at the Crawdaddy Club, Richmond.(The Yardbirds had taken over the Stones residency there.)

MONDAY MARCH 30th

An afternoon gig at the Ricky Tick "R & B Club", Guildford (3 -5:30pm). Then, after cancelling an appearance on January 5th, a re-arranged show at the Olympia Ballroom, Reading.

TUESDAY MARCH 31st

West Cliff Hall, Ramsgate.

APRIL

The Stones, as well as John Leyton, were approached by British Lions films to make a guest appearance in the Freddie and The Dreamers film, "Everyday Is A Holiday". The Stones declined the offer. Meanwhile, the N.M.E exclusively reported that negotiations were proceeding for the group to star in an as-yet untitled feature film to be made by Border Films. A ten-week shoot was expected to begin in July or early August. The group had chosen the script after sorting through several stories. Although not primarily a musical, they would perform five numbers. The plot would be of an unknown pop group, "who continually help their manager out of awkward situations".

WEDNESDAY APRIL 1st

George W. King Apprentice Association All Fools Charity Beat Ball, Locarno Ballroom, Stevenage.

FRIDAY APRIL 3rd

After a day off, the group went to Television House, Kingsway for another live appearance on "Ready Steady Go!" (broadcast between 6:10 - 6:59 pm across the ITV Network). They mimed to "Not Fade Away", in a show hosted by Keith Fordyce, also featuring Manfred Mann, Sounds Incorporated, Madeleine Bell and Billy J.Kramer and The Dakotas, while Mick was also interviewed by Cathy McGowan. The group gigged at Wimbledon Palais in the evening.

SATURDAY APRIL 4th

Leas Cliff Hall, Folkestone. In "Disc", Keith was quoted: "I think we must have written about 50 or 60 songs in the past eight or nine months, but I don't think we would record any of them as A-sides."

SUNDAY APRIL 5th

Gaumont Theatre, Ipswich. (Two shows), with The Bachelors, and compere Iain Gregory, who would both occasionally link-up with The Stones over the next six weeks.

MONDAY APRIL 6th

Royal Hotel Ballroom, Lowestoft. (1,200 audience.)

WEDNESDAY APRIL 8th

The "Ready Steady Go! Mod Ball", from the Empire Pool, Wembley,

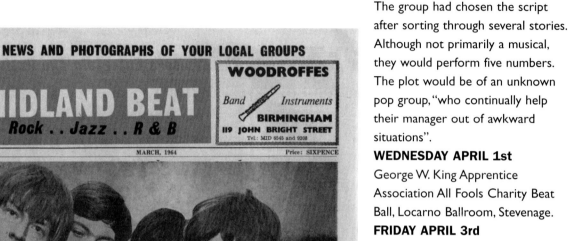

NEWS AND PHOTOGRAPHS OF YOUR LOCAL GROUPS

MIDLAND BEAT
Rock .. Jazz .. R & B

WOODROFFES
Band Instruments
BIRMINGHAM
119 JOHN BRIGHT STREET
Tel: MID 6545 and 9208

No. 6   MARCH, 1964   Price: SIXPENCE

Yes, it's the paper the long-hairs read! The Rolling Stones, riding high in the hit parade with "I Wanna Be Your Man," enjoy reading "MIDLAND BEAT" on an Oxford one-night-stand.

described as "one of the most ambitious outside events for the time ever tackled!" The idea for the show came from Elkan Allan (Entertainment Chief for Associated-Rediffusion, producers of the weekly "Ready Steady Go!" show) and Francis Hitching, (the RSG! editor) on January 3rd, when the two men met at their office at Television House, Kingsway to discuss taking the highly successful show on an outside broadcast (given the secret codename of "Operation Mod Ball"). The first official announcement was made on the March 6th edition of "Ready Steady Go!", that anyone wishing to attend should apply for tickets (£1.10s.5d) to the Variety Club of Great Britain, whose children charities would benefit from the concert. It was calculated that the event, for an audience of nearly 8,000 fans (6,000 sitting and the other 2,000 dancing, all requested to dress in "bizarre Mod fashions"), had sold out by first post on March 9th. Over 23 sacks, full of hopeful applications, had arrived and over 25,000 requests were eventually received. The doors to the Empire Pool opened at 7:30pm but the live TV broadcast did not begin across the ITV network until 9:53 (ending one hour later) and featured only selections of the line-up which included:-Cilla Black, The Fourmost, Freddie and The Dreamers, Kathy Kirby, Billy J.Kramer and the Dakotas, Kenny Lynch, Manfred Mann, The Merseybeats, The Searchers, and Sounds Incorporated. As per normal with "RSG!", the hosts were Keith Fordyce, Cathy McGowan and Michael Aldred. All acts appeared on a revolving podium, in the centre of the audience. For the live TV broadcast (which was never recorded), 10 lorries arrived at the Wembley studios, containing 7 cameras and 75 technicians. To accommodate the equipment, 450 seats had to be removed from the 200 x 80 foot area. The Stones mimed to:- "Not Fade Away", "Walking The Dog" and "Hi-Heel Sneakers". (The group were absent from the stage during "Not Fade Away", as they were mobbed, trying to reach the platform, despite being flanked by a line of security men). The group gave up miming, after being continually pulled into the audience. After finishing, they were stranded onstage for thirty minutes. The event was a success (with over £3,000 being raised for the charity), marred only by thirty people being arrested for riotous behaviour, when police tackled a gang of rockers on motorcycles waiting outside!

THURSDAY APRIL 9th
McIroys Ballroom, Swindon.

FRIDAY APRIL 10th
The Baths, Leyton. Another live BBC radio performance, this time for the popular English bandleader, Joe Loss, in his own series, aptly titled "The Joe Loss Pop Show" (broadcast 12:31-1:31 pm). The series was comparatively new, having replaced "Go Man, Go!", in February, in which the group had previously appeared (see Jan. 24th entry).
The group performed:- "Not Fade Away"/ (Robert Higgenbotham's) "Hi-Heel Sneakers" / "Little By Little" / "I Just Wanna Make Love To You" and (Hank Snow's) "I'm Moving On"
The show, besides the host, also featured Rose Brennan and Ross

McManus (father of musician Elvis Costello). The N.M.E reported that Jet Harris would record two instrumentals, written by Andrew Oldham and Brian Jones, to be issued by Decca.

SATURDAY APRIL 11th
Pier Ballroom, Hastings.

SUNDAY APRIL 12th
Fairfield Halls, Croydon.(Two shows.)

MONDAY APRIL 13th
BBC's "Saturday Club", their third appearance with host Brian Matthew. The group performed:-
"I Just Wanna Make Love To You" / "Walking The Dog" / "Not Fade Away" / (Chuck Berry's) "Beautiful Delilah" / "Hi-Heel Sneakers" and "Carol".
The recording was broadcast (10:00 -12:00am) on April 18th. The groups notoriety was spreading to such an extent, that to co-inside with this appearance, the BBC listings paper "Radio Times" ran a special feature on the group.

THURSDAY APRIL 16th
The Cubi-Club, Rochdale, abandoned halfway through due to the audience rioting. The band still received their £332.10s fee.

FRIDAY APRIL 17th
The band drove from Manchester to Coventry, for a gig at the Locarno Ballroom. "The Rolling Stones", (their first L.P), was released, with advance orders totalling over 100, 000. The start of four weeks of Radio Luxembourg's 15 minute spots,(recorded March 18th), each Friday at 9:45am.

SATURDAY APRIL 18th
Royalty Theatre, Chester. The Stones were supported by a quasi-music hall outfit, featuring a bunch of singing sailors and a female pianist, Miss Olivia Dunn!

SUNDAY APRIL 19th
The group, with Andrew Oldham and Eric Easton, flew out to Geneva from London Airport, with a tumultuous send off from hundreds of fans. The Stones were due in Switzerland to take part in another "Ready Steady Go!" special event, at the Casino, Montreux, for the annual "Golden Rose" International TV Festival, which was being held there that week. Upon arrival, they reached Montreaux via a five-hour boat trip down Lake Geneva.

MONDAY APRIL 20th
Afternoon rehearsals for the programme, which was transmitted across the ITV network on April 24th between 6:10 -6:59pm, and featured Kenny Lynch, Petula Clark and French band, Les Surfs, with regular hosts Keith Fordyce, Cathy McGowan and Michael Aldred. The idea of this overseas edition of the series, was to show delegates to the

Right: The group pose outside the Wembley Empire Pool (now Wembley Arena)
during rehearsals for the Mad Mod Ball, April 8th

"International Contest for Television Light Entertainment Programmes", how a live pop show was produced. The official (unsuccessful) ITV entry in the contest, was the all "Merseyside" edition of ABC TV's "Thank Your Lucky Stars", (originally transmitted across the ITV network on December 21st,1963). Following a heavy drinking session with Kenny Lynch and the RSG! crowd, the group were thrown out of the Palace Hotel for being "too rowdy".

WEDNESDAY APRIL 22nd

After flying back from Montreux on the 21st, (minus Charlie who was recovering from a bout of food poisoning) and assembling back in London, the group played the Carlton Ballroom, in Slough High Street. (A show that went largely unnoticed, although a picture of Bill signing autographs for local fans after the concert, appeared in the following week's edition of the "Slough Observer"). "The Daily Mirror" reported that Mr. Wallace Scowcroft, the President of the National Federation of Hairdressers, had offered a free haircut to the next number one group or soloist in the pop chart, adding "The Rolling Stones are the worst. One of them looks as if he has got a feather duster on his head!"

FRIDAY APRIL 24th

Gaumont Theatre, Norwich. (Two shows, with guest Heinz). The group's first album knocked "With The Beatles" down to No.2 in the British album charts, after being on sale for only 7 days! On Radio

Luxembourg, the second of four, fifteen minute slots was transmitted (recorded March 18th).

SATURDAY APRIL 25th

Odeon Theatre, Luton. (Two shows, with Heinz, in place of The Bachelors and Mike Sarne.)

SUNDAY APRIL 26th

The group returned to the Empire Pool, Wembley to play at the annual "NME Poll WinnersConcert", promoted by the N.M.E's Maurice Kinn and hosted by D.J's David Jacobs and Jimmy Savile. The whole event was "telerecorded" by ABC TV who transmitted the first show across the ITV network between 4:05 - 5:34pm on May 3rd. (Certain ITV regions received a repeat screening later in the year on Sunday, November 1st). The Stones, third on the running order in the first programme, performed:-

"Not Fade Away" / "I Just Want To Make Love To You" and "I'm Alright" (The latter song introduced by Charlie).

The rest of the show ran as follows: The Joe Loss Orchestra, The Hollies, The Swinging Blue Jeans, The Searchers, Freddie and The Dreamers, Brian Poole and The Tremeloes and Cliff Richard and The Shadows. (The Stones were also filmed arriving at the venue, seen during the opening titles.)

The second show transmitted the following week featured:-
Manfred Mann, Jet Harris, Kathy Kirby, Billy J. Kramer and The Dakotas, The Merseybeats, Earl Van Dyke, Joe Brown and the Bruvvers, Gerry and The Pacemakers and The Beatles.

Also on hand to cover the event were Movietone News, whose feature, "Wembley: Gathering Of The Groups", included 1 minute 54 seconds of "I'm Alright". Besides the TV show, New York American radio station WINS (hosted by "fifth Beatle", Murray The "K"), broadcast parts of the concert. After the N.M.E event had concluded, the group remained to play an evening show, ("All-Star Concert", also promoted by Maurice Kinn) at the same venue. Other acts appearing:- The Applejacks, Cilla Black, The Fourmost, Gerry and the Pacemakers, Big Dee Irwin, Eden Kane, Billy J. Kramer and The Dakotas, Manfred Mann, The Tony Meehan Combo, The Merseybeats, Tommy Quickly, The Searchers and Sounds Incorporated.

MONDAY APRIL 27th

For the third time in a week, the group participated in a TV related event, namely the BBC's "Top Beat" annual series of "Pop Prom" concerts from London's Royal Albert Hall (this year being the first mounted in tandem with BBC Light Radio).

The Stones, fifth on the running order, performed the following:-
"Not Fade Away" / "Hi-Heel Sneakers" and "I'm All Right".
The concert was transmitted live on the Light Programme, between 7:31 - 8:30pm and then between 9:10 - 9:57pm, the concert was performed a second time, where it was transmitted live on the new BBC 2 station. (The Stones performed the same three numbers.)

For their two spots, they were paid £125. This covered both TV and Radio performances in the UK. For TV screenings in the USA, the group received an additional sum of £62.10 s, while an additional sum of £31.5s was paid for use of their TV performance in the British Commonwealth and the rest of the world. For use of the radio broadcast, the group received a sum of £9 for both the USA and the rest of the world, while for use in the British Commonwealth, they received double that at £18.

The concert, hosted by Alan Freeman, also featured Joe Brown and the Bruvvers, Gerry and The Pacemakers, Big Dee Irwin, The Searchers and Susan Maughan amongst others.

TUESDAY APRIL 28th

Public Hall, Wallington.

WEDNESDAY APRIL 29th

The group again took a train to the BBC's Dickenson Road studios, to make their fourth appearance on "Top Of The Pops". Fans were waiting at the station to greet them, therefore delaying the group's arrival at the studios. This greatly angered producer Johnnie Stewart, who threatened:- "If you are late again, you will not appear on my show again!" Hosted by DJ, Alan Freeman, the group performed "I Just Wanna Make Love To You", transmitted BBC1 between 6:35- 6:59pm, later that night.

THURSDAY APRIL 30th

Majestic Ballroom, Birkenhead. The show was abandoned after one song, when fans rushed the stage.

FRIDAY MAY 1st

Imperial Ballroom, Nelson. Radio Luxembourg broadcast the third of four radio slots originally recorded on March 18th, while "Melody Maker" began a 5-part series profiling the individual members of the group entitled "1964: Stone Age". (The first featuring Bill Wyman.) The N.M.E announced that Lionel Bart would be writing the screenplay for the Stones first film, to be made by his production company, involving an eight to ten week shoot in July.

SATURDAY MAY 2nd

Spa Royal Hall, Bridlington. (Two half hour sets. 8 & 11:45pm. 3,000 audience). The group spent the night at the Queens Hotel, Manchester.

SUNDAY MAY 3rd.

Palace Theatre, Manchester.

MONDAY MAY 4th (and off & on throughout the month)

The start of more recording at Regent Sound Studios, with resident producer Andrew Oldham and Bill Farley as sound engineer. The group recorded various Jagger/Richards demo tracks, as follows:-

"Funny Guy"

"Waving Hair"

"When A Boy Meets A Girl"

"As Time Goes By" (demo for Marianne Faithfull, later modified to "As Tears Go By")

"So Much In Love" (intended for The Mighty Avengers).

"You Must Be The One" (intended for The Greenbeats).

The group went to Manchester for another live broadcast on Granada TV's "Scene at 6:30" (6:30 - 6:59pm).

WEDNESDAY MAY 6th

The Rolling Stones co-manager Eric Easton, still concerned over Johnny Stewart's threat, following their late appearance on April 29th, wrote a letter of apology to Stewart, but added:- "I am not getting on with your BBC Booking Department at present. They are so mean about money, and while I always bend over backwards to co-operate with BBC producers, the money they are prepared to pay the "Second Hottest Group in the country" is insulting. For your show (April 29th) the boys received £73.10 s, and I had quite a battle to get about £12 expenses. I think this sort of offer is too bad, and I have told the booking department that I shall have to decline any offers if the money cannot be a little more reasonable."

Meanwhile, the group visited the Southampton studios of Southern ITV for an appearance on the regional news magazine programme "Two Go Round", broadcast live (6:30-6:59pm) in Southern ITV regions only. While Mick, Keith, Brian and Charlie returned to Regent Sound Studios,

Bill went to Eel Pie Island, Twickenham for an impromptu jam session with Stu, Jeff Beck and Jimmy Page amongst others, which went late into the evening.

THURSDAY MAY 7th

Savoy Ballroom, Southsea.

FRIDAY MAY 8th

Town Hall, Hove. Radio Luxembourg broadcast the fourth and final segment in their "Nestle's Top Swinging Groups" series (recorded March 18th).

SATURDAY MAY 9th

Another concert appearance for the BBC, this time their first, and only appearance on the live, Saturday evening BBC-2 two hour music, arts and discussion programme, "Open House". The group assembled at 10:30am at the BBC's Riverside Studios, in Crisp Road, Hammersmith for a rehearsal. During this run through, and for the live show (transmitted between 4:00 - 5:59pm) the group performed:- "Put On Your Red Dress Baby" ("Hi Heel Sneakers"). For their services, they were paid £105 exactly. Backstage at the studio, BBC make-up woman, Paula James prepared Mick for the performance with a requested shampoo and set. Miss James breathlessly revealed later, that Mick didn't need a hairdrier for his hair, he just simply walked around! The other musical guests on the show, introduced by Gay Byrne, were Kathy Kirby and Kenny Lynch. No recording was made of the live broadcast. That evening, the group attended two Chuck Berry shows at the Finsbury Park Astoria (on a package with Carl Perkins and The Nashville Teens). Hoping to meet their hero, they went backstage, but found Berry acting distantly towards them. This episode made them late for their gig at the Savoy Ballroom, Catford. Arriving to find the place completely surrounded by fans, the band had to gain access via a neighbouring property. Dozens of fainting cases were reported.

SUNDAY MAY 10th

Colston Hall, Bristol. (Two shows.) (5:30 & 7:45) Promoted by Malcolm Arose, with The Avon Cities, The Ray Bush R & B Group, Christine Marlowe, The Echoes, Mike Tobin and The Magnetts, Johnny Carr and The Cadillacs, The Sensational Shouts, Gene Vincent, The No Names and Millie). Brian missed the first "house", after being delayed on the motorway. After vainly trying to gain entrance to the hall, he was finally admitted through the surrounding crowd, with the aid of police intervention. Brian's parents were backstage and he later drove back to Cheltenham with them. "Top Of The Pops" host and DJ, Jimmy Savile, was quoted in "The People":- "The Stones are a great team for having a laugh and dress very clean and smart when they relax, contrary to what lots of people think!"

MONDAY MAY 11th

Winter Gardens, Bournemouth. (Two shows.) The start of a four-date tour with Peter Jay and The Jaywalkers and Julie Grant. The bill also featured Keith Powell and The Valets, The Sunliners (with Dene Hunter),

The Gamblers, Ray Douglas, Chris Carlsen, Cliff Bennett and the Rebel Rousers and Pat Wayne and the Beachcombers. The group made the newspapers, after being refused lunch at the Grand Hotel, Bristol, because they weren't wearing ties. (They ended up dining with several fans at the Bali restaurant, Park Street). Co-manager, Eric Easton flew to the States to arrange the Stones first US tour.

TUESDAY MAY 12th

Regent Sound Studios. The group received smallpox vaccinations, for their American tour.

WEDNESDAY MAY 13th

City Hall, Newcastle-upon-Tyne (Two shows.)

THURSDAY MAY 14th

St. Georges Hall, Bradford. (Two shows.) Between shows, the group made a dash for their hotel, located across the road from the venue. Mick and Keith made it, while Bill and Charlie were forced to return backstage. Brian, trapped, was chased by a mob of girls, who tore his clothes, before reaching safety.

FRIDAY MAY 15th

Trentham Gardens, Stoke on Trent. (Two shows.)

SATURDAY MAY 16th

Regal Theatre, Edmonton, in place of Bournemouth Odeon. (Two shows, with Heinz.)

SUNDAY MAY 17th

Odeon Theatre, Folkestone, in place of Edmonton Odeon. (Two shows.) with Heinz and The Applejacks, in place of Mike Sarne and The Bachelors).

Above: Birmingham, May 26th
Left: Being interviewed for Radio Luxembourg by DJ, Jimmy Savile

MONDAY MAY 18th

The Stones returned to Scotland, for four dates. The first being at the Chantinghall Hotel, Hamilton (8pm-12pm). The police were called in after riots occured outside the venue, where 4,000 fans, many with forged tickets, were trying to get in. Inside, fans tried to climb a ten-foot high wire fence which surrounded the stage.

TUESDAY MAY 19th

Capitol Theatre, Aberdeen. (Two shows, the first of three straight evenings with Freddie & The Dreamers. At each, The Stones reluctantly closed the first half after a billing dispute). They drove on to Dundee after their set.

WEDNESDAY MAY 20th

Caird Hall, Dundee. (Two shows.)

THURSDAY MAY 21st

Regal Theatre, Edinburgh. (Two shows.)

FRIDAY MAY 22nd

Regent Sound Studios.

SATURDAY MAY 23rd

Leicester University. "Melody Maker" ran a cover story entitled "Stones Set To Invade", while inside, the paper featured a debate on the group. "For" the group were Muddy Waters and editor, Ray Coleman, while "Against" the group, was Bob Dawbarn. "As far as I'm concerned, The Stones can keep on rolling-straight past my gramophone!"

SUNDAY MAY 24th

The group made another appearance on ABC TV's, "Thank Your Lucky Stars". Returning to the Aston, Birmingham studios of Alpha Television, they mimed to "Not Fade Away" and "I Just Wanna Make Love To You". The show, hosted by Brian Matthew, also featured Adam Faith, Dionne Warwick and Kenny Ball and his Jazzmen. It was transmitted across the ITV network, May 30th, between 5:50 - 6:34pm.
Coventry Theatre. (Two shows, the start of a seven-night stand, with guests Peter and Gordon, Julie Grant and The Overlanders. For tonight

Above: Flying into New York, June 1st
Right: Brian in a music store in LA. He ordered his trademark Vox "Teardrop" pearshaped guitar while in America.

only, The Caravelles replaced Peter and Gordon.)

MONDAY MAY 25th

The group's path with Brian Matthew crossed again, as they made their fourth appearance on the BBC Light Programme's "Saturday Club". During the session, the group recorded:-

(Howlin' Wolf's) "Down In The Bottom" / "You Can Make It If You Try" / "Route 66" / "Confessin' The Blues" and "Down The Road Apiece".

The session was broadcast June 6th between 10:00 -12 :00 am, in a programme also featuring The Hollies, Dusty Springfield, Mark Wynter, The Lorne Gibson Trio, The Echoes and Matt Munro.

Two shows at the Granada Theatre, East Ham. Support acts:- The Barron Knights (with Duke D'Mond), The Cyclons and David John and The Mood. Compere: Tony Marsh. The Stones set: "Beautiful Delilah" / "Walking The Dog " / " I Just Wanna Make Love To You" / "You Better Move On" / "I`m Alright" / "Not Fade Away" /Charlie's intro and "I Wanna Be Your Man."

Fifty police and a squad of first aid attendants were called in to calm hysterical fans.

TUESDAY MAY 26th

Town Hall, Birmingham.(Two shows).The group stayed at the Grand Hotel and dressed formally for dinner,after the episode in Bristol (see May 11th entry).

WEDNESDAY MAY 27th

Danilo Theatre, Cannock. (Two shows.) The "Daily Mirror" ran a story "Beatle Your Rolling Stone Hair!", in which a headmaster ruled, "Beatle haircuts are IN - but Rolling Stones styles are OUT!" The head, Mr. Donald Thompson, had suspended eleven of his boys from Woodlands Comprehensive School in Coventry, because they wore their hair like Mick Jagger & Co. of the Rolling Stones pop group. "Long and scruffy" Mr. Thompson called it, but yesterday he said they could return, if they cut their hair neatly "like The Beatles".

THURSDAY MAY 28th

Essoldo Theatre, Stockport. (Two shows.)

THE HAMILTON
NO. 31 CHROME PLATED
CHROME PLATED STAND

Above: Brian and Charlie on the coach, June 5th
Left: Brian Jones and Andrew Oldham in tune with each other
for a change LA June 3rd

FRIDAY MAY 29th

City Hall, Sheffield. (Two shows.) The "Daily Mirror":-"Sticks and Stones: Everything seems to be against them on the surface. They are the ugliest group in Britain. They are not looked on very kindly by most parents or by adults in general..."

SATURDAY MAY 30th

Adelphi Cinema, Bath Road, Slough. (Two shows.) Compere Tony Marsh "mooned" the front row from the wings. He was reported by outraged parents and later fined.

SUNDAY MAY 31st

The group returned to the Empire Pool, Wembley for their third concert there in a month. This time it was the "Pop Hit Parade", with Adam Faith and The Roulettes, Wayne Fontana and the Mindbenders, Freddie and the Dreamers, Julie Grant, The Hollies, Eden Kane and the Downbeats, The Barron Knights (with Duke D'Mond), The Merseybeats, The McKinleys, Kevin Scott and the Kinsmen, The Swinging Blue Jeans and The Undertakers. Like the N.M.E event (see April 26th entry), the Stones remained to headline an evening show, at the venue. "AMERICAN'S BRACE YOURSELVES. IN THE TRACKS OF THE BEATLES, A SECOND WAVE OF SHEEPDOGLOOKING, ANGRY ACTING, GUITAR PLAYING BRITONS IS ON THE WAY. THEY CALL THEMSELVES "THE ROLLING STONES" AND THEY`RE DUE IN NEW YORK ON TUESDAY" (An American press release).

MONDAY JUNE 1st.

After a month of planning, the Stones, with Andrew Oldham, flew to the United States on a 1:00 pm flight. A large crowd, (which included Bill's wife Diane and son Stephen), saw them off. Co-manager Eric Easton told the press:-"the tour will earn over £30,000". They arrived 3:30pm (N.Y time) at New York's Kennedy Airport to be greeted by 500 fans. The group gave a press conference, at which, Keith and Brian were each given a bouquet of flowers and Charlie was presented with a birthday cake (for his 23rd, the following day). "Hey, are you guys wearing wigs?" and "Do you guys sing music like The Beatles?" were the level of questions, the reporters shot at them. "Not Fade Away" was at No.88, in the Billboard "Hot Hundred." The group arrived in five separate limousines at the Hotel Astor, on Broadway, where another press reception was held. A crowd of 200 fans kept vigil outside. Murray the "K" Kaufman, who was forever by the Beatles side during their visit to America in February, had the group as guests on his two hour "Murray the K's Swinging Soiree" radio show on WINS. After the show, he played The Valentinos "It's All Over Now" to the group and escorted them to the Peppermint Lounge, where they watched The Younger Brothers act and partied until 1:30am. A "curl for a souvenir" craze developed between young female fans who had converged on the hotel, where fans, armed with a pair of scissors, challenged each other to snip a piece of hair off a Stone as he left the hotel!

TUESDAY JUNE 2nd

The group woke at 8am to appear on rival radio station WMCA. A further press reception was held back at the hotel and then another after lunch. A 24-hour guard was stationed in the corridor outside their

Brian and Keith in harmony, Chess studios, Chicago, June 10th

rooms. Bill had contracted a 24-hr flu virus and remained in bed while the others were smuggled out of the hotel for some sightseeing. He was well enough to join them when they returned at midnight to appear on WABC-TV show, "The Les Crane Show". During the broadcast, viewers were invited to phone in with questions for the group (many of which they considered insulting). Crane also attempted to interview them:-
Crane: "This is your first appearance on American television?"
Keith: "Yeah!"
Crane: "Isn't it exciting?"
Keith: "Yeah, it knocks me out!" (the rest of the Stones laugh)
Crane: "You wouldn't be sending me up, would you?"
Keith: "No, I wouldn't dare" (laughter fills the room)
Crane: "You wouldn't dare. Brian Jones is the third and one of the loveliest members of the group"
Mick: "Oh, he's very lovely" (replying sarcastically). The Stones did not perform during the one-hour transmission.

WEDNESDAY JUNE 3rd

The group left New York on a 7:45am flight to California, to appear on their first major US TV show. The group were booked for an appearance on the Saturday night ABC TV variety show, "Hollywood Palace", that week hosted by legendary crooner, Dean Martin. During the show (also featuring Eydie Gorme, Zizi Jean Marie, Nicholas Brothers, Linon and Rob McBray and the Kaye Sisters), Martin insulted the group with his introductions:-"Now, something for the youngsters, five singing boys from England who's sold a lot of albiums (pretending to be drunk). albums, they're called The Rolling Stones... I've been rolled when I was stoned myself! I don't know what they're singing about, but here they are at!"
After, "I Just Wanna Make Love To You", the group immediately left the stage, and Martin re-entered:-"Rolling Stones, aren't they great?" (sarcastically rolling his eyes heavenwards), "these singing groups are under the impression they have long hair. Not true at all, it's an optical illusion, they just have low foreheads and high eyebrows, that's all". After a trampoline act, he commented:- "That's The Rolling Stones father, he's been trying to kill himself ever since!" The group, smarting, re-appeared later in the show to perform "Not Fade Away". ("Tell Me" was also performed, but never broadcast). To add insult to injury, when the programme was first transmitted across ABC TV stations on June 13th, the Stones segment had been cut to 65 seconds of "I Just Wanna Make Love To You". After numerous complaints from fans, both songs were re-instated when the show was repeated on Sept 12th. English viewers had a chance to see a version of the show on BBC-2, Saturday, Dec.16th, between 9:15 - 9:54 pm. Dean Martin had been replaced by host Ed Wynn and only "Not Fade Away" was included. After the recording, ex-Everly Brothers bassist, Joey Paige, (whom they'd met on the Everlys tour the previous year) took the group downtown to cool off. (The following year, he came to England, staying in Brian's flat in Chelsea and

1964 U.S.A Fan Club Material

recorded a Bill Wyman composition "Cause I'm In Love With You", released on Fontana, in March 1965. Bill also produced the disc.)

THURSDAY JUNE 4th

The group were photographed at Malibu Beach, attended a Phil Spector recording session at RCA studios featuring Darlene Love, Jackie De Shannon and Bob B. Soxx & The Blue Jeans and then went on to a party with The Beach Boys.

FRIDAY JUNE 5th

The group took a coach trip to San Bernadino, 62 miles away. Accompanying them was Bob Bonis, their American road manager. After more interviews for both TV and press, the group performed their first American concert at the Swing Auditorium (4,400 audience). Also on the bill were Bobby Vee (whose 20-year old saxophonist was Bobby Keys), The Chiffons, Bobby Goldsboro and Bobby Comstock. The group boarded the coach back to L.A, after the show. Back in England, a scheduled concert at the Queens Hall, Leeds, was cancelled. The N.M.E reported that "Stone Brian Jones is likely to record a single on his own, early next month, for a unique Decca single".

SATURDAY JUNE 6th

The group flew to San Antonio for the first two of four concerts at the San Antonio Teen Fair, with Billy J Kramer and The Dakotas, who were staying at the same hotel (The El Tropicano). In the "Daily Mirror", Jack Hutton reported:- "The Stones are being treated as freaks in America. People gasp in amazement when they appear at airports, in hotel lobbies and in the streets. Men have whistled and girls ask "Do they wear lipstick and eye make-up and carry purses?!" No one can take them seriously!"

SUNDAY JUNE 7th

The final two shows at the Teen Fair. During the day, the group were interviewed on San Antonio radio.

MONDAY JUNE 8th

More press conferences and local sightseeing, including a visit to the Alamo.

TUESDAY JUNE 9th

The group flew out to Chicago, via Dallas, checking into the Water Tower Inn. Upon arriving, they were eager to check out the blues clubs on the South Side, but were advised not to, due to racial tension.

WEDNESDAY JUNE 10th

The group appeared on various Chicago based radio and TV stations, including an interview for the "Jack Eigen Show" on station WMAQ. A cherished ideal was achieved by recording on 4-track, at the legendary Chess Studios, at 2120 South Michigan Avenue (where most of their R & B heroes had recorded). The suggestion to use the studio came from Phil Spector, who had met the group, following their arrival in New York. During the two day session, the group worked with Andrew Oldham and sound engineer Ron Malo. The first session (which lasted from midday to 6:00pm) produced the following:-

"It's All Over Now" (The Valentino's with Bobby Womack)

"Time Is On My Side" (first version with Stu on organ) (Irma Thomas)

"I Can't Be Satisfied" (Muddy Waters)

"Stewed And Keefed" (an unreleased blues instrumental prominently featuring Stu on piano and Keith).

During the session, Buddy Guy and Willie Dixon dropped by. Back in England, the Stones own monthly publication "The Rolling Stones Monthly" went on sale for the first time, published by "Beat Publications", who were also responsible for "The Beatles Book Monthly". (The Stones own magazine would run for 30 issues, ceasing publication in November, 1966).

THURSDAY JUNE 11th

The group held a morning press conference outside the "Chicago Tribune" newspaper building, in the middle of Michigan Avenue, facing the media, sitting in folding chairs. The police were forced to break up the conference as fans started to surge around the group, "with danger of traffic coming to a standstill". "Get out of here, or we'll lock up the whole bunch!" A senior police chief shouted. The group adjourned to the pavement. The second day at Chess, again with Andrew Oldham and Ron Malo, with Stu on piano and organ, (lasting from midday to 2:00am on the 12th), produced the following songs:-

"If You Need Me" (Wilson Pickett)

"2120 South Michigan Avenue" (originally lasting for over six minutes, but edited when released) (Nanker-Phelge)

"Empty Heart" (Nanker-Phelge)

"Confessin' The Blues" (Chuck Berry)

"Around And Around" (Chuck Berry)

"Don't Lie To Me" (based on Chuck Berry's version)

"Down The Road Apiece" (Chuck Berry)

"Look What You've Done" (Muddy Waters)

"Tell Me Baby" (based on Howlin' Wolf's "How Many More Times")

"Down In The Bottom" (Howlin' Wolf)

"Hi-Heeled Sneakers" (Robert Higgenbotham)

"Reelin` And Rockin" (Chuck Berry). The latter four remain unreleased. The group met two more heroes in Chuck Berry and Muddy Waters. Chuck was much more friendly (see May 9th entry). "I really dig these boys and their kind of music". So impressed, that the notoriously miserly musician invited them to his amusement farm "Berry Park", waiving the $2-50c admission charge! The group, during breaks, gave studio interviews for various TV and radio stations. At 3:30am, they flew on to Minneapolis.

FRIDAY JUNE 12th

Excelsior Fair Ballroom, Minneapolis. (400 audience). The venue was half-

Above: "Ready Steady Go!" June 26th
Left: Returning to Heathrow from first US tour, June 22nd

empty as the concert had only been organised two days before with a high ticket price of $3 (21s), coupled with the obvious fact that hardly anybody there had heard of them!

SATURDAY JUNE 13th

The group stopped off at Sioux Falls & Sioux City, looking in vain for native American Indians. After a press conference at the airport and appearing on a local television show, the Stones played at the Omaha Music Hall.(1500 audience). Backstage, an over-enthusiastic cop forced Keith, at gunpoint, to empty the Coke he was drinking down the "john", mistakenly convinced there was whiskey in it, despite Keith's protests!

SUNDAY JUNE 14th

The group flew from Chicago to Detroit, staying at the Holiday Inn. After another radio interview, the group played at the 13,000-seater Olympia Stadium (just under 1000 showed!). Bill, Charlie and Stu went on a "free record shopping spree" at a local store.

WEDNESDAY JUNE 17th

The group took a coach to Pittsburgh, checking into the Carlton Hotel. After being interviewed on local radio, they gave a show at Westview Park (1,300 audience). After the show, the group took an overnight 500-mile coach ride to Cleveland, arriving at 5am.

THURSDAY JUNE 18th

A 9:30am TV show and two radio shows, including an interview with future TV celebrity, Mike Douglas for his WHK radio show. Mick appeared solo, on rival Cleveland stations. A group interview appeared that night on local Cleveland TV. The group were driven on to Hershey, arriving at midnight.

FRIDAY JUNE 19th

The group flew 15 miles for radio and TV in Harrisburg and a concert at the State Farm Arena. After the show, the group took a coach to New York, checking into the Park Sheraton, at 2:30am.

SATURDAY JUNE 20th

The group appeared on "The Clay Cole Saturday Show" on WPIX Channel 11, performing "Tell Me" (their latest American single), after which Mick was interviewed by the host. In the afternoon and evening, the group performed the last two shows of the tour, at Carnegie Hall, M.C'd by Murray The "K". During the first show, fans rioted, resulting in the police insisting that another group should close the first half of the second show, in order for the group to be spirited away before the audience left the building. The disturbances created a lifetime-ban on 'rock' shows at this prestigous venue.

SUNDAY JUNE 21st

The Stones scheduled TV appearance on BBC 1's "A Swingin' Time" was cancelled, due to the group still being in America. (Their place was taken by Big Dee Irwin.)

MONDAY JUNE 22nd

The group flew home, arriving at London Airport at 7:35am. Only 50 fans were there to greet them, due to the early hour. A television interview was arranged in the conference room. While the group waited for five cars and a police convoy to escort them back to central London, Mick was met by girlfriend, Chrissie Shrimpton (sister of model Jean). Keith remarked that he had cut two inches off Bill's hair in America, "because it was too hot", while brandishing a pistol he had brought back.("You can buy them as easily as candy floss over there!") That evening, the group honoured a booking to appear at the Commemoration Ball, at Oxford's Magdalen College (made the previous year for a fee of £100).

WEDNESDAY JUNE 24th

The Stones had a business luncheon at the Savoy Hotel with Andrew Oldham, Eric Easton and a legal representative, to discuss making The Rolling Stones a limited company. Bill also formalised plans to change his surname (from "Perks" to "Wyman") by deed poll.

FRIDAY JUNE 26th

Television House, Kingsway for an "unannounced" appearance on

Associated-Rediffusion's "Ready Steady Go!" With the group recently returned from the States, schedules were hastily re-arranged to accommodate the group. The show, hosted by Keith Fordyce, was transmitted live later that night (6:08 - 6:59pm across the ITV network) and featured the group miming to "It's All Over Now" and "Good Times, Bad Times" (both sides of the group's new single released today, with advance orders of over 150,000, becoming their first No.1), as well as Bill, Brian and Mick being interviewed by Fordyce. Mick was also interviewed by Cathy McGowan, who dismissed rumours that he was about to marry her! The main subject of conversation, in both interview segments, was the group's visit to America. In the evening, the Stones attended a special "All Night Rave" at the Alexandra Palace, London. Organised by the Rolling Stones Fan Club, and promoted by John Smith, it was co-billed: "Welcome Home Stones". Starting at 9:00 pm that night and running until 6:30 the following morning, the 10 hour event, hosted by Jimmy Savile and "direct from Radio Luxembourg" Don Wardell, also

featured Alexis Korner, Millie and the Five Embers, John Lee Hooker, John Mayall's Blues Breakers, The Barron Knights featuring Duke D'Mond, Jimmy Powell and The Five Dimensions, The Downliners Sect and Tony Colton and The Crawdaddies, plus guests. The Stones performed two half-hour sets at different times, leaving the rave around 2:30pm.

SATURDAY JUNE 27th

A hectic day for the BBC. With a possible ban from "Top of the Pops" hanging over them (see April 29th entry), the group made an early journey to the Manchester studios, in Dickenson Road, to promote "It's All Over Now". The recording made on this date was included in the show transmitted Wednesday, July 1st and repeated, four weeks later, on July 29th (both BBC1 6:35 - 6: 59pm). For this performance, the Stones were paid an improved sum of £131.5 shillings (for each of the two transmissions), 5 shillings short of a £58 pay increase. Recording over, the group were driven back to London to make an appearance on the early evening, new record release judging show, "Juke Box Jury", which

MICK JAGGER   CHARLIE WATTS   BRIAN JONES   KEITH RICHARD   BILL WYMAN

had been gracing BBC television since 1959. With a regular celebrity panel of four, decreeing whether the record in question, would be a "Hit" or "Miss", the Stones appearance became the first and only time, a panel of five appeared on the show. So many people had applied for tickets for the recording, that the show, which was usually transmitted from Studio 2 at the BBC TV Centre, Wood Lane, (with an audience capacity of 125), was switched to the BBC Television Theatre in Shepherds Bush (where there was seating for 500). A week prior to the recording, applications for tickets were still flooding in and an estimated 10,000 hopeful fans were disappointed. Fans began queueing outside the BBC TV theatre, on the morning of the show, at 10am, even though the group were on their way to Manchester and were not scheduled to arrive at Shepherds Bush until around 6:45pm. Such was the interest the group were causing in the show (and in pop music in general), that producer, Barry Langford, decided to ring the changes on the programme. Extra cameras were called in, and a new set was designed. (Even The Beatles never had this, when they appeared on the programme on Dec 7th 1963). Most importantly of all, the show's "Hit" or "Miss" trademarks were temporarily scrapped, in order that each member of the group could give his own verdict on the discs in their own inimitable fashion. Langford announced: "We expect a minimum viewing audience of 20

million, as compared with the regular 11 or 12 million". The group arrived two hours behind schedule. Arrangements to film their arrival in a hired armoured car (which drove straight in through the back door on to the studio floor) went haywire, when they were driven to the wrong entrance! The group first appeared in a rehearsal at 7pm and then, before a very noisy audience, recorded the show for broadcast, from 8:15pm. From left to right, sat Mick, Charlie, Brian, Keith and Bill. The finished broadcast, (with a running time of just over 27 minutes), featured the group in judgement on: "Tobacco Road" by The Nashville Teens, "I Just Don't Know What To Do With Myself" by Dusty Springfield, "My Baby Don't Dig Me" by Ray Charles, "Play Me A Song" by Christine Holmes, "Some Day We're Gonna Love Again" by The Searchers and "The Ferris Wheel" by The Everly Brothers, (while filmclips of Freddie and The Dreamers performing "Just For You", from the British Lions Film, "Everyday's A Holiday" and Elvis Presley performing "There's Gold In The Mountains" from the MGM film "Kissin' Cousins", were also featured). During the programme, the host David Jacobs, played a 64 second audio clip of "It's All Over Now" and the group met a young female fan on the stage, who had won a competition to meet them personally. After going off-air, the group had to wait backstage for an hour, as half the audience wouldn't vacate the theatre.

Above: Keith and Brian chat to Paul McCartney at the Dorchester, July 6th
Left: Juke Box Jury, June 26th

The show was "telerecorded" on closed circuit for transmission on BBC1, Saturday, July 4th. Each Stone received a fee of £31.10 shillings. The BBC were instructed to pay all monies to "Eric Easton Ltd". The programme unfortunately no longer resides in the BBC Film/VT archives.

WEDNESDAY 1st - FRIDAY JULY 10th

Mick and Keith went to Greenford Studios to record more demos, (with producer Andrew Oldham and his orchestra):-

"Each And Every Day Of The Year" (demo for Bobby Jameson)

"We're Wasting Time" (demo for comedian Jimmy Tarbuck)

"Some Things Just Stick In Your Mind" (demo for Vashti)

"I'd Much Rather Be With The Boys" (demo for The Toggery Five)

"Blue Turns To Grey" and "(Walkin Thru The) Sleepy City" (demos for The Mighty Avengers)

"Young Love" (Bo and Peep, rumoured to be Jagger and Oldham). Among the musical directors on hand were John Paul Jones, David Whittaker and Mike Leander.

On the 3rd, Mick and Charlie went on holiday to Ibiza, Bill moved house in Kent, while Brian, initially keen to return to the States (despite the fact the group's recent tour didn't go as well as anticipated), remained in London, as did Keith. "Juke Box Jury" was transmitted on BBC-1 on July 4th. The customary early tea time slot of 5:50 had been shifted to 7:10, enabling "Summer Grandstand" to cover the close of play of the England vs. Australia third test cricket match at Headingley and the Wimbledon tennis finals. Such was the interest in the programme, that the BBC postponed another Saturday night favourite, "Dr. Who" (even going so far as to apologise in the "Radio Times"!) Unfortunately, expectations for the show were never realised, and the general consensus for the programme, was a "miss". The backlash (to both the BBC and the Stones) was particularly harsh. The group were seen smoking throughout the entire show, made little conversation, and had low opinions on all the records being judged, prompting one fan to write: "The most boring Jury I've ever seen", while another wrote:- "After seeing them on JBJ, in the words of their own song, "It`s All Over Now". The attacks even extended to the genial host David Jacobs: "I have never seen such a disgusting waste of 25 minutes, as the Rolling Stones on "Juke Box Jury". "The boys were hardly allowed to say anything constructive about the records without David Jacobs interrupting." The daily tabloids bandied adjectives such as "rude", "boorish" and "charmless" about. Adults joined in too, describing the group's behaviour as "disgusting", particularly when the girl fan came onstage to meet the group individually, only Mick bothered to stand up! The group trod on thin ice with their attack on Elvis Presley. They criticised his singing and "dated" look, which lead to more howls of protest. The show was a most valuable shot in the arm for the band's "bad boy" image, but what did they think of the programme? Bill:-"People shouldn't take these programmes so seriously. Anyway, they know where the "off" switch on the television set is, so why torture themselves by sticking with the show?" Mick "If the producer had wanted a sophisticated panel, he could have got a bunch of West End actresses!!"

JULY

The scheduled month, for shooting to begin on the group's first film. The production was shelved again, due to director, Clive Donner who would later direct "What's New Pussycat" with Peter Sellers and Woody Allen, being unexpectedly delayed in America on the latest Kim Novak film. The film, with a screenplay by Lionel Bart, was re-scheduled for October.

MONDAY JULY 6th

Brian went to Television House, Kingsway, to record an appearance as a last-minute addition to the panel (including Radio Luxembourg DJ, Muriel Young and bandleader, Johnny Franz), on the "Ready Steady Go!" spin-off show, "Ready, Steady, Win!". (A weekly judging contest to find "The best new beat group", with a first prize of £1,000 worth of musical instruments. The heats had begun on June 15th.) The show was broadcast live, over the ITV network, between 6:08 - 6:59pm. Mick, later appeared as a panellist on the series, with DJ Alan Freeman and Scottish singer, Lulu. (Taped Monday, August 17th and broadcast a week later, August 24th, between the same times.) After the show, Brian and Keith, in casual dress, arrived un-invited to a Beatles party, at the Dorchester Hotel. It was held to honour the premiere of their first film, "A Hard

Day's Night". As the pair were not permitted to enter, they instructed a messenger to take a note. It read:-"We would like to see you. Keith and Brian (of The Rolling Stones)". The messenger took the note to John Lennon and whispered to him:-
"I'm afraid, they are dressed rather untidily". "What's the difference" Lennon replied, "they're friends of ours, get them in!"

SATURDAY JULY 11th

The group taped a segment for the Southern ITV regional magazine programme, "Day By Day" (broadcast two days later, between 6:08 - 6:29 pm), before undertaking one of their more bizarre gig's at the Spa Royal Hall, Bridlington (3,000 audience). "The management reserve the right to refuse permission to anyone not wearing orthodox dress. Jeans and leather jackets will be barred." If this edict wasn't harsh enough, fans of both sexes also had to pass a cleanliness test, before being admitted! "The Rolling Stones are very clean, intelligent lads", Bridlington's deputy entertainments manager, Ron Smith told the "Daily Mirror", "but some of the fans who like to dress in the same fashion seem to think they have to be dirty too". The Stones repertoire at this time:-
"Walking The Dog" / "High-Heeled Sneakers" / "You Can Make It If You Try" / "Not Fade Away" / "Can I Get A Witness" / "I Just Wanna Make Love To You" and "It's All Over Now". Granada Television cameras filmed part of the show, for a forthcoming "World In Action" documentary (see Sept 22nd entry).

SUNDAY JULY 12th

Queens Hall, Leeds. (Two shows on a revolving stage, in the middle of the audience, with supports Ray Kennon and The Guvnors, Rose Bros (with Dallas), Lulu and The Luvvers and Ray Anton and The Peppermint Men. Compere: Garth Cawood.) Radio Luxembourg broadcast their own tribute show to the group entitled "This Is Their Life".

WEDNESDAY JULY 15th

The group made a return trip to Manchester, to appear on "Top Of The Pops" for the sixth time. They performed "It's All Over Now", on the live show (BBC-1, 6:35 - 6:59pm), which was not recorded. Again their fee was £131.5 shillings. Each member of the group received travelling expenses of £4.12 shillings, for a standard 1964 return train fare.

THURSDAY JULY 16th

While recording demos at Greenford Studios in London, the group recorded a set for Radio Luxembourg in the "Teen And Twenty Disc Club".

FRIDAY JULY 17th

A busy day for BBC Radio, with recordings for two different programmes. Firstly, the group made their second appearance on "The Joe Loss Pop Show", for the Light Programme. For this live show, also featuring Rose Brennan, Ross McManus, Larry Gretton and the Joe Loss Orchestra, the group performed:-
 "It's All Over Now" / "If You Need Me" / "Confessin' The Blues" / "Carol" and "Mona", broadcast between 12:31 - 1:30 pm.

Then, later in the afternoon, the group made their debut on "Top Gear", a new late-night radio show on the Light Programme with producer Bernie Andrews and hosted by regular "Saturday Club" host, Brian Matthew. Transmitted Thursday, July 23rd, between 10pm -12:00 midnight, they recorded:-

"Around And Around" / "If You Need Me" / "I Can't Be Satisfied" and (Bo Diddley's) "Crackin' Up".

The broadcast also featured performances by Elkie Brooks, P.J. Proby, Joe Brown and the Bruvvers and Arthur Greenslade and the Gee Men.

SATURDAY JULY 18th
A 7: 30pm show at the Beat City Club, 79 Oxford Street, London. (600 audience, with support Tom Jones and the Squires.)

SUNDAY JULY 19th
Brighton Hippodrome. (Two shows.)

MONDAY JULY 20th
Keith, Bill and Charlie visited the Fairfield Halls, Croydon for a concert by Ray Charles, which was being recorded by Rediffusion for a television special, "The Man They Call Genius" (transmitted across the ITV network on Wednesday, August 26th, 9:40 - 10:28 pm). The show was a scoop for the producers, as it was the first time Charles had appeared on British television. The three did not participate in the show, but were picked out in the audience by the TV cameras on two occasions.

TUESDAY 21st - THURSDAY JULY 23rd
Kingsway Studios, London (with Andrew Oldham and Bill Farley and orchestra).

The sessions included:-

"Heart Of Stone" (demo version)

"Try A Little Harder"

"Hear It" (featuring Keith on acoustic guitar)

"Memphis Tennessee" (often believed to be a group jam, it was in fact, the Andrew Oldham Orchestra).

"Godzi" (unreleased).

THURSDAY JULY 23rd
Brian's girlfriend, Linda Lawrence, gave birth to a son, Julian Mark. (Brian had been living at her parents house, in Reading). Another unscheduled TV appearance for Associated-Rediffusion's "Ready Steady Go!", at Television House, Kingsway. The request to appear had only been received at the Stones office, the day before. The segment was entirely pre-recorded, so the group spent the afternoon in rehearsal and taped "It's All Over Now", in the late afternoon. Keith Fordyce also interviewed Bill and Brian. The inserts were used in the following day's edition of the programme (transmitted 6:08 - 6:59pm).

FRIDAY JULY 24th
Empress Ballroom, Blackpool with Simon Scott, The LeRoys and The Executives, later to be described as "Britain's biggest rock riot ever!" During the show, when a disruptive element of the crowd started spitting at the group, Keith kicked one of the ringleaders square in the face, and a full-scale riot ensued. A Steinway grand piano was pushed off the stage and crushed, while several chandeliers were pulled from the ceiling and shattered. Events got so far out of hand that it took up to

Above: Postcards sent from Brian on the 1st US tour to girlfriend Dawn Malloy (Below).

seventy of Blackpool's policemen and approximately thirty attendants, to quell the riot. An estimated fifty were taken to hospital and the ballroom received damage totalling £4,000. Brian received a cut under his left eye. The group had to literally run for their lives, leaving behind the equipment they had borrowed from supports, The LeRoys. While the Stones laid low at the Bull and Royal Hotel, in nearby Preston, "Stu" returned at 3am, with the gear destroyed beyond recognition!

SATURDAY JULY 25th

Imperial Ballroom, Nelson. A replacement set of Vox equipment (totalling £700.) was personally delivered by Eric Easton.

SUNDAY JULY 26th

De Montfort Hall, Leicester. (Two shows.)

TUESDAY JULY 28th

The group went to the Teddington Studios of ABC TV, to record an appearance on "Lucky Stars Summer Spin", a special summer edition of "Thank Your Lucky Stars", hosted by Mike Sarne (famous for his 1962 hit "Come Outside"). The group performed "It's All Over Now" against a "Stonehenge" backdrop, in a show also featuring The Merseybeats and The Fourmost, transmitted August 8th, 5:50 - 6:34 pm across the ITV network.

FRIDAY JULY 31st

The group flew to Northern Ireland for two gigs. The first at the Ulster Hall, Belfast (A/K/A "The Boom Boom Room"). News cameras from BBC Belfast arrived to interview four group members briefly backstage (Keith was held up in the toilet due to a stomach complaint, according to BBC documentation!), for the programme "Six Ten" (transmitted in the Belfast region only, 6:10 - 6:35pm). For this service, the group were paid ten guineas. The show itself, was halted after 12 minutes, when hysterical girls were carried out in strait jackets. Newsreel footage of which, was screened on RTE TV(Dublin), the following day. The second, more restrained gig, occured at the Flamingo Ballroom, Ballymena.

SATURDAY AUGUST 1st

The group flew back to London and then drove to Hastings, for a show at the Pier Ballroom. On the town's outskirts, they switched to an ambulance van as a decoy and were driven directly down the pier, into the foyer of the ballroom, after fans gave chase.

SUNDAY AUGUST 2nd

A concert at Longleat House, Warminster, home of the Marquess of Bath, as part of the third open-air pop concert at the venue, before an audience of 25,000. After the group were introduced by the Marquess,

Below: Dawn Malloy with Brian's fifth child, John, and (right) posing with the band (second right)

200 fainted when crushed against the barriers. The Marquess was quoted:- "A delightful day, so few hospital cases, the fans were wonderful". During the day, the group gave an interview in the Green Room, for a TV news crew that was transmitted later that night.

WEDNESDAY AUGUST 5th

TV cameras from America visited London, to record an appearance for inclusion in CBS TV's Tuesday night comedy show "The Red Skelton Hour" (an American comic). An unusual performance was arranged of the Stones miming on the steps of the London Palladium."Here we are at the London Palladium, where England's latest singing sensation ,The Rolling Stones are appearing" was Red's voice-over as he walked into the venue, adorned with "Now Appearing: Rolling Stones: In Person" banners. Red entered the building to find hordes of hysterical girls screaming at the group who performed (in order):- "Tell Me" and "Carol" (at the end of which, the group made a hasty exit from the crowd). The group appeared again near the end of the show, where Red (now back in Hollywood) introduced them "Aren't those Rolling Stones really something? Hey, how do you like that hair?!" "You know, they make The Beatles look like Yul Brunner, you know England must have socialised haircuts. Hey, if all the singing groups in England would put their heads together, they could start a dandruff plantation!!" They reappeared, in the foyer of the Palladium to perform "It's All Over Now". Later in the afternoon, additional footage of the band was filmed from behind, which showed the host, being jostled by fans. (This was edited occasionally into the three song performance). The telerecording was transmitted on CBS -TV September 22nd and repeated on November 10th.

FRIDAY AUGUST 7th

The group performed on ATV-Rediffusion's "Ready Steady Go's!" first anniversary show. Bill and Brian were the week's "Amateur D.J"'s and during one of the "spoof" parts of the show, briefly parodied, in mime, The Beatles "A Hard Day's Night", which was featured in the show, transmitted live between 6:08 - 6:59 pm across the ITV network. The other guests included Brian Poole and The Tremeloes, The Nashville Teens, Kenny Lynch, Marianne Faithfull and Cilla Black. (The Beatles were rumoured to appear, but never showed). Following the show, a party

"Lucky Stars Summer Spin", July 28th

was held backstage, attended by the group, Marianne, Andrew Oldham, Eric Easton and Tony Calder. Beatles manager Brian Epstein, record producer Mickie Most and singers Jess Conrad, Elkie Brooks and Lesley Duncan were among the other guests. When the Stones left at 8:15pm, fans ripped a door off their limousine as they began to depart. Due to the size of the crowd, Brian was left stranded and frantically hailed a taxi. He later obtained a lift (to Richmond) from Eric Easton, lying on the car floor to avoid fans. Meanwhile, the other Stones had sped to a West London Police Station and in order to reach Richmond safely, had exchanged their limousine for a newspaper delivery van, entering through a tent marked "Lady Artistes Only"! That evening, the group topped the bill for the first night of the "4th National Jazz and Blues

Festival", held at Richmond Athletic Ground between the 7th & 9th of August. Their 45-minute set, before 7,000, featured "Walking The Dog", "Hi Heeled Sneakers", "It's All Over Now" and "It's Alright". The other acts that night included: Georgie Fame and the Blue Flames, Val McCallun and The Authentics, The Crebbles and The T-Bones (who played immediately before The Stones). Post show, The Stones were whisked to a hotel near London Airport for a flight to Holland, departing early the next day.

SATURDAY AUGUST 8th

The group landed at Schipol Airport, Amsterdam, for an 8:15pm concert (with supports The Jos Brinks, Trix and The Paramounts, Andre van Duyn, Richochets met Ritchie Clark, The Telstars and The Fourys

Pousze), at the Kurhaus Hall (an Opera House), Scheveningen, the Hague. The audience rioted after the first song and smashed up the seats. The group tried to carry on playing regardless, but after ten minutes, were forced to leave the stage for their own safety and the curtains were pulled. The pandemonium was captured for posterity by a Dutch TV newscrew and damage was estimated at over £1,000. Stu had to be bandaged after being hit on the head by a bottle. During the mayhem, it was reported that two girls had their clothes ripped off! The group were interviewed by the local Vara TV newscrew (included in news broadcasts that night) plus crews from Scheveningen, who captured interviews for both TV and radio, one of which featured an in-depth, (if possible), interview with Charlie Watts! The group stayed overnight at the Terminus Hotel.

SUNDAY AUGUST 9th

The group flew back to Manchester Airport from Holland to appear at the New Elizabethan Ballroom, Belle Vue. Compere: Jimmy Savile. Due to their equipment still being held in transit from Holland, the Stones used equipment loaned from The Pretty Things. During the concert, two policewomen fainted, while another was taken to hospital with rib injuries. Local barmen were called in to assist 50 police in trying to control 3,000 teenagers. Mick and Keith later sat in with The Pretty Things, at the Oasis Club.

MONDAY AUGUST 10th

An evening concert at the Tower Ballroom, New Brighton, supported by twelve finalists in a local beat contest, promoted by Ray McFall and compared by Bob Wooler (Cavern Club owner and D.J respectively). During the day, Mick Jagger received his first conviction. He was fined £32, in Liverpool, for "driving without insurance, failing to produce his driving licence and exceeding the speed limit". His solicitor explained that he "had been on an errand of mercy, driving to hospital (in Birkenhead, with the rest of the group as passengers, on April 30th) to see two fans injured in a car crash".

TUESDAY AUGUST 11th

A gig at the Winter Gardens, Blackpool, was cancelled after the trouble at the Empress Ballroom (see July 24th entry).

WEDNESDAY AUGUST 12th

Mick and Keith attended a lavish party, thrown by Brian Epstein, at his home in Whaddon House, Knightsbridge.

Brian talking to Tony Calder backstage at "Ready Steady Go!" August 7th

THURSDAY AUGUST 13th

After two days off, the group flew to the Isle of Man, their arrival being covered by local TV and radio stations. After expressing his love of cats on air, a fan gave Brian a rare Manx breed as a gift. That night they played at the Palace Ballroom, Douglas, before an audience of 7,000. The only police dog on the Isle Of Man, an Alsatian called Rex, patrolled the stage prior to the performance, but after 20 minutes, Rex had to be taken away. The screaming was so loud that he had begun to snarl at the crowd (and at the Stones, as they took the stage).

FRIDAY AUGUST 14th

The group flew back to London Airport, to keep a date at the Wimbledon Palais, for a fee of £100 (arranged the year before). In the music press, plans were announced that the group would appear in a Christmas show with their own choice of favourite American R & B stars. The idea was subsequently scrapped. Meanwhile, the "Five By Five" EP was released, to advance orders of 200,000. Plans for the Stones first film continued, with their office announcing that the film may go into production upon their return from America in November, with a release date of April/May 1965.

TUESDAY AUGUST 18th

The Stones flew to Guernsey for the first of three concerts at the New Theatre Ballroom, St Peter's Port.

WEDNESDAY AUGUST 19th

New Theatre Ballroom. The day was spent sightseeing and go-karting at nearby St Brelade's.

THURSDAY AUGUST 20th

The group were interviewed by a local TV newscrew (transmitted in the evening's newscast 6:00 - 6:10pm) and gave the last show at the New Theatre Ballroom.

FRIDAY AUGUST 21st

Springfield Hall, St Helier, Jersey.

SATURDAY AUGUST 22nd

Springfield Hall, St Helier. Trouble arose, during the last performance, when angry fans ran riot after being refused entry due to their "inappropriate attire" (blue jeans and no tie). Mick was hit by a peach and four tomatoes, as a scuffle broke out on the balcony, while a running fight raged on the floor of the ballroom between 4,000 teenage fans. 42 minders, that were hired for the night, sent female fans flying, as they attacked troublemakers, dragging them out of the hall by their hair. A girl, who was seen with a flick-knife, was dragged down two flights of stairs before being thrown out, following a struggle with officials.

group appeared again, on TWW-TV's "Here Today", transmitted between 6:08 - 6:29 pm (in that region only).

WEDNESDAY AUGUST 26th

ABC Theatre, Exeter. (Two shows, as per above.)

THURSDAY AUGUST 27th

ABC Theatre, Plymouth. (Two shows, as per above.)

FRIDAY AUGUST 28th

Gaumont Theatre, Taunton. (Two shows, as per above.)

SATURDAY AUGUST 29th

Town Hall, Torquay. (Two shows, with guests Patrick Dane and the Quiet Five and Julie Grant.)

SUNDAY AUGUST 30th

The group returned to the Gaumont Theatre in Bournemouth, twice in one week, for two more shows, with guests:- Long John Baldry and the Hoochie Coochie Men and Julie Grant.

TUESDAY SEPTEMBER 1st

Mick only, returned to Regent Sound Studios to sing lead vocal on "Da Doo Ron Ron", for the Andrew Oldham Orchestra (released on the Ace of Clubs album "16 Hip Hits", on October 2nd).

WEDNESDAY 2nd - FRIDAY SEPTEMBER 4th

Regent Sound Studios, with Andrew Oldham and engineer, Bill Farley:-
"Little Red Rooster" (Willie Dixon)
"Off The Hook" (Nanker/Phelge)
"Congratulations"
"Suzie Q"
"Under The Boardwalk" (The Drifters).

SATURDAY SEPTEMBER 5th

The group commenced their 4th British Tour, for The Robert Stigwood Organisation, with two shows at the Finsbury Park Astoria, London. For this tour, the group's set featured:-
"Not Fade Away" / "I Just Wanna Make Love To You" / "Walking The Dog" / "If You Need Me" / "Around And Around" / "I'm A King Bee" / "I'm Alright" and "It's All Over Now".
Supports:- The Mojos, Inez and Charlie Foxx, Mike Berry and The Innocents, Billie Davis, The LeRoys and Simon Scott.
Compere: Don Spencer.

SUNDAY SEPTEMBER 6th

The start of four straight nights at Odeon Theatre venues, with two shows at Leicester.

MONDAY SEPTEMBER 7th

A day-off for the group when two shows at the Norwich Odeon were cancelled.

TUESDAY SEPTEMBER 8th

Odeon Theatre, Colchester. (Two shows.)

TOWN HALL, TORQUAY

SATURDAY, AUGUST 29th, 1964
at 9.0 p.m. sharp

John Smith presents

THE ROLLING STONES SHOW

Hall
RESERVED   R   9   **12/6**

This part to be retained

SUNDAY AUGUST 23rd

An eventful flight to Bournemouth to begin a short tour of the West Country (promoted by John Smith). The group reduced an air hostess to tears, after she'd deliberately insulted them, resulting in the Stones receiving a lifetime ban from B.U.A! (British United Airlines) Two shows at The Gaumont. Supports:-The Worryin' Kind, The Overlanders and The Barron Knights (feat. Duke D'mond). Guests:-The Paramounts and Julie Grant.

MONDAY AUGUST 24th

Gaumont Theatre, Weymouth. (Two shows with guests, The Five Embers and Millie.) Footage of the group arriving at Dorchester and an interview with Mick, were included in the TWW-TV regional news programme, "Here Today", transmitted between 6:08 - 6:29pm.

TUESDAY AUGUST 25th

Odeon Theatre, Weston-Super-Mare. (Two shows, as per above.) The

WEDNESDAY SEPTEMBER 9th

Odeon Theatre, Luton. (Two shows.)

Joining them on the bill were The Riot Squad, featuring future Jimi Hendrix Experience, drummer Mitch Mitchell.

THURSDAY SEPTEMBER 10th

Odeon Theatre, Cheltenham. (Two shows.)

In between shows Brian's parents and old friends visited him. A planned party had to be abandoned because fans had converged around the hotel. The group left the Odeon through a garage to a Black Maria and drove 40 miles to a transport cafe to eat. Following this, they drove on to Monmouth, arriving at the Beaufort Arms Hotel, at 9am. "Melody Maker" readers had voted the Stones "Most Popular British Group" and "Not Fade Away", Best Song. (The awards were presented at a luncheon at the Savoy).

FRIDAY SEPTEMBER 11th

The group visited the Wye Valley and Tintern Abbey, sightseeing and buying antiques. Later the group played two shows at the Capitol Theatre, Cardiff. At Greenwich Town Hall, a "Miming Mick Jagger" competition, was won by Laurie Yarham, a 16 year-old boy from Eltham College, who had mimicked Mick correctly with every movement. But after being announced winner, "Laurie" dropped a bombshell by admitting he was in fact Mick's brother, Chris!!

SATURDAY SEPTEMBER 12th

A day off after two shows at the Gaumont Theatre in Sheffield were cancelled due to theatre damage.

SUNDAY SEPTEMBER 13th

Liverpool Empire. (Two shows.)

MONDAY SEPTEMBER 14th

ABC Theatre, Chester. (Two shows.)

TUESDAY SEPTEMBER 15th

The group visited Manchester for another live appearance on Granada TV's "Scene At 6:30" (transmitted between 6:30 - 6:59pm) and two shows at the Odeon Theatre. After the shows, the group drove to Liverpool, checking into the Adelphi Hotel. Brian, Bill, Charlie Foxx and members of The Mojos went to the Blue Angel Club, leaving around 5:30 am.

WEDNESDAY SEPTEMBER 16th

ABC Theatre, Wigan. (Two shows.) MP Tom Driberg asked the House of Commons to deplore the actions of a magistrate who called The Rolling Stones "complete morons" who wore "filthy clothes". "Jokes" doing the rounds on the band included:-"The Rolling Stones? They're the ones who look like five shots of Hayley Mills!" and "There's absolutely no truth in the rumour that Fred Flintstone was the first ever Rolling Stone!"

THURSDAY SEPTEMBER 17th

The group were interviewed for Border ITV. A short news report featured:- the group getting out of, and post-interview, getting back into their car en route to two shows at the ABC Theatre, Carlisle, the group arriving, screaming fans and a souvenir poster vendor outside the venue. This footage was transmitted in the regional news programme (6:30 - 6:59pm). After the shows, the group drove sixty miles to a country hotel in Melrose, near Edinburgh.

FRIDAY SEPTEMBER 18th

Odeon Theatre, Newcastle-upon-Tyne. (Two shows.)

SATURDAY SEPTEMBER 19th

Usher Hall, Edinburgh. (Two shows.) Following the concert, the group left the venue in the back of a (by now) customary, armoured van.

SUNDAY SEPTEMBER 20th

ABC (instead of the Globe) Theatre, Stockton-on-Tees. (Two shows.)

MONDAY SEPTEMBER 21st

ABC Theatre, Kingston-upon-Hull. (Two shows.)

Pathe News visited the venue to produce a short "Technicolour" cinema featurette entitled "Rolling Stones Gather Moss". The film, with a running time of 6 minutes 3 seconds, began with the group walking alongside the main road to Hull, pretending to hitch-hike. (Brian walking cripple-fashion.) "Just another load of hitch-hikers, that's what they look like to motorist's speeding towards Hull. You can't blame the drivers, they're keeping their eyes on the road, the way Ernie Marples (the current Minister of Transport) wants them to. Little do they know, they're having their legs pulled, because these apparent hitch-hikers, so blandly ignored, are five of the most famous young men in showbusiness, The Rolling Stones. Some of these motorists will be kicking themselves when they learn they missed a chance of a lifetime of getting to know them" ran the narrative. The rest of the film showed fans waiting outside (and then being admitted to) the venue, a backstage press conference and the group getting made up and reading fan mail in the dressing room, while Brian tuned his Vox "Teardrop" guitar. Finally footage from the second show of "Around And Around" (dubbed to the record) closed the newsreel.

TUESDAY SEPTEMBER 22nd

ABC Theatre, Lincoln. (Two shows.) Granada/ITV's weekly "World In Action" series, screened a 25 minute special, "The Flipside", on the general mechanics of the pop industry. Included in the programme (transmitted 10:45 - 11:09 pm), was a 68 second segment of the Stones performing "High Heeled Sneakers" and "Not Fade Away" live (filmed at the Bridlington Spa Royal Hall on July 11th), as well as interviews with agents Roy Tempest and Eddie Rogers, unknown group The Four plus One, record producers Mickie Most and Joe Meek, DJ, David Jacobs and "failed" ex-pop stars, Terry Dene and Ricky Valance.

WEDNESDAY SEPTEMBER 23rd

Two shows at the Rialto, York, were cancelled.

THURSDAY SEPTEMBER 24th

Gaumont Theatre (instead of the Rank cinema), Doncaster. (Two shows). The group were mobbed as fans broke through the police

"You Can't Catch Me" (Chuck Berry)
"Grown Up Wrong"
"Surprise, Surprise".

Two evening shows at the Odeon, Romford. Following which, Mick and Brian attended The Pretty Things first anniversary party at 13 Chester Square, Belgravia. (Brian had lived in the upstairs flat).

TUESDAY SEPTEMBER 29th

Regent Sound Studios and Odeon Theatre, Guildford. (Two shows.)

WEDNESDAY SEPTEMBER 30th

Two shows at the Nottingham Odeon were cancelled so the group had another day-off. Keith returned to Regent Sound to complete overdubs on songs recorded over the previous days, and added acoustic guitar to Marianne Faithfull's recording of "The House Of The Rising Sun". (Released as the B-side to her version of Bob Dylan's "Blowing In The Wind", by Decca on October 23rd.)

THURSDAY OCTOBER 1st

Colston Hall, Bristol. (Two shows.)

FRIDAY OCTOBER 2nd

Odeon Theatre, Exeter. (Two shows.)

SATURDAY OCTOBER 3rd

Regal Theatre, Edmonton. (Two shows.) The group cancelled their appearance on "Thank Your Lucky Stars". Replacements on the ABC-TV show, (transmitted that night between 5:50 - 6:34pm across the ITV network), included Shirley Bassey singing the theme from the latest James Bond film "Goldfinger", Heinz, The Barron Knights and Sandie Shaw. (The Stones re-arranged their appearance for December 5th-see entry.)

SUNDAY OCTOBER 4th

Gaumont Theatre, Southampton. (Two shows.)

MONDAY OCTOBER 5th

Gaumont Theatre, Wolverhampton. (Two shows.) Radio Luxembourg broadcast another programme in their "Battle Of The Bands" series, tonight being Part 1 of "The Rolling Stones vs. The Animals" (The 2nd part was broadcast Oct 9th).

TUESDAY OCTOBER 6th

Gaumont Theatre, Watford. (Two shows.)

WEDNESDAY OCTOBER 7th

Southend Odeon. (Two shows were cancelled.)

THURSDAY OCTOBER 8th

Another radio appearance for the BBC Light Programme, in the series "Rhythm and Blues", hosted by Alexis Korner. During the afternoon session, the group recorded the following:-

"Dust My Pyramids" / "Around And Around" / "If You Need Me" / "I Wanna Love You" / "Mona" and "2120 South Michigan Avenue".
A mystery surrounds the first track "Dust My Pyramids", which was an instrumental of less than 30 seconds duration, boasting a unique songwriting credit of Richards-Jones, which was reportedly, nothing

cordon inside and tore Mick's shirt as he tried to leave the building. Later, several members of the tour entourage went ten-pin bowling until 7am. When finishing, Brian drove everybody on to the Queens Hotel, Manchester (where the band stayed for the next three nights).

FRIDAY SEPTEMBER 25th

Gaumont Theatre, Hanley. (Two shows.) The group gave a radio interview, for the North Staffordshire Hospital Broadcasting Services. The short interview, totaling 4 minutes, was edited and transmitted across hospital radio lines on September 28th, at regular intervals throughout the day.

SATURDAY SEPTEMBER 26th

Odeon Theatre (instead of the Gaumont), Bradford. (Two shows.) In America, a new single: "Time Is On My Side" B/W "Congratulations", was released, on London Records, selling 75,000 copies within 3 days.

SUNDAY SEPTEMBER 27th

Hippodrome Theatre, Birmingham. (Two shows)

MONDAY SEPTEMBER 28th

Regent Sound Studios. Including:-

more than a short burst of Elmore James-style slide playing. "I Wanna Love You", was a Gene Pitney composition or alternatively, an early Muddy Waters song. (The latter seems more likely). The show, recorded for The General Overseas Programme (now better known as The BBC World Service), was devoted entirely to the Stones and was broadcast Saturday, October 31st. In the evening, the group performed two shows at the Odeon Theatre, Lewisham.

FRIDAY OCTOBER 9th

Gaumont Theatre, Ipswich. (Two shows.) The N.M.E reported that the group's projected Xmas tour of South Africa had been cancelled following talks between Eric Easton and the Musicians Union, who opposed South Africa's apartheid policies.

SATURDAY OCTOBER 10th

Odeon Theatre, Southend, instead of Salisbury Gaumont. (Two shows.)

SUNDAY OCTOBER 11th

The British tour ended with two shows at the Hippodrome, Brighton.

WEDNESDAY OCTOBER 14th

Charlie's marriage to Shirley Ann Shepherd, was conducted amid much secrecy, at Bradford Register Office. None of the other Stones (or Andrew Oldham) were told.

FRIDAY OCTOBER 16th

Mick was interviewed on Associated-Rediffusion's T.V's "Ready Steady Go!" by fan Ellen Grehan, while her mother waited in a side room, at the Kingsway studios, with Brian. The live show, featuring American guest, Dionne Warwick, was broadcast 6:08 -6:59 pm, across the ITV network.

SATURDAY OCTOBER 17th

"Record Mirror" reported that the Rolling Stones new single would be "Little Red Rooster", revealed by "reliable" sources at Decca Records, and with the arrival of the group in Belgium the following day, the Belgian Minister of the Interior, fearing a repeat of the riots in Holland (see Aug.8th entry), had banned the group from the country. Three days of persuasive talking by TV producer Frans Romeyns eventually changed the Minister's mind, and the visit went ahead.

SUNDAY OCTOBER 18th

The group got up at 6am to assemble at Heathrow Airport for another European jaunt. Accompanying them was Marcel Stellman, the Promotions Manager of Decca European Sales and Andrew Oldham. They arrived at Brussels Airport, to be greeted by approximately 5,000 fans. The other passengers were asked to vacate the plane first, in order for the media to get their shots. After the first of two press conferences, the Stones left the airport in a cavalcade of motor cars, and a motorcycle escort. The second press conference was held on the 29th floor of the Martini Buildings, in the city. The group later appeared live in the television studios at the American Theatre, in the Brussels World Fair Grounds. The rehearsals lasted almost three hours. Mick insisted, prior to the recording, that each member had an equal share of

coverage. The performance (interspersed with interviews by Belgian TV personalities with each member) consisted:-

"Not Fade Away" / "Walking The Dog" / "If You Need Me" / "I'm Alright" / "Carol" / "Time Is On My Side" / "Tell Me" / "It's All Over Now" and "Around And Around". (The latter song was almost terminated, when half the audience invaded the stage).

Following the show, the group's musical equipment was packed, ready for despatch to France with Ian Stewart.

MONDAY OCTOBER 19th

The group arrived in Paris from Belgium for a three-day visit, (the group currently had three records in the French Top 10), giving a press conference, at the Locomotive Club, before an audience of 2,000 fans and journalists. (The fans had been misled into thinking the group were going to perform.) In the afternoon, the group taped three tracks ("Carol" / "Mona" and "It's All Over Now") for the French music show, "Qui de Neuf", recorded at the Paris studios of ORTF 2. Due to Ian Stewart still not having appeared with their instruments, the group had to borrow equipment belonging to the TV studio. The group checked into the Hotel de Paris and finally at 10pm, Stu arrived with the gear. He had been refused entry into France with the equipment due to the tendency of English groups bringing musical instruments into the country to sell. The group went clubbing and in the early hours of the morning, Brian was found, intoxicated, desperately trying to climb the Eiffel Tower!

TUESDAY OCTOBER 20th

The group gave a radio interview as a preview for the night's concert at L'Olympia. Disappointed fans had rioted at the box office, when tickets had sold out within 36 hours, on the 16th. Backstage, the group met Johnny Hallyday and Francoise Hardy. The show (recorded in it's entirety by radio station Europe 1, and transmitted live) featured:- "Around And Around" / "Carol" / "Bye Bye Johnny" / "It's All Over Now" / "Time Is On My Side" / "Not Fade Away" / "Walking The Dog" / "If You Need Me" / "I'm Alright" / "Confessin` The Blues" and "Tell Me".
Following the concert, fans smashed seats, broke windows in the foyer and rioted in the streets outside the venue. Gendarmes made 150 arrests. At a nearby cafe, youths overturned tables and threw customers onto the pavement. The damage to the Paris Olympia was estimated at £5,000. The group escaped in the back of an armoured van. Mick unaccustomed to a longer ride than usual opened the back door when the van stopped at a red light and alighted from the vehicle, disappearing into the thronging crowd. Despite the bad publicity, Olympia owner, Bruno Coquatrix was delighted with the group's impact: "This English group can come back at any time, the sooner the better!" Charlie spent the evening at expatriate rocker, Vince Taylor's flat, (who had been on the Olympia bill), listening to jazz records.

WEDNESDAY OCTOBER 21st

The group spent the day filming, for the European Juke Box film company, "Scopitone" a colour film for "Around And Around". They flew back to England in the evening.

THURSDAY OCTOBER 22nd

On a day off before flying to America, Mick frantically searched for a new wardrobe, to replace a suitcase of clothes, lost in transit from Paris.

FRIDAY OCTOBER 23rd

The group flew to New York's Kennedy Airport to start a three-week

Charlie with Shirley Ann Shepherd on the Kings Road, Chelsea.
They married in secrecy on October 14th.

American tour, (with Eric Easton, Stu and production manager, Mike Dorsey who packed Charlie's Ludwig kit, into the hold.) Hundreds of fans turned out to greet them, despite letters being sent out, advising the group's 20,000-strong American Fan Club, not to attend! After giving an airport press conference, the group then attempted to reach the Hotel Astor. Their Cadillac became swamped with fans which resulted in Times Square (and all surrounding streets) being blocked. Eventually, the group reached their hotel rooms by taking a tradesman's lift to the basement, then walking through the kitchens to the hotel reception. Later, the group (along with Eric Easton), were interviewed in their hotel rooms for the New York radio show, "The Ed Rudy Show". In the afternoon, after three attempts to break through large crowds which had gathered outside, the group arrived at the Ed Sullivan Theatre, for camera tests.

SATURDAY OCTOBER 24th

"THE ROLLING STONES, WHO HAVEN'T BATHED IN A WEEK, ARRIVED HERE FOR THEIR SECOND U.S. TOUR YESTERDAY!" (from a promotional press release). The group reunited with Murray the "K" Kaufman, at Radio WINS, recording an interview for broadcast on his programme, "Murray The K's Swinging Soiree".

Mick: "We started broadcasting, then the weirdest thing happened. It seemed that half the people listening decided to leave their radio sets and come over to the radio station. Result was, we couldn't get out, when the programme finished". Such was the size of the crowd outside the WINS building, Bill had to re-enter the station for his own safety, as the others left the building, racing to waiting cars. Like their previous visit, Murray the "K" escorted the group to the Peppermint Lounge. New York DJ William B. Williams descibed them as "so vulgar, so bad, so embarrassing!", which only helped fan the flames. The group recorded an afternoon slot for broadcast on "The "Clay Cole Show" (for WPIX Channel 11) performing:- "Tell Me" / "It's All Over Now" / "Around And Around" / "If You Need Me" / " Confessin' The Blues" and "Time Is On My Side".

The performance was transmitted the following week, on October 31st. The group gave the first shows of the tour (before a total audience of 8,000), with two concerts at New York's Academy of Music, promoted by Sid Bernstein. The set list for the tour:- "Not Fade Away" / "Time Is On My Side" / "I'm Alright" / "It's All Over Now" / "If You Need Me" / "Carol" / "I'm A King Bee" / "Tell Me" / "Confessin' The Blues" and "Around and Around". Mick and Keith attended a birthday party, for socialite', Baby Jane Holzer, at photographer Jerry Schatzberg's apartment. Among the guests was Andy Warhol. Inez & Charlie Foxx threw Bill a 28th birthday party.

SUNDAY OCTOBER 25th

The Stones made their debut on the CBS TV Sunday night variety programme, "The Ed Sullivan Show" at the Sullivan Theatre, Studio 50, Broadway and West 53rd Street. The group arrived at 9:00am for a

9:30am camera test. At 2:00pm, they took a make-up call, before the first camera rehearsals. As per the broadcast, they performed:- "Around And Around" (in the first half) and "Time Is On My Side" (in the second).

The show was transmitted between 8:00-9:00 EST that night. The show's switchboard was jammed for hours afterwards, with calls from irate parents and kids asking for the group to be on again. Fans rioted outside the building, causing Sullivan great alarm. He told the "Newark Evening News":- "I promise you they will never be back on our show, if things can't be handled, we will stop the whole business. We won't book any more rock 'n' roll groups and we'll ban teenagers from the theatre if we have to. Frankly, I didn't see the group until the day before the broadcast. I was shocked when I saw them! Now the Dave Clark Five are nice fellows. They are gentlemen and they perform well. It took me seventeen years to build this show. I'm not going to have it destroyed in a matter of weeks". (see May 2nd 1965 entry).

MONDAY OCTOBER 26th

Following the group's notable appearance on "The Ed Sullivan Show", influential American TV critic Jack O'Brian, in his column "The Journal", described them as "slobs" and "musical riff-raff"! Unpeturbed, the group flew from New York to Sacramento, for a performance at the Memorial Auditorium (4,500 audience). After the show, the group returned to LA, taking up residence at the Hollywood Roosevelt.

TUESDAY OCTOBER 27th

Mick and Keith were interviewed on Radio KRLA's "The Gary Mack Show".

WEDNESDAY OCTOBER 28th

Brian was interviewed for local radio, by Carson Schreiber, in Santa Monica. The group were at the Civic Auditorium to film an "Electronovision" (videotape) production, entitled the "Teen Age Music International Awards Show" or "Teenage Awards Music International" (a/k/a "The TAMI Show"), directed by Steve Binder, with musical direction by Jack Nitzsche and produced by Lee Savin. The Stones had tried for two days to get the show's top billing changed around, wanting James Brown to close the concert, after hearing he was going to "make the Rolling Stones wish they'd never left England". (Luckily for them, there was a ten-minute break for the audience to cool down, after his act.)

The Stones set was as follows:-

"Around And Around" / "Off The Hook" / "Time Is On My Side" / "It's All Over Now" and "I'm Alright".

The first (shorter) version of the finished film, released in America on November 14th, (with the title "Teenage Command Performance"), contained just one Stones song:- "Time Is On My Side."

Besides the Stones, the film also featured:-Chuck Berry, Gerry and the Pacemakers, Marvin Gaye, Lesley Gore, The Miracles, Billy J. Kramer and the Dakotas, The Barbarians, The Supremes, Jan and Dean, and James

Brown and his Famous Flames. A seldom seen version of the film (running at 117 minutes) also contained The Beach Boys set (which premiered during the Christmas period in American cinemas). The film had it's belated English premiere at the Futurist Cinema, Birmingham on August 7th,1966 , sporting the alternative title of "Gather No Moss".

THURSDAY OCTOBER 29th

The group concluded their appearance in the film, by returning to the Civic Auditorium to appear with the other acts in the show, for the finale song, "Get Together".

FRIDAY OCTOBER 30th

In Los Angeles, Don Webster from the Cleveland WEWS-TV music programme, "Upbeat", interviewed Mick and Charlie. Firstly, Charlie was asked what he thought of American teenagers:-

"They're much the same all over the world".

"Not too much different at all?" Webster continued.

"No, I don't think so" Charlie replied, totally disinterested.

"You dont think there's any difference at all?" Webster's right-hand man persisted.

"They've got more money, that's all!"

The rest of the interview (interrupted by the phone ringing!) solicited Mick's opinions on "Mods and Rockers" and why English kids "don't go steady anymore" (according to American belief, anyway!) The group went to an evening party at Don Everly's house.

SATURDAY OCTOBER 31st

Swing Auditorium, San Bernadino (5,000 crowd).

SUNDAY NOVEMBER 1st

The group gave two shows, the first in the afternoon, before 13,000 at the Civic Auditorium, Long Beach (where "The Tami Show" had been filmed) and then on to San Diego for an evening show at the Balboa Park Bowl, flying back to L.A afterwards.

MONDAY NOVEMBER 2nd and TUESDAY NOVEMBER 3rd

The group recorded for the first time at the RCA Studios in Los Angeles, with regular producer Andrew Oldham, and sound engineer Dave Hassinger, in a 17 hour session (beginning at 11am), working on the following:-

"Everybody Needs Somebody To Love" (different versions/mixes) (Solomon Burke via Wilson Pickett)

"Heart Of Stone"

"Hitch-Hike" (Marvin Gaye)

"Oh Baby (We Got A Good Thing Goin')" (Barbara Lynn)

The Ed Sullivan Show, October 25th

"Down Home Girl" (Chuck Berry)
"Pain In My Heart" (Otis Redding)
(the latter two recorded with Jack Nitzche on piano/"Nitzche-Phone",
invited after working with him on "The Tami Show").

TUESDAY NOVEMBER 3rd
The group took a five hour flight to Cleveland, Ohio, to perform at the
Public Hall. A 17 year-old girl fell from the balcony, prompting the Mayor
to ban all future pop concerts. "Such groups do not add to the
community's culture or entertainment" he told the press.

WEDNESDAY NOVEMBER 4th
The group flew from Cleveland to Providence, Rhode Island, for a
concert at the Leows Theatre (3,400 audience). The show was curtailed
after five songs, when girls stormed the stage, destroying the orchestra
pit, after which, all concerts of a similiar nature were banned at the hall.
By their own request, the group travelled back to New York, after the
show, in an authentic American train, arriving at Grand Central Station at
4am. Eric Easton flew back to London, with the RCA tapes.

THURSDAY NOVEMBER 5th
Mick, Keith and Andrew went to see James Brown at the Apollo and
were asked onstage to take a bow. They later met up backstage. Bill
bumped into bluesman, Lonnie Johnson, in Greenwich Village and went
to a party at John Hammond Jr.'s apartment.

SUNDAY NOVEMBER 8th
After a few days off, the group took a midnight flight to Chicago, for
more recording at Chess Studios. The session (with Oldham and
Hassinger, with Stu on piano and organ) featured:-
"Time Is On My Side" (alternate version, a new arrangement suggested by Stu).
"What A Shame"
"Mercy Mercy" (Don Covay) (first version)
"Key To The Highway" (Little Walter)
"Good Bye Girl" (a Bill Wyman comp.) The latter three remain unreleased.

WEDNESDAY NOVEMBER 11th
The group flew to Milwaukee. The Mayor went on the radio before the
group arrived, saying the concert at the Auditorium, was an immoral
thing for teenagers to be able to exhibit themselves at. As a result of
parental pressure, hundreds of seats were empty, in the 6,266 venue.
This was the first of four shows that Brian missed (not returning until
the 15th). He had woken in the early hours of the morning, complaining
to Mike Dorsey, of feeling ill. Delirious, he was admitted to the Passavant
Hospital, in Chicago, having to be fed intravenously. He had started to
feel increasingly unwell as the tour progressed, but had not mentioned it
to the others. The American papers suggested he had taken an overdose,
while in England, it was reported he had pneumonia.

THURSDAY NOVEMBER 12th
The four-piece group drove to Indiana and were interviewed in front of
noisy fans, for cable station WANE (Channel 15). In the evening, a show
at the Coliseum, Fort Wayne, with a supporting bill, including The Shangri-La's.

FRIDAY NOVEMBER 13th
"Little Red Rooster" B/W "Off The Hook" was rush-released in the
U.K, going straight in at No 1, with advance orders exceeding 300,000.
The group drove on to Dayton, Ohio. The group checked in to the
Hotel Biltmore, giving an interview for local TV, in the afternoon and
prior to the concert, held a press conference, backstage at the
Wampler's Hara Arena. Inevitably, much of the questioning centred on
Brian's absence.

SATURDAY NOVEMBER 14th
The group drove 400 miles from Dayton to Louisville, Kentucky for a
concert at the Memorial Auditorium (1,700 audience), where James
Brown visited backstage. Following the show, the group decided, through
exhaustion, not to drive back to Chicago, but sent their equipment on
ahead.

SUNDAY NOVEMBER 15th
The group drove back to Chicago, reuniting with a recovering Brian, for
a show at the Arie Crown Theatre (5,500 audience). Prior to the concert,
a "meet and greet" session was held backstage, with hundreds of fans.
The group flew back to New York that night.

MONDAY NOVEMBER 16th
A photo-shoot in New York, later used for the cover of "Billboard"
magazine.

TUESDAY NOVEMBER 17th
Mick, Charlie and Brian flew back to London Airport, in the morning.
Upon arrival, a still peaky Brian was immediately rushed to a doctor.

THURSDAY NOVEMBER 19th
Keith, Bill and Andrew Oldham flew back to London Airport.

FRIDAY NOVEMBER 20th
The NME reported that due to Brian's illl health, he may not be able to
appear at today's "Ready Steady Go" recording, or the Glad Rag Ball.
Nevertheless, the group (with Brian), assembled in the afternoon at
Television House, Kingsway, to record another appearance on "Ready
Steady Go!" (one of three complete surviving shows).
The running order, went as follows:-
The Plebs, Paul Williams, The Zephyrs and Marvin Gaye in Part One.
The week's chart run-down, Simon Scott, "Learn a new dance step" with
Patrick Kerr (to "Yeh Yeh" by Georgie Fame and the Blue Flames),
Kenny Lynch and Jerry Lee Lewis (backed by The Plebs) in Part Two,
while Part Three featured Marvin Gaye, Them, Samantha Jones and The
Rolling Stones. After being introduced by Cathy McGowan, the group
opened with "Off The Hook", then Keith Fordyce interviewed Brian
about that night's "Glad Rag Ball". Brian revealed they were all having a
six-week holiday, and, in relation to his recent illness, his "resistance had
been low". Mick talked about the recent Corgi/Beat Publications
paperback "Our Own Story - Of The Rolling Stones. As we told it to
Pete Goodman" [published November 13th]. The group performed
"Little Red Rooster" and "Around And Around" to close the show. The

programme was "telerecorded", and shown live across the ITV network, later that night between 6:08 - 6:59pm. (The three songs were repeated in a year-end "Ready Steady Go!" special, transmitted, December 31st, between 11:05pm, into the early hours of 1965 across the ITV network) Following the show, Keith collapsed due to exhaustion, a result of going almost five days without sleep. He was well enough to appear across town, at the Empire Pool, Wembley, for the annual "Glad Rag Ball". For the show, introduced by Jimmy Savile and new female DJ, Anne Nightingale, the group performed again the same three numbers; "Off The Hook" / "Little Red Rooster" / "Around And Around". On the broadcast, transmitted across the ITV network, on Wednesday, November 25th, 9:40 - 10:24pm, only the latter two songs were transmitted. The show also featured The Animals, Susan Maughan, Humphrey Lyttleton and His Band, Long John Baldry, Lorne Lesley and Ginger Johnson and His African Drummers!

SUNDAY NOVEMBER 22nd

A BBC radio appearance, consisting of a brief interview with Mick at Broadcasting House, on the weekly Light Programme show, "Teen Scene". The interview, conducted by Chris Hutchins, lasted only 2 minutes and was later broadcast on Friday, November 27th, between 10:45 - 11:31pm. Mick took the opportunity to deny that Charlie's recent marriage had caused friction within the group.

MONDAY NOVEMBER 23rd

Co-manager Eric Easton signed, on the group's behalf, contracts for two radio appearances on "Saturday Club". The first for transmission on the 28th of November, the other to be scheduled. The other contract was

Bill at "Pop Inn" November 24th

for appearances on "Top Gear" (December 3rd) and "The Joe Loss Show" (December 11th). This was unbeknown to the group, who later claimed they knew nothing about the bookings. They failed to turn up for the 28th of November sessions being replaced by Alex Harvey's Soul Band, while on the December 3rd edition of "Top Gear", they were replaced by Alexis Korner's Blues Inc.) Relationships between the group and the BBC turned sour. "Melody Maker" headlined:- "BBC Storm - 6 Month "Saturday Club" Ban!". Mick:- "I understand the bookings were made on our behalf but we never consented to them. That is partly the reason we didn't turn up". Again, in circumstances similiar to the group's late appearance on "Top Of The Pops" (see May 6th entry), Eric Easton wrote an apology letter to BBC radio executives explaining the unfortunate mix-up. The BBC, in realisation of the group's popularity, reluctantly accepted the explanation, replying to Easton's letter on December 18th (see entry). The group would return to BBC radio on March 1st, 1965.

TUESDAY NOVEMBER 24th

Before the BBC storm broke, Bill was interviewed by host Keith Fordyce on the Light Programme's "Pop Inn", broadcast live between 1:00 - 1:59 pm.

THURSDAY NOVEMBER 26th

Mick was fined for motoring offences in Tettenhall, Wolverhampton. His solicitor, Mr. Dale Parkinson, pleaded for the retention of his license. "It's loss" he said "might damage one of Britain's invisible exports. Jagger would be less mobile and exceptional inconvenience would be caused to millions of fans". The chairman, Mr. Jack Bradburn replied by telling Mr. Parkinson, "...today's endorsement would not mean the loss of Jagger's licence".

SUNDAY NOVEMBER 29th

The group went to the Alpha Television Studios, Birmingham, to headline a re-arranged appearance on "Thank Your Lucky Stars", aptly titled "Lucky Stars Special", thus illustrating the TV pulling-power of the group in a scheduled appearance. (An October 3rd appearance had been cancelled). For the telerecorded programme, transmitted Saturday, December 5th 5:50 - 6:34pm, the group mimed an unprecedented four tracks (taking over the second half of the programme):-
"Around And Around" / "Little Red Rooster" / "Off The Hook" and "Empty Heart".
The show, hosted by Brian Matthew, also featured Sandie Shaw, Herman's Hermits, Mark Wynter, Clinton Ford and Petula Clark. This special appearance by the Stones on the programme, gave rise to the group taking over the complete cover of weekly listings paper, "Television Weekly".

DECEMBER

Bill returned to Regent Sound Studios, to produce and play bass on The Cheynes single "Down And Out" / "Stop Running Round", released January 29th, 1965, on Columbia.

THURSDAY DECEMBER 3rd

"Little Red Rooster", despite still being at No.1, was not featured on today's edition of "Top Of The Pops". The BBC denied this was due to the current dispute. A BBC spokesman:- "There is no battle between the BBC and the Rolling Stones. The BBC doesn't ban artists, nor does it ban records". (A montage of the song was used instead.)

FRIDAY DECEMBER 4th

Fairfield Halls, Croydon. (Two shows, with The Squares, The Barracudas, The Worryin' Kind, The Rattlers, Dave Dee and The Bostons and The Overlanders.) A new E.P for release on today's date, in time for the Xmas market, was scrapped. Mick and Brian spent the weekend in Paris. (On the 5th, Brian went to a party given by The Animals after their Olympia concert).

SUNDAY DECEMBER 6th

Minutes before broadcast, Andrew Oldham was told that because of the radio ban, he could not appear on the BBC Light Programme show, "The Teen Scene".

FRIDAY DECEMBER 11th

Decca released the Bobby Jameson single "All I Want Is My Baby" B/W "Each And Every Day", co-written by Keith and Andrew Oldham and produced by Oldham. In the N.M.E end-of-year polls, the Stones were voted runners-up to The Beatles in the "World Group" section.

SATURDAY DECEMBER 12th

The group went to Haliford Studios, at Shepperton Film Studios, London to record "inserts" for the USA ABC TV show "Shindig!", with producer, Leon Mirrell. Following afternoon camera rehearsals, the group mimed to playback: "Heart Of Stone" / "Suzie Q" / "Oh Baby (We Got A Good Thing Goin')" and "Down The Road Apiece".
The songs were spread over two editions of the show; "Oh Baby (We Got A Good Thing Goin'")" and "Down The Road Apiece", on Wednesday, December 16th, 8: 30 - 8: 59 EST. "Susie Q" and "Heart Of Stone", two weeks later on December 30th (same times).

FRIDAY DECEMBER 18th

"Disc" printed Brian's denial, that because of his recent illness, he would be leaving the group, under a heading "I'll Stick With Stones". He was also interviewed on Radio Luxembourg. G. M. Turnell, the Head of BBC Programme Contracts, replied to Eric Easton`s letter, regarding the group's failure to honour their radio appearances (see Nov.23rd entry). The letter went on to say:- "If the Rolling Stones fail to honour any future commitment, we shall cease to offer them engagements in radio. Signed G. M. Turnell."

MONDAY DECEMBER 21st

Beat Publications published "Ode To A High Flying Bird", by Charlie Watts. Written in 1961, the book was about Charlie "Yardbird" Parker (accompanied by Charlie's own drawings). Charlie: "It doesn't matter if you don't know anything about Charlie Parker, because it's just about this little bird. In fact it's the kind of book you can buy for a kid".

MONDAY DECEMBER 28th

Radio Luxembourg, continuing with it's "Battle Of The Giants" series, broadcast the programme "Rolling Stones vs. Gene Pitney" at 8:15 pm.

THURSDAY DECEMBER 31st

The group visited Television House, Kingsway, to appear on a year-end special edition of "Ready Steady Go!", entitled "The New Year Starts Here!". The programme also featured:- The Kinks, The Animals, The Dave Clark Five, Freddie and the Dreamers, Kenny Lynch, Manfred Mann, Susan Maughan, Sandie Shaw and Dusty Springfield. As well as appearing in the audience, the Stones three-song segment, originally transmitted November 20th (see entry), was repeated. Mick also demonstrated "this week's dance", with regular show dancer, Patrick Kerr. Hosted by Keith Fordyce and Cathy McGowan, it was transmitted across the ITV network from 11:05pm into the early hours of 1965.

Mick struts his stuff on "The New Year Starts Here" with Patrick Kerr (left) and Mike (McCartney) McGear (right)

TELEVISION WEEKLY

CHANNEL 10 **TWW**
ITV Programmes for
WEST of ENGLAND

Vol. 7, No. 49
DECEMBER 3, 1964

DECEMBER 5—11

SIXPENCE

THE ROLLING STONES
See them in LUCKY STARS SPECIAL on Saturday

NINETEEN SIXTY FIVE

JANUARY

The Rolling Stones were invited to appear on the ATV show "Sunday Night At The London Palladium". Co-manager Eric Easton turned down the request with a statement: "This is a family show, after all, and I sincerely don't think the country is quite ready to have the boys in their living rooms."

The group would eventually appear on the show on January 22nd, 1967 (see entry) and appeared in performance at the venue on August 1st (see entry). Decca released Bobbie Miller's "What A Guy" / "You Went Away" single, produced by Bill Wyman, who co-wrote the B-side.

WEDNESDAY JANUARY 6th

The first assignment of the year was a tour of Ireland, for promoter, John Smith, with supports:- The Sack O' Woes, The Quiet Five, Cliff Bennett and the Rebel Rousers and Twinkle. After landing at Belfast's Aldergrove Airport (without Keith who missed the flight), the group were interviewed by BBC Radio. Later, at the afternoon soundcheck, presenter Maurice Smith briefly interviewed each group member for the UTV magazine programme "Six Five". The cameras also caught 70 seconds of the group rehearsing "Little Red Rooster" (with Andrew Oldham in attendance). This appearance, for which they were paid 10 guineas (£10-10 shillings) was transmitted on the programme between 6:05-6:30pm. In the evening, the group played two shows at the ABC Theatre.

THURSDAY JANUARY 7th

Adelphi Theatre, Dublin. (Two shows.) The group travelled down from Belfast by train and Mick gave a brief interview for RTE Television's Mike Burns on the station platform.

FRIDAY JANUARY 8th

Savoy Theatre, Cork. (Two shows.) The group travelled on the Cork-Dublin road. Brian:- "I got out of the car to ask a couple of locals, with a donkey, if they would mind Keith filming them with his cine' camera. They thought I was going to attack them, or something. Next moment, they came at me with shovels. I just made it to the car!" Keith:- "We stopped outside a fabulous old shop one morning to buy some gear. It was kind of an old army surplus store, right out in the sticks.

There was an old fella behind the counter who screamed that we'd been sent by Oliver Cromwell. He chased us out of the shop and jumped on the bonnet of our car. Then he proceeded to try and boot the windscreen to pieces. He must have been at least eighty!!"

SUNDAY JANUARY 10th

The group returned to London on the 9th and played two concerts (5:45 & 8:15pm) at the ABC Commodore, Hammersmith (with supports Marianne Faithfull, Julie Grant, Tony Jackson and The Vibrations, Zoot Money's Big Roll Band, The Quiet Five and The Original Checkmates). Hilton Valentine, from The Animals, visited Brian backstage and NME journalist Keith Altham interviewed the group about their forthcoming album. Brian revealed his favourite track as "I Can't Be Satisfied", while Keith chose "You Can't Catch Me". Following the performances, Mick, Bill and Brian went ten-pin bowling with Julie Grant.

MONDAY 11th and TUESDAY JANUARY 12th

Two days recording initial takes of:- "(This Could Be) The Last Time" (working title), at Regent Sound Studios. Further work would resume on the track in Los Angeles (see January 17th and 18th entries).

WEDNESDAY JANUARY 13th

The group pre-recorded another appearance on the Saturday night ATV pop show, "Thank Your Lucky Stars". They mimed "Down Home Girl" and "Under The Boardwalk" and were interviewed by Brian Matthew, included in the broadcast (also featuring Wayne Fontana and The Mindbenders, Cliff Bennett and The Rebel Rousers, Craig Douglas, Sandra Browne and Jan Panter), on January 30th (ITV 5.50 - 6.34 pm).

FRIDAY JANUARY 15th

A live guest slot on Associated-Rediffussion's "Ready Steady Go!", at Television House, Kingsway, to mark the release date of their second (U.K) album "The Rolling Stones No.2". The group performed "Time Is On My Side" and "Down The Road Apiece" and were interviewed by host Cathy McGowan, in a show also featuring The Kinks, The Righteous Brothers, Del Shannon, The Mark Leeman Five, Jimmy Radcliffe and Sandra Barry. The programme was transmitted that night between 6:08 - 6:59pm, across the ITV region. After the

Keith, Brian and Mick with the Righteous Brothers at a Decca press reception.

show was wrapped up, Brian went (with The Righteous Brothers and the "R.S.G!" team) to the Hampstead residence of "Melody Maker" writer, Bob Dawbarn, for an all-night "Thank You" party for "the artists who helped to make 1964 a record pop year". Other guests included George Harrison, Ringo Starr, Brian Epstein, Cilla Black and Dusty Springfield.

SUNDAY 17th and MONDAY JANUARY 18th

The group left London Airport on the afternoon of the 16th to fly to Australia via Los Angeles, resuming recording at RCA Studios (with Andrew Oldham, and engineer Dave Hassinger). During the two day sessions, they continued work on the following tracks (started in London - see Jan.11th/12th entry):-

"The Last Time"

"A Mess Of Fire" (later re-titled "Play With Fire", featuring only Mick and Keith, with Jack Nitzsche on percussion/harpsichord and Phil Spector on "zoom" bass and acoustic guitar, as Brian, Bill and Charlie had fallen asleep in the studio). Also recorded (according to a contemporary N.M.E report from Oldham), were "three old blues numbers".

TUESDAY JANUARY 19th

The group left Los Angeles en route to Sydney, at 8pm, landing to refuel at Honolulu and Fiji. In total, the journey lasted 18 hours (missing the 20th altogether, due to crossing the International Dateline).

THURSDAY JANUARY 21st

The group landed at Kingsford Smith Airport in Sydney, Australia at 8:15am to start a 26-day tour.(The previous year, Eric Easton had tentatively confirmed an 11-day tour, starting November 20th, which had to be postponed, due to the group's busy schedule.) The group were signed, by Harry M. Miller of Pan Pacific Promotions Ltd, for $12,500 per week, for which they had to give thirteen performances. This paid for accommodation and economy air fares for the five Stones, Andrew Oldham, Ian Stewart and Mike Dorsey. When re-confirming the details of the tour, Miller refused to allow them to bring their gear as excess baggage. "They can bring their guitars but that's all I'm paying for" Miller told Oldham." We've got perfectly good amplifiers in Australia. Christ, who are we working for -Scrooge??!!" was Oldham's retort! 3,000 fans, mostly girls, rioted as the Qantas plane landed, some tearing through a chain-wire fence and smashing into the quarantine area, ripping a steel Customs Hall rail. Five girls were cautioned by quarantine officials and told that they were liable to a £100 fine and a series of inoculations. "It was worth it, we touched them!!" was their ecstatic reply. (One enterprising youth sold two empty soda-pop bottles, for £5 each, claiming that "Stones leader, Mick Jagger had touched them!") The arrival and press conference was covered in depth by TV & Radio. Movietone News captured the events to show in English cinemas. This short 2 minute 38 second film, entitled "Stones Roll Down Under", also featured "Not Fade Away", dubbed over highlights from the following evening's 6:00pm concert, at The Manufacturer`s Hall. Newspaper reports on the group's arrival carried headlines such as:- "Shockers!" "Ugly Looks!" "Ugly Speech!" "Ugly Manners! (Negative press coverage would continue to plague them on this tour.) The group stayed on the fifth floor of the Chevron-Hilton Hotel, Macleay Street, which overlooked Sydney Harbour, recording interviews for TV and Radio 2 UE. Mick met up with his aunt and cousins on his mother's side.

FRIDAY JANUARY 22nd

The morning was spent in a private house, backing on to Sydney Harbour, owned by a relative of Harry Miller's. The press hovered in boats at the water's edge, so the group staged a water fight for their benefit. Brian, Keith, Charlie and Andrew took a boat out into the harbour and were heckled by three schoolboys in a fishing boat. Things turned nasty, when one dived into the water and tried to capsize the Stones boat. Oldham:- "The attack was quite unprovoked.We didn't want to fight, but we were forced into it." The first night of the tour featured two shows (6:00 & 8:45pm) at the Agricultural Hall, Manufacturer's Auditorium. The concerts were sold out, with a total of 10,500 fans in attendance. The tour's set list:-

"Not Fade Away" / "Walking The Dog" / "Under The Boardwalk" / "Little Red Rooster" / "Around And Around" / "Heart Of Stone" / "Time Is On My Side" / "It's All Over Now" and "I'm Alright."

The package tour featured Roy Orbison, The Newbeats (from America) and Ray Columbus and The Invaders (from New Zealand). Dionne Warwick, originally announced as being on the bill, had to pull out due to an injury. (On these first shows, Roy was suffering from acute tonsilitis and general nervousness).

SATURDAY JANUARY 23rd

Agricultural Hall, Manufacturer's Auditorium. (Three shows.) (2:15, 6:15 & 8:45pm.) The group embarked on a morning cruise, accompanied by ten girls aged between 14 and 16, aboard the boat "Seabird" around Sydney Harbour and swam in drizzling rain, at Seven Shillings Beach, near Redleaf Pool. Before their departure on the cruise, 30 fans waited for them outside the hotel. Later, the group arrived at the venue via an armoured van from their hotel. The journey to the hall was escorted by two other armoured vans, manned by security officers. Audience figures revealed that 4,000 watched the afternoon matinee performance, while an additional 1,000 were present for the final show. As a security precaution, an extra 100 police were on duty. During the third concert, several girls fainted while at least one was taken to hospital. In attendance, were around 100 police-squad and rescue men. Before the 6pm show, plain-clothed policemen walked the aisles, looking for a surfer suspect in a local murder case.

SUNDAY JANUARY 24th

The group flew on to Brisbane, to be greeted by 1,500 fans. The Stones checked into the Lennon's Hotel, Mick:- "Does he own this as well?" where a rival package tour, comprising The Kinks, Manfred Mann and The Honeycombs, were also staying. During a tropical storm, both promoters threw a party for the groups, at the hotel. A drunken Brian rang a local radio station, requesting The Honeycombs hit, "Have I The Right", be played at 78rpm!

MONDAY JANUARY 25th

In the morning, the Stones (minus Bill) went water ski-ing on a nearby lake, with Brian piloting the boat. Bill and Manfred Mann lead singer, Paul Jones visited a wildlife zoo. (Jones also watched the evening show from the wings.) Keith confounded the hotel room service, by asking for an electric heater for his room, despite the 90 degree heat! ("Its just that I've got cold blood!") The group gave a press conference and then played two sell-out shows (6:00 & 8:45pm) at the City Hall. During the second show, 40 fans stormed the stage. Mick: "I almost got torn to pieces and Keith's shirt was torn so much, that it looks as though he's been living in it on a desert island for two years." 25,000 had attended the Australian shows, thus far and the group had ten records in the Australian Top 100 (with "Under The Boardwalk" at No.1).

TUESDAY JANUARY 26th

City Hall, Brisbane. (Two shows.) The group (minus Bill, who explored the outback desert with Paul Jones) hired two cars for a 50 mile drive to Surfer's Paradise. They spent the afternoon sunbathing, before returning to Brisbane. During the journey back, one of the cars was involved in an accident, when Andrew Oldham was forced to swerve out of the way of a speeding motorist. Keith was the only casualty, banging his head on the windscreen.

WEDNESDAY JANUARY 27th

Agricultural Hall, Manufacturer's Auditorium, Sydney. (Two added shows.)

THURSDAY JANUARY 28th

The group flew to Melbourne, giving a press conference at Essendon Airport. Fearing a repeat of the trouble in Sydney, airport officials had banned fans from the terminal. 2,000 still turned out to greet them. Police escorted the group from the airport to the John Batman Motor Inn (which was covered in "Welcome To The Rolling Stones" flags). The afternoon was spent around the pool of a house owned by a lawyer friend of Harry Miller's. The group were then driven to the Palais Theatre, St. Kilda for two shows. Backstage, they were interviewed by Radio "DB", broadcast live between 4:30 - 4:37pm. All tickets for the shows had sold out prior to the group's arrival. (Miller had taken the curtains down at the back of the stage, put out extra chairs, charging £2 10s a ticket).

FRIDAY JANUARY 29th

Palais Theatre, St. Kilda. (Two shows). During the afternoon, the group visited the studios of ATV-O in Melbourne, to record a special, entitled "The Rolling Stones Special" (televised February 12th, 7:00 - 8:00pm. The show also featured Ray Columbus & The Invaders, The Newbeats and Roy Orbison). The Stones mimed four tracks, in studio time running from 12:00 midday to 5:30pm (including camera rehearsals):-

Sydney airport press conference January 21st

Above and below: Invercargill, "the arsehole of the world", February 2nd.

"Walking The Dog" / "Heart Of Stone" / "Little Red Rooster" and "Around and Around".

SATURDAY JANUARY 30th

Palais Theatre, St.Kilda.(Three shows.) Melbourne radio station 3KZ featured an exclusive interview, recorded by Neville Wragg and Stan Rofe. The group took the opportunity to meet the staff and to personally thank them for plugging their records. They also filmed television plugs for their upcoming New Zealand dates. A homesick Brian rang his father, in Cheltenham, during the early hours of the morning (U.K time), after listening to the radio coverage of Winston Churchill's funeral.

SUNDAY JANUARY 31st

The group landed at Harewood Airport, Christchurch at 6:40pm to commence a 10 day tour of New Zealand. Despite persistent rain, a crowd of 1,000 screaming teenagers turned out to greet them. Upon their arrival, the group gave an NZBC radio and TV interview. The group had to gain entrance to the United Service Hotel, on Cathedral Square, via a laundry entrance, such was the size of the surrounding mob.

MONDAY FEBRUARY 1st

Theatre Royal, Christchurch. (Two shows, featuring the same bill as in Australia.) "Daily Express" columnist, John Drew wrote a report headlined "STONES UNWASHED", from Christchurch. In it, he reported the group had complained that their hotel had too few bathrooms, with each having to do his own washing. Mick: "You can't blame us if we smell!"

TUESDAY FEBRUARY 2nd

The group flew to Invercargill, the southernmost tip of New Zealand (or "the arsehole of the world", as Keith remembers it!), for two shows (6 & 8:30pm) at the Civic Theatre (with local support, The Echophones). The older audience response was lukewarm, while some fans threw paper at the group, from the balcony, before being warned off by Mick. He complained their 28-room hotel, The Kelvin, only had two bathrooms, with supper finishing at 7pm!

WEDNESDAY FEBRUARY 3rd

The group flew in to Momona Airport, Dunedin to perform two shows (6:00 & 8:30pm) at the Town Hall.

THURSDAY FEBRUARY 4th

The group arrived in the afternoon at Whenuapai Airport, Auckland, with two days off. The group met reporters at their hotel and went sight-seeing. ("Little Red Rooster" was at No.1 in the NZBC Top 20).

FRIDAY FEBRUARY 5th

In the morning, the group visited the local hot springs for an outdoor swim, with Roy Orbison. Mick: "It's just like taking a bath out in the open", while Bill decided to visit the mud baths in Rotorua, with Invaders bassist, Billy Kristian. The others went horse-riding.

SATURDAY FEBRUARY 6th

Three shows (2:15, 6:00 & 8:30pm) at the Town Hall, Auckland.

*The Stones (without Bill) and Andrew Oldham
at Waikiki Beach, Perth, Australia February 14th*

The afternoon matinee performance was added due to the impossibility of playing a concert the previous day. Tickets were on sale for 20/6, 28/6 and 35/6.

MONDAY FEBRUARY 8th

The group arrived in the afternoon, at Rongotai Airport, Wellington, to play two shows (6:00 & 8:30pm) at the Town Hall. Due to the successful venture of keeping Stones activities a secret, only two fans were there to greet them at the airport, where they gave a low-key press conference. Bill was driven by Stu and a security man to Titahi Bay to visit an old

friend, George Smith, from Penge, who had emigrated. An announcement was made before both shows started, that anybody leaving their seats would be ejected from the hall. This annoyed the group, particularly Mick, who felt he wasn't able to "get through to the fans." Following the two shows, the group were driven straight to the airport, leaving Wellington in a specially chartered plane to fly back to Christchurch. Due to inclement weather, they were 90 minutes late in arriving at their pre-booked hotel, who refused them accommodation. The owners of the Black Cat Restaurant opened up especially, upon their arrival at 2am, serving the group steaks all round.

TUESDAY FEBRUARY 9th

The group flew from Christchurch, back to Melbourne. In the evening, they attended a barbeque party given in their honour by Mr & Mrs Ham, two local lawyers.

WEDNESDAY FEBRUARY 10th

Another press conference, and in the evening two more performances (6:00 & 8:45pm) at the Palais Theatre, St. Kilda.

THURSDAY FEBRUARY 11th

The group flew to Adelaide, staying at the Akabar Hotel.

FRIDAY FEBRUARY 12th

Centennial Hall, Adelaide. (Two shows, the last to feature The Newbeats, who flew back to America, the following day.)

SATURDAY FEBRUARY 13th

A four and a half-hour flight to Perth. The group booked into the Adelphi Hotel, before performing three shows at the Capitol Theatre. (2:30, 6:00 & 8:45pm.) Bill met his great aunt and family at the hotel, after the matinee show.

SUNDAY FEBRUARY 14th

The group hired two cars and drove 30 miles up the coast to Waikiki Beach, to enjoy some privacy. Their relaxation was ruined when press and fans converged. They later went to a "farewell" barbeque at nearby Mt. Pleasant and ended the evening at a drive-in movie. Bill had picked up an eye infection, forcing him to visit three local specialists, who instructed him to wear dark glasses at all times, including concerts, and not to go out in the daylight, unless absolutely necessary.

MONDAY FEBRUARY 15th

The group flew from Perth in the afternoon to Singapore, checking into the Singapura Hotel.

TUESDAY FEBRUARY 16th

An unusually quiet meeting with the press. Due to the dictatorship of Eastern etiquette, all reporters were told they must not shout or get angry. By doing so, they would appear to be "losing face". Later, the group attended a luncheon with the High Commissioner of Singapore and his family, at Government House. (The meal lasted almost three hours). After which, they were taken on a guided tour of the gardens, before undertaking a shopping expedition in China Town. In the evening, they gave two shows at the Badminton Hall.

THURSDAY FEBRUARY 18th

The group flew to Los Angeles making stop-overs in Hong Kong (where they went shopping), Tokyo (giving a press conference for Japanese television), Honolulu and San Francisco. Gaining a day, by crossing back over the International Dateline, the group arrived in L.A, booking into the Ambassador Hotel. Mick, Keith and Charlie returned to RCA Studios to finish work on "The Last Time". (Vocal and guitar overdubs were needed to be added to the recordings begun on January 17th/18th). Not being required, Brian and Bill continued to socialise. Brian met back up with Joey Paige (see June 3rd 1964 entry) and invited Paige to stay with him, when he visited London.

SATURDAY FEBRUARY 20th

Mick flew back to London, unannounced, in the early hours of the morning. He spent his first night back, at the Ad-Lib Club in Leicester Square, where he met The Beatles. "We had a long chat about their next film ("Help!"), the Bahamas and things". Meanwhile, Keith had flown from LA to New York, with Andrew Oldham and Stu.

SUNDAY FEBRUARY 21st

Keith and Andrew Oldham flew from New York to Paris, while Stu returned to England.

MONDAY FEBRUARY 22nd

Bill returned to England. Charlie and Shirley (who was waiting for him in LA) visited Miami (arriving back on the 25th).

TUESDAY FEBRUARY 23rd

Keith arrived back in London, from Paris, with Andrew.

WEDNESDAY FEBRUARY 24th

Mick and Keith begin searching for a new flat, after fans had found out the whereabouts of their Mapesbury Road, Hampstead address.

FRIDAY FEBRUARY 26th

"The Last Time" B/W "Play With Fire" was rush-released (the tapes arrived in the country on the 20th), becoming the group's first self-composed single (and third No.1). Brian returned to London Airport early in the morning, after several days in L.A. He'd already cancelled three flights back after staying and partying with Jack Nitzsche. Amongst other things, he'd attended a Phil Spector mixing session with The Righteous Brothers (the Stones had been plugging "You've Lost That Loving Feeling" incessantly in Australia), visited Brian Wilson at a session and caught back up with Phil Everly at his home. He arrived in time to perform with the rest of the suntanned group on "Ready Steady Go!", at Television House, Kingsway. During this session they rehearsed (for the cameras) and recorded the following:-

"Play With Fire" / "The Last Time" and "Everybody Needs Somebody To Love" (plus an interview between Mick and Cathy McGowan.)
The latter song was largely an instrumental, as a gang of teenage girls mobbed Mick, making him hurt his ankle as he crashed to the studio floor. ("I was stamped on by scores of stiletto heels!")
The show (for which they were paid £42.10s) was broadcast, between

6:08 -6:59pm, and also featured The Dave Clark 5, The Animals, Jackie Ross, Jon Mark and Little Frankie.

SUNDAY FEBRUARY 28th

The group's first appearance on the late-night ITV chat show, "The Eamonn Andrews Show", at Teddington Studios. The group took part in camera rehearsals (7:30 - 8:30pm), a dress rehearsal (8:45 - 9:30pm) and then, in the "live from London" broadcast slot (11:06 -11:59pm), they mimed to "The Last Time". Prior to the performance, Andrews interviewed Mick for all of 30 seconds and mentioned it was Brian's birthday, displaying the sackfuls of cards and presents that had flooded into the studio. Immediately following the show, the group (minus Charlie) attended a special "Jones" party, thrown by "Disc", in Kensington. Brian was one of the guests of honour, along with Paul Jones, also celebrating the same birthdate and Tom Jones, who was currently at No.1 with "It's Not Unusual". Other guests included The Animals, Lulu, The Downliners Sect, The Kinks, The Nashville Teens, Georgie Fame, The Blue Flames and Mick's girlfriend Chrissie Shrimpton.

MARCH

Brian was interviewed for pirate station, Radio London. He was currently esconsed in a Kensington hotel, while flat hunting, eventually moving into a bachelor pad in Elm Park Mews, Chelsea.

MONDAY MARCH 1st

After the storm over the group's failure to turn up for radio bookings (see Nov. 24th 1964 entry), they returned to the BBC Playhouse Theatre Studios to record for "Top Gear". During the afternoon session, the group recorded:-

"Down The Road Apiece" / "Everybody Needs Somebody To Love" / "The Last Time" and "If You Need Me". Mick and Brian were also interviewed. The radio programme (also featuring Goldie & The Gingerbreads), was hosted by Brian Matthew and transmitted Saturday, March 6th 10pm -12:00 midnight, on the BBC Light programme.

TUESDAY MARCH 2nd

Mick and Brian made an appearance on "Pop Inn" for the BBC Light Programme, (broadcast 1:00 - 1:59 pm), being interviewed by Keith Fordyce, from the BBC "Studiolympia", at the "Daily Mail" Ideal Home Exhibition, Earls Court.

THURSDAY MARCH 4th

The group returned to Dickenson Road, Manchester to appear on BBC TV's "Top Of The Pops". With rehearsals running from noon, they ran through (for the benefit of the cameras), "The Last Time". The live show, transmitted 7:32 - 8:01pm, hosted by Jimmy Saville, also featured in the studio:- Twinkle, The Hollies, Herman's Hermits and The Searchers, while Wayne Fontana & The Mindbenders, Gene Pitney, Sandie Shaw, Petula Clark and Tom Jones all appeared by way of Ampex TOTP/VT repeated inserts. The Stones performance, (with Manchester United football wonderboy, George Best, among the audience) closed the show. The clip received a second, albeit brief, showing on July 13th, as part of a BBC-1 tribute to Jimmy Savile, aptly titled "Jimmy Savile" (see June 10th entry) and a third (complete) showing on the "Top of the Pops" review of 1965, "Top Of The Pops '65" transmitted Christmas Day, between 10:35 - 11:50 pm (repeated Boxing Day 12:15 - 1:30 pm). "The Last Time" appeared on TOTP again (March 25th, 7:31 - 8:01pm), but this insert clip was not repeated, due to a BBC non-agreement over payment of a repeat fee. Instead, the song was played over shots of the audience dancing, while photos of the band (taken by official TOTP photographer, Harry Goodwin) were relayed over a studio screen. With the group leaving the studio late in the evening, the BBC arranged to pay for their return fares to London, including sleeping berths on the train, costing £1-6 shillings. The group had enough time to squeeze in a visit to local nightclub, "Mrs Smiths", with Jimmy Savile, before departing.

FRIDAY MARCH 5th

The beginning of a two week British tour, starting with two shows at the Regal, Edmonton. The package tour also included:- The Hollies, Dave Berry & The Cruisers, The Konrads, The "Original" Checkmates and Goldie & The Gingerbreads. The Righteous Brothers and Donovan were acts originally announced to the press as appearing. Compere:-Johnny Ball. The group performed:-

"Everybody Needs Somebody To Love" (short version)/ "Pain In My Heart" / "Down The Road Apiece" / "Time Is On My Side" / "I'm Alright"/Charlie's intro/"Little Red Rooster" / "Route 66" / "I'm Moving On" and "The Last Time".

Glyn Johns recorded both shows for a forthcoming live E.P ("Got Live If You Want It!" released June 11th). Due to a fault in the balancing, the results were deemed unsatisfactory, so the following nights at Liverpool and Manchester were also recorded.

SATURDAY MARCH 6th

Liverpool Empire. (Two shows, with Glyn Johns recording both - see March 5th entry.) Following the shows, the group were taken by police jeep to their waiting car, to Manchester. The Grand Hotel turned down their booking, without an explanation, so the group stayed at the Midland, turning in for an unusually early night, except for Brian who went on to a nightclub.

SUNDAY MARCH 7th

Palace Theatre, Manchester.(Two shows.) During the second show, a fan fell 15 feet from the Dress Circle. Other than losing three teeth, she escaped uninjured. Prior to the shows, the group and Andrew Oldham, gathered in the dressing room to listen to a playback of the previous nights concerts. These shows were also being taped by Glyn Johns for the EP.(see March 5th entry.)

MONDAY MARCH 8th

The group received a "No Ties, No Meals" ultimatum at the Midland Hotel. (They were intending celebrating "The Last Time" being at No.1, In America it was at it's highest position of No 8.) The group lunched in Mick's room, instead. Mick and Keith then drove on to Scarborough, in

Mick's car. The others followed later for two shows at the Futurist (6:15 & 8:40pm).

TUESDAY MARCH 9th

Odeon, Sunderland. (Two shows.)

WEDNESDAY MARCH 10th

ABC Theatre, Huddersfield. (Two shows.)

THURSDAY MARCH 11th

The group appeared again on Granada TV's "Scene At 6:30pm" in Manchester. After participating in camera rehearsals, they recorded "The Last Time" for transmission between 6:30 - 6:59pm. They then played two shows at the City Hall, Sheffield. During the second performance, the noise generated was so loud that it drowned out Portuguese pianist

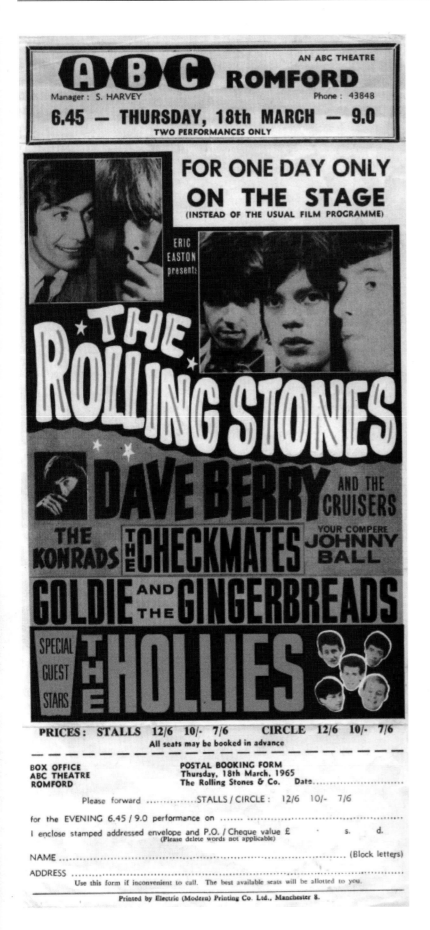

Sergio Varella-Cid who was playing to an audience of only 150 at a nearby venue. "If I had known, I would have asked for another date" he whined later. Backstage at The City Hall, prior to the first show, Brian was interviewed by the BBC World Service for the programme "The Sights and Sounds Of London" (transmitted May 9th).

FRIDAY MARCH 12th

Trocadero (in place of the ABC) Theatre, Leicester. (Two shows.)

SATURDAY MARCH 13th

Granada Theatre, Rugby. (Two shows.)

SUNDAY MARCH 14th

Odeon Theatre, Rochester. (Two shows.)

MONDAY MARCH 15th

Odeon Theatre, Guildford. (Two shows.)

TUESDAY MARCH 16th

Granada Theatre, Greenford. (Both shows recorded by Glyn Johns - see March 5th entry.) Backstage, Brian gave an interview for the BBC Light Programme's "Melody Fare" (transmitted two days later between 3:00 - 3:31 pm).

WEDNESDAY MARCH 17th

Odeon Theatre, Southend, in place of Chelmsford Odeon.(Two shows.)

THURSDAY MARCH 18th

ABC Theatre, Romford.(Two shows.) After rushing from the venue to avoid fans, the group's Daimler stopped at the Francis Service Station, Romford Road, Forest Gate,the scene of the infamous filling station incident. (See July 22nd entry.)

SUNDAY MARCH 21st

The group recorded a late-afternoon appearance on the "new-styled" (complete with live audience) "Thank Your Lucky Stars", at the ABC TV Alpha Studios, in Aston, Birmingham, miming four songs including "The Last Time" and "Off The Hook" (with Brian on piano).The programme, hosted by Brian Matthew, also featured Bobby Vee, Dave Berry and Susan Maughan and was broadcast March 27th, between 5:50-6:34 pm.

WEDNESDAY MARCH 24th

The group flew to Copenhagen, Denmark, for the start of a short Scandanavian tour.

THURSDAY MARCH 25th

Contrary to popular belief, the Stones did not make another appearance on "Top Of The Pops" on this date (see March 4th entry).

FRIDAY MARCH 26th

Fyens Forum,Odense.(Two shows). During the soundcheck prior to the shows, Mick came into contact with two live microphones at once. They short circuited, throwing him against Brian, who collided with Bill, knocking him unconscious by the 220-volt shock. The show's promoter Knud Thorbjoersen said "Bill came to, after a few minutes. The thing that saved them was an electric plug pulled out by Mick Jagger's fall". The tour's set list was as follows:-

"Everybody Needs Somebody To Love" / "Tell Me" / "Around And

Around" / "Time Is On My Side" / "It's All Over Now" / "Little Red Rooster" / "Route 66" and "The Last Time".

SUNDAY MARCH 28th

Tivoli Konsertal, Copenhagen. (Two shows.) The group attended a concert given by jazz legends Ella Fitzgerald and Oscar Peterson and were guests of honour of the Danish Branch of The Rolling Stones Fan Club. The group went clubbing and photographs of a drunken Brian, at the British Servicemen's club, appeared in the morning papers.

TUESDAY MARCH 30th

Tivoli Konsertsal, Copenhagen. (Two shows.)

WEDNESDAY MARCH 31st

Masshalen, Gothenburg, Sweden. (Two shows.)

APRIL

With the group on tour in Europe, Decca Records in England announced that their contract with The Rolling Stones had been extended by ten years (the current contract was not yet two years old!) despite tempting offers from Pye, CBS, Reprise and ABC. During the month, 19-year old photographer, Gered Mankowitz (son of noted author/critic Wolf Mankowitz) was invited by Oldham to take his first session with the group, after being impressed with his work for the sleeve of Marianne Faithfull's "Come My Way" album. A shot from the resulting session (shot outside Gered's studio in Masons Yard, Mayfair) would grace the sleeve of the U.K "Out Of Our Heads" and U.S. "December's Children (And Everybody's)" albums.

THURSDAY APRIL 1st

Kungliga Tennishallen, Stockholm. (Two shows.)

FRIDAY APRIL 2nd

The group were interviewed by host, Klaes Burling, for his radio show "Pop' 65" (on station P2). The short interview was transmitted April 4th. The evening's concert at the Kungliga Tennishallen, was filmed by April TV for the programme, "Popside". The following tracks:-
"Everybody Needs Somebody To Love" / Mick's introduction - "Tell Me" / Charlie's intro - "Around And Around" / "Little Red Rooster" and "The Last Time", were transmitted April 8th.

SATURDAY APRIL 3rd

Bill visited a local hospital as he had suffered further problems with his eye infection. In the afternoon, the group played at an open air festival in Helsinki, Finland.

MONDAY APRIL 5th

The group returned to London Airport. During the week, John Lennon and Beatle roadie, Neil Aspinall, spent the night at Mick and Keith's new flat, at 10A Holly Hill, Hampstead, chatting and listening to records.

FRIDAY APRIL 9th

In what was considered another make-over, "Ready Steady Go!" re-titled itself for a new "live" format as "Ready Steady Goes Live!" (Regardless of the fact that many of the shows over the previous 19 months had been transmitted live anyway!) Original host Keith Fordyce,

stepped down with Cathy McGowan becoming chief compere and operations were moved from the stifling surroundings at Television House, Kingsway, to Studio One at Wembley. (This shift in production meant an estimated 50% on the show's budget.) This revamped second edition (broadcast 6:08 - 6:59pm) was sub-titled "Ready Steady Stones!", with the group performing:-
"Everybody Needs Somebody To Love" / "Pain In My Heart" / "I`m Alright" and "The Last Time".
The programme also featured:- The Animals, Goldie and the Gingerbreads, Madeline Bell and Roger Miller.

SUNDAY APRIL 11th

The group returned to the Empire Pool, Wembley to close the first half of the annual "NME Poll Winners Concert" ("Big Beat '65", 10,000 audience). The bill featured The Moody Blues, Freddie and The Dreamers, Georgie Fame and The Blue Flames, Twinkle, The Seekers, Hermans Hermits, The Ivy League, Sounds Inc., The Bachelors, Wayne Fontana and The Mindbenders, The Rockin' Berries, Cilla Black, Donovan, Them, Tom Jones, The Searchers, Dusty Springfield, The Animals, The Kinks and The Beatles. Comperes: Jimmy Savile, Keith Fordyce and Cathy McGowan. The Stones performed:-
"Everybody Need`s Somebody To Love" - "Pain In My Heart" / "Around and Around" / "The Last Time" and "Everybody Need's Somebody To Love" (complete). They also won awards (presented by Tony Bennett) for "Best New Group", "Best British R & B Group" and runners-up as "World & British Vocal Group". Mick was voted "Best New Disc or T.V Singer". As with the 1964 event, ABC TV filmed proceedings and broadcast the Stones set in "Poll Winners Concert" (Part 1) on Easter

Below: "Ready Steady Stones!" April 9th

Sunday, April 18th, (over most of the ITV network between 3:15 - 4: 39pm, while London viewers received the show between 4:10 - 5: 34pm). The first part of the broadcast, also featured Georgie Fame and The Blue Flames, Twinkle, The Ivy League & Division Two, The Bachelors, Cilla Black, Donovan, Them, The Searchers, Dusty Springfield, The Animals and The Beatles. Movietone News again covered the event, in a feature entitled "With It At Wembley", featuring a 1 minute 17 second extract from "The Last Time".

MONDAY APRIL 12th

Brian attended a private Rank Cinema screening of "The TAMI Show" (see October 28th & 29th 1964 entries) with Mary Wilson and Florence Ballard of The Supremes. It was the first time that any of them had seen the show, except on monitors during the making of the film. Despite favourable press reaction, the film would not be officially distributed to

Above: Breakfast at Heathrow, April 22nd
Bottom left: Brian backstage at the Olympia, April 16th

British theatres, until August 7th, 1966.

FRIDAY APRIL 16th

The group flew to Paris, staying at the Hotel de Paris, for the first of three sell-out concerts at L'Olympia. Set list:-
"Everybody Needs Somebody To Love"- "Around And Around" / "Off The Hook" / "Time Is On My Side" / "Carol" / "It's All Over Now" / "Little Red Rooster" / "Route 66" / "Everybody Needs Somebody To Love" (Full version)/ "The Last Time" / "I'm Alright" and (Bo Diddley's) "Crawdad".

SATURDAY APRIL 17th

The second of three concerts at the Paris Olympia.

SUNDAY APRIL 18th

The third and last of the three shows. This performance was recorded and transmitted live on the French radio station, Europe 1, in the programme "Musicorama". The group were interviewed for the programme that afternoon. In answer to a query about his current three favourite discs, Brian replied "Gloria" by Them, "Don`t Let Me Be Misunderstood" by Nina Simone and "Mr. Tambourine Man" by The Byrds.

MONDAY APRIL 19th

A scheduled concert at Blokker, 40 km north of Amsterdam, Holland was cancelled. Instead, the group flew back to London.

THURSDAY APRIL 22nd

The group arrived at London Airport early in the morning to fly out to Montreal, Canada, to begin their third North American Tour. Chaos ensued as Mick, Keith & Brian insisted on finishing their breakfast before boarding the plane. A policeman stood by as fans began to converge and later, extra police were drafted in to make a safe passage for the group, from the breakfast bar area to the departure lounge. The group departed on a 9:00am flight, arriving (via Manchester and Prestwick), some ten hours later at 1:00pm (Canadian time) the same day in Montreal to a large airport reception of fans and media. The group were interviewed for TV and Radio and in the evening, Bill went clubbing with local DJ "Lord Tim"(Hudson).

FRIDAY APRIL 23rd

Charlie and Bill went sightseeing by taxi and in the evening the group performed at the Maurice Richard Arena, Montreal. (6,500 audience.)

SATURDAY APRIL 24th

A two-hour drive to Ottawa arriving at 5pm, with a crowd of 200 fans surrounding the Chateau Laurier Hotel. At 8:30pm, the group left for the evening's show at the YMCA Auditorium (4,000 audience). Ten minutes after the show had begun, the stage was besieged. The noise was so loud, that no one noticed Brian's amp kept cutting out, as well as the power for the stage cutting out altogether. A fifty strong police cordon, completely surrounded the stage, making the group practically invisible, by the end of the concert.

SUNDAY APRIL 25th

A drive to Toronto. During the journey, a song idea came to Keith,

"I gotta plane ta catch!!", Heathrow, April 22nd

becoming "Satisfaction". The group arrived at their hotel at 5pm, with around 10 police stationed on their floor. The group left again at 8:30pm for the evening's show at the Maple Leaf Gardens, giving press, radio and TV interviews backstage. The show (in front of the tour's biggest audience of 16,000) featured the by-now usual stage invasion spectacle, despite the group being flanked by 60 police. Getting out of the venue, back to their hotel was also a problem.

MONDAY APRIL 26th

The group drove on to London, Ontario. These car journeys were spent filming the local scenery and/or reading. Mick & Keith's preference was for Ian Fleming's James Bond novels, Brian & Bill's science fiction by Ray Bradbury, while Charlie devoured anything on the American Civil War. They arrived in time for a pre-concert press conference at the Treasure Island Gardens and then played before an audience of 4,500 (many who had come from nearby Detroit as the group weren't playing there, on this tour). Unhindered by a 5-foot fence and fifty police surrounding the stage, a dozen fans made the stage. The show was stopped halfway through the third song ("Off The Hook") by the police who turned on the house lights and cut the power. When the authorities refused to restore it, the group continued to play for a few

minutes (Mick on maraccas, Brian on tambourine with Keith and Bill handclapping). After apologising, the group left the stage. They had appeared for only fifteen minutes, causing the disappointed crowd to start tearing the place apart. Mick: "We just felt sorry for the fans suddenly not having a show to watch. So we ganged up on the police."

TUESDAY APRIL 27th

Upon departure from Canada, the radio station WRTY interviewed the group. Meanwhile local Ontario radio stations were bombarded with complaints from angry fans, following disruptions to the previous nights concert. The group received their first major headlines on the tour. "CRUDE AND RUDE ROLLING STONES HURL INSULTS AT POLICE" and "ROLLING STONES CREATE HAVOC AT GARDENS - DAMAGES IN THOUSANDS REPORTED."

The group flew to New York, staying in Suite 709 at the Gorham Hotel, on 55th Street, with a 24-hr security guard on their floor. Oldham and Easton, who had just flown in from London, were there to meet them. (Oldham later flew on to L.A to make preparations for their West Coast arrival.) The group went to a party at Bob Crewe's (of The Four Seasons) apartment, where they met English jazz pianist, George Shearing.

WEDNESDAY APRIL 28th

The group rehearsed for their upcoming return appearance on "The Ed Sullivan Show". Sullivan had sent a telegram to Andrew Oldham, saying he would "appreciate it, if the boys would make some determined effort to smarten themselves up", so the band went clothes shopping, prior to rehearsals. The group met Big Dee Irwin outside the Gorham and Wayne Fontana and The Mindbenders, who were also staying at the hotel. During the Stones stay in New York, fans camped outside the Gorham, disguising themselves as Chrissie Shrimpton, Murray the "K", their mothers and even as room service, carrying piles of dirty laundry! Mick, Keith and Brian saw Wilson Pickett at the Apollo, in Harlem, where they received a note from James Brown:- "Missed you once again on this tour. Just wanted to pay my respects and say how much I like your new records."

THURSDAY APRIL 29th

Palace Theatre, Albany, New York State. (Two shows.) The group were interviewed for Radio WTRY Albany.

FRIDAY APRIL 30th

The group were interviewed for Hartford radio station WDIC and in the evening, a concert at the Memorial Auditorium, Worcester.

SATURDAY MAY 1st

Two concerts at different venues. The first, at 1pm, at the Academy of Music, New York. Compere:-DJ Scott Ross (with a fan club "get together" organised backstage) and in the evening, an 8pm show at the Convention Hall, Philadelphia. The show, promoted by Dick Clark, was attended by 15,000 and also featured Freddie Cannon, Bobby Vee, Little Anthony and The Imperials and Herman's Hermits (featuring a rather nervous Peter Noone, who had to be reassured by Mick).

SUNDAY MAY 2nd

Under pressure from his audience, Ed Sullivan ate his words (see Oct 24th 1964 entry) and the group made their second live appearance on his top rated CBS TV variety show ("The Ed Sullivan Show"). During the afternoon, the group ran through three numbers for the cameras, (a fourth track, "2120 South Michigan Avenue" was rehearsed, but did not make the final broadcast) while the doors of the TV studios on Broadway and West 53rd Street, were locked shut for almost 12 hours! The broadcast (featuring "The Last Time", in the first half of the show, and "Little Red Rooster" and "Everybody Needs Somebody To Love" in the second), went out later that night between 8:00 - 9:00pm (CET). The show also included Tom Jones and British comedians, Morecambe and Wise in the studio, while Dusty Springfield appeared on film. Following the broadcast, the group attended a party given in their honour by London Records, at The Playboy Club. Roy Orbison was among the guests.

MONDAY MAY 3rd

The group recorded an ABC-TV hour long special: "The Beatles vs. The Rolling Stones" hosted by Clay Cole in New York. The group were interviewed by the host, and performed six tracks to be broadcast on May 29th. Naturally, the show was a comparison contest between both groups, with The Beatles appearing via film clips and interviews. The audience contained an equal mix of Beatles/Stones fans, all screaming hysterically whenever their respective group was mentioned. Afterwards, Bill, Charlie, Stu and Mike Dorsey went to the all-night Tower Records store, in Times Square.

TUESDAY MAY 4th

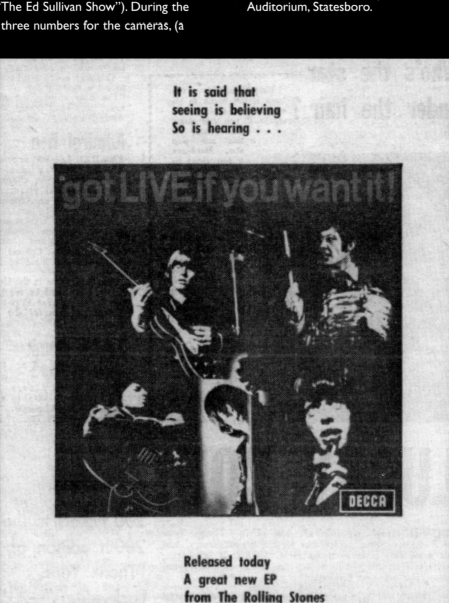

It is said that
seeing is believing
So is hearing . . .

got LIVE if you want it!

DECCA

Released today
A great new EP
from The Rolling Stones

Produced by Andrew Loog Oldham for Impact Sound

The group had a nasty landing when their plane's hydraulic brakes failed, upon arrival in Atlanta. They changed planes and flew to Savannah, before driving 50 miles to perform at the Georgia Southern College Auditorium, Statesboro.

WEDNESDAY MAY 5th

A day spent sightseeing and swimming, in 90 degree temperatures. Whilst the group were eating at their motel, the manageress asked for an autograph for one of the kitchen maids. When Mick hesitated, they were horrified by the woman's assurance:-"It's alright, she's a white woman". That night, the group flew on to Tampa, stopping at Jacksonville, Daytona and Orlando.

THURSDAY MAY 6th

Jack Russell Baseball Stadium, Clearwater, Florida. (4,000 audience). Owing to fan fervour, the police insisted the group stopped playing only five numbers. The group were staying at the Gulf Motel, where Keith first played Mick the riff to "Satisfaction". Brian wore a corset after cracking two ribs, during a brawl with roadie, Mike Dorsey. A story was hastily concocted that he had slipped and fallen after practising karate by the motel swimming pool.

FRIDAY MAY 7th

Legion Field Stadium, Birmingham, Alabama (20,000 audience). The group arrived at the venue in three small planes, to top a bill, which also included Sonny James, Marty Robbins, The Righteous Brothers and The Beach Boys.

SATURDAY MAY 8th

The group arrived in Jacksonville at 3:30am, only to find their hotel already surrounded by fans. They eventually found alternative accommodation at 6am, at the Thunderbird Hotel.

THE ROLLING STONES FAN CLUB

OFFICIAL MEMBERSHIP CARD

ROLLING STONES FAN CLUB

CLUB HEADQUARTERS:
c/o 10 Blenheim Street,
New Bond Street,
LONDON. W.1

NAME...GREG PIPPET

ADDRESS...EAST PERDEX

...MELROSE. ROX SCOTLAND

MEMBERSHIP NUMBER 17.061

VALID UNTIL March...1970

1965 U.K. Fan Club membership card
and badge

SUNDAY MAY 9th

The group flew to Chicago, staying at the Sheraton Hotel. A press conference was held backstage, before the show at the Arie Crown Theatre, McCormick Place.

MONDAY MAY 10th

Chess Studios, for more recording sessions, with Andrew Oldham and Ron Malo. The mammoth seventeen hour session, (12am-5am, including overdubbing) featured:-

"Mercy, Mercy" (second released version) (Don Covay)
"(I Can't Get No)Satisfaction" (First version)
"That's How Strong My Love Is"(Otis Redding)
"The Under Assistant West Coast Promotion Man"
"Try Me"(James Brown)
"Fanny Mae"(Buster Brown)
"Key To The Highway"(Little Walter)
"Get Back To The One You Love"
"Leave Me Alone"

"Go On Home" (Arthur Alexander).
The latter six remain unreleased.

TUESDAY MAY 11th

The group flew to LA, staying at the Ambassador Hotel, where they were interviewed on Radio KHJLA. During their stay, an invitation to visit Elvis Presley on the Paramount film set, fell through.

WEDNESDAY 12th and THURSDAY MAY 13th

Two days of recording at RCA Studios, with Andrew Oldham and Dave Hassinger. The sessions (10:00am - 2:30am and 1pm-9pm) produced the following:-

"(I Can't Get No)Satisfaction" (A further three versions, including the finished master featuring a different drum track from Charlie and Keith`s Gibson fuzzbox double tracked)
"My Girl" (Two versions) (The Temptations via Otis Redding)
"Cry To Me"(Solomon Burke)
"One More Try"
"Good Times"(Sam Cooke)
"I've Been Loving You Too Long"(Otis Redding)
"The Spider And The Fly" (Two versions)
"Tracks Of My Tears"(The Miracles) (unreleased).
Additional musicians:-
Jack Nitzche (Piano, organ, percussion) with J.W. Alexandra on percussion.

FRIDAY MAY 14th

New Civic Auditorium, San Francisco. (5000 audience with The Byrds, who supported the Stones on each of the West Coast dates.)

SATURDAY MAY 15th

Swing Auditorium, San Bernadino. (4,500 audience.)
The group went to the Los Angeles studios of ABC-TV to record their only appearance on the show "Hollywood A Go-Go", transmitted Wednesday, May 26th, between 6:30 - 7:30 EST. During the programme, also featuring Chuck Berry, the group mimed "Little Red Rooster", "The Last Time" and "Play With Fire".

SUNDAY MAY 16th

Civic Auditorium, Long Beach, before an audience of 9,000 fans. The group narrowly escaped getting crushed when their getaway was halted by fans, who had surrounded the car, hundreds of them climbing onto the roof. The group had to push up from inside with their legs, to stop the roof caving in. During the confusion, a girl lost a finger, and another had her foot crushed. The shaken group were helicoptered back to L.A, before driving to the studios of ABC-TV to telerecord four songs for "Shivaree". The group mimed "Play With Fire", "The Last Time", "Down The Road Apiece" and "Little Red Rooster". "The Last Time and Play With Fire" were used in Show 19 of the 1965 season, which also featured Jody Miller, Rick Lancelot, Esther Phillips and The O'Jays, transmitted June 5th (being repeated August 28th)." Down The Road Apiece" and "Little Red Rooster" were used in Show 26, transmitted

July 10th (repeated December 11th), which also featured The Dixie Cups, Jimmy Witherspoon, Vicki Gomez and Jerry Fuller. After the recording, Bill and a "tripping" Brian went to the Action Club, on Sunset Strip, where Brian jammed with the house band on harmonica .

MONDAY MAY 17th

Community Concourse, Convention Hall, San Diego. The group were half an hour late getting to the venue when their car broke down, so The Byrds kept playing to pacify the crowd. They had started to play Stones songs, after they'd exhausted their own set, by the time the group eventually arrived.

THURSDAY MAY 20th

The group returned to the ABC TV studios to make an appearance on Jack Good's show "Shindig!". They mimed to live pre-recordings of: "Little Red Rooster", "Play With Fire" (posed in front of a Rolls-Royce) and "The Last Time".

Good had asked the group who they would like as their guest on the programme. They chose Howlin' Wolf, who performed the song "How Many More Years?" as they sat at his feet and watched. The group also met organist, Billy Preston, for the first time. The show, featuring Sonny and Cher and Jimmie Rodgers, was first transmitted by ABC TV on Saturday, May 22nd, between 8:30 - 8:59 EST.

FRIDAY MAY 21st

Civic Auditorium, San Jose. In England, the Decca charity compilation album, "14", was released, featuring "Surprise, Surprise" (which had been left over from the Regent Sound sessions - see Sept.28th, 1964 entry). All royalties were donated to the National Playing Fields Association.

SATURDAY MAY 22nd

Two shows, the first at the Convention Hall, Ratcliffe Stadium, Fresno, which was cut short, with a ring of 75 police surrounding the stage. The second at the Municipial Auditorium, Sacramento. Due back in New York, the group split up to make their own ways there. Mick and Keith hired a car and drove via the Arizona desert, while Charlie travelled to Gettsyburg, looking for his beloved Civil War memorabilia. Bill and Brian stayed on in L.A, flying in to New York, on the 28th.

THURSDAY MAY 27th

Eric Easton announced that the Stones first film would begin shooting in July.

SATURDAY MAY 29th

An additional three sell-out shows were added at New York's Academy of Music by promoter Sid Bernstein (3,500 capacity at each). At the end of the shows, the group partied at Ondine's with The Animals.

TUESDAY JUNE 1st

The group returned to London Airport. Mick and Keith had vacated their Hampstead flat, before leaving for the States, so the pair stayed at the Hilton. Mick temporarily lodged with his fashion photographer friend, David Bailey, while Keith also stayed with friends, before buying a flat, in St. Johns Wood.

FRIDAY JUNE 4th

The group visited Studio One at Wembley, for another appearance on ATV's "Ready Steady Goes Live!", hosted by Cathy McGowan, transmitted live between 6:08 and 6:59 pm, over the ITV network. The group performed "Oh Baby (We Got A Good Thing Going)", "Good Times" and "I'm Moving On". Also appearing were The Kinks, The Yardbirds and French band Les Surfs.

Below: Mick with Georgie Fame

Above and Below: Glasgow, June 15th

SUNDAY JUNE 6th

"Thank Your Lucky Stars", at Alpha Studios, Astor, Birmingham. The group mimed to "I'm Alright" and "I'm Moving On" (from the new "live" E.P. "Got Live If You Want It", released Friday, June 11th). The show, hosted by Brian Matthew and transmitted across the ITV network, on June 12th, (between 5:50 - 6:34pm) also featured:- The Kinks, Lulu and The Luvvers, Ian Whitcomb, Little Frankie, The Boys Blue and The Fortunes. "(I Can't Get No) Satisfaction" had been released in the States, but because of the release of the live E.P., it was not released in England until August 20th. (see entry.)

THURSDAY JUNE 10th

To Manchester, to appear on "Top of the Pops". The group participated in afternoon camera rehearsals, and then between 7:29 - 7:59pm, live on

BBC-1, mimed "I'm Alright" (from the live E.P). The show, hosted by Alan Freeman, also featured "disc-girl" Samantha Juste, The Who, Burt Bacharach and The Breakaways, Donovan, Unit 4 plus 2, Gene Pitney, The Hollies, The Kinks, Dave Clark 5 and Sandie Shaw.

On this appearance, the group received a payment of £157. 10 shillings, an increase of £26. 5 shillings from their usual BBC appearance fee. During a break from the afternoon rehearsals, Brian was interviewed in the dressing rooms for a BBC1 special on DJ, Jimmy Savile. Entitled simply, "Jimmy Savile", Brian spoke of "Jimmy's attitude to pop star's and their's to him". A brief clip of "The Last Time" from the March 4th edition of "Top Of The Pops" was featured also. The rest of the Savile tribute programme included Peter Noone, (also in the TOTP dressing room from today's edition), Jimmy's parents at home, Jimmy wrestling (!) and Johnny Stewart directing the show. The music featured The Hollies, Twinkle (who had recently claimed she had turned down a song written by Brian), The Seekers and Petula Clark amongst others. The programme, which carried the description: "A documentary about ten days in the hectic life of Britain's No.1 DJ", was transmitted on BBC1, Tuesday, July 13th, between 9:16 -10:14pm.

FRIDAY JUNE 11th

Mick met John Lennon at the Scotch of St. James club, who told him of The Beatles getting their M.B.E awards (a day before the story broke in the press). Mick: "He seemed a bit embarrassed".

SATURDAY JUNE 12th

Brian declared in "Melody Maker":-"I reckon Mick's twice as good as (Eric) Burdon." The same issue reported that Brian intended visiting Bob Dylan's New York home in the summer, as well as buying a house for himself in the States. He also had plans to record an unknown girl singer.

TUESDAY JUNE 15th

A four-show Scottish tour, for promoter Albert Bonici, beginning with two concerts at the Glasgow Odeon, with support bands:- The Hollies, The Moody Blues, The Cannon Brothers and The Checkmates. Mounted police kept crowds within 250 yards of the theatre. The group's set list included:- "Route 66" / "Pain In My Heart" / "Little Red Rooster" / "Not Fade Away" / "It's All Over Now" / "The Last Time" / "Play With Fire" /

"Come On" and "Off The Hook".

WEDNESDAY JUNE 16th

Usher Hall, Edinburgh. (Two shows.) The group drove overnight to Aberdeen.

THURSDAY JUNE 17th

Aberdeen Capitol. (Two shows.)

FRIDAY JUNE 18th

Dundee Caird Hall. (Two shows.) The group stayed at the Gleneagles Hotel, in Perthshire, where they posed for a photo session on the putting green. The group flew back to London the following day, except for Mick, who remained an extra night, suffering from exhaustion and Charlie, who stayed to keep him company.

MONDAY JUNE 21st

Interviews recorded in Scotland were transmitted on two BBC Light radio programmes "The Teen Scene" (broadcast between 10:35 - 11:15 pm) and bizarrely, "Woman's Hour" (between 2:00 - 3:00 pm).

WEDNESDAY JUNE 23rd

The group flew to Oslo to begin another short Scandanavian sojourn, being interviewed at the airport for local Norwegian television.

THURSDAY JUNE 24th

A press conference was held at their hotel, the "Viking". During the show at the Sjolsthallen, the 3,000 capacity crowd became uncontollable, sparking a police baton charge. One girl slipped through the police cordon, jumping onstage to plant a kiss on Charlie, after which she promptly passed out! The tour set list:-
"Everybody Needs Somebody To Love"-"Pain In My Heart" / "I'm Moving On" / "I'm Alright" / "The Last Time" / "Little Red Rooster" / "Time Is On My Side" / "Around and Around" and "Route 66".

FRIDAY JUNE 25th

The Stones held a press conference at the Hotel Turku, Helsinki, before giving an open-air concert before 15,000, on Yyteri Beach, Turku-Pori, Finland. Due to the nearest road being several miles away, the group were driven to the venue over sand dunes in a jeep!

SATURDAY JUNE 26th

K.B. Hallen, Copenhagen, Denmark. (Two shows.)

SUNDAY JUNE 27th

The group sailed from Copenhagen to Malmo, Sweden and were interviewed by pirate station "Radio Syd" for the programme "Sondagsportrattet".

TUESDAY JUNE 29th

The final two shows of the tour at Baltiska Hallen, Malmo. Charlie was interviewed for local radio.

WEDNESDAY JUNE 30th

In Glasgow Central Juvenile Court, magistrate Mr. James Longmuir, called the group "long-haired morons", when dealing with a youth who'd smashed a shop window near where the group were appearing (see June 15th entry). "They wear their hair down to their shoulders, wear filthy clothes, act like clowns and you buy a ticket to see animals like

that?! Do you think that if people come here with their banjo's and hair to their waist, you should go and smash window's?!"

THURSDAY JULY 1st

As the group (minus Brian who had flown to Paris for a brief holiday) returned to London Airport, "The Evening News" reported that private summonses had been issued against Mick, Brian and Bill for alleged insulting behaviour at an all-night filling station (see March 18th entry). The case reached trial on July 22nd (see entry).

WEDNESDAY 2nd - MONDAY 12th JULY

The group flew to Los Angeles for further recording and mixing at RCA with Andrew Oldham and Dave Hassinger. Tracks included:-
"Get Off Of My Cloud" (first versions)
"The Singer Not The Song"
"She Said Yeah"(Chuck Berry)
"I'm Free"
"Talkin About You"(Chuck Berry)
"Gotta Get Away" (alternate versions and arrangements)
"Blue Turns To Grey".

SATURDAY JULY 10th

In "Disc", it was reported that shooting on the group's first film had been delayed until December, where eight weeks had been set aside. Eric Easton:- "The delay is because we couldn't co-ordinate the availability of people we want, like director, cameramen, etc". "(I Can't Get No) Satisfaction" was at No.1 in the "Billboard" Hot Hundred chart, making it the group's first American chart topper. Radio Luxembourg broadcasted a special "Battle Of The Giants" - The Rolling Stones vs The Beatles, at 8:15pm (see July 15th entry).

TUESDAY JULY 13th

The group and Andrew Oldham flew back to London.

THURSDAY JULY 15th

After pipping The Beatles at the post, in Radio Luxembourg's contest (see July 10th entry), an awards ceremony was organised aboard the Thames River pleasure cruiser, "Kingswood". Brian, Keith and Charlie were on hand to receive the awards on behalf of the group, presented by singer Anita Harris. Movietone News shot 4 minutes of film for a feature entitled "Rolling Stones Get Award".

FRIDAY JULY 16th

The first of a series of summer appearances with two shows at the Odeon Theatre, Exeter with:- The Walker Brothers, Steam Packet, (featuring Long John Baldry, Brian Auger, Rod Stewart and Julie Driscoll), Tommy Quickly (& The Remo 4), Elkie Brooks and Thee (of London). Compere: Simon Oates.

SATURDAY JULY 17th

Guildhall, Portsmouth. (Two shows.)

SUNDAY JULY 18th

Gaumont Theatre, Bournemouth. (Two shows, without The Walker Brothers and Elkie Brooks. The Paramounts & Twinkle were their replacements.) Compere: Ray Cameron.

STONES ROLL DOWN UNDER
Left: Sydney, January 23rd
Right: New Zealand tour programme
Bottom right: Rare New Zealand E.P

HARRY M. MILLER
presents

BIG BEAT '65

★ THE ROLLING STONES ★ ROY ORBISON

★ THE NEWBEATS

★ RAY COLUMBUS AND THE INVADERS

NEW ZEALAND TOUR — 1965

mono

FIVE BY FIVE   DECCA
THE ROLLING STONES

THE MUSIC BOX
83 Cathedral Square
CHRISTCHURCH

July West Country tour programme

THURSDAY JULY 22nd

Mick, Bill and Brian (with Keith giving evidence and Charlie observing) attended West Ham Magistrates Court, with their lawyer, Mr. Dale Parkinson and pleaded "not guilty" to alleged insulting behaviour, whereby a breach of the peace may have occured. Bill also denied using obscene language to the annoyance of passengers. They were all found "guilty" of the charge and fined £5 each (plus 15 guineas costs). Bill was found "not guilty" on the obscene language charge. The Magistrate summed up:- "Just because you have reached an exalted height in your profession, it does not mean you can behave in this manner." All three gave notice of appeal. More than 20 police were at the court to control about 200 teenagers gathered outside and in the public gallery. Mick, Brian and Bill were interviewed about the trial for the World Service radio programme "The Streets Of London", transmitted the following day.

FRIDAY JULY 23rd

Mary Malone, in the "Daily Mirror", reported on the previous day's trial:- "The Stones Daimler pulled into the Petrol station in Romford Road,

West Ham (the night of March 18th) with several friends inside. Bill asked an attendant if he could use the lavatory, but was refused. A mechanic, at the garage, Mr. Charles Keeley, asked Jagger to get the group off the forecourt. He (Mick) brushed him aside saying, "We will piss anywhere man". This was taken up by the group as a chant. As one of them danced, Wyman, Jagger and Jones were seen to urinate against a wall of the garage. The car drove off with people inside sticking their hands through the windows in a well-known gesture!"

SATURDAY JULY 24th

Mick, Keith and Andrew Oldham met American business manager Allen Klein (of ABKCO) for the first time, in his suite at the Hilton.

SUNDAY JULY 25th

ABC Theatre, Great Yarmouth. (Two shows.) After returning to London, Bill and Brian attended Rik Gunnell's (manager of Georgie Fame and co-owner of The Flamingo Club) all-night birthday party at The Scotch of St James.

MONDAY JULY 26th

ABC Theatre, Leicester. (Two shows.) The group gathered at Andrew Oldham's office at 138 Ivor Court, Gloucester Place, before a business meeting with Klein, at the Hilton. Much to Brian, Bill and Charlie's dismay, Mick, Keith and Oldham had already effectively agreed to allow Klein to run the Stones affairs, without consulting them first.

TUESDAY JULY 27th

All five Stones met at 138 Ivor Court and then went with Oldham, to Decca House on the Albert Embankment, where the hardnosed pair of Klein and his lawyer, Marty Machat, set about negotiating the band a favourable new English record deal.

WEDNESDAY JULY 28th

The Stones videotaped six songs for ABC-TV's "Shindig" on Stage 3 at Twickenham Studios, London. (Georgie Fame and The Blue Flames were also there to tape inserts for the programme). The group arrived late in the morning and left mid-evening after spending over 5 hours onstage. Brian Epstein and Andrew Oldham visited the set. The day's taping went, as follows:-

2pm:

"Mercy Mercy" Rehearsed then taped in one live take.

"Hitch Hike" (live)

"That's How Strong My Love Is" (live, with Brian playing the organ used by Georgie Fame). Costume changes in Dressing Room 7.

"Satisfaction" (mimed)

"Good Times" (mimed). Break until 7pm then impromptu jam session (off camera).

"She Said Yeah" (live).

The performances were spread over two editions. "Satisfaction" on Thursday, August 5th (between 8:30 -8: 59 EST), "Good Times" and "Mercy Mercy", in the edition two weeks later on August 19th (same times). "Satisfaction", when broadcast, had the line, "trying to make some girl", censored by ABC. "Hitch Hike", "That's How Strong My Love Is" and "She Said Yeah", remain un-aired.

THURSDAY JULY 29th

The Stones and Andrew Oldham signed a ten-year contract in the boardroom at Decca House, for what Oldham claimed to be "the most generous terms yet afforded by any record company for any artist" (including royalties for Oldham as producer). Klein now set about re-negotiating the group's deal with London Records, in America.

FRIDAY JULY 30th

A press release announced that Charlie had bought a 16th-century mansion near Lewes, Sussex from Lord Shallcross, a former British Attorney General, for £8,850. While Bill had bought a £12,000 house in Keston. The N.M.E reported that so far, 25,000 copies of "Satisfaction", had been pressed, in England, with the wrong B-side. Oldham:-"The factories have been pressing "Satisfaction" with the same B-side as it had in America, "The Under Assistant West Coast Promotion Man", but the song would not have meant a thing in Britain".(These copies were exported to the Continent.)

SATURDAY JULY 31st

Radio Luxembourg broadcast a special "Meet The Rolling Stones" at 8:15pm .

AUGUST

A busy socialite, Mick attended the opening of ex- "Ready Steady Go!" dancer, Patrick Kerr's , "Hem and Fringe" boutique in Pimlico and a function at The Queens Head pub, in Pinner, Middlesex, with Paul McCartney, Peter Asher, Marianne Faithfull and John Dunbar.

SUNDAY AUGUST 1st

London Palladium (Two shows. 5:30 & 8pm). Guests:-The Moody Blues (who replaced The Walker Brothers, originally billed to appear), The Fourmost, Steampacket, The Quiet Five, Sugar Pie de Santo (with The Shevelles) and Julie Grant. Compere: Ray Cameron.

MONDAY AUGUST 2nd

All five Stones attended a meeting of directors of "Rolling Stones Ltd", at Andrew Oldham's office, after which, the group took a three week break. Brian and Bill were in the celebrity packed audience at Blaise's club in Kensington to see a special British tour "warm-up" show by American group, The Byrds. Afterwards,the group went to a party at Brian's Chelsea flat.

WEDNESDAY AUGUST 4th

Brian flew to Tangier, for a "peace-making" holiday with his ex-girlfriend, Linda Lawrence. (She had sought a court order against Brian as the father of her one year-old son, Julian). Mick and Chrissie Shrimpton accompanied them, Bill visited his brother in the army in Germany, Charlie and Shirley went to Majorca while Keith (and girlfriend Linda Keith), chose the Mediterranean. (Keith was refused entry to one Athens hotel due to his long hair). The Stones office announced that Brian and Bill had formed a company, "Mossy Music", with producer Shel Talmy.

WEDNESDAY AUGUST 11th

Keith interrupted his holiday in the South of France, flying back to London and then flying directly on to New York with Andrew Oldham for talks with Allen Klein about the group's new record deal in the States. (Mick flew from Tangier to meet them on the 13th). Mick:-"The whole British music scene is dead boring now. There hasn't been anything new or exciting for ages...first there was The Beatles, then us, now there's nothing!" The trio stayed at the Drake Hotel.

SUNDAY AUGUST 15th

Mick, Keith and Oldham were amongst the 56,600 audience for The Beatles historic concert at Shea Stadium. Following the show, they visited the "Fabs" at the Warwick Hotel.

MONDAY AUGUST 16th

After a business meeting with Decca/London lawyers, Mick, Keith and Oldham flew back to London in the evening.

TUESDAY AUGUST 17th

A further meeting of directors, at the Ivor Court office, minus an unaware Brian and Bill, who were still abroad. (They both returned that evening, for the meeting scheduled the following day, with German tour promoter, Helmut Voss).

WEDNESDAY AUGUST 18th

Mick and Chrissie Shrimpton were guests at David Bailey's wedding to actress Catherine Deneuve. (Mick was best man.)

THURSDAY AUGUST 19th

With "(I Can't Get No) Satisfaction" finally being released in England, the group went to Manchester to plug it on "Top Of The Pops" (for the last time. From now on, all future appearances would be recorded in London). They mimed to "Satisfaction" in an insert, first shown on September 2nd, with further showings on September 9th and 16th (all on BBC1 7:31 - 8:00pm). A fourth showing appeared in the year end "Top Of The Pops '65" on BBC1 Christmas Day, between 10:35 - 11:35 pm (and repeated Boxing Day 12:15 - 1:30 pm).

FRIDAY AUGUST 20th

"(I Can't Get No) Satisfaction" B/W "The Spider And The Fly" was released in the U.K, after it had already received heavy rotation on pirate radio. Within a fortnight, it went to No.1, after having spent 5 weeks at No.1 on the U.S charts. Andrew Oldham complained to the music press, about Decca's poor distribution of the single, claiming they hadn't pressed enough singles to meet the demand. The group recorded their last radio sessions with two seperate programmes, for the BBC.

ALL-VOX MAN ...that's BILL WYMAN

The Wyman Bass was specially created by VOX for Bill Wyman of the Rolling Stones.

It's an entirely new semi-acoustic version of the famous VOX Mark IV BASS. A truly great guitar. Retail £73.10.0

Bill Wyman also features the VOX foundation bass illustrated here. Retail £173.5.0

Send for full details and address of your nearest stockist.

The first was a Bank Holiday Special:- "The Rolling Stones" (A/K/A "Yeh! Yeh!"), hosted by Tony Hall, for which they performed:- "Mercy Mercy" / "Oh Baby (We Got A Good Thing Goin')" / "Satisfaction" and "The Spider And The Fly".

The programme, also featuring Herman's Hermits and The Three Bells, was transmitted Monday, August 30th, between 4:00 - 5:00 pm, on the BBC Light Programme. Later in the day, the group recorded their fifth and last appearance on "Saturday Club" for transmission September 18th, between 10:00 - 12:00 am, again on the Light programme. The Stones performed:-

"Satisfaction" / "The Spider And The Fly" / "Oh Baby (We Got A Good Thing Goin')" / "Cry To Me" and Buster Brown's "Fannie Mae". Mick was also interviewed by host, Brian Matthew. (The songs common to both shows, were in fact, the same versions). The broadcast, also featured Buddy Greco, Lou Johnston, The Fortunes and Sonny Childe and the Cool School. In the evening, Mick attended the launch party for Andrew Oldham and Tony Calder's new record label, Immediate Records. Guests included Eric Clapton, Byrd Michael Clarke and German chanteuse, Nico (one of the label's first signings).

SUNDAY AUGUST 22nd

Another concert in Blackpool was cancelled, fearing a repeat of the events of July 24th, 1964 (see entry). Instead the group performed two shows at the Futurist Theatre, Scarborough, with Lulu and The Luvvers.

MONDAY AUGUST 23rd

The group went to the Manchester studios of Granada Television to record "Scene at 6:30pm". Studio security guards were forced to spray 200 fans with fire hoses when they broke through safety barriers. The Stones mimed "Satisfaction", in Studio 4, broadcast later that night between 6:30 - 6:59pm (in the Granada ITV region only).

TUESDAY 24th and WEDNESDAY AUGUST 25th

The group and Oldham, met Allen Klein for two days of business talks at the London Hilton.

FRIDAY AUGUST 27th

Another appearance on "Ready Steady Go!", at Studio One, Wembley. The group performed "The Spider And The Fly", "Mercy, Mercy" and "Satisfaction". The programme, transmitted later that night between 6:08 -6:59pm, also featured Lulu, The Hollies and Chubby Checker. Following the live show, Brian and (ex-dancer on the show) Patrick Kerr went to the Scotch of St. James until 3:30am and then on to an all-night party at Le Kilt discotheque, leaving at around 5:30am. After hailing a taxi, they stopped at the Chelsea Bridge tea stall. Brian:- "I came here the other day with John Lennon and George Harrison. The customers didn't know what to say, but I always keep my taxi on though, just in case!"

Right: "I Got You Babe", "Ready Steady Go!", September 2nd

SATURDAY AUGUST 28th

Decca Chairman Sir Edward Lewis sent personal letters to each of the group outlining a new deal, and a personal "thank you" for previous successes. They had signed a £5 million contract, with Decca agreeing to finance five films, to be made over the next three years, with a total budget, estimated at well over £1 million (premature reports suggested Bob Dylan might co-star in one of them). Meanwhile, an official announcement was made that The Rolling Stones had a new agent, Tito Burns (who also represented Dylan in the U.K.) and that Allen Klein would now act as co-manager with Andrew Oldham (in place of the ousted Eric Easton).

SUNDAY AUGUST 29th

Judith Simons in "The Daily Express" reported the group would stay with London Records, for the States. Andrew Oldham:- "Under the terms of a deal concluded by our American business manager, Mr. Allen Klein, the Stones are guaranteed three million dollars over the next five years." The Stones went to the ABC TV Studios, Birmingham, to record an appearance on the "Thank Your Lucky Stars" summer spin-off series, aptly titled "Lucky Stars Summer Spin". Following afternoon rehearsals, the group mimed "Satisfaction". The show, now hosted by "Carry On" film stalwart, Jim Dale, also featured Herman's Hermits, Unit Four Plus Two, Lulu and Chubby Checker. The programme, now reduced to a running time of only 39 minutes, was transmitted across certain ITV regions on Saturday, September 4th, between 5:50 - 6: 29pm.

THURSDAY SEPTEMBER 2nd

A hastily organised (that week) taped appearance on "Ready Steady Go". (So fast, that the week's "TV Times" made no mention of the fact the group would be appearing.) The Stones took over the show (transmitted across the ITV network between 6:08 - 6:59pm, on Friday, September 10th), with guests including record producer Mickie Most (singing "Johnny B. Goode"!), Manfred Mann, Chris Farlowe and Goldie and the Gingerbreads. Bill specially introduced his protégés', The Preachers (featuring ex-Stones drummer, Tony Chapman - see Jan. 11th 1963 entry) performing their new single "Hole In My Soul" (released the following day B/W "Too Old In The Head", on Columbia. Bill produced the disc). Other highlights included the Stones (with Andrew Oldham and host Cathy McGowan), camply parodying Sonny and Cher's "I Got You Babe" and each of the group listing his best and worst records of the year. Mick:- Best "In The Midnight Hour"-Wilson Pickett. Worst:- "Is It Because"-The Honeycombs. Keith:- Best:- "Like A Rolling Stone"-Bob Dylan. Worst:- "Snakes and Snails"-Alma Cogan. Charlie:- Best-"The In Crowd"-Ramsay Lewis Trio. Worst:-"Where Are You Now?"-Jackie Trent. Bill:-Best-"Hey Good Lookin' "-Bo Diddley. Worst:- "Midnight Special"-Johnny Rivers. Brian:- Best-"The Same Old Song"-The Four Tops. Worst-"Crying In The Chapel"-Elvis Presley. The group performed a three-song live set: "Oh Baby (We Got A Good Thing Goin')", "That's How Strong My Love Is" and "Satisfaction" to close the show.

FRIDAY SEPTEMBER 3rd

The group with Andrew Oldham, flew out from London to Dublin, their movements being captured on celluloid by documentary filmmaker, Peter Whitehead, who had been specifically hired by Oldham, after he had seen Whitehead's "Wholly Communion" documentary (on the Beat Poets gathering at the Albert Hall, in June). Over the next two days, he filmed interviews by Oldham, with both the group and fans, backstage scenes and live footage (of "The Last Time" and "I'm Alright"). Whitehead's hand-held filming style, with just a film crew of three, captured a unique "life on the road" portrait, which would eventually form the documentary, "Charlie Is My Darling".

Whitehead:-"Andrew Oldham asked me if I wanted to film the Stones and I said "yes", not realising there were probably 999 other film-makers who would have done it. "Right", Oldham told him, "grab your camera, we leave for Dublin tomorrow... It was as simple as that!". A short extract from the unedited film was first screened on BBC-1's "Top Of The Pops", on October 14th (see entry). The rarely-seen film, would not be given a (limited) release, until the Spring of 1966.

The first night of the two day visit, the group gave two shows at the Adelphi Theatre, Dublin. (with The Ivy League). During the second show, 30 fans stormed the stage. Mick was dragged to the floor, Brian wrestled with three punching teenagers and Bill was forced back against a piano at the side of the stage. Keith fled, while Charlie, a professional to the end, carried on playing while the pandemonium raged around him (as documented in Whitehead's film).

SATURDAY SEPTEMBER 4th

The group, with Whitehead still filming, travelled to Belfast, Northern Ireland via train for two shows at the ABC Theatre (with The Ivy League). Again the concerts were marred by riots, with 80 seats smashed and thrown at the stage as the group performed. Two fans sustained serious leg injuries. Whitehead continued to film off-duty moments, including interviews with Bill, Charlie and Brian and a rather drunken sing-a-long around the hotel piano, involving Mick, Keith and Oldham. The group flew back to London, the morning of the 5th (where Whitehead concluded filming).

SUNDAY SEPTEMBER 5th and MONDAY SEPTEMBER 6th

The group flew to Los Angeles, directly after the Irish tour, for recording sessions at RCA, finishing the tracks originally started 7 -12th July, 1965 (see entry). A show at the Coventry Theatre (on the 5th) was subsequently cancelled.

WEDNESDAY SEPTEMBER 8th

The group arrived back in London, at 6am on an 8am flight from L.A. They had scarcely enough time to recover, before catching a 1pm flight to the Isle of Man to make their last ever ballroom appearance, "because of the danger of people getting injured", at the Palace Ballroom, Douglas, for a fee of £946.15s. Mick was forced to gain access to the venue through a bathroom window. Following the show, the group went gambling in a casino.

THURSDAY SEPTEMBER 9th

The group had discussions with agent, Tito Burns, about future plans, including the possibility of the Stones own television special at Christmas.

FRIDAY SEPTEMBER 10th

The N.M.E exclusively reported on a behind-the-scenes dispute over the management of the Rolling Stones. Eric Easton:- "My contract as agent and co-manager of the Rolling Stones still has nine months to run." (Oldham claimed that he was sole manager and Tito Burns, agent.) Easton added he was willing to negotiate a settlement of the matter, but had been unable to get together with the other parties involved. He'd placed the matter in the hands' of his solicitors.

SATURDAY SEPTEMBER 11th

The group landed at Dusseldorf Airport to begin a short tour of West Germany and Austria. Fire hoses had to be used on 200 fans, who attacked police after breaking through barriers set up. Fearing similiar chaos, hotels refused accommodation for the group. Munsterlandhalle, Munster. (Two shows.)

The song line-up for the tour included:-
"Everybody Need's Somebody To Love" / "Pain In My Heart" / "Around And Around" / "Time Is On My Side" / "I'm Moving On" / "The Last Time" / "Satisfaction" and "I'm Alright".

SUNDAY SEPTEMBER 12th

Gruga Halle, Essen.(Two shows.)

Above and Below: Scenes from "Charlie is My Darling"
September 3rd and 4th

Above and right: Bill gets "sticky fingers" backstage at the Finsbury Park Astoria (Tom Keylock at right), September 24th Left: Bill at home (taken by Tom Keylock).

MONDAY SEPTEMBER 13th

Ernst Merck Halle,Hamburg. (Two shows,with an audience total of 14,000.) The group stayed overnight at the Hotel Lilienhof.

TUESDAY SEPTEMBER 14th

Cirkus Krone Bau, Munich. (Two shows.) Brian met 22-year old model,Anita Pallenburg backstage for the first time. Promoter Karl Buchmann later received a £1,200 bill for amusement tax.The authorities in question, claimed the Stones made noise, not music!

WEDNESDAY SEPTEMBER 15th

The group flew into West Berlin and were given a police escort to the Hotel Garhus. (The Berlin Hilton had cancelled their reservations for security reasons). After a visit to the Berlin Wall, the Stones arrived (and left) through underground tunnels (left over from World War Two) at the Waldbuhne, for an outdoor show in front of 23,000 people,with 500 police. Arguably, it was the worst night of audience rioting in the group's career. Fifty rows containing 20,000 seats were destroyed,to a total of £40,000 and police, armed with rubber truncheons, battled with the 70% male audience. The group had to exit the stage for fifteen minutes

while calm was restored, before continuing. After the concert, the rampage continued with fans smashing up an East German train, causing £18,000 damage. (The Communists later claimed compensation.) A total of 32 fans and 6 policemen were detained in hospital for injuries, some serious (one policeman apparently lost an eye). A temporary hospital was erected behind the stage to deal with the casualties. Short excerpts from "Everybody Needs Somebody To Love" and "The Last Time" was featured in the German TV programme "Berliner Abendschau", transmitted on station SFB, on the 16th. The report also included an interview with Heinrich Albertz, the director for "Security and Order", showing the severity of the rioting.

FRIDAY SEPTEMBER 17th
The group drove to Vienna for the final show of the tour at the Wiener Stadthalle (12,500 audience).

SATURDAY SEPTEMBER 18th
The group (minus Brian, who went to Paris for a few days holiday) returned to London Airport, from Vienna, arriving at 4pm.

MONDAY SEPTEMBER 20th
All five Stones were present at an afternoon business meeting, at 138 Ivor Court. In the evening, Bill and Glyn Johns produced four tracks for

American group, Moon's Train, at Olympic Studios.

THURSDAY SEPTEMBER 23rd
The group returned to a familiar haunt, namely Ken Colyer's club, "Studio 51", in Great Newport Street, for a day's rehearsal, before their upcoming tour.

FRIDAY SEPTEMBER 24th
The start of a 24-date British tour, to coincide with the release of the group's third (U.K) album, "Out Of Our Heads", commencing with two shows (6:40 & 9:10 pm), at the Finsbury Park Astoria. The tour was very much an "in-house" affair, featuring acts connected with either the group or Andrew Oldham:-The Checkmates, Charles Dickens, The Habits (later managed by Tom Keylock), The End and Unit 4 Plus 2. The shows were compered by Canadian comedian Ray Cameron. Special guests were The Spencer Davis Group. The Stones set consisted:- "She Said Yeah" / "Mercy Mercy" / "Cry To Me" / "That's How Strong My Love Is" / "Oh Baby (We Got A Good Thing Goin')" / "I'm Moving On" / "The Last Time" and "Satisfaction".

SATURDAY SEPTEMBER 25th
Gaumont Theatre, Southampton. (Two shows, in place of Portsmouth Guildhall. 6:15 & 8:40 pm.) "Disc" announced that Richmond's Station

Hotel was to be demolished to make way for a modern multi-storey block of flats. Mick:- "I haven't been in the place for ages, but I'll always remember the fun we had there." (The building had a stay of execution and is still on it's original site.)

SUNDAY SEPTEMBER 26th

Colston Hall, Bristol. (Two shows.) (5:30 & 7:45 pm.) The group attended a special after show party.

MONDAY SEPTEMBER 27th

Odeon Theatre, Cheltenham. (Two shows.) (6:15 & 8:45 pm.) The group jammed with The Spencer Davis Group, at their hotel afterwards.

TUESDAY SEPTEMBER 28th

Capitol Theatre, Cardiff. (Two shows.) (6:00 & 8:30 pm.)

WEDNESDAY SEPTEMBER 29th

Granada Theatre, Shrewsbury. (Two shows.) (6:15 & 8:30 pm.)

THURSDAY SEPTEMBER 30th

Gaumont Theatre, Hanley. (Two shows.) (6:30 & 9:00 pm.) Tonight (and for the two following nights), The Moody Blues replaced Unit 4 plus 2 on the bill.

FRIDAY OCTOBER 1st

ABC Theatre, Chester. (Two shows.) (6:15 & 8:30 pm.) Two singles produced by Bill Wyman were released. Bobbie Miller's "Every Beat Of My Heart" B/W "Tomorrow", on Decca and John Lee's Groundhogs "I'll Never Fall In Love Again" B/W "Over You Baby" (co-produced by Glyn Johns), on Shel Talmy's Planet label.

SATURDAY OCTOBER 2nd

ABC Theatre, Wigan. (Two shows.) (6:20 & 8:35 pm.)

SUNDAY OCTOBER 3rd

Odeon (instead of the Palace) Theatre, Manchester. (Two shows.) (5:15 & 8:00 pm.) Rioting fans smashed and threw seats, debris of which hit Keith, rendering him unconscious for five minutes. He was carried off, but soon recovered. Mick sustained a cut eye, but carried on singing. The group were staying at the Piccadilly Hotel, where Bill denied rumours, in the music press, that he was leaving the group.

MONDAY OCTOBER 4th

Gaumont Theatre, Bradford. (Two shows.) (6:15 & 8:40 pm.)

TUESDAY OCTOBER 5th

ABC Theatre (instead of the Gaumont), Carlisle. (Two shows.) (6:15 & 8:30 pm.)

WEDNESDAY OCTOBER 6th

Odeon Theatre, Glasgow. (Two shows.) (6:15 & 9:00 pm.) Joan Baez watched the late show from the wings.

THURSDAY OCTOBER 7th

City Hall, Newcastle. (Two shows.) (6:15 & 8:45 pm.)

FRIDAY OCTOBER 8th

ABC Theatre, Stockton-on-Tees. (Two shows.) (6:15 & 8:30 pm.) Mick received a cut over his right eye, when a coin struck him.

SATURDAY OCTOBER 9th

Odeon Theatre, Leeds. (Two shows.) (6:00 & 8:30 pm.)

SUNDAY OCTOBER 10th

Liverpool Empire. (Two shows.) (5:40 & 8:00 pm.)

MONDAY OCTOBER 11th

Gaumont Theatre (instead of City Hall), Sheffield. (Two shows) (6:15 & 8:50 pm).

TUESDAY OCTOBER 12th

Gaumont Theatre, Doncaster (instead of Derby Gaumont.) (Two shows.) (6:15 & 8:30 pm.)

WEDNESDAY OCTOBER 13th

De Montfort Hall, Leicester. (Two shows) (6:15 & 8:35 pm).

THURSDAY OCTOBER 14th

Odeon Theatre, Birmingham. (Two shows. 6:45 & 9:00 pm). The first public screening of Peter Whitehead's Irish tour footage (see Sept. 3rd and 4th entries) was shown on "Top Of The Pops" (BBC1 7:30 - 8:00pm). (The Stones current American single, "Get Off Of My Cloud", was dubbed over the soundtrack. The song wasn't released in Britain until the 22nd).

FRIDAY OCTOBER 15th

Regal Theatre (instead of the ABC), Cambridge. (Two shows) (6:15 & 8:30 pm.)

SATURDAY OCTOBER 16th

ABC Theatre, Northampton. Two shows at 6:30 & 8:45 pm in place of two shows at the Southend Odeon, which were cancelled at the request of the local police, who were unable to provide sufficient protection). On BBC-1's "Juke Box Jury" (broadcast between 5:15 - 5:45 pm), host David Jacobs criticised "Get Off Of My Cloud", by echoing a common complaint that the lyrics were inaudible, suggesting the record company were at fault.

SUNDAY OCTOBER 17th

Granada Theatre, Tooting (in place of Hammersmith Commodore). (Two shows.) (6:00 & 8:30 pm.)

MONDAY OCTOBER 18th

At Olympic Sound Studios, Carton Street, Marble Arch, the group recorded a set of American radio ads for use on Los Angeles station KHJ, to promote their upcoming tour, while Mick, Brian and Bill gave an interview for "Teen Time Radio".

TUESDAY OCTOBER 19th

The group recorded an insert for "Top Of The Pops" (in London for the first time). After afternoon rehearsals in Studio 2, at the BBC TV Centre, Wood Lane, they mimed to "Get Off Of My Cloud", first transmitted on the November 4th show, repeated on November 11th (both BBC1 7:30 - 7:59pm) and finally in the year end "Top Of The Pops '65" on Christmas Day (BBC1 10:35 - 11:50 pm, repeated Boxing Day BBC-1 12:15 - 1:30 pm). The insert had a fourth showing, albeit one minute, on the BBC-2 news documentary programme, "Man Alive" (December 30th

8:26 - 8:54pm). This edition (entitled "Love Me And Leave Me"), focused on the plight of illegitimate children. Amongst the single mothers under the spotlight was 20 year-old Patricia Andrews, who spoke with Brian's 4 year-old son Mark, on her lap. She revealed that over the previous four years, Pat and Mark had been living rough, with hardly any money, and that she actually felt sorry for Brian. He was "... estimated to earn around £1,000 a week", but "if Pat Andrews was to take Brian to court and win an affiliation order against him, the maximum amount she could receive was £2 .10 shillings a week" (which is exactly what was awarded when she won a paternity order against Brian, in his absence, the following January).

FRIDAY OCTOBER 22nd

"Get Off Of My Cloud" B/W "The Singer Not The Song" was rush-released, only nine weeks after "Satisfaction", to avoid clashing with the next Beatles single. It had already been released in the States, (with "I'm Free" as the B-side) where it leapt from No.64 to No.1 in three weeks. The End released "I Can't Get Any Joy" B/W "Hey Little Girl", on Phillips, with production credited to Three Way Music, a company formed by manager Bill Wyman and producer, Glyn Johns. The Stones made another appearance on "Ready Steady Goes Live" at Studio One, Wembley (hosted by regular presenter Cathy McGowan), performing live "Cry To Me", "She Said Yeah". and "Get Off Of My Cloud". The live show, transmitted across certain ITV regions later that night between 6:08 - 6:59pm, also featured:- The Animals, The Searchers, David and Jonathan and Chris Farlowe. Andrew Oldham and Peter Whitehead went along to watch.

SUNDAY OCTOBER 24th

The group's scheduled appearance on "The Eamonn Andrews Show" was cancelled because Oldham wanted the group to film an insert for the show, but ABC TV insisted on a live appearance.

MONDAY OCTOBER 25th

Andrew Oldham flew to New York to finalise arrangements for the group's imminent American tour. Mick took Chrissie Shrimpton to Paris for the day.

TUESDAY OCTOBER 26th

Back in London, Mick (with Keith) recorded "As Tears Go By" at IBC Studios with Mike Leander (and his orchestra).

WEDNESDAY OCTOBER 27th

After a four hour flight delay, the group eventually departed to New York from London Airport, for a six-week, 35 date American tour with Andrew Oldham and Stu. Accompanying them to document the tour (at Oldham's invitation), was photographer, Gered Mankowitz (see April entry). Upon landing at Kennedy Airport, the entourage was driven to the City Squire Hotel, after the Warwick Hotel had turned down their reservations, where two floors were taken over as a base for operations during their stay. The promoters, The William Morris Agency, estimated the Stones would earn around £600,000 for the tour.

THURSDAY OCTOBER 28th

Press call at the Hilton Hotel. ("Get Off Of My Cloud" was at No.1 in the States). Pete Hamill, of the "New York Post" described them: "There is something elegantly sinister about the Rolling Stones. They sit before you at a press conference, like 5 unfolding switchblades, their faces set in rehearsed snarls, their hair studiously unkempt and matted, their clothes part of some private conceit and the

the one you've been waiting for
... all new recordings

out of our heads
THE ROLLING STONES *

a great new LP

① SKL 4733 ② LK 4733

DECCA

12" LP RECORD

produced by andrew loog oldham

The Decca Record Company Limited · Decca House · Albert Embankment · London SE1

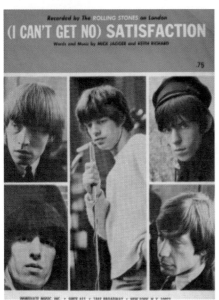

way they talk and the songs they sing all become part of some long, mean reach for the jugular!" The group went on a shopping spree, firstly at a clothes warehouse, then onto various record stores, after purchasing portable record players to use in their hotel rooms, whilst on tour.

FRIDAY OCTOBER 29th

The group flew to Montreal (via private plane, which they utilised throughout the tour). There was panic on the flight when Keith discovered he'd lost his passport. Subsequently, he had to be smuggled into Canada. (After several frantic phone calls, his passport was traced back to New York.) The group later held a press conference, backstage at the Forum. During the concert (8000 audience), around 450 fans rushed the stage. One fan managed to steal Charlie's bass drum, while another attempted to run off with Keith's guitar. Stu chased the youth halfway out of the building, before retrieving it. Charlie's jacket was ripped as he left the stage and after seats were thrown, Brian received a cut on the forehead. The sheer size of the crowd backstage, had Bill and Keith trapped onstage for 20 minutes. There were some 30 injuries. The setlist for the tour:-

"Everybody Needs Somebody To Love" / "Play With Fire" / "Mercy Mercy" / "Around And Around" / "The Last Time" / "That's How Strong My Love Is" / "Get Off Of My Cloud" / "I'm Alright" and "Satisfaction". The group were driven to the airport and flew back to New York, immediately following the show.

SATURDAY OCTOBER 30th

The group held another press conference at the Hilton. They arrived from the Warwick Hotel via limousine, which transported them into the freight elevator, thus becoming the only personalities to be taken directly inside the Hilton in a vehicle, since the late President, John. F. Kennedy. That afternoon, the tour continued with a show at Cornell University in The Barton Halls, Ithaca, New York State, while in the evening, the group performed at the War Memorial Hall, Syracuse. Supports:- The Rockin' Ramrods, The Vibrations and Patti La Belle and the Bluebelles. Following the show, Bob Dylan and friends visited Brian, in his room at the City Squire. Times Square currently boasted a 100 foot-high billboard promoting the November release of the album "December's Children (And Everybody's)" (in America only). The display featured a 60 X 40ft David Bailey picture. Meanwhile, in Britain, "Disc" reported the group had signed a "Youth Against Hunger" declaration, would not be appearing in the annual Royal Variety Show and that Mick and Keith had been awarded the paper's "Silver Quills'" for the songs, "(I Can't Get No) Satisfaction" and "Get Off Of My Cloud" (to mark 250,000 sales).

SUNDAY OCTOBER 31st

The group experienced a bumpy plane ride to Canada. Maple Leaf Gardens, Toronto. (15,000 audience), followed by a flight back to New York.

MONDAY NOVEMBER 1st

Memorial Auditorium, Rochester. The show was stopped after seven numbers, despite the Stones protests. Brian's face was bruised, during the stage skirmishes. The group recorded further (ad-libbed) Radio Ads for the tour and went to Ondine's club for the evening. "Get Off Of My Cloud" was at No.1 in both Britain and the States.

WEDNESDAY NOVEMBER 3rd

After a day-off, the group played the Auditorium, Providence, Rhode Island.

THURSDAY NOVEMBER 4th

The Arena, New Haven, Connecticut. (Two shows.)

FRIDAY NOVEMBER 5th

The Boston Gardens, Boston, Massachusetts.

SATURDAY NOVEMBER 6th

In the afternoon, the group played New York's Academy of Music and The Convention Hall, Philadelphia, in the evening, being interviewed by a television news crew backstage. Mick and Keith caught up with James Brown at the Apollo, Brian met Bob Dylan and Al Kooper at the Phone Booth for a night of clubbing, ending up at a Wilson Pickett recording session, while Charlie toured the Greenwich Village jazz clubs.

SUNDAY NOVEMBER 7th

Mosque Theatre, Newark, New Jersey. (Two shows.)

TUESDAY NOVEMBER 9th

Brian met up with Dylan and his confidantes, Robbie Robertson and Bobby Neuwirth for a legendary jam session ("The Lost Jam"), held on the fifth floor of the Lincoln Square Motor Inn, New York, on the night of the infamous city "blackout".

WEDNESDAY NOVEMBER 10th

Reynolds Coliseum, Raleigh, North Carolina.

THURSDAY NOVEMBER 11th

The group recorded their only appearance on the TV show, "Hullabaloo" at NBC's New York studios. After a camera rehearsal, in the afternoon, they videotaped two songs, in colour. As well as appearing in the show's introduction, the Stones segment opened with the "Hullabaloo" orchestra's version of "Satisfaction", set to 45 seconds of footage from "Charlie Is My Darling". (although, at this stage, no title had been given to the film - see September 3rd and 4th entries). Following host Barry McGuire's studio introduction ("That was the Rolling Stones, and so is this"), the group performed "She Said Yeah", followed by "Get Off Of My Cloud".(Mick's live vocals over both songs, backing tracks.) The show, also featuring:- The Kingsmen, Brenda Lee and Barbara McNair, was transmitted Monday, November 15th, across the NBC TV network, between 7:30 - 7:59 EST.

FRIDAY NOVEMBER 12th

The War Memorial Hall, Memorial Auditorium, Greensboro, North Carolina.

SATURDAY NOVEMBER 13th

Another two concerts, the first being at the Washington Coliseum,

Washington D.C., during the afternoon and then later, at the Civic Center, Baltimore, Maryland. Brian had a newly-purchased dulcimer stolen backstage by a fan.

In "Disc", Mick talked about the current American tour and older people's reaction to them: "...in the hotel lobby the other day, an 80 year-old woman asked me if I was one of The Supremes. She wasn't kidding! Also, in the same paper, it was reported that the group would start shooting their film debut, over the winter and early spring of 1966. Mick and Keith would be writing the songs for the film and Decca recording manager, Mike Leander, was currently writing additional background music. Mick hoped that David Bailey would do camera work on the picture. Two American scriptwriters were travelling with the group on their current US tour, to do preliminary work.

SUNDAY NOVEMBER 14th

Civic Auditorium, Knoxville, Tennessee.

MONDAY NOVEMBER 15th

Charlotte Coliseum, North Carolina. Andrew Oldham returned to London, to supervise editing, on the as-yet untitled "Charlie Is My Darling" film documentary (see Sept.3rd and 4th entries). Andrew Loog Oldham Orchestra versions of "Play With Fire" / "Heart Of Stone" / "Satisfaction" and the trad. "Maybe It's Because I'm A Londoner" (!) (after a brief ad-lib in the film) were dubbed onto the finished print. (Oldham flew back to the States in time for the final Californian leg of the tour).

Mick and Keith give an interview for "pirate" Radio London at the Marquee

TUESDAY NOVEMBER 16th

Municipial Auditorium, Nashville, Tennessee.

WEDNESDAY NOVEMBER 17th

Mid South Coliseum, Memphis, Tennessee. After the show, the group flew to Miami for a break, where Anita Pallenburg was waiting for Brian.

FRIDAY NOVEMBER 19th

In England, the "Farlowe In The Midnight Hour" E.P was released, on Immediate, credited to "We 3 Producers" (Mick, Keith and Andrew Oldham). Keith played guitar on the tracks.

SATURDAY NOVEMBER 20th

State Fair Youth Centre, Shreveport, Louisiana (A 15-foot wide moat seperated the crowd from the stage). Oldham, in "Disc":-"This is the boys' fourth American tour, but the first one that is going to pay dividends. During this six-week period of concerts and TV appearances, we will gross an unprecedented $1,500,000". In the same issue, a graphologist, Frank Hilliger, examined and analysed each of the Stones autographs.

SUNDAY NOVEMBER 21st

Two Texan concerts, the first being at the Will Rogers Memorial Center, Fort Worth in the afternoon, while in the evening, the Memorial Auditorium, Dallas.

TUESDAY NOVEMBER 23rd

Assembly Center, Tulsa, Oklahoma.

WEDNESDAY NOVEMBER 24th

Civic Arena, Pittsburgh, Pennsylvania.

THURSDAY NOVEMBER 25th

Auditorium Arena, Milwaukee, Wisconsin. Anita returned to London, having spent a weeks holiday with Brian. She was asked to reply to strong rumours sweeping London and Paris, of her imminent marriage to Brian (some saying Bob Dylan would be best man!) "It will be soon, otherwise it won't be at all!" She told reporters.

FRIDAY NOVEMBER 26th

Cobo Hall, Detroit, Michigan. During the afternoon, the group attended a Tamla Motown recording session.

SATURDAY NOVEMBER 27th

Another two concerts, the first, in the afternoon, at Wampler's Hara Arena, Dayton, Ohio, then an evening concert at the Cincinatti Gardens.

SUNDAY NOVEMBER 28th

Arie Crown Theatre, McCormick Place, Chicago. (Two shows.) The group flew on to Denver, Colorado, where a seven and a half-hour poker game ensued!

MONDAY NOVEMBER 29th

A sell-out show at the Coliseum, Denver. The group were suffering from the constant climate changes (the temperature was 20 below freezing in Denver). "Disc" rang Mick at his hotel room and asked him to comment on the accusations that they were deserting their British fans, with overseas touring:-

"We've been away for about 12 weeks out of this whole year. I don`t think that's an awful lot and to say we are deserting Britain is absolutely ridiculous". Brian went on to deny marriage rumours (see Nov.25th entry). "I've obviously contemplated marriage. Anita is the first girl I've met, I've been serious about. This interview is a bit embarrassing to me, because it's all very private. We're very fond of each other. Obviously, it's more than a casual acquaintanceship." Meanwhile, the Governor of Colorado, John. A. Love, declared tomorrow (the 30th), "Rolling Stones Day", throughout the State.

TUESDAY NOVEMBER 30th
Veterans Memorial Coliseum, Pheonix (in a temperature of 68 degrees).

WEDNESDAY DECEMBER 1st
The Agrodome, Vancouver. The concert was captured for posterity by a film crew (featuring the crowd, more than the group) for the local police force. The intention was to show how "a large excitable crowd could be contained".

THURSDAY DECEMBER 2nd
Coliseum, Seattle, Washington.

FRIDAY DECEMBER 3rd
Memorial Auditorium, Sacramento (4,500 audience). Keith received a massive electric shock and was knocked unconscious, during "The Last Time", when he attempted to move an ungrounded microphone with the neck of his guitar. The concert ground to an emergency halt and the curtains were pulled as doctors rushed to revive him. They announced later: "If Keith had been wearing his Spanish heels and not wearing his Hush Puppies shoes, he would most certainly have died with his boots on." Brian (in the N.M.E):-"We generate more excitement than The Beatles, because we go on, casually dressed like the audience. The Beatles are idols now. The kids can't really identify with them, but we identify with the kids".

SATURDAY DECEMBER 4th
Civic Center Auditorium, San Jose. (Two shows.) Keith appeared against his doctor's advice. Following the concert, Mick, Brian and girlfriends flew on ahead to San Diego, while the others stayed on for a party. Reports in England claimed that Brian was expected to be a director of one of a chain of new boutiques, "House Of Pooh Corner", to be opened in Copenhagen, later that month.

SUNDAY DECEMBER 5th
The tour ended with two Californian concerts. In the afternoon, the group played at the Convention Hall, San Diego, while the final concert took place at the Los Angeles Sports Arena, in front of 13,500, with takings exceeding £26,000. Following the show, Mick, Chrissie, Charlie and Shirley went with Jack Nitzsche to session drummer, Hal Blaine's mansion, while Brian, Anita, Keith and Linda Keith attended the second Acid Test party, held by Ken Kesey and the Merry Pranksters. The following day, Keith, Gered Mankowitz and Allen Klein's nephew, Ronnie Schneider flew to Phoenix for an overnight camping trip on horseback.

TUESDAY 7th to FRIDAY DECEMBER 10th
Four days of evening recording at RCA (with Andrew Oldham and Dave Hassinger. Brian, Stu and Jack Nitzche alternated on piano, organ and harpsichord).
"Mother's Little Helper"
"19th Nervous Breakdown" (two alternate versions)
"Take It Or Leave It"
"Doncha Bother Me"
"Think"
"Goin` Home"
"Sad Day"
"Sittin' On A Fence"
"Ride On Baby"
"Looking Tired" (unreleased completed master, as slated to appear on the finished "Aftermath" album).
(The title to "19th Nervous Breakdown", apparently came from Mick:-"We had just done five weeks hectic work in the States, and I said, "Dunno about you blokes, but I feel about ready for my nineteenth nervous breakdown"). In the end-of-year NME polls, the group were voted "Best British R & B Group", second to The Beatles in the "World Vocal Group", while "Satisfaction" was voted "Best Disc Of The Year" and "Get Off Of My Cloud" third.

SUNDAY DECEMBER 12th
Bill and Charlie were first to return to London. Customs men thoroughly searched Charlie's luggage, to the extent of checking the lining of his cases! Mick and Chrissie flew to Jamaica, while Brian and Anita went to the Virgin Islands.

TUESDAY DECEMBER 14th
Andrew Oldham returned to London, with the R.C.A tapes.

FRIDAY DECEMBER 17th
The N.M.E reported that the group's first film, provisionally titled "Back, Behind And In Front" would now begin shooting on April 10th, 1966, and would not star Marianne Faithfull (as erroneously reported on Dec.10th in the same paper). It would take place in Britain and four Iron Curtain countries, with music being written by Mick and Keith, who had begun work on it the previous week, in Hollywood. The movie was being produced by Allen Klein and Andrew Oldham.

WEDNESDAY DECEMBER 22nd
Keith flew back from Los Angeles to London to spend Christmas.

FRIDAY DECEMBER 24th
Mick returned home to London, also to spend Christmas with his family. Amongst the presents he'd bought was a Mini-Cooper for his brother Chris.

SATURDAY DECEMBER 25th
Brian spent Christmas in New York, with Anita. Whilst there, they met Bob Dylan at the Chelsea Hotel, who greeted Brian: "How's your paranoia meter?!"

"The New Year Starts Here!"

MONDAY DECEMBER 27th

Brian and Anita returned to London. Brian was suffering from a tropical virus he'd picked up on holiday.

FRIDAY DECEMBER 31st

The group went to Studio One, Wembley to appear on what was originally planned as the farewell edition of "Ready Steady Go!", a special "The New Year Starts Here" (transmitted live across the ITV network between 10:52 and the early hours of 1966, with a brief break to catch the chimes of Big Ben). The group arrived in the afternoon for camera rehearsals and later mimed to "Satisfaction" and "Get Off Of My Cloud", on the live ATV-Rediffusion broadcast. The programme had an informal party atmosphere, with no script to follow, hence there was no set time for the show to be "wrapped-up", and basically continued until all the acts had finished performing. The programme, hosted by Cathy McGowan and Dusty Springfield, featured a "Who's Who" of the current pop scene (like the previous year's special), namely: The Animals, Chris Andrews, Dave Berry, The Dave Clark 5, Tom Jones, The Kinks, Lulu, Kenny Lynch, The Searchers, Dusty Springfield and The Who.(The cameras all carried "Ready To Go in 66" slogans).

new MUSICAL EXPRESS

WORLD'S LARGEST CIRCULATION OF ANY MUSIC PAPER

No. 974 EVERY FRIDAY PRICE 6d. SEPT 10, 1965 Registered at the G.P.O. as a Newspaper

ELVIS exclusive

STONES
• DONOVAN
and
DYLAN
• WALKERS

THEY'RE COMING YOUR WAY !!!

ERIC EASTON FOR ROLLING STONES LTD., presents

THE SENSATIONAL

ROLLING STONES

YOUR ONLY OPPORTUNITY TO SEE THE STONES IN PERSON BEFORE SPRING, 1966

THE CHECKMATES • RAY CAMERON

'SPENCER DAVIS GROUP

CHARLES DICKENS • THE HABITS • THE END

UNIT FOUR + 2

WHERE and WHEN

FINSBURY PARK, Astoria Fri., Sept. 24th, 6.40 & 9.10
  12/6, 10/6, 8/6, 6/6, 4/6
SOUTHAMPTON, Gaumont Sat., Sept. 25th, 6.15 & 8.40
  12/6, 10/6, 8/6, 6/6
BRISTOL, Colston Hall Sun., Sept. 26th, 5.30 & 7.45
  12/6, 10/6, 8/6, 7/6, 5/-
CHELTENHAM, Odeon Mon., Sept. 27th, 6.15 & 8.45
  12/6, 10/6, 9/6, 8/6
CARDIFF, Capitol Tue., Sept. 28th, 6.00 & 8.30
  12/6, 10/6, 8/6
SHREWSBURY, Granada Wed., Sept. 29th, 6.15 & 8.30
  12/6, 10/-, 7/6
HANLEY, Gaumont Thur., Sept. 30th, 6.30 & 9.00
CHESTER, A.B.C. Fri., Oct. 1st, 6.15 & 8.30

WIGAN, A.B.C. Sat., Oct. 2nd, 6.20 & 8.35
  12/6, 10/-, 7/6
MANCHESTER, Odeon Sun., Oct. 3rd, 5.15 & 8.00
  12/6, 10/6, 8/6, 6/-
BRADFORD, Gaumont Mon., Oct. 4th, 6.15 & 8.40
  12/6, 10/6, 8/6
CARLISLE, A.B.C. Tue., Oct. 5th, 6.15 & 8.30
  12/6, 10/-, 7/6
GLASGOW, Odeon Wed., Oct. 6th, 6.15 & 9.00
  12/6, 10/6, 8/6, 6/6
NEWCASTLE, City Hall Thur., Oct. 7th, 6.15 & 8.45
  12/6, 10/6, 8/6, 7/6, 5/-
STOCKTON-ON-TEES, A.B.C. Fri., Oct. 8th, 6.15 & 8.30
  12/6, 10/6, 8/6, 6/6
LEEDS, Odeon Sat., Oct. 9th, 6.00 & 8.30
  12/6, 10/6, 8/6, 7/6, 6/6, 5/6

LIVERPOOL, Empire Sun., Oct. 10th, 5.40 & 8.00
  12/6, 11/6, 10/6, 9/6, 8/6, 7/6, 7/-, 5/-
SHEFFIELD, Gaumont Mon., Oct. 11th, 6.15 & 8.50
  12/6, 10/6, 8/6, 6/6
DONCASTER, Gaumont Tue., Oct. 12th, 6.15 & 8.30
  12/6, 10/6, 7/6
LEICESTER, De Montfort Hall Wed., Oct. 13th, 6.15 & 8.35
  12/6, 10/6, 7/6, 5/6
BIRMINGHAM, Odeon Thur., Oct. 14th, 6.45 & 9.00
  12/6, 10/6, 8/6, 6/6
CAMBRIDGE, A.B.C. Fri., Oct. 15th, 6.15 & 8.30
  12/6, 10/-, 7/6
NORTHAMPTON, A.B.C. Sat., Oct. 16th, 6.30 & 8.45
  12/6, 10/-, 7/6
TOOTING, Granada Sun., Oct. 17th, 6.00 & 8.30
  12/6, 10/6, 8/6, 6/6

PLEASE NOTE: AT HANLEY, CHESTER and WIGAN — THE MOODY BLUES will appear in place of UNIT FOUR + 2 | BE ADVISED—BOOK EARLY !

HUBBUB PRODUCTIONS
PRESENTS

ONLY NEW ENGLAND CONCERT
FIRST U.S. APPEARANCE 1966

THE
ROLLING
STONES

FRI., JUNE 24
8:00 P.M.

MANNING BOWL
LYNN, MASS.

TICKETS: $5.00 - $4.00 - $3.00

MAIL ORDERS - HUBBUB, 2 Park Sq., Boston   (Check or Money Order only)

ON SALE AT:
LYNN - Ben Brown Music, 136 Monroe Street   BEVERLY - King's Rook Honda, 277 Rantoul Street
SALEM - Ted Cole's Music, 170 Essex Street   IPSWICH - King's Rook Coffee House
SAUGUS - King's Rook Honda, Route 1   MARBLEHEAD - King's Rook Coffee House
                    GLOUCESTER - Sterling Drug, 171 Main Street

NINETEEN SIXTY SIX

JANUARY

By way of a belated Christmas present to himself, Keith took delivery of a dark blue Bentley Continental (he didn't pass his driving test until February 8th). Mick and Chrissie, back from a holiday in the Bahamas, went on a two day clothes buying trip to Paris. Mick entered I.B.C. Studios, in London, to record an Italian version of the Stones latest American single, "As Tears Go By", ("Con Le Mie Lacrime"), but the session was temporarily aborted after he lost his voice!

MONDAY JANUARY 3rd

Brian flew out to Copenhagen for another holiday.

TUESDAY JANUARY 4th

Mick, Keith and Bill went to a preview of Peter Whitehead's "Charlie Is My Darling" (see Sept 3rd and 4th, 1965 entries). The hour long film, produced by Andrew Oldham, was being offered to British T.V. companies.

FRIDAY JANUARY 7th

The release date for a scrapped E.P, featuring "As Tears Go By" as it's title track. In the States, the song was at No.9 on the "Billboard" Hot 100. Allen Klein arrived in London, for further script consultations on "Back, Behind And In Front".

SATURDAY JANUARY 8th.

Mick held a party at his townhouse at 13a Bryantson Mews East, near Baker Street. Beatles, John, George and Ringo were among the guests.

FRIDAY JANUARY 14th

Chris Farlowe's version of "Think" was released on Immediate, produced by Mick, Keith and Andrew Oldham.

SATURDAY JANUARY 15th

"Record Mirror" reported that Mick had been seen recently, in the Soho Record Centre, buying a copy of The Beatles latest album, "Rubber Soul".

SATURDAY JANUARY 22nd

Geneva City Council labelled the group as "undesirables" and banned them from giving a concert at a civic ice rink, when representatives were booking venues for an upcoming European tour (in March). The council relented enough to allow a show in a circus marquee, in a public square, if a quarter of the takings were given to the city poor - and the council! The group passed.

SUNDAY JANUARY 23rd

The press reported the Rolling Stones and their managers, were involved in a "backstage" row with Decca Records, over the title of their next L.P. which the group wanted to call "Could You Walk On The Water?" (with a sleeve of their heads just visible above a Hollywood reservoir). Decca executives objected to the title, because of it's Biblical connotations and feared much ill-feeling in high places; exactly what Oldham was hoping for! (The sleeve was also to be a gatefold, illustrated with ten pages of colour Gered Mankowitz photos, shot on the last American tour - see Oct.27th 1965 entry.) This idea was put on hold, resurrected for the design of the "Big Hits (High Tide and Green Grass)" album sleeve (see March 26th entry).

FEBRUARY

Bill passed his driving test and he, Diane and Stephen, moved into a nine-roomed house in Farnborough, Kent. Keith bought "Redlands", a thatched roof, Tudor-style estate, surrounded by a moat in West Wittering, Sussex, for £17,750 moving in on April 16th.

THURSDAY FEBRUARY 3rd

The group's first 1966 television appearance, being for "Top Of The Pops", at the BBC TV Centre, Wood Lane. Rehearsals and camera tests began at midday and continued until 6pm. During the afternoon, they recorded "19th Nervous Breakdown" (released the following day), for inclusion in an upcoming show, provisionally scheduled for March 3rd, but due to a special film being sent back from Australia (see Feb 21st), this insert was screened (for the only time) in the earlier edition of February 24th (BBC1 7:31 - 8:00pm). For the live broadcast that evening, (BBC-1 7:30 - 8:00 pm), the group performed the song against a different studio backdrop. The show (hosted by Jimmy Savile), also featured in the studio: Petula Clark, Eddy Arnold, The Overlanders, Crispian St. Peters and the St. Louis Union, while Herb Alpert and The Tijuana Brass appeared by way of specially shot 16mm BBC film and The Spencer Davis Group, via a repeated insert. The dance group, The Go-Jos danced to Nancy Sinatra's "These Boots Are Made For Walking". The Stones clip was repeated in the February, 10th edition

(BBC1 7:30 - 8:00pm) and in the year-end "Top Of The Pops '66" on Boxing Day (BBC1 6:15 - 7:00 pm, repeated the following day between 6:17 - 7:00 pm). For their services, the group were paid £183.15 shillings for each performance and each subsequent repeat. Producer Johnnie Stewart gushed to "Disc": "Mick Jagger is the most photogenic star I've ever seen!"

FRIDAY FEBRUARY 4th

The group's ninth British single, "19th Nervous Breakdown" B/W "As Tears Go By", was released, while in America (with "As Tears Go By" already released as an A-side), the B-side became "Sad Day" (not released in Britain until 1973).

Previous Pages: "Top of The Pops" February 3rd
Above and Below: Leaving Heathrow for New York February 11th

SATURDAY FEBRUARY 5th

With the group preparing for another tour of Australia, it was announced that a rumoured film idea, entitled "The Assassination Of Mick Jagger", was merely a joke on his friend, David Bailey's, part!

SUNDAY FEBRUARY 6th

The group went to Teddington Studios to record their second appearance on ABC TV's "The Eamonn Andrews Show", for a fee of £200. A camera test between 7:30 - 8:30pm, was followed by a dress rehearsal between 8:45 - 9:30pm. The show was transmitted live across the ITV network, that night between 11: 05 -11:49pm. The group mimed to "19th Nervous Breakdown", while a subdued Mick joined the panel to answer questions (for a duration of 4 minutes 30 seconds, for which he was also paid £200 for the privilege!)

THURSDAY FEBRUARY 10th

The group returned again to the BBC TV Centre in Wood Lane, to record a third performance of "19th Nervous Breakdown", for "Top Of The Pops", broadcast February, 17th (BBC1 7:30 - 8:00pm). The show, hosted by Alan Freeman, also featured:- The Small Faces, The Animals, Lulu, The Mindbenders and The Truth.

FRIDAY FEBRUARY 11th

The group (minus Mick who'd caught an earlier flight with Chrissie Shrimpton) flew to New York's Kennedy Airport. The Daily Mail reported:-"The Rolling Stones refused to be photographed when they flew into New York tonight. After one of the group shouted at photographers, a cameraman yelled "Say that again, and we'll take your picture lying down!" Due to intrepid fans, the group were forced to stay individually at different New York hotels.(Mick stayed at the Delmonico, Bill and Brian at the Holiday Inn and Keith and Charlie at the Essex House). Meanwhile, "Disc" featured an article:-"The Stones By The Stones", where each member gave his impression of another. (Mick by Bill, Keith by Mick, Brian by Charlie, Bill by Brian and Charlie by Keith.)

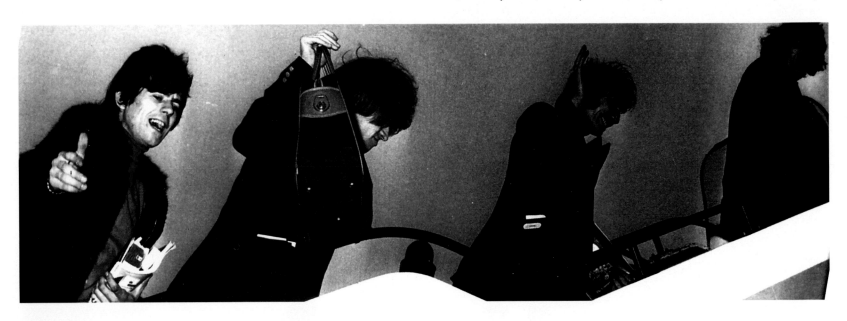

SUNDAY FEBRUARY 13th

The group appeared (for the third time) on CBS-TV's "The Ed Sullivan Show". The group had a near escape, when arriving at the Sullivan Theatre, in the afternoon, for rehearsals. A disbelieving doorman refused to open the stage door, as fans came charging towards them. When the shaken group were finally admitted, an enraged Keith emptied a wastepaper basket over the hapless jobsworth's head! The live broadcast, (their first performance in colour), was transmitted between 8:00 - 9:00pm EST and featured the group performing:- "Satisfaction", against a red background in the first half and a light blue backdrop for "As Tears Go By" (with the lights dimmed as Mick, with Keith, on guitar, took centre stage) and "19th Nervous Breakdown", in the second.

MONDAY FEBRUARY 14th

The group left New York for two days in Los Angeles, prior to their Australasian tour. (Promoter Harry M Miller had cabled an offer for the group to tour the previous September, but this clashed with their U.K. tour. Plans for a concert in Hawaii on the way over had to be abandoned due to lack of time). "19th Nervous Breakdown" reached No.2 in the U.K.

WEDNESDAY FEBRUARY 16th

The group arrived via Honolulu and Fiji at Mascot Airport, Sydney at 7:00am (Australian time), greeted by a large crowd, despite pouring rain. Travelling with the entourage was Charlie's wife, Shirley. Their arrival and airport press conference was covered by Radio & T.V. crews, including Channel 7, who interviewed the group as they passed through Customs.

THURSDAY FEBRUARY 17th

A press reception was held at the Chevron-Hilton, during which the group met the five winners of a "Meet The Stones" contest, organised by the "Sun Herald" newspaper. The competition winners received 5 individual Stones portraits, painted by the paper's artist Tony Rafty, with each member signing his respective drawing (entries to the competition had totalled over 3,000). They also met the presidents of their Australian Fan Club, who presented each of them with kangaroo-skin fur coats. While in Sydney, the group taped an appearance on Channel 7 TV's "Bandstand" show, (hosted by Brian Henderson) miming to "Satisfaction", amongst others, surrounded by a streamer-throwing audience.

FRIDAY FEBRUARY 18th

The group opened the tour, with the first of five shows (6:00 & 8:45pm) at the Manufacturers Hall, Commemorative Auditorium. The Searchers were the only other overseas act on the tour, while local acts Max Merritt & The Meteors, Tony Barber and Marty Rowan, were the supports, in Sydney. For this tour, the Stones set consisted:- "Mercy, Mercy" / "She Said Yeah" / "Play With Fire" / "Not Fade Away" / "The Spider And The Fly" / "The Last Time" / "That's How Strong My Love Is" / "Get Off Of My Cloud" / "19th Nervous Breakdown" and "Satisfaction".

Mick besieged backstage, Sydney, February 18th

SATURDAY FEBRUARY 19th

The second of two days of concerts at the Manufacturers Hall, with three shows, at 2:30, 6:00 & 8:45pm. A total 25,000 had seen the five Sydney shows.

SUNDAY FEBRUARY 20th

The group landed in Brisbane to a waiting crowd of 5,000. The group made clear to fans and press alike, their displeasure at the persistent rain! Local Radio Station 4BC, had become "Stonesville" and made February, "Rolling Stones Month", building up anticipation for their concerts.

MONDAY FEBRUARY 21st

City Hall, Brisbane. (Two shows.) (6:00 & 8:45pm.) Local supports:- Max Merritt and The Meteors, The Feelgoods and Down And Out). The sun had come out at last, and at Surfers Paradise, a visiting BBC crew shot footage of the group for "Top Of The Pops". The film that resulted, featured a formally dressed waiter, serving them champagne from a tray, as well as the group frolicking in the sea, minus Bill, who sat watching from the beach. Deciding to join the others, he waded into the water, still fully clothed! This silent black & white 16mm film (running only 1 minute 15 seconds), was screened the once on the March 3rd edition (BBC1 between 7:30 -7:59pm). For their appearance in this zany piece of cinema verite', the group were paid £105 exactly. Unfortunately, the film was later assigned to the BBC "junk bin"!

TUESDAY FEBRUARY 22nd

Centennial Hall, Adelaide. (Two shows.) (6:00 & 8:45pm.) Rival Brisbane station 4BH broadcast (between 8:00 & 8:45pm), a recording of the previous evening's show from the City Hall, presented by Newmarket Music Centre.

WEDNESDAY 23rd - SATURDAY FEBRUARY 26th

The group flew to Melbourne, staying at The Southern Cross Hotel, for four days of shows at the Palais Theatre, St. Kilda. (Two per day, starting on the 24th; 6:00 & 8:45pm, with a party being thrown each night, by promoter Harry Miller). The late show from the 24th, was recorded and later transmitted by radio station 3UZ.

SUNDAY FEBRUARY 27th

The group flew to New Zealand, arriving at Rongotai Airport, Wellington (covered by NZBC news cameras). Some of the 400 fans there to greet them, climbed along a roof and tried unsuccessfully to climb down a 15-foot wall, to reach the tarmac.

MONDAY FEBRUARY 28th

The group (minus Bill, who'd gone sailing) gave a press conference around the White Heron Lodge pool, before travelling to the Town Hall for two shows (6:00 & 8:30pm) with The Searchers and N.Z. supports The Four Fours, Sandy Edmondes, Ralph Cohen & Mike Leyton. At the late show, during "Satisfaction", a girl leapt onstage from a balcony. The mass cue for 300 fans to rush the stage. The group stopped playing and fled. Keith received a cut eye and birthday boy Brian, badly hurt his ankle, when three girls pounced on him. (Both were treated at a local hospital). Many fans were taken away by ambulancemen but only several had (minor) injuries. A policeman sustained a sprained wrist. The Town Hall bore the brunt of the damages. Rabid fans in cars, chased the group's getaway car back to the hotel. The night's ordeals weren't yet quite over for Charlie. A stranger kept knocking on his door, continually insulting him to the extent of getting a punch on the nose, from the normally placid Mr Watts. When the guy came back to extract revenge, Charlie was ready and waiting, with tour manager, Mike Rispoli. Mick rang "Disc" in London, about the local record scene:- "...it's very funny over here, because in Australia at present, our top number is "Fortune Teller", which is three years old, yet it's No.1 over there. In New Zealand, our most popular number is still "Little Red Rooster".

TUESDAY MARCH 1st

The group flew on to Whenuapai Airport, Auckland, giving an interview to Merv Smith, for the N.Z.B.C. In the evening, the group played the

final two shows of the tour (6:00 & 8:45pm) at the Civic Theatre. (Contrary to previous sources, the group did not play two final shows, at the Capitol Theatre, Perth, Australia, the following day). Afterwards, Bill and Brian went to the Top 20 Club, in Durham Lane.

WEDNESDAY MARCH 2nd

Mick, Keith, Charlie, Shirley and Stu flew from Auckland to Fiji for a three day holiday, while Brian and Bill flew directly on to L.A, checking into the Ambassador Hotel. A visit to Japan en-route for a major T.V. show was cancelled.

FRIDAY MARCH 4th

Chris Farlowe's album, "14 Things To Think About" (produced by Mick, Keith and Andrew Oldham) was released on Immediate.

SUNDAY 6th - WEDNESDAY MARCH 9th

Lengthy sessions at RCA Studios, to finish what would become the "Aftermath" album. Over the next four days, the group completed (with Andrew Oldham and Dave Hassinger):-

"Flight 505"

"High And Dry"

"It's Not Easy"

"Under My Thumb"

"I Am Waiting"

"What To Do"

"Long Long While"

"Lady Jane"

"Stupid Girl"

"Out Of Time" (two versions)

"Paint It Black"

Jack Nitzsche played harpsichord on "Lady Jane" and "I Am Waiting", as well as organ and piano with Stu.

FRIDAY MARCH 11th

The release of the Immediate album "The Aranbee Pop Symphony Orchestra (Conducted by Keith Richards)", produced by Keith, with sound engineer Glyn Johns, recorded at Olympic Studios. (The 10 tracks ranged from Lennon-McCartney's "There's A Place" and "We Can Work It Out" to (with an eye for royalties!):-"Play With Fire" / "Mother's Little Helper" / "Take It Or Leave It" and "Sittin' On A Fence". Also, the Bobbie Miller / Ian Stewart and the Railroaders Decca single "Everywhere I Go" B/W "Stu Ball" was released. The single, produced by Bill (on bass), also featured a line-up of Keith on guitar, Stu on piano and ex-Shadow, Tony Meehan on drums.

SATURDAY MARCH 12th

Mick, Keith, Bill, Stu, Charlie and Shirley flew home to London from L.A. while Brian and Andrew Oldham flew to New York.

MONDAY MARCH 14th

Brian returned to London from New York, where he had spent time clubbing with a character named "Hari Hari" (a pupil of Ravi Shankar's, he was teaching Brian the basic rudiments of the sitar). Brian had to

break into his Earls Court flat, after losing his keys somewhere between Sydney and New York. Later, he entertained guests Steve Winwood, Spencer Davis (The Spencer Davis Group having used the Stones limo, while they were away), Tom Keylock and N.M.E's Keith Altham. "19th Nervous Breakdown" was at No.2 in the States and Peter Whitehead's "Charlie Is My Darling" (produced by Lorimer Films and Andrew Oldham) was given a limited release in Europe (see Sept. 3rd and 4th 1965 entries). Two finished versions were prepared; a 48 minute cinema version, while a version running at 26 minutes found it's way (unofficially) onto European T.V. stations during the 1970's. A further excerpt of "I'm Alright" from the film, was shown on BBC-1's "The Movies", on Monday, August 11th, 1969 6:00 - 6:19 pm. Much un-used footage lies on the cutting room floor and at the time of writing (1996), a "director's cut" is planned.

MONDAY MARCH 21st

The press announced that The Rolling Stones had won the Carl Alan Award for the "Most Outstanding Group of 1965".

FRIDAY MARCH 25th

A tie-less Mick and Andrew Oldham were refused entry to a Mayfair restaurant, where they were due to be interviewed by DJ Alan Freeman for "Rave" magazine. The trio went instead to the trendy Trattoria Terrazza Italian restaurant, in Soho.

SATURDAY MARCH 26th

"Big Hits (High Tide And Green Grass)" was released in the U.S. (A revised version was released in the U.K on November 4th - see entry.) The group flew to Schipol Airport, Amsterdam, for the start of a ten day European tour. Vara-TV covered the airport press conference, along with a short interview with Brian, both featured in news broadcasts. In the evening, the group's concert at the Brabanthal Danbosche (with supports:-The Ferraris, Peter and The Blizzards, The Bumble Bees, The Outsiders and The Bintangs) was cut short after the audience rioted.

SUNDAY MARCH 27th

The group flew via helicopter to Brussels, giving a press conference at the airport, before playing at the Palais Des Sport. RTBF-TV filmed a special report, including backstage footage, support act Ronnie Bird and the group descending the stairs, enroute to the stage. 2,000 were involved in fist fights with the police. Due to a lack of nightlife, the group flew directly onto Paris a day early, checking into the Georges V.

MONDAY MARCH 28th

The group spent the morning in their hotel suite (with Anita Pallenburg), listening to an acetate of "Aftermath". Deciding to go shopping, they were mobbed as they left the Georges V. (Bill narrowly avoided being run down by a Cadillac by vaulting clean over it's bonnet). As the two limos accelerated off, a fan clung tenaciously to the tail fin of one of the cars, before finally being shaken off by Mike Gruber, the group's American roadie. At a café, a journalist gave each member a copy of the Marcel Proust questionnaire (which The Beatles had filled out the year previous), the answers to be printed in a French magazine. (John Lennon's answers were apparently so X-rated, that Brian Epstein had threatened to sue if they were printed. Likewise, Brian Jones's answers were never printed). On the way back to the hotel, they bumped into Georgie Fame, who they arranged to meet later that night. After lunch (photographed by the press), Chrissie Shrimpton arrived in time for an evening's clubbing, which ended at the Castelles Club.

TUESDAY MARCH 29th

The group, minus Charlie, who was suffering from blood poisoning, gave an afternoon press conference at the hotel. That evening, there were two sold-out shows at the Paris Olympia (2,500 at each) with supports, Ian Whitcomb and Wayne Fontana. The set-list for the early show:-
"The Last Time" / "Mercy Mercy" / "She Said Yeah" / "Play With Fire" / "Not Fade Away" / "That's How Strong My Love Is" / "I'm Moving On" / "The Spider And The Fly" / "Time Is On My Side" / "19th Nervous Breakdown" / "Around And Around" / "Get Off Of My Cloud" / "I'm Alright" and "Satisfaction"
For the evening show, the set was varied to:-
"The Last Time" / "Mercy Mercy" / "She Said Yeah" / "Play With Fire" / "Not Fade Away" / "The Spider And The Fly" / "Time Is On My Side" / "19th Nervous Breakdown" / "Get Off Of My Cloud" / "I'm Alright" and "Satisfaction". Ex-RAF Bill Wyman stamped out a smoke bomb thrown onto the stage, before it exploded. 57 arrests were made and five gendarmes received medical attention, one being bitten by a fan. (Local radio station, Europe 1, transmitted both concerts in the series "Musicorama".) Charlie played both shows against doctor's orders. Following the concerts, at midnight, a party was held for the group at the Georges V, with Marianne Faithfull, Francoise Hardy and Brigitte Bardot in attendance. Bardot had specially asked to meet the group and the outcome of their meeting was her asking Mick and Keith to write a song for her next film "Two Weeks In September". They agreed to "have a bash at it".

WEDNESDAY MARCH 30th

The group (minus Keith who drove) flew to Marseilles, spending the day sunbathing, playing the Salle Valier (1,200 audience) in the evening. During "Satisfaction", seats were wrecked and Mick was hit in the eye by a chair, resulting in eight stitches. 85 arrests were made.

THURSDAY MARCH 31st

The group chartered a plane to Lyon for two shows at the Palaise d`Hiver (4,000 total audience). Following which, Brian and Bill took a sleeping car train back to Paris. Mick, Keith and Charlie flew back to London for a two day break.

FRIDAY APRIL 1st.

Mick and Jack Nitzche went to a Troggs recording session at Pye Studios, where the band were recording their hit, "Wild Thing". In Paris, Brian and Bill were in the audience for a special edition of "Ready Steady Go!":- "Ready Steady Allez!" from Lá Locomotive Club. The show, which featured The Who and The Yardbirds, was transmitted across the ITV network between 7:00 - 7:30 pm. Following the live transmission, Bill and Brian (along with the RSG! crowd), went to the Castelles Club.

SATURDAY APRIL 2nd

Bill and Brian flew to Sweden to rejoin the rest of the group, who had left England that afternoon. In "Disc", Mick talked about the new album, "Aftermath":- "The average album lasts between 15 and 17 minutes, but we've put a lot more into this one. It runs to about 24 or 25, so at 52 minutes, it will probably be the longest pop L.P ever produced. We cut 22 sides altogether and it's been quite a job choosing the right ones. As before, we recorded some in America, thirteen in L.A." On the album's release delay:-"There's been a lot of trouble one way or another. The title's been changed again and we ran into a lot of problems over the printing. Some negatives got lost and now we've re-designed the sleeve completely. I should think it'll be two to four weeks, before it's actually in the shops."

SUNDAY APRIL 3rd

Kungliga Tennishallen (a tennis stadium), Stockholm, Sweden.

TUESDAY APRIL 5th

The group flew from Stockholm to Denmark to perform two shows at the K.B. Hallen, Copenhagen.

WEDNESDAY APRIL 6th

The group flew back to London. Mick & Charlie were interviewed, at the airport, featured on the early evening news. (BBC-1 5:50 pm).

MONDAY APRIL 11th

The date scheduled for "Back, Behind And In Front" to go into production (see May 10th entry).

THURSDAY APRIL 14th

The group went to the BBC TV Centre, in Wood Lane, to record "Mothers Little Helper" (from "Aftermath") which closed "Top Of The Pops", broadcast on BBC1 that night, between 7:30-8:01pm. The programme, hosted by David Jacobs, also featured in the studio: The Alan Price Set and The Searchers, while The Who, Chrispian St. Peters, The Seekers, Dusty Springfield and The Spencer Davis Group appeared by way of previously transmitted appearances. (Simon & Garfunkel also appeared via a CBS promotional film for "Homeward Bound"). This first version of "Mothers Little Helper" received three further TOTP transmissions, in the shows broadcast on the 12th, 19th and 26th of May (all BBC1. 7:30 - 8:01pm). The group returned to the BBC TV Centre to record another version for "Top of the Pops", on April 28th (see entry).

FRIDAY APRIL 15th

A full-page "Aftermath" advert, appeared in "Record Mirror", captioned "Released today: the new Rolling Stones ellpee(sic)/14 new songs"(all Jagger-Richards compositions, for the first time). The same issue also carried a review of the album by Richard Green, headlined "The smash LP of the year?". In "Disc", Mick talked about the album. "I'm not

Above: "Mother's Little Helper", "Top of The Pops", April 14th

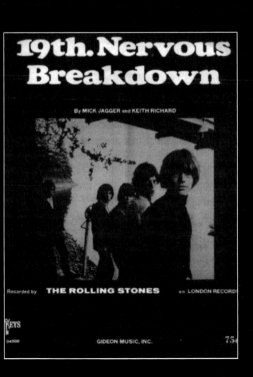

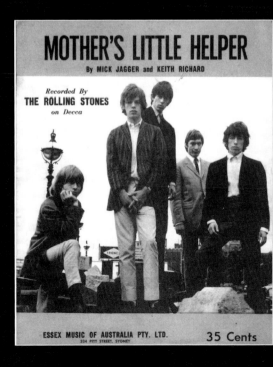

completely satisfied with it, but then I never am. I like it better than any of our other albums, because we've put a lot more into it. I enjoyed doing the ballad songs like "Lady Jane" for example. It's a change for me and gives the others something different to play with. Some of the songs Keith and I wrote months ago but most were done recently for the session. I hope the fans enjoy it!" The Searchers "Take It Or Leave It" became the first of many cover versions, released from the album. (Mick and Keith had given them the song, on the Australian tour, earlier in the year).

WEDNESDAY APRIL 20th
Mick and Chrissie went on holiday to Paris.

SUNDAY APRIL 24th
Brian and Anita, plus Mick and Chrissie were among the guests at the 21st birthday party of Guinness heir, Tara Browne, held at the Luggala estate, in Ireland.

WEDNESDAY 27th - SATURDAY APRIL 30th
Chris Farlowe sessions at Pye Studios, London, with Mick acting as producer. Tracks included "Out Of Time" (with Mick on guide vocal. Farlowe added his vocal at I.B.C Studios, on Friday May 6th). The line-up of musicians during the sessions featured:-
Jimmy Page (guitar), Joe Moretti (guitar), Reg Guest (piano), Eric Ford (bass), Andy White (drums) and Sidney Sax (string leader).

THURSDAY APRIL 28th
BBC TV Centre, Wood Lane, to tape another "Top Of The Pops" insert for "Mother's Little Helper", transmitted the once, in that night's programme between 7:31-8:00pm, on BBC1. "Aftermath" was at No.4 in the "Record Mirror" LP charts, and had sold 180,000 copies, according to Andrew Oldham's figures.

SATURDAY APRIL 30th
Bill and Brian went to see The End at "Tiles" Club, Oxford Street.

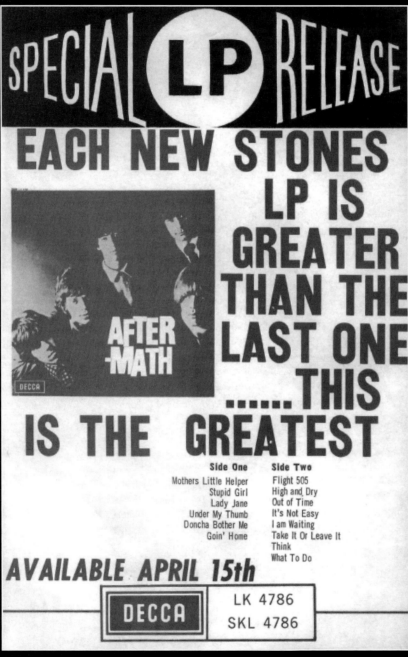

SPECIAL LP RELEASE
EACH NEW STONES LP IS GREATER THAN THE LAST ONE .... THIS IS THE GREATEST

AFTER-MATH

DECCA

Side One	Side Two
Mothers Little Helper	Flight 505
Stupid Girl	High and Dry
Lady Jane	Out of Time
Under My Thumb	It's Not Easy
Doncha Bother Me	I am Waiting
Goin' Home	Take It Or Leave It
	Think
	What To Do

AVAILABLE APRIL 15th

DECCA   LK 4786   SKL 4786

SUNDAY MAY 1st
The group played at the Empire Pool, Wembley, for the annual "NME Poll Winners Concert" which ran (in order):- Sounds Incorporated, The Overlanders, The Small Faces, The Spencer Davis Group, Roy Orbison, The Walker Brothers, The Yardbirds, The Seekers, The Alan Price Set, Cliff Richard and The Shadows, The Fortunes, Crispian St. Peters, Hermans Hermits, Dave Dee, Dozy, Beaky, Mick and Tich, Dusty Springfield, The Who, The Rolling Stones, the Poll Awards (presented by Clint Walker) and The Beatles. Introduced by DJ, Pete Murray. The Stones performed:-
"The Last Time", "Play With Fire" and "Satisfaction". In contrast to the previous two years, the group did not allow the ABC TV cameras to film their set (ditto billtoppers, The Beatles). Conflicting reasons were given. The press were told that both groups said the sound system in the vast Empire Pool, filled with 12,000 screaming fans, was not good enough, while the more likely reason was contractual disputes between ABC Television and the respective management of both groups. The only time both groups did appear in the TV broadcast (for which ABC-TV paid the NME, £8,000, for the exclusivity of covering the show), was during the awards ceremony, included in Part Two of the "Poll Winners Concert" programme. (Transmitted by only certain ITV regions, May 15th 3:50-4:59pm, due to the fact that the two main attractions weren't included).

TUESDAY MAY 3rd
Mick appeared in the "Hot Seat" of BBC 1's youth programme "A Whole Scene Going", introduced by artist Barry Fantoni (who painted and drew for the "Observer" and "Private Eye") and Wendy Varnals (an aspiring young actress whose previous claim to fame was her "carefully rehearsed lines" being edited out of the 1965 Beatles film, "Help!") The

show, transmitted on BBC1 the following day between 6:30 - 6:59pm, also featured a report on "Modesty Blaise-Is she the female James Bond?" and music by the Slade Brothers (no relation to the '70's group, Slade).

SUNDAY MAY 8th

The group went to the Alpha Television Studios in Aston, Birmingham, for what was to be their last appearance on ABC-TV's "Thank Your Lucky Stars". Since their television debut on the show almost three years ago, the series had undergone many changes. The Saturday night "prime time" slot of 45 minutes, had been changed to a Sunday afternoon slot of 30 minutes (running from 3:30-3:59pm, and then in only certain ITV regions). For the show (telerecorded and transmitted May 15th), the group mimed to "Lady Jane" and the group's new single, "Paint It Black" (the latter featuring experimental film negative effects during the second half of the song). In between songs, Mick was interviewed by host, Jim Dale, who asked him:- "There's one question that I want to ask you, that is an acquaintance of yours by the name of Ringo was asked "What sort of time do they get off?" and he replied "We had an hours holiday yesterday!"". "Oh, that's not what I heard!" was Mick's offhand retort. The show also featured The Kentuckians, Lorne Lesley, Ronnie Carroll, The Koobas, Deano, The Morgan-James Duo and The Londonaires, alongside the week's other special guest star, Tom Jones. "Thank Your Lucky Stars" would run for another four shows, with it's final transmission appearing on June 12th, 1966.

TUESDAY MAY 10th

The press officially announced that the first proposed Rolling Stones film "Back, Behind And In Front" would now, not be made.

THURSDAY MAY 12th

The group travelled to the BBC TV Centre for yet another taped appearance on "Top Of The Pops" that evening. After a camera rehearsal, they recorded their first performance of "Paint It Black", featured in the 7:31-8:00pm broadcast on BBC1. (The group would record a second version on May 26th - see entry.) Following the recording, Brian flew to Marbella, Spain, for a weeks holiday at a friends villa.

FRIDAY MAY 13th

"Paint It, Black" B/W "Long, Long While" was released, with advance orders of 300,000.

SATURDAY MAY 14th

Mick and Chrissie went shopping in Portobello Market, with John and Cynthia Lennon after an all-night party. "Record Mirror" carried a full page advert for "Paint It, Black" with the caption:- "A different kind of single from The Rolling Stones". While some papers incorrectly titled the song as "Painted Black", others questioned the use of the comma. An interview with Mick by Judith Simons, appeared in "The Daily Express":- "When I was 16, I wanted to be a journalist, but it seemed too much like hard work. When I went to the L.S.E. (London School of

Charlie swapping drumming tips backstage at the Wembley Empire Pool, with Brian Bennett of the Shadows, and Keith Moon of the Who, May 1st

Economics), I thought of going into politics, but I believe it is harder initially to get into politics and then get to the top, than it is in the pop world". In "Disc", it was announced that the group would get one million dollars to make "Only Lovers Left Alive", a dramatic imaginary story of the conquest of England, by violent and rebellious youth, with a musical score by Mike Leander and songs by Jagger-Richard. The Stones would all have leading roles and eight weeks of shooting would start on location in Britain, in early autumn. The film was an adaptation of a book of the same name by schoolteacher, Dave Wallis, written and published two years before. The story was chosen for them by Andrew Oldham ("The book could have been written for them!"), who, with business manager, Allen Klein, would produce the picture. (Klein had been negotiating for the property for the past six months). Both were currently looking for a screenwriter, director and distributor. Favourite choice for director was Nicholas Ray ("Rebel Without A Cause"), whom Klein had bought the screen rights for the novel from. "Rumours that Charlie Watts had requested the picture to be a silent movie, were unfounded!!"

MONDAY MAY 16th

"Paint It Black" reached No.1 in England, having sold 400,000 copies. "The Daily Mail" carried an interview with the wife of David Wallis (on his behalf), condemning The Rolling Stones role in the forthcoming film of "Only Lovers Left Alive". The book had a serious subject "...but with these people in it, I don't see it being taken as a serious film". Mick angrily replied in "Disc":- "If I'd written a book, I'd be very pleased that somebody of box-office appeal was going to act in the film version.

and himself would write the film's soundtrack heard over the film, with musical numbers done in such a way that they would not look like stage performances. Mick would take the lead role of Ernie (the central character in the book).

WEDNESDAY MAY 25th

Keith and Brian visited Bob Dylan at the Mayfair Hotel, along with Paul McCartney and Marianne Faithfull. Later that night they met up again at Blaise's club, in South Kensington, to see John Lee Hooker, continuing on to "Dollys" in Mayfair, where Keith and Brian got into a heated row with Dylan.

THURSDAY MAY 26th

In the afternoon, the group went back to the BBC TV Centre in Wood Lane, to tape their fourth clip in six weeks for "Top Of The Pops". Assembling in the studio, first for the cameras, then for a recorded performance, the group mimed to "Paint It Black", transmitted that night, on the show, between 7:31 - 8:00pm on BBC1. Hosted by Jimmy Savile, the show also featured:- Chris Andrews, The Animals, Wayne Fontana, The Small Faces and Ken Dodd. The insert was repeated in the year-end "Top Of The Pops '66", on Boxing Day (BBC 1 6:15 - 7:00 pm, repeated the following day between 6:17 - 7:00 pm). In the evening, the group with respective wives and girlfriends, attended the first of two controversial "electric" concerts by Bob Dylan (and The Hawks), at the Royal Albert Hall, watching from a pre-booked box.

FRIDAY MAY 27th

The group travelled to Studio One, Wembley for a live appearance on "Ready Steady Go!". After Cathy McGowan's introduction, the group performed: "I Am Waiting", "Under My Thumb" (from "Aftermath") and "Paint It Black". The show, also featuring Chris Andrews, The Animals and The Yardbirds (in a bid to boost viewing figures), was transmitted across certain ITV stations later that night (6:07 - 6:34 pm). A probable factor as to why this 12 minute segment is one of the few Rolling Stones "Ready Steady Go!" performances surviving, is due to the fact that on Nov.12th 1966, "RSG!" director, Michael Lindsay-Hogg, wrote to Rediffusion Television Limited, requesting a copy of the performance "for private use only". On November 15th, "The Director of Programmes" for Rediffusion Television granted his request. At a cost £55, a 16mm black & white "telerecording" of the programme extract was hand delivered to Hogg on the 30th.

SUNDAY MAY 29th

Brian again jetted off to Marbella, Spain for a week's holiday with Anita. He returned looking exhausted.

THURSDAY JUNE 2nd

Keith accompanied Canadian fashion artist and model Karen Moller, to the premiere of Roman Polanski's film "Cul-de Sac". The event was filmed by Peter Whitehead, for inclusion in his "Swinging London" documentary, "Tonite Lets All Make Love In London" (see Oct.1968 entry).

Anyhow, I wouldn't condemn a film as bad, until I'd seen it, ...if we wanted to make a funny film, we would have got a funny storyline. We have every intention of treating this film, as seriously as the subject demands." Meanwhile, Mick, Keith and Brian visited Allen Klein at his suite on the 26th floor of the London Hilton.

THURSDAY MAY 19th

Mick met "Disc" reporter Bob Farmer, for a future "Day In The Life Of Mick" article. They lunched in Soho with David Bailey, were chauffeured to Harrod's, inspected the empty premises of Mick's new flat in Marylebone Road (he moved in later that month), called in to Andrew Oldham's Baker Street offices, went back to Mick's current digs in Montague Square to watch "Top Of The Pops", had dinner in Chelsea and then ended the evening at "Dollys" nightclub, leaving around 2:30am.

FRIDAY MAY 20th

Keith Altham of the NME interviewed Mick and Keith at Andrew Oldham's office, about "Only Lovers Left Alive". Mick confirmed that the Stones would not be seen as a group in the film, adding that both Keith

TUESDAY JUNE 14th

Mick collapsed from nervous exhaustion, brought about by overwork, at his Harley House flat, forcing him to cancel his second appearance in the "Hot Seat" on the BBC TV programme, "A Whole Scene Going", due for transmission on the 15th. He was ordered to take total rest, until departing for the States on June 23rd.

FRIDAY JUNE 17th

Mick joined Chris Farlowe at Studio One, Wembley for his appearance on "Ready Steady Go!", to plug "Out Of Time". (Released today on Immediate B/W "Baby Make It Soon".) Mick was interviewed regarding his role as producer by Cathy McGowan, while Farlowe mimed to a pre-recorded live version of the song. Other guests included Gene Pitney, The Hollies and Herman's Hermits. The show went out live that night between 6:15 - 6:59pm, across certain ITV regions.

SUNDAY JUNE 19th

"The Sunday Times" reported that the The Rolling Stones were suing fourteen of New York`s leading hotels (including The Waldorf-Astoria and Hilton) for £1,750,850 damages, because of refused bookings. (The group were trying to fix a base for their American tour). Allen Klein filed a writ (on June 21st), alleging that the hotels had injured the group's reputation. It claimed that the refusal of bookings amounted to "discrimination on account of national origin", which was a violation of New York's civil rights law. (Each member of the group was claiming £357,000 for alleged damage to their reputation and £170 for alleged civil rights violations). He also sent a strong protest to the New York State Attorney-General, Mr Lefkowitz. The hotels had 20 days to file their answers. Meanwhile, The Holiday Inn on West 57th Street had come to the rescue, by publicly offering the group accommodation.

THURSDAY JUNE 23rd

The group left London Airport en route for New York, to begin their fifth American Tour (their last until 1969). The group solved their accommodation problem, by renting Allen Klein's yacht, SS Sea Panther (anchored in New York harbour) as their headquarters. That evening, Bill played bass on a John Hammond Jr. session at A & R Studios. Also joining Hammond (guitar, organ and vocals), were Robbie Robertson (guitar) and Charlie Otis (drums). They recorded:-
"I Wish You Would" and "I Can Tell".

The session was produced by songwriters Jerry Lieber and Mike Stoller and engineered by Phil Ramone. Brian and Bob Dylan arrived halfway through the session to watch. Mick later met up with Dylan, who played him the completed "Blonde On Blonde" album.

FRIDAY JUNE 24th

An afternoon press conference on board the Sea Panther, circling Manhattan Island. Linda Eastman (McCartney) took photographs of the group on board for "Town and Country" magazine, whose current issue featured a cover story:- "Alexandra E. Chace (a N.Y. socialite) Meets The Rolling Stones." In the evening, the tour started with a show at the

Above: Meeting Bob Dylan, May 25th, with Tom Keylock (top left).

Manning Bowl, in Lynn, Massachusetts, 20 miles north of Boston.(15,000 crowd). Police hurled tear gas when a riot broke out during the concert and after, when fans chased the group's two getaway cars, bound for the airport. As gas grenades fell among the crowd, thousands fought to get out of the way and many were trampled. The set list for the tour:-
"Not Fade Away" / "The Last Time" / "Paint It Black" / "Stupid Girl" / "Lady Jane" / "The Spider And The Fly" / "Mothers Little Helper" / "Get Off Of My Cloud" / "19th Nervous Breakdown" and "Satisfaction" .
Back in New York, custom-built Vox equipment, belonging to the group,

Leaving for New York, June 23rd

was stolen. Amongst the items, was an electronic dulcimer (the world's first).

SATURDAY JUNE 25th

The first of five extra dates added to the tour with an afternoon concert at the Cleveland Arena and an evening show at the Pittsburgh Civic Arena.

SUNDAY JUNE 26th

Added dates. Washington Coliseum (afternoon) and Civic Centre, Baltimore (evening).

MONDAY JUNE 27th

Dillon Stadium, Hartford, Connecticut (added date).

TUESDAY JUNE 28th

Buffalo, New York State (added date).

WEDNESDAY JUNE 29th

The group flew to Canada to appear at the Maple Leaf Gardens, Toronto (11,000 crowd).

THURSDAY JUNE 30th

Montreal Forum (12,000 crowd), originally scheduled for the previous night. The group stopped a song to join in booing a bunch of bouncers, who were beating people up indiscriminately. The organiser, who leapt on stage, ordering Mick to leave, was told where to go. After the show, the group had to exit sharply, when the same bouncers came looking for them!

FRIDAY JULY 1st

Marine Ballroom, Atlantic City.

SATURDAY JULY 2nd

The "Music Festival", held at the 9,500 seat capacity Forest Hills Tennis Stadium, headlining a bill which featured: The McCoys, The Tradewinds and The Standells. After the Stones finished their set, a crowd of fans broke through a cordon of 125 private and 250 city police. Within minutes, the group had left the stadium in a helicopter, heading for Manhattan. The concert grossed $50,000, with the Stones receiving half that sum, although some newspapers were quick to point out that many of the $5 and $10 seats were empty. After the show, at Linda Keith's (Keith's girlfriend) urging, the group caught Jimmy James and The Blue Flames act, at the Cafe Wha, in Greenwich Village. Jimmy James was soon bound for England (and glory) as Jimi Hendrix.

SUNDAY JULY 3rd

Convention Hall, Asbury Park, New Jersey.

MONDAY JULY 4th

"Under the Dome" Theatre, Virginia Beach.

WEDNESDAY JULY 6th

War Memorial Hall, Syracuse, New York. Police investigated reports from angry residents who claimed that "a member of the Rolling Stones (Brian) had dragged an American flag along the floor, on their way to the stage... he had snatched the flag from a chair where it had been spread to dry. During a brief scuffle, it was grabbed back by a member of staff". The police reported "...the singer wanted the flag as a souvenir, and had apologised for the incident". Radio Luxembourg's 208 station broadcasted the first of three Rolling Stones "Battle Of The Bands". Tonights being against The Beatles. (The second, against The Walker Brothers, on the 16th, the third, against Cliff Richard, on August 15th, each show broadcast at 8:15 pm).

FRIDAY JULY 8th

Cobo Hall, Detroit.

SATURDAY JULY 9th

State Fairground Coliseum, Indianapolis.

SUNDAY JULY 10th

Arie Crown Theatre, Chicago.

MONDAY JULY 11th

Sam Houston Coliseum, Houston (10,000 audience).

TUESDAY JULY 12th

Kiel Convention Hall, St. Louis, Missouri. Airport authorities initially refused to let the group's chartered flight land, due to their appearance!

THURSDAY JULY 14th

Winnipeg, Canada.

FRIDAY JULY 15th

Civic Auditorium, Omaha, Nebraska. The group flew onto Los Angeles after the show, checking into the Century Plaza Hotel, in secrecy for a few days rest, before continuing the tour.

SATURDAY JULY 16th

Brian visited Sunset Strip, for a night on the town, spoilt by constant hassles from tourists.

TUESDAY JULY 19th

Pacific International Exhibition Forum, Vancouver, Canada.

WEDNESDAY JULY 20th

Centre Coliseum, Seattle, Washington.

THURSDAY JULY 21st

Memorial Coliseum, Portland, Oregon.

FRIDAY JULY 22nd

Sacramento Memorial Auditorium, California. (Two shows.) (6:30 & 9:30pm.)

SATURDAY JULY 23rd

Lagoon, Davis County, Salt Lake City, Utah.

SUNDAY JULY 24th

Bakersfield, California. (Two shows.)

MONDAY JULY 25th

Hollywood Bowl, L A (promoted by Radio KHJ, with supports including The Buffalo Springfield, 17,500 audience). Large "Aftermath" posters hung on stage behind the group as they played.

TUESDAY JULY 26th

Cow Palace, San Francisco. The group flew back to L A after the show.

WEDNESDAY JULY 27th

The group flew to Hawaii, checking into the Kahala Hilton, Honolulu.

THURSDAY JULY 28th

International Sports Centre, Honolulu. Set:- "Not Fade Away" / "The Last Time" / "Paint It Black" / Charlie's intro / "Lady Jane" / "Mothers Little Helper" / "Get Off Of My Cloud" / "19th Nervous Breakdown" and "Satisfaction". The entire concert was transmitted live by local based Honolulu radio station K-POI.

MONDAY AUGUST 1st

New York DJ Harry Harrison interviewed Mick and Keith, at the Beverley Wilshire in L A, by phone, for his radio programme "The In-Sound". Another interview, recorded for the show that afternoon, featured Keith only. It was transmitted two weeks later, on August 15th.

WEDNESDAY 3rd - SUNDAY AUGUST 7th

RCA Studios (with Andrew Oldham and Dave Hassinger. Jack Nitzsche on piano):-

Hollywood Bowl, July 25th

"Have You Seen Your Mother, Baby, Standing In The Shadow?" (Three versions, including backing tracks.)

"Panama Powder Room" (unreleased)

"Who's Driving Your Plane?"

"Can't Believe"(unreleased)

"She Smiled Sweetly"

"Something Happened To Me Yesterday"

"My Obsession"

"Cool, Calm, Collected"

"Complicated" (the latter three; backing tracks-the vocals were added at Olympic-see Nov.10th to Dec.6th entry).

Upon conclusion of recording at RCA, the group took a month's holiday.

MONDAY AUGUST 8th

Mick and Keith flew from L.A to Acapulco to spend a few days songwriting (they returned to London on August 14th). Charlie stayed on for another five days, Brian, another six, while Bill and Diane went to Palm Springs, Florida.

SATURDAY AUGUST 13th

Charlie arrived back in London, flying out to Greece, with Shirley, two days later. Pirate station, Radio Caroline, slapped an airplay ban on all records by the Rolling Stones (and Andrew Oldham's Immediate label) until further notice, as a direct result of a court order by Oldham against station owner, Phillip Solomans.

SUNDAY AUGUST 14th

Brian returned to London.

TUESDAY AUGUST 16th

Mick produced a session at I.B.C Studios, for an aborted Immediate single, "Come Home Baby", featuring Rod Stewart and P.P Arnold on vocals, with Keith on guitar.

THURSDAY AUGUST 25th
Mick's Aston Martin DB6 was involved in a car crash, near his Marylebone flat. Neither he nor Chrissie were injured, but damage to the car was estimated at £700.

SUNDAY AUGUST 28th
Brian, Anita and friend, antiques dealer, Christopher Gibbs, left for a holiday in Tangiers.

WEDNESDAY AUGUST 31st
Brian cabled Andrew Oldham from Morocco telling him he had broken two bones in his left wrist, after a climbing accident and that he would be unable to play for at least two months.

FRIDAY SEPTEMBER 2nd
Mick and Keith were at I.B.C Studios, with Mike Leander, working on song arrangements.

SUNDAY SEPTEMBER 4th
Brian and Anita returned to London. (Brian's hand was in a cast, but the damage was not as extensive as originally thought).

MONDAY SEPTEMBER 5th
Although unable to play, Brian went to I.B.C Studios, to supervise the start of work on the soundtrack to the film "Mord und Totschlag" ("A Degree Of Murder"), starring Anita Pallenburg which went into production in Munich, early the following year. The loose line-up of musicians for the sessions were:-

Brian Jones:-sitar, organ, dulcimer, harp, auto-harp, clarinet and harmonica. Jimmy Page:-guitar / Nicky Hopkins:-piano / Peter Gosling:-vocals on one track / Kenney Jones:-drums. (Mike Leander produced the orchestral score).

WEDNESDAY 7th - FRIDAY SEPTEMBER 9th
Mick, Keith, Stu and Andrew Oldham were at RCA Studios to finish

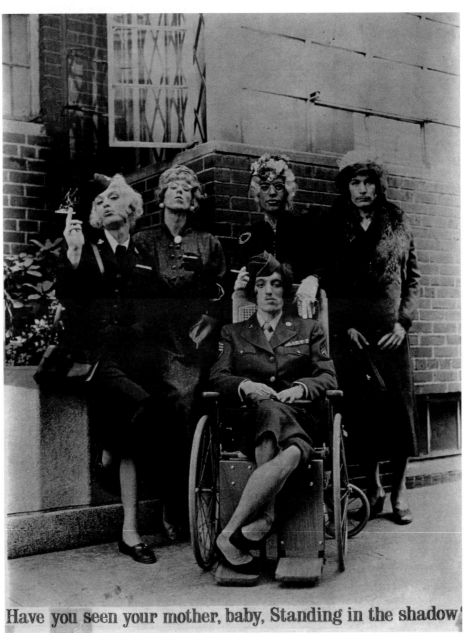

Have you seen your mother, baby, Standing in the shadow'

work on "Have You Seen Your Mother, Baby, Standing In The Shadow?". The original recordings from 3rd -7th of August were overdubbed with additional guitar tracks, Mick re-recorded his vocals and a brass arrangement, suggested by Mike Leander, was added.

In London, on the 8th, Brian's doctor removed the plaster cast, replacing it with a bandage. He advised Brian to exercise his hand with guitar practice. He was therefore able to accompany Bill and Charlie next day, to New York, for the Stones "Ed Sullivan" appearance.

SATURDAY SEPTEMBER 10th
Mick and Keith, flew to New York, meeting up with the others, at their hotel. That afternoon, New York society photographer, Jerry Schatzberg, took the infamous "drag" pictures, to promote "Have You Seen Your Mother, Baby...", footage of which became the basis of a Peter Whitehead promotional film to accompany the single. (The group would now become accustomed to shooting a "promo" film, for distribution to T.V stations, in their absence). The group posed in a back street, off 3rd Avenue (standing left to right: "Flossie" Jones, "Molly" Richard, "Sarah" Jagger, "Millicent" Watts, with "Penelope" Wyman out front, perched in a wheelchair!) Photo shoot completed, the group adjourned to a nearby bar ordering a round of beers, still in costume. Nobody blinked!!

SUNDAY SEPTEMBER 11th
At 9am, the group went to the Sullivan Theatre to appear in the first of a new season of "The Ed Sullivan Show". After their arrival through an hysterical crowd (filmed by Peter Whitehead - see Sept 10th entry), they headed straight to their dressing rooms for a 10 am make-up call and then appeared at 10:45 am for the first camera tests.

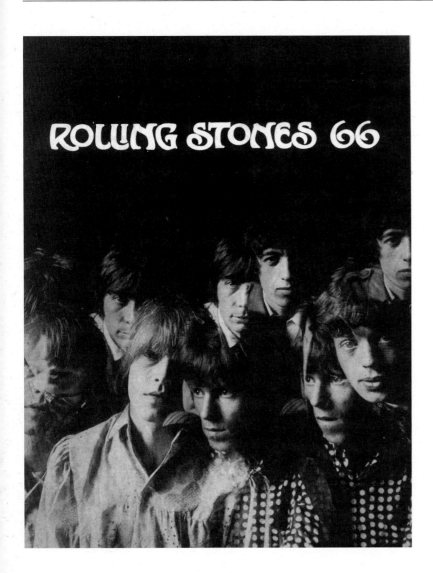

ROLLING STONES 66

Previous Page: Royal Albert Hall, September 23rd
Above: UK tour programme

ROLLING STONES LTD. PRESENTS
ROLLING STONES 66
STARRING
THE ROLLING STONES
IKE & TINA TURNER
THE YARDBIRDS
PETER JAY & THE NEW JAY WALKERS
THE KINGS OF RHYTHM ORCHESTRA
THE IKE-ETTES   JIMMY THOMAS
BOBBY JOHN   RAY CAMERON
SOUVENIR COLOUR ROLLING STONES ALBUM FREE WITH EVERY PROGRAMME

AN ABC THEATRE
A.B.C., ARDWICK
Manager: T. A. GRIFFITHS   Telephone 1141
ON THE STAGE
(Issued of the usual film programme)
Two performances only
Wednesday 28 September at 6.30 and 8.45
One day only   P.T.O.
Prices 15/- 12/6 10/- 7/6 All seats may be booked in advance

Between rehearsals, the group were filmed by Whitehead's roving camera, including shots of Mick walking through the Village, Keith playing piano backstage, Brian looking through a card full of holes and the group posed outside the back of the theatre, again for Jerry Schatzberg's camera - a fish-eye lens shot used for the American single and later, the U.K "Big Hits (High Tide And Green Grass)" album sleeve. During the afternoon, pre-recorded backing tracks, sent from RCA Studios in L.A, were delivered. It was agreed that the group should mime, due to Brian's inability to play, with Mick's vocals live. Between 5:00 - 5:25 pm, the first run through, was videotaped. (This rehearsal contained notably different camera shots from the actual broadcast). The group performed "Paint It Black", which opened the first half and "Lady Jane" and "Have You Seen Your Mother, Baby..." to close the show. It was transmitted live between 8:00 -9:00 EST on CBS. The Beatles ex-PR man, Derek Taylor went to the taping and became the Stones US publicist (up until his return to the UK, and The Beatles, in 1968).

WEDNESDAY SEPTEMBER 14th

Decca announced The Rolling Stones had helped add £231,000 to their profits over the last year.

MONDAY SEPTEMBER 19th

Mick and Keith were interviewed at the Mayfair Hotel, by both Keith Altham (from the NME) and Jimmy Savile (for his Radio Luxembourg 208 radio show, transmitted later that night). Mick played Altham the new single "Have You Seen Your Mother, Baby..." telling him: "I'm not going to burst into tears if this doesn't go to No 1. At least, it's the best we could do and I'm satisfied that we have given our best".

THURSDAY SEPTEMBER 22nd

The "Have You Seen Your Mother, Baby..." film received it's premiere on BBC TV's "Top Of The Pops" (7:30 -7:59pm). The film would also receive another screening the following week. (September 29th, BBC1 7:30 - 8:01pm). The BBC paid £183.15 shillings for each showing of the film. Incidentally, the BBC requested a film for "Lady Jane", but one had not yet been made! (see Sept 23rd entry). When submitted by Peter Whitehead, it was a case of too little, too late and the film was subsequently never screened on "Top Of The Pops". (It was eventually included in Whitehead's film "Tonite Let's All Make Love In London" -see Oct.1968 entry).

FRIDAY SEPTEMBER 23rd

"Have You Seen Your Mother, Baby, Standing In The Shadow?" B/W "Who's Driving Your Plane?" was released simultaneously, in the U.K & U.S.A. The group began another British tour (their last until 1971), with support acts Ike and Tina Turner (and The Ike-ettes), The Yardbirds, Peter Jay and The New Jay Walkers (featuring 16 year-old singer Terry Reid), The Kings of Rhythm Orchestra, Jimmy Thomas, Bobby John, Ray Cameron and compere' Long John Baldry. Radio London DJ, Mark Roman accompanied the tour, recording programmes for the "Big L" spot every night. (Beginning on September 26th between 6:30- 7:00pm,

Above: Royal Albert Hall, September 23rd. Stones PR man Les Perrin (right) acts as bouncer.
Below: Backstage at Glasgow, September 30th

inspired by Kenny Everett's coverage of The Beatles recent tour of America). The opening show was at London's Royal Albert Hall (7,000 crowd), at 8:00pm. Again, director Peter Whitehead filmed the group, to make a less controversial promo for "Have You Seen Your Mother, Baby...". He filmed (using fast and normal speeds) in the dressing room (even taking film of himself, by shooting his reflection in the mirror!), Long John Baldry's introductions and then 20 minutes of the concert. At one point on the tour, he also filmed an interview with Mick discussing his current philosophies, to be included in Whitehead's "Swinging London" film study, "Tonite Let's All Make Love In London" (see Oct. 1968 entry). The song line-up for the show featured:-"Paint It Black" / "Under My Thumb" / "Get Off Of My Cloud" / Charlie's intro "Lady Jane" / "Not Fade Away" / "The Last Time" / "Who's Driving Your Plane?" / "19th Nervous Breakdown" / "Have You Seen Your Mother, Baby..." and "Satisfaction".

The tracks: "Under My Thumb" / "Satisfaction" / "The Last Time" (along with Long John Baldry's introduction) were later used for the album "Got Live If You Want It", with recordings from Newcastle (October 1st) and Bristol (October 7th). The concert itself put the group's fears of a low-key reception to rest. (They hadn't toured Britain for a year). The minute the Stones appeared, fans rushed the stage on two occasions, forcing the group to retreat backstage. Stage "bouncers" included Andrew Oldham, Les Perrin, Tito Burns, D.J Chris Denning and Larry Page (ex Kinks, current Troggs manager). The security provided by the Albert Hall, were over zealous in protecting their charges, with girls getting kicked, punched and even physically picked up and thrown back into the crowd (as evidenced by Whitehead's footage). Fifty fainting

cases were reported. Afterwards, the group attended a post-show party held at the Kensington Hotel, thrown by Decca-London Records, to mark the Stones receiving 20 gold discs (4 each), presented by Decca executive Mr. W. Townsley. (The discs signified sales of more than a million dollars in the States for each of their last four albums. Plans for the presentation being made onstage at the Albert Hall, had to be scrapped, due to the fans' exuberance.) Guests included:- John Maus and Gary Leeds (from The Walker Brothers), ex-Searcher Chris Curtis, Jonathan King, Lionel Bart and from "Ready, Steady, Go!", Cathy McGowan, Vicki Wickham and Michael Lindsay-Hogg. The events at the Kensington Hotel were captured by BBC TV (for use on "Top Of The Pops", in the edition broadcast, September 29th on BBC1 7:30 - 7:59pm) and by Peter Whitehead on 16mm black & white film.

SATURDAY SEPTEMBER 24th
Odeon Theatre, Leeds. (Two shows.) (6:00 & 8:00pm.) The group's chauffeur on this tour, John Binney, started a regular stage-door ritual, by distributing to waiting fans, the pages of the newspapers the group had read, during the journey!

SUNDAY SEPTEMBER 25th
Empire, Liverpool. (Two shows.) (5:40 & 8:00pm.) The group's Daimler was replaced by an Austin Princess, after it's sides were buckled in by fans.

TUESDAY SEPTEMBER 27th
Mick was interviewed by BBC Radio News, for the Light Programme.

WEDNESDAY SEPTEMBER 28th
ABC Ardwick, Manchester. (Two shows.) (6:15 & 8:45pm.) Mick contracted heavy flu during the tour break, which, luckily, hadn't affected his singing. Backstage, the group were forced to stick a poster over their dressing room window when plain-clothes police kept trying to peer through. After the evening show, Brian cut his eyelid, when hurriedly taking his guitar off to dash from the hall (adding to his injured hand). Mick, Keith and Brian went to the Phonograph Club with Radio London's Mark Roman and Ike-ettes, Rose and Pat (alias P.P) Arnold.

THURSDAY SEPTEMBER 29th
ABC Theatre, Stockton-On-Tees. (Two shows.) (6:15 & 8:30pm.) Due to wrong directions, both the Stones and the Yardbirds arrived 20 minutes late for the first house. There was a near-riot when Long John Baldry announced they may not perform. Peter Jay and The Jaywalkers and Ike and Tina Turner played an extra set, to cover for them. The Stones eventually arrived, but played for only 20 minutes. After the shows, Mark Roman drove Bill's Mercedes from the theatre, as a fan decoy, while Bill left with the others in the Austin Princess. A few miles out of town, the two vehicles met and Bill took over the Mercedes. (Bill had been driving himself between venues, since the tour resumed in Manchester).

Right: "Ready Steady Go!", October 4th
Above left: Gold Record presentation at the Kensington Hotel, September 23rd

FRIDAY SEPTEMBER 30th

Odeon Theatre, Glasgow. (Two shows.) (6:40 & 9:00pm, 5,000 sell-out.) The police found it necessary to clear several streets around the venue, to ensure the group's arrival and departure was without incident.

SATURDAY OCTOBER 1st

City Hall, Newcastle-on-Tyne. (Two shows.) (6:15 & 8:30pm, 5,000 sell-out.) Leaving Glasgow, Bill was involved in a pile-up, when his Mercedes hit an accident that had already happened. Luckily, the others were following close behind, so Bill climbed into the Austin Princess, that was now carrying ten people! Peter Whitehead filmed the group (from behind Charlie) at the afternoon's rehearsal. The black & white 16mm film utilised "fast-motion" shots, similar as to that shot at the Albert Hall (see September 23rd entry). The footage remains unseen. Recording equipment, (stored in the Yardbirds cramped dressing room) was used for the second show, of which "Get Off Of My Cloud" (original version) and "19th Nervous Breakdown" (remixed) were later used on the album "Got Live If You Want It". Following the shows, the group gathered in Mick's hotel room (a nightly ritual) whiling away the hours by building mechanical toys and playing with them on the floor!

SUNDAY OCTOBER 2nd

Gaumont Theatre, Ipswich. (Two shows.) (5:30 & 8:00pm.) The music press described the shows as the worst received on the tour (not all of the shows had sold out).

MONDAY OCTOBER 3rd

Brian, Keith and Marianne Faithfull went to an art opening at the Robert Fraser Gallery, 69 Duke Street, Mayfair. Other guests included Paul McCartney and Pete Townshend.

TUESDAY OCTOBER 4th

"The Daily Sketch" reported that top-writing team, Keith Waterhouse and Willis Hall ("Billy Liar", "Whistle Down The Wind" and "All Things Bright and Beautiful") were to write the filmscript for "Only Lovers Left Alive". Meanwhile, the group took a break from the tour, to record two important TV appearances to help promote their slow-moving chart single. The first being at Studio One, Wembley, in what was to be their last appearance on "Ready Steady Go!". The group appeared at 2:00pm for a camera rehearsal, then later mimed to "Paint It Black", "Lady Jane" and "Have You Seen Your Mother, Baby, Standing In The Shadow?" to close the show. Hosted by Cathy McGowan, the show (also featuring Eric Burdon, Paul and Barry Ryan, Robert Parker and The Breakaways), was transmitted on October 7th between 6:15 - 6:59 pm on certain ITV regions.

WEDNESDAY OCTOBER 5th

Another TV appearance on "Top of the Pops". The group arrived at the BBC TV Centre, Wood Lane for camera rehearsals which ran from 2:00 -3:00pm and then recorded "Have You Seen Your Mother....." The insert appeared in the programme, transmitted on October 6th (BBC1 7:30 - 7:59pm).

THURSDAY OCTOBER 6th

Odeon Theatre, Birmingham. (Two shows.) (6:45 & 9:00pm.)

FRIDAY OCTOBER 7th

Colston Hall, Bristol. (Two shows.) (6:15 & 8:30pm.) There was an incident at a local hotel when the support acts were refused admittance due to racial prejudice over Ike and Tina's backing band. In revenge, during the second performance that night, Long John Baldry announced that the Stones were having a party at this particular hotel and everyone was invited!! Also from the second show, remixed versions of "Lady Jane", "I'm Alright" and "Have You Seen Your Mother Baby, Standing In The Shadow?" as well as original raw versions of "Not Fade Away" and "Time Is On My Side" were used for the "Got Live If You Want It" album. (The album was mixed solely by Mick and Keith at Olympic Studios, later in the month and was released in the U.S only, on December 10th). Brian's parents visited him backstage, but ".. all his spark seemed to be gone. He was very unhappy." Later, the entourage gathered in Mick's room at the Ship Hotel to watch Roman Polanski's "Repulsion" (supplied by Michael Cooper, a recent acquaintance who was photographing the band on the road) on a hired 16mm-film projector. It was here that Mick and Marianne's affair began. (She had been casually invited to the shows by Brian and Keith).

SATURDAY OCTOBER 8th

Capitol Theatre, Cardiff. (Two shows.) (6:00 & 8:30pm.) Following the concerts, at their motel, Brian and Keith (along with guests) watched "House Of Wax", starring Vincent Price. "Disc" announced that the Stones were scheduled to do three albums, within the next few months, one later in the month and then the others would follow in January and

March (the latter, the soundtrack of songs from "Only Lovers Left Alive"). The Stones, according to Allen Klein, would get more than £300,000 for their parts in the film, estimating they would bring 20 million dollars (£6.5m) into Britain, during the next twelve months, from film, stageshows and recordings.

SUNDAY OCTOBER 9th

Gaumont Theatre, Southampton. (Two shows.) (6:00 & 8:30pm.) Following the final concert, The Stones gave a bottle of Scotch to everyone who had been part of the tour. Upon departing from the venue later that night, Bill was driven back to Kent by his wife Diane in the Mercedes, Charlie and Shirley were chauffeur driven back to Lewes, while the other three were driven back to London by Tom Keylock.

TUESDAY OCTOBER 11th

"Have You Seen Your Mother, Baby, Standing In The Shadow?" was at No.2 in the "Disc" chart, despite being officially listed at No.5 (it's highest chart position in the U.K). In the States, it had jumped 33 places to No 7. "N.M.E" revealed that the group were undergoing some kind of preliminary dramatic coaching, which involved acting techniques in London (that week) for their new film "Only Lovers Left Alive". The girls in the film would be unknowns (so girl fans could identify themselves with them) and the planned motorbike sequences "may be substituted for fast open cars!"

FRIDAY OCTOBER 14th

Mick went to Studio One, at Associated-Rediffusion's Wembley complex to be interviewed live on "The Frost Programme" (ITV regions, between 10:40 - 11:16 pm). Chris Farlowe released his third consecutive Jagger / Richards composition, "Ride On Baby" B/W "Headlines", on Immediate (with Mick as producer).

SATURDAY OCTOBER 15th

Mick appeared with Marianne Faithfull in public for the first time, at the launch party for the "Underground" newspaper "International Times", held at the Roundhouse, Chalk Farm. (Chrissie Shrimpton still shared Jagger's flat at 52, Harley House, Marylebone Road.) In "Record Mirror", Jeff Beck (of The Yardbirds) claimed to Richard Green, that two girls who had jumped onstage at the Royal Albert Hall concert on September 23rd were paid to do this. (The remark was subsequently retracted by the paper as being untrue.) The N.M.E reported that the group's next L.P. titled (as per the States), "Big Hits (High Tide And Green Grass)", would be a hits collection in a gatefold sleeve, with 10 pages of colour pictures, priced at 38 shillings (released Friday, November 4th). "It was planned to release an L.P. of entirely new tracks before Xmas, but time has prevented it's completion. Instead, it will be issued in the New Year." In "Disc", Keith discussing songwriting, revealed:- "Really, what I'd like to do would be to write a song jointly with John Lennon or Paul McCartney" (hastily adding that he still enjoyed writing with Mick!).

FRIDAY OCTOBER 21st

Keith Altham, of the NME reported on his visit to Brian's new flat in

Courtfield Road, near Gloucester Road tube station, in London. Keith Richard was also present. "Brian played me some of the experiments in sound he has been conducting in the privacy of his new home", Altham wrote, "...but impressed on me that they were purely personal attempts and that the mixing and dubbing were far from perfect. He seemed enthusiastic, but embarrassed about his efforts!"

SATURDAY OCTOBER 22nd

In "Disc", Keith claimed the group had been told to take elocution lessons for their upcoming film "because we mumble too much!".

TUESDAY OCTOBER 25th

Mick and Keith attended a party given for American singer Bobby Darin, who was in London.

FRIDAY NOVEMBER 4th

"Big Hits (High Tide And Green Grass)" with an amended track listing and sleeve, was released in the U.K. with a deluxe gatefold sleeve and booklet (see Jan 23rd & March 26th entries). Immediate released "The Art of Chris Farlowe" album (with Mick credited as producer). Keith arranged Farlowe's version of Otis Redding's "I've Been Loving You Too Long".

MONDAY NOVEMBER 7th

The first projected shooting day for "Only Lovers Left Alive" at Boreham Wood Studios. None of the Stones turned up and the film was eventually scrapped altogether. Brian attended a party at the Playboy Club, in Mayfair.

THURSDAY NOVEMBER 10th

"The Rolling Stones Monthly" ceased publication after thirty issues.

SUNDAY NOVEMBER 13th

Mick, Keith and Charlie were guests at Brian Epstein's party, given for The Four Tops, at his house in Belgravia. Other celebrities present included John Lennon, George Harrison, Eric Burdon and Donovan.

WEDNESDAY 16th NOVEMBER - MONDAY DECEMBER 5th

Recording sessions at Olympic Sound Studios (which had now officially moved to it's present site at 117 Church Road, Barnes, South West London) with Andrew Oldham and engineer Glyn Johns. These sessions (with Jack Nitzsche and/or Ian Stewart on piano/organ) formed the "Between The Buttons" album:-

"If You Let Me"

"Yesterday's Papers"

"Ruby Tuesday" (initially with a working title "Title 8". Brian played recorder, with Bill and Keith on cello. Due to it's bulk, Bill held the instrument, while Keith played the notes).

"Back Street Girl"

"Connection"

"Miss Amanda Jones"

"Let's Spend The Night Together" (Keith - piano)

"Who's Been Sleeping Here"

"Please Go Home"

"All Sold Out"

"Dandelion" (initially with a working title "Sometimes Happy, Sometimes Blue")

"Cool, Calm And Collected" (vocals added)

"Complicated"(vocals added)

"My Obsession" (vocals added) (the latter three's backing tracks were cut at RCA - see Aug 3rd to 7th entry)

"Trouble In Mind" (a nonsense jam, largely instigated by Brian on kazoo, of the old blues standard).

"Can't Believe" (second version)

"Looking Tired" (second version)

"English Summer"

"Gold Painted Nails"

The latter five remain unreleased.

During the sessions, Peter Whitehead filmed the band at work. (Footage of a "Yesterday's Papers" session formed the visuals to the promotional films for "Ruby Tuesday" and "Lets Spend The Night Together"). Photographers, Michael Cooper and Gered Mankowitz were also on hand to document the sessions. At the conclusion of one session (date unknown),the group and Mankowitz piled into Andrew Oldham's Rolls-Royce, driving to Primrose Hill at dawn, to shoot a series of shots for the front sleeve. (A distinctive "foggy" effect achieved by smearing a glass filter with vaseline).

THURSDAY DECEMBER 1st

Keith, Brian, Bill and Marianne were amongst the celebrity audience at The Young Rascals gig at the Scotch of St. James.

TUESDAY DECEMBER 6th

Jack Nitzche flew back to Los Angeles. Brian and Keith went with him for a ten-day break.

SATURDAY DECEMBER 10th

The N.M.E end-of-year poll results revealed the Stones had been voted "Top R & B Group" and "Satisfaction", the best song of the year.

TUESDAY DECEMBER 13th

Andrew Oldham flew to Los Angeles to start mixing and editing tracks cut at Olympic, at RCA Studios.

THURSDAY DECEMBER 15th

Mick cancelled a planned vacation to Jamaica (with Chrissie still seemingly unaware of Marianne). Instead, he spent the day in London with Marianne, having lunch in Knightsbridge and then buying Christmas presents at Harrods. Bill and Glyn Johns went to the star-studded opening night of the Speakeasy, 48 Margaret Street, W1.

FRIDAY DECEMBER 16th

Comedian John Bird drafted a programme idea, involving the Rolling Stones and himself, to the BBC "Head of Planning" (see Dec 21st entry).

SATURDAY DECEMBER 17th

Brian's friend, Tara Browne, the 21-year old Guiness heir, was killed when his Lotus Elan crashed into a stationary van, in Redcliffe Gardens.

His girlfriend, Suki Poitier escaped unhurt (see Jan.10th 1967 entry).

SUNDAY DECEMBER 18th

Bill attended ex-Animal, Chas Chandler's birthday party at 34 Montagu Square, W1. Other guests included Eric Burdon, Zoot Money and Jimi Hendrix.

MONDAY DECEMBER 19th

Mick and Chrissie's three year romance officially ended. Mick released a statement to the press: "Three years is a long time to be spent with somebody, but although we were unofficially engaged, we hadn't set any date for a wedding". Chrissie put on a brave face: "We were very much in love but we argued all the time. As time goes on you begin to feel different about life and each other. There wasn't a row. We broke by mutual agreement." Bill and Diane also separated (see July 9th 1969 entry).

TUESDAY DECEMBER 20th

Mick went to Studio One, Wembley to appear on the last ever edition of "Ready Steady Go!", aptly titled "Ready Steady Goes!". It consisted of past performers, who had appeared on this much-missed show, featuring (in the first half):- The Breakaways, Paul Jones, Dave Dee, Dozy, Beaky, Mick and Tich, Eric Burdon, Alan Price, Donovan, Kenny Lynch and The Who. The second half featured Lulu, Keith Relf, Paul Samwell-Smith, Julie Felix, Cat Stevens, The Merseys, Peter and Gordon, The Small Faces and The Spencer Davis Group who all took turns to perform brief snatches of their hits (i.e two of The Yardbirds performed a one minute version of "For Your Love", The Who a 47-second "I'm A Boy", etc.) Mick appeared in a duet with Chris Farlowe on two tracks:- "Out Of Time" (lasting 1 minute 12 seconds) and "Satisfaction" (1 minute 30 seconds. The two longest performances in the second half of the show). The show was broadcast over certain ITV regions on Friday, December 23rd, between 6:08 - 6:34 pm.

WEDNESDAY DECEMBER 21st

A memo within BBC Chief Executives announced that "...today, BBC1 accepted, in principle, an idea submitted by John Bird for a special involving himself, The Rolling Stones, Malcolm Muggerige and others. It is in fact, a satirical send-up of the whole pop scene. It is estimated that the filming requirements would be 10 days, and 2 days in Studio 3, 4 or 1 (at the BBC TV Centre, London) to make this programme and the time suitable for all concerned is May/June". That was as far as the idea ever got!

SATURDAY DECEMBER 24th

With Chrissie recuperating in Greenway Nursing Home, Hampstead (after an apparent suicide attempt), Mick arranged for a removal van to collect her belongings and returned her hospital bills unpaid. Marianne moved in shortly thereafter, the couple spending Christmas together at Harley House (with Marianne's young son, Nicholas). Keith, Brian and Anita spent a Parisian Christmas in a luxury suite at the Georges V.

Bill and friend at Olympic Studios

JANUARY

The group spent the early part of the month, completing final mixes of tracks, at Olympic Studios. A publicity photo shoot was held at Green Park, Mayfair.

MONDAY JANUARY 2nd

Mick and Marianne were among the guests attending Ian Stewart's wedding (to Andrew Oldham's secretary, Cynthia) and reception at St Andrew's Church, Cheam, Surrey.

WEDNESDAY JANUARY 4th

Bill saw the little-known Jimi Hendrix Experience play the Bromel Club, at the Bromley Court Hotel, Kent.

SATURDAY JANUARY 7th

Mick as "Saturday Boy" gave an interview (conducted on January 4th), to "Saturday Girl", Anne Nightingale in her regular weekend column for "The Daily Sketch". (The article was captioned "I can't believe that people listen to one and a half hours of Palm Court on the Home Service!".)

TUESDAY JANUARY 10th

Keith, Brian and Anita attended the memorial service for Tara Browne (see Dec.17th 1966 entry) at St Pauls Church, Knightsbridge.

WEDNESDAY JANUARY 11th

Bill was among the rock aristocracy present at the Bag O'Nails Club, Kingly Street, Mayfair to see the Jimi Hendrix Experience.

THURSDAY JANUARY 12th

Superstitious Keith, Bill and Brian changed flights, flying out a day early from Heathrow Airport to New York to appear on "The Ed Sullivan Show" (therefore avoiding flying on Friday the 13th). Mick and Marianne went to the opening of a new club, the "7 & 1/2", in Whitehorse Street, W1, where The Jimi Hendrix Experience were playing. (Marianne went back to catch their act the following night.)

FRIDAY JANUARY 13th

"Let's Spend The Night Together" B/W "Ruby Tuesday" was released (reaching No 2). In the U.S, sensitive radio programmers plugged "Ruby Tuesday", where it reached No 1 in March. Having spent the previous day, ordering new clothes, Mick left Heathrow Airport on a morning flight, joining the other three, at their hotel in New York. (Charlie flew out the following day).

SUNDAY JANUARY 15th

The group made their fifth appearance on "The Ed Sullivan Show", broadcast live from the CBS TV studios, between 8:00 - 9:00 EST. Mick sang live (over the original backing tracks): "Ruby Tuesday" and reluctantly, "Let's Spend Some "Time" Together". The first afternoon camera rehearsal (between 2 - 3 pm, before a live audience), was videotaped. (During which, Mick mischievously kept to his original lyric, smirking at the camera as he did so). The camera shots at this rehearsal substantially differed from the evening's broadcast, where the group appeared as the final act in the second half of the programme.

THURSDAY JANUARY 19th

Controversy was brewing over the group's forthcoming appearance on ATV's "Sunday Night At The London Palladium". An ATV spokesman told "Disc": "There have been some discussions as to whether the song's ("Let's Spend The Night Together") lyrics should be altered or even if they should sing it at all, on the show, but nothing can be decided until the Stones return". (They arrived back that afternoon.) In the evening, Mick and Marianne went to see The Jimi Hendrix Experience at the Speakeasy.

FRIDAY JANUARY 20th

"Between The Buttons" was released in the U.K (in the U.S.A on Feb. 11th). Charlie: "Andrew told me to do the drawings for the L.P. and told me the title was between the buttons. I thought he meant the title was "Between The Buttons", so it stayed". Mick and Marianne attended an evening function, at the Savoy Hotel, to mark the 20th anniversary of London Records.

SATURDAY JANUARY 21st

Keith, Brian and Anita went shopping in the Kings Road, buying garments from the "Granny Takes A Trip" boutique (for the following day's "Palladium" appearance). Whilst there, Brian bumped into ex-Decca and Stones publicist, Tony King. In an earnest, in-depth interview with Richard Lennox of "Disc", Brian revealed that he had been working on a film. "It's been something I've been working on for a long time and I've got my first offer within the last few days. It's very new and I haven't had the chance to talk to anybody about it. That's why I have to be

vague. There's really nothing more I can say because you must realise that everything we do exists within the framework of The Rolling Stones".

SUNDAY JANUARY 22nd

The group made their controversial bill-topping appearance, for a fee of £1,500, on the live ATV/ITV variety show "The All New Sunday Night at the London Palladium", transmitted between 8:25 - 9:24pm across the ITV network. (Italian television were also present, filming the group backstage, as part of an R.A.I T.V. special, screened on Feb.12th).

The group mimed to pre-recordings (taped at Olympic on the 20th) of (in order):- "Connection", "Ruby Tuesday", as a bow to the past, a radical rearrangement of "Its All Over Now" and "Let's Spend The Night Together". Other guests included:- actress, Shani Wallis, The Carmenas, The London Palladium Dancers, Jack Parnell & His Orchestra and Irish comedian, Dave Allen, who made jokes at the group's expense, before they appeared. The group had the last laugh, by refusing to appear in the traditional end-of-show "revolving stage" finale' (to the tune of "Startime"), despite coaxing from Andrew Oldham. Mick: "That revolving

Left: Three superstitious Stones leaving for New York, January 12th to avoid flying on Friday 13th
Below: Returning to Heathrow, January 19th

stage isn't an altar - it's just a drag!" This caused an uproar. "They're insulting me and everyone else" ranted Albert Locke, the show's producer. Mick later told the NME: "The only reason we did the show at the Palladium was because it was a good national plug, anyone who thought we were changing our image to suit a family audience was mistaken." An ATV spokesman attempted a cover-up by saying: "It was simply a security measure. They aren't the first artists on the Palladium, who haven't been on the finale. The Beatles also left early, so they would not be mobbed. Before the show, it was agreed that the Stones should leave the theatre early so that fans could not mob them outside." (The group left the theatre via a side entrance, under police escort.) Immediately following the recording, Mick and Keith went to Paul McCartney's home in St. John's Wood, to watch a videotape recording of the show (which had received it's highest viewing figures in a year). A week later (on Jan 29th), the furore was still simmering. "Entertainer", Max Bygraves sprayed the hallowed stage with aerosol, when the group's name was mentioned. On Feb 5th, Peter Cook and Dudley Moore appeared on the revolving stage with large paper dummies of the group (drawn by cartoonist Gerald Scarfe), to wave a humourous farewell, to the whole incident.

WEDNESDAY JANUARY 25th

The group went to the Lime Grove Studios of BBC Television, to record inserts for both "Let's Spend The Night Together" and "Ruby Tuesday", for use on "Top Of The Pops". After a noon camera rehearsal, they videotaped both songs in one session. "Let's Spend The Night Together" would be transmitted for the first time on the following day's broadcast (7:30-8:00pm) and repeated in the year-end "Top Of The Pops '67" (Boxing Day BBC1 5:10-5:59 pm), while "Ruby Tuesday" would be broadcast on the February 2nd and 9th editions (again between 7:30 - 8:00pm).

FRIDAY JANUARY 27th

Marianne flew to Nice to begin a week long series of rehearsals for her appearance in the annual San Remo Pop Festival. (Mick joined her on the 30th). Chris Farlowe's "My Way Of Giving" (written by Steve Marriott and Ronnie Lane, of The Small Faces) B/W "You're So Good For Me", produced by Mick, was released on Immediate. The same label also released Nicky Scott's version of "Back Street Girl", produced by Mick and Andrew Oldham.

SATURDAY JANUARY 28th

Bill produced the Hamilton and The Movement single "I'm Not The Marrying Kind" B/W "My Love Belongs To You" at Olympic (released Friday, February 10th, on CBS). The following day, he flew to Madrid, with Glyn Johns, for a week of business discussions, on their joint productions. His Swedish girlfriend, Astrid Lundstrom accompanied them.

SATURDAY FEBRUARY 4th

Mick and Marianne, whilst still on the Riviera, attended the International Record and Music Publishing Market in Cannes, where Mick accepted an

Above and below: Tom Keylock pictures of work in progress at Olympic Studios.

award on behalf of the Stones for "Best Selling British Act".

SUNDAY FEBRUARY 5th

In a series on "Pop Stars And Drugs", "The News Of The World" reported: "Mick Jagger has taken LSD at the Moody Blues house in Roehampton." He was also quoted as saying: "I dont go much on it now the cats have taken it up. It'll just get a dirty name. I remember the first time I took it, it was on tour with Bo Diddley and Little Richard." The report continued: "During the time we were at Blaises Club, in Kensington, Jagger took about six benzedrine tablets." I just would not keep awake in places like this if I didn't have them"...Later at Blaise's, Jagger showed a companion and two girls a small piece of hash and invited them to his flat for "a smoke". The source for the story was in fact, a year-old interview with Brian. The "News of the World" reporter had mistaken him for Jagger. In the evening, the group went to the Teddington Studios of ABC TV, to appear for the third time (for the usual payment of £200) on "The Eamonn Andrews Show". Following camera (7:30 - 8:30pm) and dress (8:45 - 9:30pm) rehearsals, the Stones played and sang live "She Smiled Sweetly", which was substituted in place of "Ruby Tuesday" at the last minute, when Musicians Union officials refused to let the group mime to the same tape they had used on the Palladium show (see Jan 22nd entry). The programme was transmitted live across the ITV network between 11:05- 11:49pm. During the show, Mick joined the panel (lasting approximately 4 minutes, for which he was again paid £200), where he announced that he would be suing the "News of the World" paper for libel. Other guests on the programme included singer, Susan Maughan and comedy character actor, Terry Scott.

TUESDAY FEBRUARY 7th

True to his word, Mick's lawyers issued a libel suit against the "News Of The World" (see Feb 5th entry). For the rest of the week, Mick complained of being constantly under surveillance.

THURSDAY 9th - FRIDAY FEBRUARY 24th

"She's A Rainbow" sessions at Olympic Studios (working titles included "She Comes In Colours" and "Lady Fair"), with Andrew Oldham and Glyn Johns. Brian and Keith were absent from the first session. (Brian had gone to Munich with Anita, on the 8th, to discuss her role in "A Degree Of Murder", with Keith tagging along). Nicky Hopkins played piano and John Paul Jones scored the string arrangement.

FRIDAY FEBRUARY 10th

Keith, Brian and Anita arrived home from Munich in the morning. That night, Keith joined Mick and Marianne at a special Beatles session in Studio One, at EMI's Abbey Road Studios, which was being filmed. The occasion was the orchestral crescendo being recorded for the climax of "A Day In The Life", conducted in an informal party atmosphere. Among the other pop celebrities present were "Monkee" Mike Nesmith and Donovan. Mick, Keith and Marianne were featured in the finished film.

SATURDAY FEBRUARY 11th

The Stones recorded two versions of a track, given the working title "Blues I", at Olympic. After the others had left, Brian continued his "A Degree Of Murder" soundtrack sessions, as the movie deadline was approaching. At 10pm, the "News Of The World" received a "tip-off" about a weekend party at Keith Richard's house, Redlands, in West Wittering, Sussex. They duly telephoned Scotland Yard, as the first guests started arriving at 11pm.

SUNDAY FEBRUARY 12th

A search warrant issued under the "Dangerous Drugs Act 1965", was obtained from a local magistrate, and shortly after 8pm, eighteen police officers (including two policewomen) raided Redlands (after allegedly waiting for George and Patti Harrison to leave). Mick, Keith, Marianne, Michael Cooper, art dealer Robert Fraser, his Moroccan servant Mohammed, antique dealer Christopher Gibbs, scenester Nicky Kramer and a mysterious stranger (whom Keith only recalled meeting on two separate occasions before) by the name of David Schneiderman (invited down by Fraser), were all searched and samples were taken for examination. These included four Benzedrine tablets, actually belonging to Marianne, prescribed by a doctor, when the couple were in Italy for the San Remo Festival. Mick claimed ownership after they were found in his jacket pocket. 24 heroin "jacks" (tablets), were found on Robert Fraser, who claimed they were diabetic tablets, prescribed by his doctor. A briar pipe-bowl was also taken away and on analysis, it's contents were found to contain traces of cannabis resin. The police did not search Schneiderman's suitcase (full of drugs), being satisfied with his claim that it contained irreplaceable film, that would become exposed to light, if opened. Marianne was wrapped in a fur rug after a bath just as the police swooped. She was taken upstairs and searched by the policewomen. The police regarded Christopher Gibb's outfit as "unorthodox", until it was pointed out that it was the Pakistani National Dress. As the police left, Keith was told that should investigations show dangerous drugs had been used on the premises and were not related to any individual, he would be held responsible. "I see, they pin it all on me" was his response. Shortly after, Brian rang to say he and Anita were on their way down. (They had been due the night before but Brian was still in the studio). "Forget it, man", Keith told him, "we've been busted!".

TUESDAY FEBRUARY 14th

David Schneiderman, highly suspected of being a "plant" at the party, for the "News Of The World", discreetly left the country. For the group, it was business as usual with a session at Olympic Studios.

SUNDAY FEBRUARY 19th

An unincriminating report on the Redlands raid was printed in the "News of the World", titled "Drugs Squad Raid Pop Stars Party". The

Right: Keith and Bentley, "The Blue Lena" (named after singer, Lena Horne), outside the Georges V Paris, February 25th

following day, Mick and Keith went to the Hilton Hotel for a legal meeting with Timothy Hardacre (Keith's lawyer), Victor Durand QC (appointed counsel for the pair) and Allen Klein. Andrew Oldham was conspicuous by his absence.

THURSDAY FEBRUARY 23rd
Mick and Marianne caused an uproar by arriving 8 minutes late for the world premiere of Roland Petit's ballet "Paradise Lost", starring Rudolph Nureyev and Margot Fonteyn at the Royal Opera House, Covent Garden. It was considered a lack of protocol due to the presence of H.R.H. Princess Margaret.

SATURDAY FEBRUARY 25th
Feeling the pressure from the aftermath of the bust, Mick, Brian and Keith decided on a "get away from it all" holiday, to Morocco. Keith, Brian, Anita and Deborah Dixon (girlfriend of film director, Donald Cammell) flew to Paris, to meet Tom Keylock at the Georges V. Keylock would drive them (in Keith's Bentley, "The Blue Lena") to Tangier, where they planned to rendezvous with Mick, Marianne, Christopher Gibbs and Michael Cooper.

MONDAY FEBRUARY 27th
After feeling ill during the journey, Brian was hospitalised at The Centre Hospitalier D'Albi in Tarn, near Toulouse. The rest of the party checked into a hotel for the night.

TUESDAY FEBRUARY 28th
Brian spent his 25th birthday hospitalised. With Deborah Dixon flying back to Paris, Keith and Anita began their affair on the drive across the French-Spanish border, stopping for the night at Valencia. After a misunderstanding over Keith's Diners Club card, Keith, Anita and Tom were hauled off to a police station and spent the night being interrogated, before Keylock was escorted to the hotel for their passports.

WEDNESDAY MARCH 1st
Returning to the hotel at dawn, a telegram from Brian awaited Anita, instructing her to return to Toulouse, as he was being discharged from hospital. She ignored it and the trio drove on to Marbella.

THURSDAY MARCH 2nd
Brian sent a telegram to the Stones office in London: "Feeling almost fully recovered. Must leave here as soon as possible for Tangier, assuming no complications. Very, very unlikely. Please book flights, first class, Toulouse/Paris/Tangier early next week and mail tickets immediately. Also notify others of arrival and ask them to wait for me. Will recuperate fully in sun. Love Brian".

SUNDAY MARCH 5th
After four nights with Keith in Marbella, Anita flew back to get Brian, in Toulouse. Tom drove Keith to Gibraltar, where they crossed over to North Africa and on to Tangier, meeting up with Mick, Christopher Gibbs, Robert Fraser and Michael Cooper, at the Hotel El Minzah.

MONDAY MARCH 6th
Brian was discharged, fit enough to fly back to London with Anita, so

that he could have some tests done. He went for a chest X-ray at the Harley Street Nursing Home, before entering the West London Hospital, discharging himself in a matter of days. While in London, he did a live phone-in interview for Harry Harrison's New York radio show "The In Sound". (A further interview was broadcast March 13th).

FRIDAY MARCH 10th
The sole Moon's Train single, "Deed I Do" B/W "It's My Mind", produced by Bill, was released on MGM.

SATURDAY MARCH 11th
Brian, Anita and Marianne flew to Marrakesh via Madrid and Gibraltar, reuniting with the others at their hotel.

WEDNESDAY MARCH 15th
Sir Cecil Beaton, the royal photographer, who the party had met the previous evening in the hotel lobby and had dined with, took photographs of Mick, Keith and Brian, as they lounged around the hotel pool. That evening, Brian inflicted a savage beating on Anita, marking the end of their tempestuous relationship.

THURSDAY MARCH 16th
In the afternoon, Brian went with Brion Gysin into the Atlas Mountains to the "Djemaa el Fna" Public Square, recording "ethnic trance" music and smoking hashish with the Mejdoubi Brothers. While he was away, Keith and Anita fled from Tangier, being driven to Barcelona by Tom Keylock, without informing Brian of their whereabouts.

FRIDAY MARCH 17th
A distraught Brian flew from Morocco to Paris, staying with Donald Cammell and Deborah Dixon. Mick, Marianne and Christopher Gibbs arrived back in London from Morocco.

SATURDAY MARCH 18th
Brian returned to London Airport alone, while "The Daily Mirror" reported on the Redlands raid, in detail, for the first time, revealing that Mick and Keith faced summonses for alleged drug offenses. Their lawyer, Mr Timothy Hardacre accepted the summonses on their behalf, the following week. "Disc" announced the Rolling Stones had been awarded a Gold Record in America for "Ruby Tuesday" and "Let's Spend The Night Together", plus their sixth consecutive Gold Record for the "Between The Buttons" album.

FRIDAY MARCH 24th
The group flew to Malmo, Sweden via Copenhagen from London Airport to begin the first leg of an European tour (their last until 1970). Accompanying them were Tom Keylock, Les Perrin and new recruit, Alan Dunn, to help Stu with the gear. Custom's officials in Sweden, strip-searched Mick and Bill and searched all sixteen pieces of luggage, causing an hour's hold up. Mick: "They were looking for pot, and they went through every bit of clothes we had, even our underclothes."

SATURDAY MARCH 25th
Idrottens Hus Paskafton, Helsingborg. (Two shows.)
The tour set list:-

"The Last Time" / "Paint It Black" / "19th Nervous Breakdown" / "Lady Jane" / "Get Off Of My Cloud" / "Yesterday's Papers" / "Ruby Tuesday" / "Let's Spend The Night Together" / "Goin' Home" and "Satisfaction". Mick was nearly beaten up, as police, with dogs and batons, attacked fans, who stampeded the stage, curtailing the concert prematurely, prompting him to complain: "Why do you have to hit girls on the head with batons?".

MONDAY MARCH 27th

Vinterstadium, Orebro, Sweden. (Two shows.)

TUESDAY MARCH 28th

The group flew to Germany.

WEDNESDAY MARCH 29th

Stadhalle, Bremen. (Two shows, with supports, The Creation, The Easybeats and The Hollies, on each German date). Olympic Gold Medalist Lyn Davies was staying at the same hotel and later whined to "The Daily Express": "I felt sick and was ashamed to be British as they poured out swear words at the breakfast table ...they are tarnishing the name of our country in a foreign land". Mick: "The accusations are disgusting and completely untrue. We deny that we were badly behaved. I cannot remember when we have behaved better. We hardly used the public rooms in this hotel. They were crammed with athletes behaving very badly!!"

THURSDAY MARCH 30th

Sporthalle, Cologne. (Two shows.) Prior to the concert, Mick was interviewed for the German TV station WDR, included in evening newscasts, as well as footage of the early show.

FRIDAY MARCH 31st

Westfallenhalle, Dortmund.

SATURDAY APRIL 1st

Ernst Merck Halle, Hamburg. (Two shows.)

SUNDAY APRIL 2nd

Stadthalle, Vienna, Austria. (Two shows, 14,000 at each.) During the late show, a smoke-bomb was thrown, causing another riot. A total of 154 fans were arrested. A report from the first show, with "Get Off Of My Cloud" live, was later included in Show 19 of the NDR German television show, "Beat Club", transmitted in the news section, on May 1st.

MONDAY APRIL 3rd

The group (minus Keith, who checked into the Georges V, in Paris, to meet Anita, who had completed filming "A Degree Of Murder") flew back to Heathrow, their arrival being covered by a BBC TV newscrew. Brian spent the day shopping at the Chelsea Antique Market and the evening at the Bag O'Nails.

WEDNESDAY APRIL 5th

The four Stones flew to Italy, rejoining Keith for two shows at the Palazzo dello Sport, Bologne. (The Move supported on each Italian date).

THURSDAY APRIL 6th

Palazzo dello Sport, Rome. (Two shows.) The group dropped "19th

Brian and Keith's getaway, Holland, April 15th

Nervous Breakdown" and "Goin' Home", re-arranging the set list as follows:-
"The Last Time" / "Paint It, Black" / "Ruby Tuesday" / "Get Off Of My Cloud" / "Yesterday's Papers" / "Lady Jane" / "Let's Spend The Night Together" and "Satisfaction".

Actresses Brigitte Bardot, Jane Fonda and Gina Lollobrigida were amongst the matinee' audience. The group flew to Milan the following day.

SATURDAY APRIL 8th

Pallazzo dello Sport, Milan.(Two shows.) The group were bombarded with missiles, after police manhandled a girl trying to get on stage. Marianne had flown in to be with Mick.

Mick with Peter Asher

SUNDAY APRIL 9th

Palazzo dello Sport, Genova. (Two shows.)

MONDAY APRIL 10th

Mick flew back to London for 24 hours, with Marianne, while the rest of the group flew to Zurich, changing planes before flying to Paris. At Orly Airport, the group received a heavy customs inspection. (their arrival and departure from the airport in two limos was filmed by a local newscrew).

TUESDAY APRIL 11th

Mick flew into Orly Airport, rejoining the others at the Georges V. The group played two shows, with the Move, at L' Olympia, with the following set list:- "Paint It Black" / "19th Nervous Breakdown" / "Lady Jane" / "Get Off Of My Cloud" / "Yesterday's Papers" / "Under My Thumb" / "Ruby Tuesday" / "Let's Spend The Night Together" / "Goin' Home" and "Satisfaction".

Riot police dispersed 2,000 fans. A live broadcast of the concerts was made by French radio station, Europe 1, on the programme "Musicorama". While the Stones were performing, their hotel rooms were ransacked and many personal belongings were stolen. (The group later filed a £150 insurance claim.)

WEDNESDAY APRIL 12th

As the group flew out of Le Bourget airport, Mick and Keith were punched by an angry official, before Tom Keylock intervened, after a communication breakdown involving the groups passports. The flight to Warsaw, via Vienna, ran 90 minutes late.

THURSDAY APRIL 13th

The group held a press conference at the Hotel Orbis-Europejski, before two concerts at the Sala Kongresowej, a 2,741 seater hall, inside The Palace of Culture. In the square outside the Palace, ten thousand Polish teenagers demonstrated against being locked out, while students protested that the ticket distribution had been "fiddled", with most of the tickets being sold through ministries, party officials and factories, rather than through a normal box-office channel. The reason for this was so that the "selected" audiences would comply with an official request to "behave culturally". During the 5pm show,150 police were on duty inside the hall, while outside, the hundreds of police lining the square, made baton charges on the students. During the 8pm show, the crowds outside finally erupted into violence. 2 to 3,000 teenagers charged the massive iron gates, trying to get into the hall. The police and troops shot tear gas shells into the crowd, who threw stones and bottles back. Some 30 kids were arrested. The Official Polish News Agency reviewed the concerts, not mentioning the riots once:-"One of the famous modern music big teams, The Rolling Stones, gave two concerts in Warsaw. The young English artists performed their best things and the audience, consisting of mainly young people, received the performance with an enthusiasm which was too noisy, too loud. In the first part of the concert, the Polish team of Red-Black performed. Two performances in the Sala Kongresowej were not enough. Some of the viewers tried to mislead the vigilance of the checking officers, to get into the Sala. More than 200 tickets were confiscated. Inventful ones had forged them, selling the tickets later with an enormous profit. (Genuine tickets had fetched ten pounds each on the black market).

FRIDAY APRIL 14th

The group flew from Warsaw to Zurich, Switzerland. Swiss police used fire hoses to disperse fans who had run amok at the airport. At the Dolder Grand Hotel, Vienna a press conference was held, where Mick was interviewed by a local Swiss TV station, broadcast on that night's news programme. In the evening, the Stones gave a concert at the Hallenstadion on a 13-foot high stage, before 12,000 fans. Mick was thrown to the ground from behind, by a fan who had somehow broken through a 300-strong police cordon. The group stopped playing, while he clung to Mick, who was now looking over the edge of the precipice. After being shaken off, the persistent fan was finally felled by a blow to the jaw from Tom Keylock, who broke his hand! Mick signalled and the band resumed playing.

SATURDAY APRIL 15th

The group flew to Schipol Airport, Amsterdam to play a show at the Houtrusthallen, the Hague, returning to the ten-song set performed at the start of the tour. The concert, attended by Dutch minister, Joseph Luns, was covered by VARA-TV (a short clip of "19th Nervous Breakdown", with Luns watching from the balcony, appeared in news reports the following day) and Radio NTS (with a report that evening and the following day). The group stayed at the Rotterdam Hilton.

SUNDAY APRIL 16th

The Stones flew back to London, en route for Greece. Brian, who had a doctors appointment, remained behind, having lunch at the Alvaro restaurant and a night at the Speakeasy.

MONDAY APRIL 17th

Brian flew to Athens, to play the tour's final show at the Panathinaikos Stadium (on a stage in the middle of the pitch). Amongst the crowd of 40,000, was the Queen of the Hellenes. Tom Keylock had five teeth knocked out, while gallantly defending Brian onstage, from a crazed fan. After the tour ended, Bill and girlfriend Astrid stayed on in Greece for a holiday, with Glyn Johns, returning on the 23rd, while Keith went to Rome, where Anita was auditioning for her role as the Black Queen, in Roger Vadim's "Barbarella".

TUESDAY APRIL 18th

Mick, Brian and Charlie arrived back at London Airport.

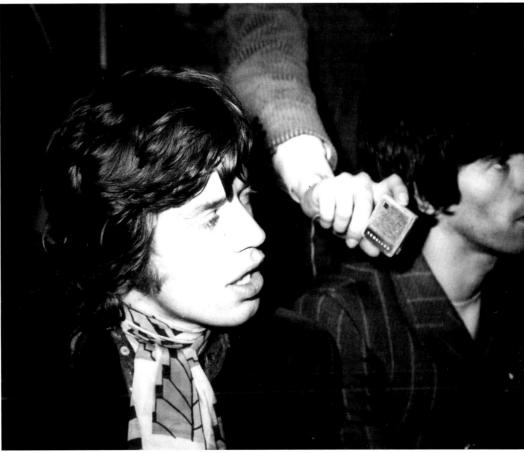

Warsaw press conference, April 13th

WEDNESDAY APRIL 19th

Brian and Linda Keith (Keith's ex-girlfriend) were driven by Brian's new chauffeur, Brian Palastanga to the Lygon Arms Hotel, Broadway (near Worcester) for a four-day break. Whilst there, Brian expressed an interest in buying Aston Somerville Hall, a £12,500 property ten miles north of Cheltenham.

SATURDAY APRIL 29th

Bill attended a press reception at the New Forest on behalf of his company, Power Of Two Promotions, to promote Moon's Train.

MAY

Mick produced a Marianne Faithfull session at Decca's West Hampstead studios, with Paul McCartney in attendance. Glyn Johns engineered, while Mike Leander handled the string arrangements.

FRIDAY MAY 5th

Chris Farlowe's version of "Yesterdays Papers" (produced and featuring backing vocals by Mick) B/W "Life Is But Nothing", was released on Immediate. The Warren Davis Monday Band single "Wait For Me" B/W "I Don't Wanna Hurt You" was released on Columbia, both sides produced by Bill. Brian and Anita, temporarily reconciled, attended the Cannes International Film Festival for the premiere of Volker Schlondorff's

Heathrow, April 18th

"Mord Und Totschlag" ("A Degree of Murder", distributed by Universal - see Sept 3rd, 1966 entry). The film was the official German entry. Keith was also there, but was keeping a low profile.

TUESDAY MAY 9th

Keith returned to London from Cannes, while Anita flew to Munich. He met Mick for lunch at "Simpson's" restaurant, to discuss the following day's case, before Tom Keylock drove the pair to Redlands for the night.

WEDNESDAY MAY 10th

Mick, Keith and Robert Fraser had breakfast at Redlands before Tom Keylock drove them to a layby near Chichester, where the trio transferred to a police car which drove them into the rear of the court

at West Sussex Quarter Sessions, half an hour before their hearing (meeting Allen Klein, who had just flown in and Les Perrin). Twelve fans had arrived the night before (some 14 hours before the case was due to start), to camp on the steps to ensure their places in the gallery (only 42 seats were available to the public). Coachloads of fans from London, had been expected; "Stones Fans - See You In Chichester On May 10th!" had been scrawled on Underground station walls. Extra police were called in to control the crowd of 500, (some of them anti-Stones) that had gathered outside, as Mick and Keith left the court during the luncheon adjournment. When court resumed, they elected trial by jury and were each remanded on £100 bail, for trial on June 22nd. With this, they slipped through the back door, where Keylock was waiting in the Bentley. The crowd outside had dwindled to 100, by the time they sped away to Redlands. Keith left London in the evening, for a week in Paris with Anita. At 4 pm, Brian was arrested at his flat at No 1 Courtfield Road. He and houseguest, 24-year old Prince Stanislas Klossowski de Rowla, were taken to Chelsea Police Station and charged with possession of Indian hemp. Detective Sergeant Norman Pilcher, of Scotland Yard, ordered a large amount of property be taken from the flat for analysis. After being released, the pair went straight to Allen Klein, who had just returned from Chichester, in his suite at the Hilton. Advised to give Courtfield Road a wide berth, Brian and "Stash" finished the evening at the Odeon Cinema, Marble Arch, watching "The Professionals" (starring Burt Lancaster).

THURSDAY MAY 11th

Brian and "Stash" arrived at West London Magistrates Court in Marlborough Street, an hour before their three minute hearing and were each remanded on £250 bail until June 2nd. Brian sent his parents a telegram, reading:- "Please don't worry. Don't jump to hasty conclusions and don't judge me too harshly. All my love. Brian." At Olympic Studios, Mick attended a Beatles session, adding backing vocals to "Baby, You're A Rich Man".

FRIDAY MAY 12th

Brian went on a shopping spree at Chelsea Antique Market.

TUESDAY 16th - FRIDAY MAY 19th

Olympic Studios. John Lennon and Paul McCartney attended the session on the 18th, adding their high harmonies to "We Love You".

SUNDAY MAY 21st

Mick appeared on BBC-1's "Look Of The Week", discussing hysterical audiences, with the Professor of Psychology, at Manchester University, John Cohen. To illustrate this, a 2 minute 5 second excerpt of the Albert Hall "Have You Seen Your Mother, Baby..." promo film (see Sept 23rd 1966 entry) was screened, as well as clips from the film "Privilege" and footage of the recent 36 hour "Technicolour Dream" event staged at Alexandra Palace (with "Paint It Black" played over the soundtrack). The programme, hosted by Robert Rubinson, was broadcast between 11:00 - 11:25 pm.

Above: Brian and "Stash" leave court, May 11th after being busted at his flat, No. 1 Courtfield Rd, Kensington (right).

FRIDAY JUNE 2nd

Brian and "Stash" appeared at West London Magistrates Court and elected to be tried by judge and jury. The two sat together in the dock as detectives told magistrate, Mr E.R Guest, of finding cannabis (Indian hemp), methedine and traces of cocaine at Courtfield Road. When Jones was shown a phial which was believed to contain cocaine, he said: "No man, I'm not a junkie! That's not mine at all." When shown a cigarette end which "appeared to contain cannabis", he said "Yes, it's hash. We do smoke, but not the cocaine, that's not my scene!". (The charge against "Stash" of being in possession of cocaine was dismissed). They were both committed for trial at Inner London Sessions, on bail of £250 each (see Oct 30th entry).

SATURDAY JUNE 3rd

Marianne collapsed on stage during her performance of Irina, in Chekov's "The Three Sisters" at The Royal Court Theatre, Sloane Square

(the play had opened April 14th. Mick attended most nights).

SUNDAY JUNE 4th

Brian and Jimi Hendrix went to see The Turtles, at the Speakeasy.

THURSDAY JUNE 8th

Paul McCartney invited Brian down to play on a Beatles session at Abbey Road. McCartney later recalled:- "We expected him to bring down a guitar, instead he turned up with just a saxophone!" This he played "just how we wanted", on "You Know My Name (Look Up The Number)".

MONDAY 12th and TUESDAY JUNE 13th

Further sessions at Olympic Studios.

TUESDAY 13th - SUNDAY JUNE 18th

Brian flew to California (with The Jimi Hendrix Experience) via New York and San Francisco, to attend the legendary Monterey International Pop Festival, held at the Monterey County Fairground, organised by Lou Adler and John Phillips. Andrew Oldham was also present, being on the board of directors. (Artists included:- The Association, The Jefferson Airplane, The Byrds, The Grateful Dead, Big Brother and the Holding Company, The Buffalo Springfield, Hugh Masekala, Lou Rawls, Canned Heat, The Blues Project, Simon and Garfunkel, Country Joe and The Fish, Ravi Shankar, Eric Burdon and The Animals, Otis Redding, The Who, The Jimi Hendrix Experience and The Mamas and The Papas). The event was captured by film-maker D. A. Pennebaker, in his documentary "Monterey Pop" (released 1969), in which, footage of Brian wandering around the festival grounds, appeared (for 4 seconds) during Eric Burdon and The Animals version of "Paint It Black". Brian also introduced the Jimi Hendrix Experience's incendiary set (the footage appearing some 20 years later in the "Jimi Plays Monterey" film). Jimi was Brian's constant companion over the weekend, as was Nico. In the lead-up to their trials, Mick and Marianne went back to Tangier, while Keith and Anita flew to Paris.

SUNDAY JUNE 25th

Back from holiday, Keith, Mick and

Marianne were among the friends summoned by The Beatles to Studio One at Abbey Road Studios, as guest backing vocalists on "All You Need Is Love" being transmitted live, via satellite for the first time, as part of the global TV event, "Our World".

TUESDAY JUNE 27th

Early in the morning, Mick, Keith and Robert Fraser were driven by Tom Keylock, in Keith's Bentley, from Redlands to a secret rendezvous nearby, where they transferred to a police car. They arrived at a court back entrance, for the first day of trials at West Sussex Quarter Sessions, in Chichester, under Mr.Justice Block. Firstly, Robert Fraser admitted being in unlawful possession of 24 heroin tablets. He was remanded in custody for sentence. The court agreed to the defence's application to hear Jagger and Richards cases separately, with different juries. Mick pleaded "Not Guilty" to the charge of being illegally in possession of four amphetamine tablets.His defence,based on a legal submission, from his lawyer Michael Havers QC, was that he had them lawfully because they had been prescribed, albeit orally, by a doctor, to combat exhaustion. When summing up, Judge Block ruled: "I have no hesitation whatever in saying that the evidence given by Dr Firth (Jagger's London doctor) would not, in law, amount to the issue of a prescription by a qualified practitioner...It therefore follows that the defence, such as is

Left: Brian at the Monterey Pop Festival, with Nico (above), June 17th

open to Jagger is not available. So really, as a matter of law, I have to direct you to say there is no defence to the charge." The all-male jury took six minutes to return a "Guilty" verdict and Jagger too, was remanded in custody for sentencing, until after the hearing of the charge against Keith. Mick spent his first night in Lewes jail, taking with him 3 books (about art and Tibet), cigarettes, chocolate, a jigsaw puzzle and a suitcase full of clothing.

WEDNESDAY JUNE 28th

Keith and Michael Havers were driven from Redlands to Chichester by Tom Keylock. Mick and Robert Fraser (handcuffed together) were driven from Lewes in a grey prison van to Chichester, in the event of an opportunity for sentencing arising. Keith pleaded "Not Guilty" to the charge of allowing his home to be used for the smoking of cannabis resin. Havers went to great lengths to protect Marianne's identity, after the prosecution had evidence admitted regarding her condition, draped in nothing but a fur rug. "I am not going to tear that blanket of anonymity aside and let the world laugh and scorn as they will". (Alas, he was too late as the infamous "Mars Bar" story was already circulating). When the court adjourned for lunch, Keylock drove Keith to a local hotel. At midday, a nearby hotel proprietor arrived on the court steps carrying Jagger and Fraser's lunch. Their menu (as dutifully reported in the press) consisted: Fraser: iced melon, fresh salmon salad, fresh fruit and strawberries and cream. Jagger: prawn cocktail, roast lamb and mint sauce, fresh strawberries and cream. They both shared a bottle of Beaujolais. After the conclusion of the prosecution's case and Havers opening address to the jury, Keith was remanded on bail for his trial to continue at 10am the following day. Marianne visited Mick at his cell, below the courtroom, for 15 minutes, bringing newspapers, cigarettes, fruit and a draughtsboard, which he had specifically asked for. She was

then driven back to Redlands. Michael Cooper visited, taking the opportunity to shoot a portrait of Mick through the cell door, for a possible album sleeve. (His efforts were thwarted when police found and confiscated the film as he left.) Keith also visited before Mick and Fraser were driven back to Lewes jail, handcuffed separately to prison officers. Earlier in the day, police and an ambulance crew had gone to Brian's Courtfield Road address, after a hoax call told them he had taken an overdose. Brian awoke startled to find them climbing through, over the balcony of his first floor flat, after the front door bolt had got stuck. Fearing further police reprisals, Brian moved out of the flat into a room at the Royal Garden Hotel, Kensington.

THURSDAY JUNE 29th

Mick and Robert Fraser arrived from Lewes (handcuffed again to each other) in a prison van, a few minutes before Keith's trial continued, at West Sussex Quarter Sessions. Keith took the stand to give evidence. During cross-examination, Keith confirmed his defence that Schneiderman had been planted by the "News Of The World", in order to get Mick convicted of smoking hashish (in retaliation to his libel suit - see Feb 5th entry). The prosecution advised the jury to disregard this, in their closing address, as there was "not the slightest shred of evidence to support this story". The jury of 11 men and one woman returned after five minutes with a "Guilty" verdict. Keith was dealt with first by Judge Block, being sentenced to one year's imprisonment (and £500 costs), Fraser received six months imprisonment (and £200 costs), while Mick received three months imprisonment (and £100 costs). When Mick was sentenced, he swayed and reeled in the dock. Girls in the gallery cried "Oh No!". He turned and looked at them, as he approached the staircase leading to the cells. Keith and Fraser both clicked their heels as they heard their sentences. Marianne arrived weeping, shortly after the sentencing, and was allowed to see Mick in his cell for 15 minutes. The news was phoned to Allen Klein who immediately flew to London to arrange their release, while a cable was sent to Anita, in Rome. At 8pm, Mick was delivered to Brixton prison, while Keith and Robert Fraser were transferred to Wormwood Scrubs, to begin their sentences. Some papers gleefully reported that prison medical officers had the authority to order the two Stones to have their hair cut short! They would be able to send and receive one letter a week and visitors would be allowed once every two weeks. With a maximum remission of sentence, Richard would serve only eight months and Jagger two months. Les Perrin announced that both Stones would be appealing.

FRIDAY JUNE 30th

Mick and Keith were granted bail in the High Courts for the sum of £5,000 each, plus two sureties of £1,000 each, pending their appeals. (Robert Fraser remained to serve his sentence, reduced to four months, with full remission). Tom Keylock collected Mick from Brixton at 4pm, in the Bentley and there on to Wormwood Scrubs, for Keith, taking them to the Embankment for a three hour meeting with Michael Havers.

Later, they met Les Perrin and the press at "The Feathers" pub, off Fleet Street. "It's great to be out!" the pair told newshounds "and now we are going to get down to some hard work". Both admitted they were treated no differently from the other prisoners and Mick kept pop gossip columnists happy by revealing one of the first people he had called was Paul McCartney. Meanwhile, several newspapers, including the "Evening Standard" carried advertisements placed by The Who:-"The Who consider Mick Jagger and Keith Richard have been treated as scapegoats for the drug problem and as a protest against the savage

press. Michael Cooper and his son, Adam were also houseguests.

JULY

The group announced that plans to open a "top London TV and recording studio" were nearing completion, with an accompanying record label provisionally titled "Mother Earth" (the group would be contractually unable to appear on the label, although Decca would handle the distribution). Marianne Faithfull would be the first artist to appear under the new "banner". The press also reported that another film proposal had been accepted by Mick (on behalf of the group), with

Left: Mick and Keith at Redlands before their trials, June 27th, and with PR Les Perrin at Chichester (middle).
Right: Brian, Suki, Poitier and Nicky Browne leave for Marbella, July 27th

sentences imposed upon them at Chichester yesterday, The Who are issuing today the first of a series of Jagger/Richard songs to keep their work before the public until they are again free to record themselves". (They had recorded "The Last Time" and "Under My Thumb", the previous night, in a single session, with royalties going to the Stones legal costs. Keith Moon even joined the throng demonstrating outside the offices of the "News Of The World", after hearing the news). Stones fans also gathered at Piccadilly Circus, chanting "Free The Stones, Free The Stones". Teeny favourites, The Monkees wore black armbands at their Empire Pool concert to show where their sympathies lay (they later met Brian, who was staying on the same floor, at the Royal Garden Hotel, Kensington). Carnaby Street was quick to cash in with sets of handcuffs on display with the invitation: "Be Faithfull with a pair of Jagger links"! Mick spent the weekend with Marianne and Nicholas at her father's manor, "Brazier's", in Oxfordshire, away from the prying

shooting, mainly on location abroad, to begin February, 1968. An unnamed French director had already been approached.

SATURDAY JULY 1st

"The Times" editor, William Rees-Mogg, risking prosecution, published his "subjudice" editorial leader: "Who Breaks A Butterfly On A Wheel?" (from "The Trials Of Oscar Wilde"), which criticised the severity of Judge Block's sentence passed on Jagger, because of his celebrity. It drew attention to the fact that if it had been the Archbishop of Canterbury, "he would have risked commiting precisely the same offence. It should be the particular quality of British justice to ensure that Mr. Jagger is treated exactly the same as anyone else, no better and no worse. There must remain a suspicion in this case that Mr. Jagger received a more severe sentence than would have been thought proper for any purely anonymous young man".

MONDAY JULY 3rd

Brian and new girlfriend, Suki Poitier visited Dr Leonard Henry, who recommended Brian be admitted to a health clinic in Liphook, Hampshire. Brian followed the doctor's advice (checking in as "Mr L Howlett"), only to discharge himself two days later.

TUESDAY JULY 4th

Mick and Keith were at Redlands, resting and songwriting, where they heard that their court appeals, originally scheduled for October, had been speeded up and would now be heard on July 31st, the last day of the legal year. Mick: "It's a great relief."

THURSDAY JULY 6th

Brian collapsed at the Hilton Hotel, suffering from "mental strain and severe exhaustion". He and Suki were admitted to the Priory Nursing Home, Roehampton where Brian underwent three weeks of treatment with psychiatrist, Dr Anthony Flood. Dr Flood later described him, on admittance, as "anxious, considerably depressed and potentially suicidal". Three weeks later, Brian's condition had improved. He checked out of the clinic, on the 24th, continuing to see Dr Flood about once a week.

FRIDAY 7th - SATURDAY JULY 22nd

The group returned to Olympic Studios with Glyn Johns. (Sessions booked 11pm - 5am.Keith was absent from some, while Brian attended the session on the 12th). The following songs were completed:-
"Acid In The Grass" (working title of Bill Wyman's "In Another Land", featuring Nicky Hopkins on piano and harpsichord. Bill and Charlie were the only Stones to turn up at the booked session on the 13th, so Bill seized the moment, roping in Small Face, Steve Marriott, from a neighbouring studio, to add guide backing vocals, which are audible on the finished master.)
"2000 Light Years From Home" (Brian on mellotron. Nicky Hopkins on piano)
"Sing This All Together" (both versions)
"Citadel" (alternate versions and arrangements, with Nicky Hopkins on piano)
"We Love You" (final overdubs, including a slamming cell door, from a BBC sound effects record)

THURSDAY JULY 27th

Brian left Heathrow to recuperate in Malaga, Spain, for 3 weeks with Suki Poitier and Nicky Browne, Tara Browne's widow. They stayed with Belgian artist, Phillip Mack.

SUNDAY JULY 30th

Mick, Keith and Marianne went to a disused church in Essex, with Peter Whitehead, to film a promotional film clip for "We Love You". Whitehead: "We filmed on a Sunday, not knowing whether they would go to jail on the Monday". It was Whitehead's idea to base the film on the "The Trials Of Oscar Wilde", (with the recent "... Butterfly On A Wheel" editorial in mind). Dressed in period costume, Mick played Wilde, replete with green carnation in his buttonhole, being sentenced while Marianne (hair hidden under a short wig) portrayed Lord Alfred Douglas ("Bosie", Wilde's friend), head bowed, in the witness box. Keith, resplendent in his 1967 finery, played The Marquess of Queensbury, complete with spectacles and a wig made up of rolled newspapers. To add a touch of irony, Bosie (Marianne) presented to the court a large fur rug, underneath which, a naked Mick emerged. At the editing stage, Whitehead added fast motion and double-exposure shots of the Stones, filmed at Olympic, during the recent sessions (see July 8th - 20th entry), as well as a 12 second extract of his footage from the Albert Hall concert (see Sept 23rd, 1966 entry). "Top Of The Pops" producer, Johnnie Stewart, viewed the film several times, finally deeming it unsuitable to screen, as he felt the courtroom scenes were ridiculing British justice. Instead, for the episode transmitted 24th August (between 7:30 - 8:00pm), the song was played over shots of the studio audience dancing, while pictures of the Stones were relayed over a studio screen. The film's world premiere (in colour) occurred on Munich's ZDF channel's "experimental weekend" of colour programming, on September 1st and received a monochrome screening during Show 23 of German NDR's "Beat Club", on August 26th. (It later reappeared, albeit in edited form, as part of Peter Cifton's "Popcorn: An Audio Visual Thing" film -see April 28th 1968 entry). During the last week of August, Whitehead started work on a revised version of the forbidden film (in a vain attempt to get it shown on "Top Of The Pops"), featuring scenes from the original film, being projected onto a woman's dancing hands, but the idea was abandoned before completion.

MONDAY JULY 31st

Mick and Keith appeared at the Law Courts, before Lord Parker, Lord Justice Winn and Mr Justice Cusack to appeal against their convictions

Brian and Suki in Marbella with Belgian artist, Phillip Mack

Above: Battersea Heliport, July 31st
Right: Faithful fans outside the Appeals court, July 31st

and sentences. (Robert Fraser lost his appeal on July 22nd and his sentence was upheld). To screams and cheers from the gallery, Mick received a twelve month conditional discharge, while Keith's conviction for allowing his house to be used for the purpose of smoking cannabis resin was quashed. (Keith had chicken pox and waited in the Crown Office for the verdict.) Lord Chief Justice, Lord Parker told Jagger: "Whether you like it or not, you are the idol of a large number of young people in this country and have very grave responsibilities. It is only natural that if you do commit another offence, it will carry a higher penalty because of those responsibilities." As the relieved pair left the court, Mick told waiting reporters: "I feel great!",while Keith quipped "I feel spotty!" When hearing the outcome of the appeals, in Marbella, Brian ordered a celebratory beer, saying "Thank God, justice has prevailed". At Heathrow, Paul McCartney (returning from Greece) commented: "I am always pleased about the idea of people not going to jail." Marianne waited at home, to hear the verdicts. Keith was driven directly to Heathrow by Tom Keylock, where he flew to Rome to join Anita on the film set of "Barbarella". A press conference, attended by Mick only, was held at Granada TV`s London Office in Soho (covered by BBC and ITN crews for news broadcasts that night on both stations). While Marianne posed for photographers outside, Mick replied to Lord Parker's address: "One doesn't ask for responsibilities. One is given responsibilities, when one is pushed into the limelight. My private life is my own responsibility. I simply ask for my private life to be left alone". Mick and Marianne were then whisked straight from the conference to Battersea Heliport, flying to Spains Hall, the home of Sir John Ruggles-Brise, near Ongar, Essex to appear in a "World in Action" special for Granada Television. While Marianne waited outside in a mini-

car, Mick was filmed in serious discussion with Lord Stow-Hill (a former Home Secretary), William Rees-Mogg, Dr John Robinson, The Bishop of Woolwich and Father Thomas Corbishley (a leading Jesuit priest). The programme (transmitted August 7th, between 8:00 - 8:30 pm) was directed by John Birt (now the current Head of BBC Television). Following the filming, the couple were flown back to Battersea Heliport.

FRIDAY AUGUST 4th

Mick was interviewed by Keith Altham of the NME, at Andrew Oldham's New Oxford Street office. During the session, Altham was played the new Stones single, "We Love You", backed by "Dandelion". Mick denied any Beatles involvement with the record (see May 12th entry).

SATURDAY AUGUST 5th

The Stones began lengthy sessions at Olympic (between 11pm - 5am), lasting (off and on) through to September 7th (to complete what would become "Their Satanic Majesties Request"). The recordings (with Nicky Hopkins on piano) included:-

"2000 Man"

"On With The Show"

"The Lantern"

"Gomper"

"Cosmic Christmas" (a 30-second oscillator arrangement of the traditional "We Wish You A Merry Xmas" carol, slowed down by Bill Wyman, which was included uncredited on the finished album.)

"Gold Painted Fingernails" (originally titled "Gold Painted Nails" when first attempted during the November 16th - December 5th sessions at Olympic, the previous year)

"Bathroom/Toilet" (possibly a working title).

FRIDAY 11th - MONDAY AUGUST 14th

Mick broke from recording to fly to Dublin, for a weekend with Marianne and Christopher Gibbs. On the 13th, they arrived uninvited at a party given by the Butler Society, in Kilkenny Castle. With them were Desmond Guiness and his wife. After twenty minutes of the cream of Irish society snubbing them, they made their excuses and left.

FRIDAY AUGUST 18th

"We Love You" B/W "Dandelion" was released in the U.K (reaching No.7) and "The Rolling Stones File", a "cash-in" paperback on the recent drugs trials, was published by Panther Books.

SATURDAY AUGUST 19th

"Disc" exclusively reported the Stones may do some free concerts in Britain, before Christmas. Mick: "People are offering us enormous amounts to play again, but if I do a show, I'd like to do it for nothing. I'd like to do a show where the kids don't have to pay for a change".

FRIDAY 25th - SUNDAY AUGUST 27th

Mick and Marianne went to Euston Station to join The Beatles and their wives in a Bank Holiday visit to the Teacher's Training College in Bangor, North Wales, for a seminar studying Transcendental Meditation given by the Maharishi Mahesh Yogi. (The visit was cut short by the news of Brian Epstein's death, on the 27th). Mick returned unconvinced: "Maybe he is the reincarnation of the Buddha for all I know. I never really got into it that much…"

FRIDAY SEPTEMBER 1st

Keith arrived home from Rome, (where he had been visiting Anita), while Brian flew out to Amsterdam to meet the Maharishi and then on to Libya for a holiday. Andrew Oldham flew to New York to discuss possible promotion for the BBC-banned "We Love You" film.

SATURDAY SEPTEMBER 2nd

The N.M.E reported that Mick and Marianne had £1,000 worth of clothing and jewellery stolen from their London home.

SUNDAY SEPTEMBER 3rd

Brian struck fear into the heart of the aviation industry, when his intention to apply for a pilot's licence, was reported.

TUESDAY 5th - THURSDAY SEPTEMBER 7th

The final sessions at Olympic, for "Satanic Majesties", after which Mick and Marianne went to Amsterdam and Paris, Keith flew back to Rome to rejoin Anita on the film set, while Brian went to Spain.

FRIDAY SEPTEMBER 8th

Bill continued work at Olympic (with Glyn Johns), producing The End. The session produced the single: "Loving Sacred Loving" B/W "Shades Of Orange", released on Decca, on March 8th, 1968. (Nicky Hopkins played harpsichord on Side A, while none other than Charlie Watts played tabla on Side B). (See also Sept 1969 entry).

WEDNESDAY SEPTEMBER 13th

Mick flew to New York from Heathrow (after flying in from Paris, in the morning), for four days of business talks. The other Stones had flown out earlier in the day (with Michael Cooper) and had been detained half an hour by immigration officials, questioning Keith's status. Mick received the same treatment, when he arrived. Both were ordered to appear at the I.N.S. the following morning. ("We Love You" currently stood at No 86 in the "Billboard" chart, while "Dandelion" leapt 33 places to No 42.)

THURSDAY SEPTEMBER 14th

Mick and Keith appeared before immigration officers in Broadway, who asked them about their recent drugs trials in England. (Brian and Michael Cooper were also present). The group later had a long business meeting with Allen Klein at his Broadway office. Following the meeting, Mick and Michael Cooper visited Mt. Vernon in New York to supervise the 3-D sleeve production at Pictorial Productions Limited (this being the only factory, aside from a plant in Tokyo, where 3-D images could be manufactured). First estimates for the sleeves were set at $50,000 (as the 3-D plastic images would cost $1 apiece to make). In a 2-part interview for "Disc", Bill was quoted:-"If 'We Love You' doesn't make No 1, I don`t think we'll worry. After all, if The Beatles "Penny Lane" can't make it- what can?". He also went on to talk about "In Another Land": "Mick said that, as I'd written it, I could damn well sing it!".

SUNDAY SEPTEMBER 17th

After persuading a costumier's in Manhattan to open especially, for the group to choose their regalia, Michael Cooper took the front sleeve picture (for "Satanic Majesties"), at a nearby warehouse, using an expensive Japanese 3-D Polaroid. The group had pitched in to help create the artificial surroundings, which took 3 days to construct. The Beatles heads peered from the shrubbery as a reciprocal "Thank You" for the doll seen wearing a Rolling Stones T-shirt, on their "Sgt. Peppers Lonely Hearts Club Band" sleeve (also photographed by Cooper on March 30th).

FRIDAY SEPTEMBER 29th

The Rolling Stones office confirmed that, after months of rumour and speculation, they had parted company with their original producer/manager, Andrew Oldham. (For the near future, they would produce their own records. Mick also ceased production for Immediate Records).

OCTOBER

The group made a colour promotional film for "2000 Light Years From Home", directed by Peter Clifton, at Kevin Brownjohn's (who had designed the film titles for "Goldfinger" amongst others) studio. The group mimed to the song (with Brian on mellotron), against a backdrop of changing hues of red, green and blue (with shots of their faces in close profile). All of the group were dressed in their standard 1967 garb, the exceptions being Charlie who wore outsized glasses and a beaded cowl over his head (!), while Mick sported facial paint and Egyptian headgear. The resulting film received one of it's few screenings (in monochrome) during Show 29 of German NDR TV's "Beat Club", on March 9th, 1968 and in colour, as part of Peter Clifton's "Popcorn-An Audio Visual Thing" (see April 28th 1968 entry). Clifton also took the

the Costa Del Sol in Spain, to relax and get in shapee, in the run-up to his court appearance, returning on the 29th.

FRIDAY OCTOBER 27th

"Disc" quoted Mick that there were no plans to replace Brian, nor would the group break up, should he be imprisoned. He also revealed that the group were considering touring the following year. "It won't be the usual Rolling Stones sort of tour. We won't be doing any more of those. But we do want to do something really different, visiting everywhere we can. It wouldn't even be a concert hall tour, in the sense of the word, either. More than that I can't say at the moment."

SUNDAY OCTOBER 29th

Mick flew out to Frankfurt, to visit Marianne on the "Girl On A Motorcycle" set, returning to London the following day, to fly to New York with Keith, for further business discussions, with Allen Klein.

MONDAY OCTOBER 30th

Brian and Prince Stanislas Klossowski de Rola appeared in the dock at

Below: Departing for New York, September 13th

opportunity to interview Mick on the set, (filmed in black and white) also for inclusion in "Popcorn" (see Jan 1968 entry).

THURSDAY OCTOBER 5th

Keith flew to Rome to visit Anita.

FRIDAY OCTOBER 6th

Mick flew to Geneva, to visit Marianne on the "Girl On A Motorcycle" film set.

MONDAY OCTOBER 9th

Keith was backstage at the Jimi Hendrix Experience concert at the L'Olympia, Paris.

FRIDAY OCTOBER 13th

P.P Arnold's Immediate album "The First Lady Of Immediate" was released, with three tracks ("Am I Still Dreaming?", "Treat Me Like A Lady" and "Though It Hurts Me Badly") produced by Mick.

SUNDAY OCTOBER 15th

"The People" newspaper announced: "The Beatles and The Rolling Stones are planning to get together on a business venture." (projects which never got beyond the discussion stage included a joint London studio, to record unknown artists and the possibility of making films together.) Les Perrin issued a press statement on the 17th: "In view of the statement made over the weekend, but not emanating from the Rolling Stones, that a business merger between them and the Beatles is imminent, it is felt that the position should be clarified. Mr Mick Jagger states that preparatory conversations of a purely exploratory nature were held between himself and Mr Paul McCartney. Discussed was the possibility or advisability, of opening a recording studio, at some unspecified future date. These conversations have not been resolved and any assumption to the contrary should be considered premature."

THURSDAY OCTOBER 20th

After a motoring holiday around the West Country, Brian flew out to

Inner London Sessions, before Mr R.E Seaton, both having been remanded on charges of possessing cannabis and methedine. The prosecution offered no evidence against "Stash", as being a resident in Switzerland, he was only a guest in Jones flat and no drugs had been found on him when searched. Brian pleaded guilty to permitting his flat at Courtfield Road, West Kensington, to be used for smoking cannabis and to unlawfully possessing a quantity of cannabis resin. He denied two charges of unlawfully possessing methedine and cocaine and these pleas were accepted by the prosecution. In a plea of mitigation, Brian's counsel, James Comyn QC, asked that he should not be sent to prison. "He has instructed me to say he had never taken hard drugs. As for cannabis, he will cut it out completely. It has never helped him solve any problems. In fact, it had created problems. He says that no one should take an example from him. He has never peddled or pushed drugs and never carried them around. But he has had many people at his flat, who have smoked cannabis and he sometimes has smoked it himself." He described Brian as "a young man with a brilliant career", who was a versatile musician, playing many instruments and winning fame as a composer. Dr. Leonard Henry, Brian's psychiatrist, when asked what effect the possible likelihood of a prison sentence would have on him, replied: "I have reached the conclusion that it would completely destroy his mental health. He would go into a psychotic depression as he could not possibly stand the stigma of a prison sentence and he might well attempt to injure himself." Brian was then called to the witness box. In answer to his counsel, he said he very much wanted to go on with his composing, that he intended to have nothing more to do with drugs and admitted he had been very lax on those "very rare occasions" when cannabis had been smoked at his flat. The court then adjourned, while Brian waited 90 minutes in a room below the court for the chairman's decision. When court re-opened, he was brought back to the dock. Mr Seaton told him that he had given the case "very careful and anxious consideration. The offence of permitting your premises to be used for smoking cannabis to which you have pleaded guilty is a very serious one. It means that people can break the law in comparative privacy and avoid detection of what is a growing canker in this country at the moment... I have listened to what has been said by your counsel. You occupy a position by which you have a large following of youth and it behoves you to set an example. You have broken down on that. I should be failing in my duty if I did not indicate the seriousness of the offence by passing a sentence of imprisonment." To cries of "Oh no, no" from the gallery, Brian was sentenced to nine months imprisonment for allowing his flat to be used for smoking cannabis and three months for possessing a quantity of cannabis (the sentences to run concurrently). He was also ordered to pay 250 guineas towards the prosecution costs. Notice of appeal against sentence was immediately given, but Mr Seaton refused an application for bail. Half an hour later, Brian was driven in a prison van, past his silver Rolls-Royce, on the way to Wormwood Scrubs.

The news was phoned through to Mick and Keith, in New York. Fans demonstrated in the Kings Road for nearly two hours, handing out "Release" leaflets, near The Worlds End pub, with several being arrested (including Chris Jagger, who was charged with obstructing the police, using abusive behaviour and damaging a police van). Others arrested included "underground" luminaries Suzy Creamcheese and Caroline Coon.

TUESDAY OCTOBER 31st
Brian left Wormwood Scrubs in the evening, after a successful High Court application in Chambers, by his counsel, Mr Peter Howard. He was released on £750 bail pending appeal against sentence. After leaving the prison, Howard and a relieved Brian stopped for a drink at The White Horse, in Longford, Middlesex.

WEDNESDAY NOVEMBER 1st
Chris Jagger, appeared at Marlborough Street Magistrates Court and was released on £25 bail (see Oct 30th entry). The Stones office issued a statement saying the group would continue as a four-piece if Brian had to have medical treatment. Allen Klein issued a statement saying "There is absolutely no question of bringing in a replacement".

MONDAY NOVEMBER 13th
Bill and Asrid flew to New York for a week's holiday.

SATURDAY NOVEMBER 18th
"Melody Maker" reported on Judge Leslie Block's recent "sub-judice" remarks about the Rolling Stones, during an after-dinner speech, he was giving to farmers at Rudgewick, Sussex. "We did our best, your fellow countrymen, I and my fellow magistrates, to cut those Stones down to size, but alas, it was not to be because the Court of Criminal Appeal let them roll free". A spokesman told the paper: "All the group are angry about these remarks. We have asked for a transcript of the speech to pass on to the group's legal advisers. We are making no comments because Brian Jones' case is still sub-judice." The NME printed the full track listing for the new album (the first to be completely produced by the band, provisionally titled at this stage "Her Satanic Majesty Requests and Requires", a pun on the wording of a British passport). The same issue revealed how the group fared in the end-of-year polls:-
Mick was 19th in the "World Male Vocalist" poll with 112 votes and The Stones, 4th in the "World Male Vocal Group" poll with 448 votes.

SATURDAY NOVEMBER 25th
"Their Satanic Majesties Request" album was released in America (already having reached Gold Record status), in a lavish 3-D gatefold sleeve (which cost Decca/London £10,000 in total, for production and design). "In Another Land" (a 2:48 edit, credited solely to "Bill Wyman") B/W "The Lantern" was extracted from the album as an American single (reaching No.64).

THURSDAY NOVEMBER 30th
Mick, Brian and Charlie visited the studios of BBC Radio One to appear on the programme "Top Gear", hosted by Tommy Vance (produced by

Above and below: "Top Gear" with Bernie Andrews and Tommy Vance, November 30th

Bernie Andrews). The three took over the last half hour of the two hour show, promoting and playing selected tracks from the new album. Mick described them as "mid tempo shufflers" and "dirgy knee-tappers" and that "Brian played almost every instrument on the album". (Contrary to popular belief, Brian contributed much to this album, but little to the next, "Beggars Banquet".) The programme was broadcast between 2:00 - 5:00 pm on Sunday, December 3rd, five days before the album's U.K release.

SATURDAY DECEMBER 9th

In the N.M.E, "Satanic" Mick, interviewed by Keith Altham (who the previous week had described the album as "a trip to infinity between the stars and beyond!"), revealed the group had made a 15 minute colour promotional film for the album. In America, a second single from the album, "She's A Rainbow" B/W "2000 Light Years From Home" was released (reaching No.10, in the Billboard Hot Hundred).

SUNDAY DECEMBER 10th

Brian and Jimi Hendrix went to see The Moody Blues at the Speakeasy.

TUESDAY DECEMBER 12th

Brian was at the Court of Appeals, before Lord Parker. His counsel, James Comyn talked of Brian's suffering since sentencing (see Oct 30th entry), "which cannot be removed and may be regarded as penalty enough". Three psychiatrists then gave evidence for Brian. Dr Anthony Flood, who had treated Brian (see July 6th entry), described him as "an extremely frightened young man…", "I think if one put a reefer within half a mile of Brian Jones, he would start running", adding that a prison sentence would be "disastrous". Dr Leonard Henry told the court he had seen Jones eight times, during the year and considered him "a very emotional and unstable person who, in circumstances not intolerable to a less neurotic personality, might well make an attempt on his life". Dr. Walter Neustatter told of four interviews with Jones: "He came in most extraordinary clothes which one could only describe as flamboyant. I think he had gold trousers and something which looked like a fur rug". Asked about his outfit, Jones said "uniformity in males rather frightened him". After a twenty-minute retirement with Lord Justice Edmund Davies and Mr Justice Widgery, Lord Parker set aside the prison sentence and Brian was fined £1,000 and put on three years probation, with a condition that he continued to receive psychiatric treatment under the direction of Dr Flood, Lord Parker told him: "Remember, this is a degree of mercy, which the court has shown. It is not a let-off. You cannot go boasting, saying you have been let off. You are still under the control of the court. If you fail to co-operate with the probation officer or Dr Flood, or you commit another offence of any sort, you will be brought back and punished afresh for this offence and you know the sort of punishment you will get." After Brian was released, he spent some time in a court official's room, talking to Mr.Comyn, his probation officer, Dr Flood and Mick, who, on the way to the Law Courts, was involved in a brawl, when his chauffeured Aston Martin was involved in a near collision with a Mercedes. Brian then left to be driven to his dentist, as he had been suffering a raging toothache, during the two hour hearing. A press conference was cancelled, with a spokesman making the statement: "Brian is very mindful of what the Lord Chief Justice said and because of this is saying nothing." Brian paused long enough to say: "I am very happy to have my freedom." Mick added: "We are all pleased he is free. All we want to do now is put it behind us and get down to some hard work."

THURSDAY DECEMBER 14th

Brian collapsed at his flat, after an evening at the Middle Earth club in Covent Garden and was taken to St. George's Hospital. "There is no cause for alarm. He is just tired and suffering from over-strain. He has also had some teeth out" a doctor told waiting journalists. Within an hour, Brian discharged himself, telling stunned doctors "I'm going home".

SATURDAY DECEMBER 16th

Norman Jopling, in "Record Mirror", gave "Their Satanic Majesties Request" one of it`s few positive reviews, calling it "the best album by far that The Rolling Stones have ever recorded", while in the same issue, a telegram from the States to Sir Edward Lewis (head of Decca Records) was reproduced, proclaiming "It's not a hit, it`s an epidemic!!", in view of sales for the new LP totalling 470,000 to date. (An estimated $2,500,000 worth of copies were sold by Christmas.)

WEDNESDAY DECEMBER 20th

The group visited the BBC's Lime Grove Studios in London, to record an appearance for "Top Of The Pops". For a fee of £183.15 shillings, they mimed to "2000 Light Years From Home", included in the December 28th edition (BBC1 7:30 - 8:00 pm). During the afternoon rehearsals, Mick was interviewed for his views on the music scene of 1967. The brief interview, along with comments from other contemporary artists, such as Jimi Hendrix, was featured in "Top Of The Pops '67" Part One, transmitted Christmas Day (BBC 1, 2:05 - 3:00 pm). Meanwhile, the end of year NME Polls for 1967 revealed that:-

Mick was 16th in the "World Male Singer" section with 602 votes.
The Rolling Stones were 4th in the "World Vocal Group" section with 1626 votes.
1st in the "British R & B Group" section with 8428 votes.
2nd in the "British Vocal Group" section with 3420 votes.
Mick and Marianne spent Christmas in Barbados and South America. Keith and Anita flew to Paris, en route to Tangier and Marrakesh, Bill and Astrid went to Sweden, while Brian spent the festive season, in Ceylon with Linda Keith.

Brian at the Court of Appeals, December 12th

THEIR SATANIC MAJESTIES REQUEST

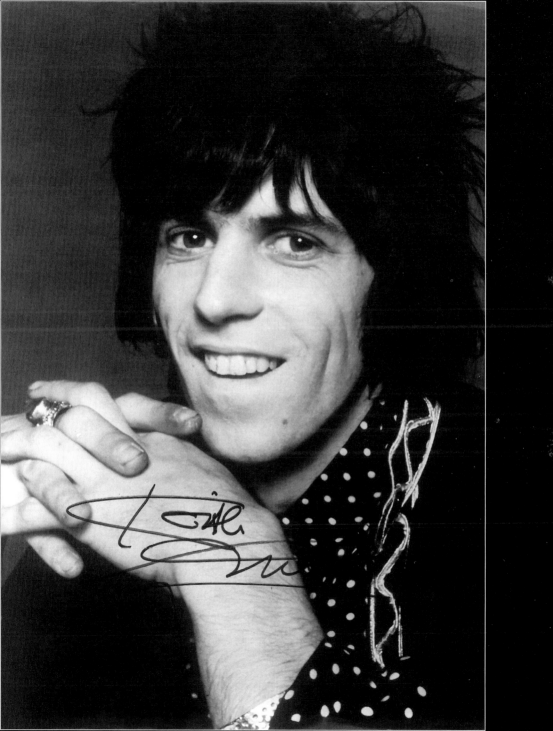

JANUARY

Mick, Marianne and Nicholas, went on holiday to the Bahamas, staying at the Emerald Beach Hotel, in Nassau, before going onto the island resort of Eleutherer. Mick was also interviewed (exact date/location unknown) for the second time (see Oct 1967 entry), by documentary filmmaker, Peter Clifton, (in black and white), for inclusion in his documentary "Popcorn: An Audio Visual Thing". Dressed in a trendy "haircoat" and black hat, he discussed whether or not, the Stones had progressed within the current pop scene.

THURSDAY JANUARY 4th

"The Daily Sketch" reported that U.C.L.A. were insisting that "students taking a degree in music, must study The Rolling Stones".

THURSDAY JANUARY 18th

Brian attended a launch given for the band, Grapefruit. The party, held at the Hanover Grand, in Hanover Street, was also attended by Beatles John, Paul and Ringo, (Terry Doran of Apple Publishing had discovered them, making the group the Beatles first signing to Apple), Cilla Black and Donovan. Also, this month, Brian, Mick and Marianne attended The Duke of Bedford's party for The Supremes, at John Bull's in the Kings Road, Chelsea (both Stones were sporting beards).

SATURDAY JANUARY 20th

Brian (and "Stash" Klossowski) joined Paul McCartney in the recording studio to add saxophone to tracks for the "McGough and McGear" album. Others present included:-Jimi Hendrix, Graham Nash, Dave Mason and Zoot Money.

SUNDAY JANUARY 21st

Brian attended a Jimi Hendrix Experience session at Olympic Studios, where "All Along The Watchtower" was being recorded.

FRIDAY JANUARY 26th

Brian went back to Olympic Studios for a Jimi Hendrix Experience session, playing sitar on two takes of "Little One" (unreleased).

SUNDAY FEBRUARY 4th

Mick went to the ABC TV studios in Teddington to make a solo appearance on "The Eamonn Andrews Show". The programme was transmitted between 11:15 pm-12 midnight across the ITV network (11:05 - 11:50 pm across certain ITV regions).

MONDAY FEBRUARY 5th

The Rolling Stones new office premises opened at 46a Maddox Street, Mayfair.

WEDNESDAY FEBRUARY 28th -
THURSDAY MARCH 14th

While Brian celebrated his 26th birthday in Paris, the group (with Stu) commenced two weeks of solid rehearsal at R.G Jones studio, in Morden, Surrey, with new American producer, Jimmy Miller (who they had met the previous year, while he was producing Traffic at Olympic Studios) and Glyn Johns. (Bill was absent from some sessions also). Amongst the jams (with Mick on guitar), preserved on tape, were:-

"I'll Be Coming Home"

"No Expectations" (working version)

"Stray Cat Blues" (working version)

"Rock Me Baby" (Howlin' Wolf)

"Shoot My Baby" (Jimmy Reed)

"Hold On, I'm A-Comin' " (Sam and Dave)

"Jumping Jack Flash" (working version).

SATURDAY MARCH 9th

"Disc" reported that The Rolling Stones had agreed to act as "working sponsors" of the first European International Pop Festival in Rome (between May 4th-10th) in aid of orphans and young victims of the Vietnam War. Mick had written to the festival committee promising the Stones "advice, aid and assistance" in publicising and staging the event. In the same issue, Mick reviewed The Beatles new single Lady Madonna: "It could have been groovier if Paul had done it like "Long Tall Sally", but the words are very nice. In fact, the words are the best part. But I feel it is too relaxed, with not enough excitement." Jimmy Miller was also interviewed:- "At the moment, I'm increasing the atmosphere for them and at the same time, doing a little subtle coaxing. With luck, we'll have the album and possibly a single ready around the end of March or early April."

FRIDAY 15th - SUNDAY MARCH 31st

The group block booked sessions at Olympic Sound Studios, with Jimmy Miller and Glyn Johns, working from 7pm to 8am, without a break. The following tracks had reached the recording stage (with Mick on guitar for the first time):-

Above: Brian at the Grapefruit party, January 19th, with the Beatles, Donovan and Cilla Black, (Below) with Jimi Hendrix and girlfriend Kathy Etchingham.

"Jumping Jack Flash"

"Family" (various versions)

"Parachute Woman"

"Jigsaw Puzzle"

"Child Of The Moon" (two versions; the first with "country" piano and acoustic guitar. At Keith's insistence, it was re-made as the finished version)

"Primo Grande" (early version of "Did Everybody Pay Their Dues?", the backing track recorded on a Phillip's cassette machine, with Charlie playing a child's toy drum, transferred from 4-track onto 8-track tape and subject to overdubs - see May 13th entry). This track would eventually become "Street Fighting Man" (see May 4th entry).

The session on March 31st, ran from midnight to 9am, making Mick miss the opening night of Marianne Faithfull's new play "Early Morning" at London's Royal Court Theatre. (He eventually saw it on April 14th).

SATURDAY MARCH 16th

After an all-night session at Olympic (on the 15th), Brian returned to find the police (acting on a tip-off) at his flat in Chesham Street, Belgravia. They had smashed the door down to get to his girlfriend, Linda Keith, who had collapsed, after taking an overdose of tranquillisers. She was taken to St. George's Hospital, where her condition "seemed to be satisfactory". The same afternoon, the landlord called the police to have Brian removed, with his clothes and equipment still inside the flat. (Brian stayed temporarily at the Imperial Hotel, Queensgate.)

SUNDAY MARCH 17th

Mick was among the estimated 10,000 anti-Vietnam war demonstraters, outside the American Embassy, in Grosvenor Square. He eventually retreated when recognised. The experience helped shape "Street Fighting Man" (see May 13th - 21st entry). During the late-night Olympic session, Charlie's wife Shirley went into labour and on the 18th, their daughter Seraphina was born.

APRIL

Mick and Marianne went on a caravan holiday to Ireland, Keith and

Anita, to Rome, while Brian flew to Spain.

SUNDAY APRIL 28th

The group were at Olympic Studios to film two alternate colour promotional films for their forthcoming single, "Jumping Jack Flash", with director, Michael Lindsay-Hogg, hired for a fee of £670. The two films were largely the same (a dark back-dropped studio with the band miming to a pre-taped backing track), except for minor differences. The more widely seen Version One, opened with Mick, face adorned with war paint, walking slowly towards the camera (through a gap in the studio setting). His vocals were performed straight to camera. Brian and Keith wore dark glasses. (Brian's face was given a light-green covering to match his green frames). Both Bill and Charlie wore dark eye make-up; Bill's face painted white while Charlie wore a triangular Indian symbol on his forehead. Version Two featured similar camera shots, the major difference being the group were wearing different clothing (Mick; a glittery jacket, Brian and Keith without shades) and no distinctive facial make-up. Mick: "The song "Jumping Jack Flash" was made a hit by the film we did to promote it. Straight performance, nothing else, no freakin' about on the heath and that whole trip. That was what really helped the record, made it commercial, 'cos it was shown all over the world." The first version went on to receive numerous TV showings, including three broadcasts on BBC TV's "Top Of The Pops", transmitted May 23rd, June 6th and Part One of the end-of-year "Best of '68" on Christmas Day (all BBC1 7:30 - 8:00pm). Although shot in colour, the transmissions were in monochrome. ("Top Of The Pops" was not shown in colour until November 27th, 1969). On the June 27th edition, the film was not shown. Instead, still pictures of the Stones faces were superimposed, over the Go-Jo's dancing. For each screening, the BBC paid £52.10 shillings. (The BBC also requested and received, a 16mm copy of the "Child Of The Moon" film -see May 11th entry- for inclusion on "Top Of The Pops", but it was never screened). All dealings for the film's screenings were handled by Sandford Lieberson of "Creative Management Associates", London. The "Jumping Jack Flash" film (in colour) was given another lease of life, when it was featured, (alongside the films for "Have You Seen You Mother, Baby...?", "We Love You", "2000 Light Years From Home", and two exclusive interviews with Mick - see Oct.1967 & Jan.1968 entries), in the 1968 Peter Clifton film "Popcorn-An Audio Visual Thing", a pot-pourri of pop images, shot by various filmmakers. Following the film shoot at Olympic, Brian visited the Revolution Club, Mayfair to see the Ike and Tina Turner Revue perform.

THURSDAY MAY 2nd

Brian moved into flat No.15 at Royal Avenue House, Kings Road, Chelsea, rented from Lord Eliot. The previous tenant had been actress Joanna Pettet, who had moved out earlier in the day. Later, Brian went to Cornwall for the weekend. The press also reported that Mick had bought a house at 48 Cheyne Walk, overlooking Chelsea Bridge, and a £25,000 mansion, "Stargroves", in Newbury, Berkshire.

Mick at the "Jumping Jack Flash" promo shoot, April 28th

SATURDAY MAY 4th

"Disc" reported that the new Rolling Stones single (to be released May 26th) would be the Jagger/Richard composition: "Did Everybody Pay Their Dues?" The track (featuring Dave Mason playing flute and members of Family on backing vocals) was cut at a midnight session, three weeks previous at Olympic, with producer, Jimmy Miller. "We were invited down by Jimmy Miller. Keith and Mick just told us what they wanted and we got together and did it. The track is slightly influenced by the Stones old style, but with a new approach."
The London "underground" newspaper "International Times" published an interview with Mick, conducted at the time of the anti-Vietnam War demonstrations outside the American Embassy in Grosvenor Square, in which he took part (see March 17th entry). Mick's experiences on "the frontline", his interest in the month's Paris student riots and the realisation that his celebrity couldn't affect change directly ("What can a poor boy do, except to sing for a rock and roll band?"), inspired him to write a set of rabble-rousing lyrics, which when married to the completed backing track of "Did Everybody Pay Their Dues?", became "Street Fighting Man". ("Did Everybody Pay Their Dues?" was added to the growing stockpile of unreleased Stones offcuts.)

TUESDAY MAY 7th

Kenneth Hyman, executive vice-president of Warner Brothers-Seven Arts (in charge of Worldwide Productions), announced in a press release: "Mick Jagger has been signed to make his motion picture dramatic acting debut in "The Performers"(sic), starring opposite James Fox. Shooting is scheduled to begin in and around London locations in mid- July".

WEDNESDAY MAY 8th

Jimmy Miller flew to New York, to complete editing on the new single.

SATURDAY MAY 11th

The group (with several extra's) ventured into the Surrey countryside, to film a surrealistic, rarely seen promotional film for "Child Of The Moon". The film, shot in colour on 16-mm film, centred around a village pathway, where individuals of different ages, encountered the Stones, dressed gypsy-style, blocking their passage. The film was again directed and produced by Michael Lindsay-Hogg and Sanford Lieberson, respectively. (See April 28th entry.) Film out-takes survive featuring longer profile shots of each Stone, re-takes and aerial shots of the band in position and a rejected scene, involving Mick lip-synching the song's lyrics. To date, only a mere few seconds have been publicly seen, namely in Tony Palmer's 1968 BBC-2 documentary, "All My Loving" and in the Stones own official rockumentary, "25 X 5" (1989).

SUNDAY MAY 12th

The group made their first British live appearance in eighteen months (and Brian's last) at the "NME Poll Winners" concert at the Empire Pool, Wembley, as the surprise finale'. As the group took the stage, the 10,000 crowd were silent in amazement at first, but then went wild as the group started to play. They performed: "Jumping Jack Flash" and "Satisfaction" (during which, Mick threw his white shoes into the audience). In the front row, a delighted Marianne threw red roses onto the stage. The show, which would be the last of the annual concerts, was hosted by DJ's, Jimmy Savile and Tony Blackburn and also featured: Status Quo, Don Partridge, The Love Affair, The Showstoppers, The Association, The Paper Dolls, The Breakaways, Lulu, Amen Corner, The Herd, The Tremeloes, The Move, Dusty Springfield, Scott Walker, The Bee Gees, Cliff Richard and The Shadows and Dave Dee, Dozy, Beaky, Mick and Tich (who closed the show following the awards). Backstage, Mick was ecstatic: "It was just like old times. In fact, it was better than old times- one of the best receptions we have ever got. We were all delighted. We intended doing "Jumping Jack Flash" only and then just accept our Poll Award (voted "Best R & B Group" for the fifth year running, the award presented by Roger Moore), unless there was a worthwhile reaction, in which case, we would also do "Satisfaction". We played "Satisfaction!". Les Perrin: "They're back - bigger than ever before!". Although ABC-TV had stopped covering the annual event in 1966, the Southern ITV show "Time For Blackburn" (hosted by Tony Blackburn), covered the event in a fifteen minute segment, with clips of the groups live (including "Jumping Jack Flash"), the award presentations and interviews (including Mick) backstage. The show, produced by Mike Mansfield was transmitted across Southern ITV regions only, on Saturday, May 18th between 5:50 - 6:14pm and also featured music from Scott Walker, Sandie Shaw and Paul Jones. The band returned to Olympic Studios for another midnight to dawn session, after the event.

Mick with Roger Moore, NME Pollwinners concert, May 12th

MONDAY 13th - TUESDAY MAY 21st

Olympic Studios sessions with Jimmy Miller and Glyn Johns, commencing or completing work on:-

"No Expectations"

"Blood Red Wine"

"Street Fighting Man" (retitled from "Did Everybody Pay Their Dues?" - see March 15th entry-) with a new vocal from Mick, Brian on tamboura and additional guitar from ex-Traffic's Dave Mason.

"Stray Cat Blues"

"Sister Morphine" (early version of the jointly composed Mick, Keith and Marianne song, without Ry Cooder's slide overdubs)

"Memo From Turner" (various demos, including Traffic members Steve Winwood and Jim Capaldi. A re-cut slower version, with Ry Cooder on slide, taped at R.C.A - see July 5th-25th entry, was later used in the film "Performance")

"Factory Girl" (Rick Grech, from Family, on fiddle)

"Love In Vain" (Robert Johnson) (early version)

"Downtown Suzie" (a Bill Wyman comp.)

"Dear Doctor"

"Prodigal Son" (Rev. Robert Wilkins)

"Salt Of The Earth" (a street choir from Watts, Los Angeles were overdubbed, during the final sessions at R.C.A - see July 4th-25th entry)

"You Got The Silver" (Mick on vocal)

"Hamburger To Go" (A/K/A "Stuck Out All Alone")

"I'm A Country Boy"

Above: A harassed Brian leaves court, May 21st

Below: Mick and Jean Luc-Godard during the "One plus One" filming, June 4th

"Lady" (possibly a working title)
"Silver Blanket"
"Still A Fool" (Muddy Waters).

WEDNESDAY MAY 15th

Brian and Mick, went to the BBC studios of Radio One, to record interview material. Firstly, Brian only, was interviewed by host, Johnny Moran for his weekly show, "Scene And Heard". Brian recorded up to 40 minutes of interview material, that would feature in three future shows (that night's, plus the May 18th and July 17th editions all between 6:32 - 7:30 pm). Brian and Mick were then interviewed jointly by John Peel, for "Top Gear" (transmitted May 19th between 2:00 pm - 4:00 pm). Asked if "Jumping Jack Flash" was the obvious choice for a single, Mick replied: "We didn't do it as a single. We are over halfway through the new album and it was difficult picking which track should be the new single, because they are all quite good for singles."

THURSDAY MAY 16th

All five Stones, plus wives and girlfriends, went to see Stanley Kubrick's "2001: A Space Odyssey" at the Casino Cinerama, in Gerrard Street.

TUESDAY MAY 21st

At 7:20 am, a raid was carried out at Brian's rented flat at Royal Avenue House, in the Kings Road. For ten minutes, four police officers (including a woman detective) rang the bell and knocked repeatedly, finally gaining access via a refuse hatch. They found Brian, just returned from an all-night session at Olympic, in the bedroom, wearing a dressing gown, dialling his lawyer. Asked why he had not answered the door, Jones said: "You know the scene, man. Why do I always get bugged?!" He was taken to the living room, which was being searched. In the top drawer of a bureau, a ball of wool was found, on top of a Stones album, containing an amount of cannabis resin. Brian was shown the ball of wool and before it was opened, exclaimed: "Oh no! This cannot happen again just when we were getting on to our feet." Asked if the ball of wool was his, he replied "It could be". He was taken to Chelsea police station and formally charged. "I never take this stuff. It makes me so irate", he protested. Brian later appeared, pale-faced and unshaven, at Marlborough Street Court, charged under his full name of "Lewis Brian Jones, 26, a musician", with possessing an unknown quantity of cannabis. He was released on bail to June 11th, on his own recognisance of £1,000 and with a surety of £1,000 by the Stones accountant, Frederick Trowbridge. A crowd of 100 waited outside, but Brian left court via the backyard, slumped, with hand over face, in the back of a chauffeur-driven Humber. He was driven directly to the Priory, in Roehampton, for a few days rest.

FRIDAY MAY 24th

"Jumping Jack Flash" B/W "Child Of The Moon" was released. "Disc" reported that Mick may star in a movie adaptation of a mad Welsh fairy tale, "Mobinogion", specially re-written for the screen by Spencer Davis and also to feature John Lennon, Donovan, Arthur Brown and Pete Townshend and Keith Moon of The Who.

Jumpin' Jack Flash
Rolling Stones

released 24 May   produced by Jimmy Miller   b/w 'Child of the Moon'   F12782

The Decca Record Company Limited   Decca House   Albert Embankment   London SE1

DECCA

45 rpm record

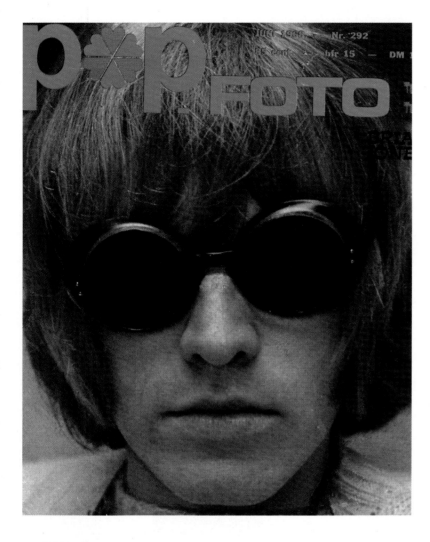

SUNDAY MAY 26th

Charlie, in an un-accustomed solo role, visited the BBC TV Centre, Wood Lane, for an appearance on the late-night arts/entertainment programme "Late Night Line -Up". He was interviewed, by presenter Joan Bakewell. Camera rehearsals took place at 3pm, with the finished interview being included in the show transmitted later that night between 11:20pm -12:05 am on BBC 2.

MONDAY MAY 27th

Plans to start shooting the Jean Luc-Godard film, "One Plus One" were postponed due to Brian's drug bust. (Work commenced June 4th). With some free time, Mick, Marianne and Nicholas went to Ireland for a short break.

FRIDAY MAY 31st

The group held a press call, at their offices at 46a Maddox Street, Mayfair, to promote "Jumping Jack Flash".

TUESDAY 4th - TUESDAY JUNE 11th

The group continued work at Olympic Studios with French "nouvelle vague" director Jean-Luc Godard's cameras filming them for his "One Plus One" movie (produced by Cupid Films). It was his first film in

English and dealt with the parallel themes of construction and destruction. (Destruction was typified by a love triangle which ended in death, while construction was illustrated by the Stones recording a new song in the studio.) With this synopsis, the eavesdropping cameras caught the evolution in process of "Sympathy For The Devil", from it's simple sparse acoustic beginnings (as "The Devil Is My Name", inspired by Mikhail Bulgakov's "The Master and Margarita", a novel Marianne had given to Mick) through to the final samba-flavoured master. The idea for the "whoo whoo" chorus apparently came from Jimmy Miller. "When I started going "whoo whoo" in the control room, so did they" Miller recalled. "I had the engineer set up a mike, so they could go out in the studio and "whoo whoo". (They being Keith, Anita, Brian, Suki Poitier, Bill, Charlie, Glyn Johns and Nicky Hopkins.) At the editing stages, this fascinating footage was intercut with non-related scenes of black revolutionaries executing three white women in a car dump, while their leader Frankie Dymon, spouted Eldridge Cleaver (the leader of the Black Panthers) propaganda, the inside of a seedy pornographic bookshop, an unknown actress being interviewed while walking through a forest and a graffitist scrawling slogans on everything in sight. (see Nov. 29th entry). While filming a late-night session on the final day (11th), a fire broke out at approximately 4:15am. The group, Marianne and film technicians ran for safety when the roof of the studio burst into flames and started to collapse, causing thousands of pounds worth of damage. Mick: "It was a pretty fantastic blaze. It was a good job it was the roof. We saw it coming. The fire brigade were so thorough that our Hammond organ and all the electrical equipment, was completely drenched" (causing some scenes to be re-shot). Even Charlie was moved enough to comment: "It was bloody frightening!" The tapes were salvaged by Bill Wyman and Jimmy Miller. Meanwhile, "Jumping Jack Flash" was at No.1 (their first since "Paint It Black" two years previous. In America, it stalled at No.3.) During the sessions on the 6th, Mick was interviewed by John Peel for BBC Radio One's "Top Gear" (broadcast on June 9th between 3:00 pm - 5:00 pm).

THURSDAY JUNE 6th

Mick and Marianne were guests at the wedding of Lord Christopher Thynne and Antonia Palmer at the Queens Chapel, St James's and then went onto the reception at St James's Palace.

SATURDAY JUNE 8th

The "Beggars Banquet" sleeve photo, with the group dressed as tramps, was taken by Michael Joseph, at a mansion, Sarum Chase in Hampstead, hired for the day (with props), at a cost of £45.

SUNDAY JUNE 9th

A further photo session idea, for the "Beggars Banquet" sleeve, had the group dressed in costumes, hired from theatrical agency, Berman and Nathan, at an old ruin, near Derby and also playing cricket in the long grass nearby. (Although never used on the sleeve, these Michael Joseph shots were put to good use for the album's publicity campaign).

TUESDAY JUNE 11th

At a five minute hearing at Marlborough Street Magistrates Court, Brian was sent for trial to Inner London Sessions on June 25th. He was given unrestricted bail, after the magistrate, Mr Aubrey Fletcher, was told that Jones had several engagements abroad before the trial. Brian left court via a back exit, evading 30 girl fans who had gathered at the front entrance.

FRIDAY JUNE 14th - THURSDAY JUNE 20th

The group were on holiday; Brian in Malaga, Keith in Rome and Mick in Paris. The Stones office announced that Mick would begin work on his first solo film appearance on July 29th. The Warner Brothers-Seven Arts film had now been re-titled "Performance".

SATURDAY JUNE 15th

Keith was interviewed in "Melody Maker", under the heading:-"U.F.O's are landing in my garden"! Apart from claiming Redlands was a U.F.O landing site, he found time to talk about more earthly matters: "We've got enough recorded to bring out the album, but we want to get another 4 or 5 things completed, so we can have a good mixture of things on it. It'll definitely be out next month and we are still aiming to release it on the 26th, which is Mick's birthday." On live shows: "We are developing some ideas we've had for some shows, that are different. They may just be crazy ideas, but they involve combining us with a circus."

SATURDAY JUNE 22nd

A message to Rolling Stones fans appeared from the group in the NME. It read:-"Dear readers of NME. Jumpin' Jack Flash is really gassed that he made number 1. So are the Rolling Stones. Thank you. We are slaving over a hot album which is coming out next month. Until then..."
Bill returned to Olympic Studios, with Glyn Johns to produce more tracks for The End (see Sept. 1969 entry).

TUESDAY JUNE 25th

Brian's trial was adjourned to September 26th (see entry).

WEDNESDAY JUNE 26th

The group jammed and recorded at Redlands in the "Fifth Dimension" (the name given to Keith's basement, after he'd knocked out three walls into one large room), with Jimmy Miller, Glyn Johns and American musician, Ry Cooder on slide guitar. Songs recorded included:-
"Highway Child"
"Still A Fool" (Muddy Waters).

THURSDAY JUNE 27th

Mick was a one-off guest reviewer, in the "Discs" column of the "Daily Mirror", as regular columnist, Don Short, was on holiday.

FRIDAY JULY 5th

Mick flew to Los Angeles, with Jimmy Miller, to supervise with Keith who arrived on the 8th), the final overdubs and mixing of "Beggars Banquet" at RCA Studios. In the evening, the pair went out to dinner with The Doors, before their sell-out performance at the Hollywood Bowl for which the pair had tickets front row centre stage. Jagger later described "the Lizard King's" performance as "a bore".

SUNDAY JULY 7th

The Stones office had booked three boxes for the group at the Royal Albert Hall, to see a charity show featuring:- The Byrds, The Move, Joe Cocker, The Easybeats, Grapefruit and the Bonzo Dog Doo Dah Band. (They had turned down a request to appear as "they didn't give charity shows"). At the event, only Keith and Bill showed up.

MONDAY JULY 8th to FRIDAY JULY 26th

Charlie (with Shirley), flew out to L.A to join Mick in the studio. Keith, Anita and Marianne flew out, later the same day. Whilst at R.C.A. Mick produced the backing tracks for Marianne's version of "Sister Morphine" and "Something Better" (featuring Jack Nitzsche on piano, Ry Cooder on slide and Charlie on drums. The vocals were added at a later session at Olympic), as well as the "film" version of "Memo From Turner".

WEDNESDAY JULY 17th

Keith and Anita, with Robert Fraser, attended the film premiere of The Beatles "Yellow Submarine". (Mick and Marianne had also been invited, but were still in L.A.)

FRIDAY JULY 19th

Chris Farlowe's version of "Paint It Black" B/W "I Just Need Your Lovin'" was released on Immediate. (The single had been produced by Mick at Olympic Studios, some 18 months before.)

FRIDAY JULY 26th

The original planned release date for "Beggars Banquet" (a title suggested by Christopher Gibbs). Decca refused to release it with it's original "graffitied lavatory wall" sleeve (photographed by film director Barry Feinstein and designed by New York artist Tom Wilkes of A & M Records). The delay, due to a stalemate between Decca and The Stones, would go on for another four months. Meanwhile, Mick returned from L.A, on his 25th birthday, in time for the opening party of the Vesuvio Club, in Tottenham Court Road. (He and Keith had a vested interest in the club, managed by Stones assistant, "Spanish" Tony Sanchez). Guests included John Lennon and Paul McCartney. Mick played an acetate of the finished "Beggars Banquet" over the sound system. (The club later burned down in a "mysterious" fire.)

MONDAY JULY 29th

The scheduled date for Mick to commence shooting his role as Turner, in the film, "Performance". Due to exterior shots being covered first, he wasn't required now until early-September, on a six week shooting schedule (between 8am - 7pm daily).

FRIDAY AUGUST 2nd

Mick and Marianne went on a week's holiday to Ireland, returning on the 8th. Brian went to Tangier, with engineer George Chkiantz, to record the Pipes of Pan played by the Master Musicians of Joujouka (which formed the posthumous album, "The Pipes of Pan of Joujouka", released 1971). The tracks included:-
"Keimonos"

"Incantation" (from the Koran)

"Aatini Mak"

"Music For Bou Jeloud"

"Men's Song"

"Pipes Tunes"

Brian and Suki returned to London on August 23rd.

SATURDAY AUGUST 10th

The N.M.E reported the Stones "are to make regular use of new rehearsal/recording studios at 47 Bermondsey Street, South East London, to be run by road manager, Ian Stewart". (The premises had been leased by the Stones, since April 1st.)

SATURDAY AUGUST 24th

The story broke of the group and Decca's stalemate over the original sleeve design to "Beggar's Banquet". Both Decca in England and London Records in America, refused to release the album until a new sleeve design was submitted. In "Disc", Mick adamantly denied Eric Clapton would be replacing Bill Wyman. Speaking from Ireland, he said "The five Rolling Stones remain the five Rolling Stones - there is no alteration whatsoever in the personnel." Clapton: "I know nothing about it. It's all pretty strange to me and I'd have to play lead guitar anyway."

SEPTEMBER

Bill purchased Gedding Hall, a 14-acre estate near Bury St Edmunds, in Suffolk for £41,000.(Bill, Astrid and Stephen moved in on October 30th).

MONDAY SEPTEMBER 2nd - FRIDAY NOVEMBER 1st

Mick began six weeks of filming "Performance", co-directed by Donald Cammell (who wrote the screenplay) and Nicholas Roeg, with Sanford Lieberson as Executive Producer. His hair was dyed dark brown, for the role of Turner, a one-time rock star, now a recluse, composing ultra-modern forms of music (on a Moog synthesiser, on which Jagger scored the incidental music for the film). Turner co-habitates with two women, Pherber and Lucy, (played by Anita Pallenburg and Michele Breton respectively), in a bizarre, decaying Notting Hill mansion (actually shot in a mansion in Lowndes Square, Knightsbridge), where he shelters Chas (played by James Fox), a gangster on the run from mob bosses. Turner becomes fascinated with Chas's macho exterior and villainous lifestyle and after Chas eats hallucinogenic mushrooms, their characters intertwine.

TUESDAY SEPTEMBER 3rd

Mick taped a guest appearance on Rediffusion Television's "Frost On Friday". He arrived at the Wembley studios for a rehearsal, which began at 7:00pm and then from 8:00pm recorded the show which was transmitted on September 6th, across the ITV network between 9:15 - 10pm (11:05 - 11:45 pm in certain ITV regions). Mick also appeared on BBC Radio One's "Scene And Heard" (transmitted between 6:32 -7:30 pm on September 14th, repeated two days later between 7:45 - 8:43 pm), being interviewed live by host Johnny Moran. "Street Fighting Man" had been banned by some Chicago stations, following the recent riots at the Democratic Convention in the city. (Initial copies of the single were housed in a hastily withdrawn sleeve, depicting an L.A street riot). Mick:- "I'm pleased to hear they've banned it, as long as it's still availiable in the shops. The last time they banned one of our records in America, it sold a million!" (The single climbed as high as No 48).

THURSDAY SEPTEMBER 5th

Even though a suitable sleeve for "Beggar's Banquet" had yet to be found, advertising boards for the album were erected in London, Manchester and Birmingham. "The Daily Mirror" eloquently reported: "A lavatory wall is standing between the Stones and the release of their new LP "Beggar's Banquet."

Left: Brian arrives at Inner London Sessions, September 26th
Below: With accountant, Fred Trowbridge

MONDAY SEPTEMBER 9th

Mick and Keith were interviewed by the N.M.E's Keith Altham at the Stones' office. Keith: "The job of the record company is to distribute. All they've got to do is put it in the shops, not dictate to people what they should or should not have." Mick: "It is our job to produce and make the records. The record company is not there to tell us what we can make. If that's the way they feel about it, then they should make the records and we'll distribute them." Keith: "They told me that "Street Fighting Man" was subversive. "Course it's subversive" we said. It's stupid to think that you can start a revolution with a record. I wish you could! The fact that a couple of American radio stations in Chicago banned the record just goes to show how paranoid they are..." Mick: "What it all comes down to is that we design the sleeves and make the records-just like we have been doing for the last five years...we'll get this album distributed somehow even if I have to go down the end of Greek Street and Carlisle Street at two O'clock on Saturday morning and sell them myself!"

SATURDAY SEPTEMBER 14th

Mick told "Disc's" Mike Ledgerwood that the Stones would "definitely make, at least, one live appearance in Britain before Christmas. We've got this new album, all of which we're dying to play live. All we want is for someone to give us the opportunity to play somewhere. It could work out very groovy". Mick also commented on the delayed "Beggar's Banquet" album: "I don't know when it will be out now. I don't think it's (the sleeve) offensive and I haven't met anyone who finds it offensive. It's all a drag really. I even suggested that they put it out in a brown paper bag labelled "unsuitable for children" if they felt that bad about it". Mick remained adamant that the sleeve would not be changed at all, declaring "The Stones are standing by their guns". The same issue also reported that there were no plans to issue "Street Fighting Man" as a single in the UK and that Anita Pallenburg was co-starring with Mick in "Performance". Mick: "Lucky old Anita, she's OK. We're all one big family!"

SATURDAY SEPTEMBER 21st

Another proposed film idea for the Stones was announced. Entitled "Maxigasm",(a "sort of black comedy/science fiction Western"!), it would be directed by Carlo Ponti in Hollywood. Shooting would begin late December in North Africa. Mick: "It's Keith's baby. It should be fun and we hope to have Anita (Pallenburg) and John Phillip Law (the blind angel in "Barbarella") and a host of other stars". Meanwhile, Mick was interviewed by Radio One DJ John Peel on a special "Voice of Pop" discussion show about pop lyrics and censorship. Also appearing in the programme were Tim Rose, Barry Mason, Marc Bolan, DJ Pete Murray, Mick Farren, Clive Selwood, Alan Keen, the former Radio London programme director and Radio One boss Robin Scott. (The programme was transmitted between 6:32- 7:30pm and was repeated two days later.)

THURSDAY SEPTEMBER 26th

Brian was driven by Tom Keylock to Inner London Sessions, arriving 30 minutes before court was due to sit. He pleaded "Not Guilty" to unlawful possession of 144 grains of cannabis resin and his trial commenced. Brian, in evidence, gave his address as "Redlands", West Wittering, Sussex (where he was temporarily lodging. Keith had moved into Robert Fraser's Mount Street flat, during Anita's "Performance" filming commitments). He said he never used the bureau in which the ball of wool was found. Asked by his counsel, Michael Havers QC (who had defended Mick and Keith the previous year) what effect it had on him, when the police officer showed him the wool, he said: "I just could not believe it. I was absolutely shattered... I don't knit. I don't darn socks. I don't have a girlfriend who darns socks." Asked "Had you the slightest knowledge that the resin was in that wool?" Jones replied "No. Absolutely none until that moment." In his summing up, the chairman, Mr R.E Seaton, said that the case depended mainly on circumstantial evidence. When the jury of ten men and two women returned, after 45 minutes, with a "Guilty" verdict, there were gasps in the court. (Mick and Keith had arrived to hear the verdict). Brian had to be helped back to his seat in the dock. He admitted being in breach of his probation order, following his conviction the previous October (see Dec 12th entry). Mr Seaton: "I am going to fine you relatively, according to your means. But you must keep clear of this stuff. At the moment you are on probation from this court and you really must watch your step. For goodness sake, don't get into trouble again. If you do, there will be some real trouble." Brian was fined £50 with £105 costs. Brian and Suki left court, hand in hand, to meet waiting pressmen: "It's great not to be in jail. I was sure I was going to jail for at least a year. I never expected that I would be going home. It was such a wonderful relief. I still protest my innocence. I had no idea the cannabis resin was in the ball of wool. I didn't even know the wool was there, but I am not interested in an appeal at this moment. It's great to be free." Mick "We are very pleased that Brian didn`t have to go to jail. Money doesn't matter".

SATURDAY SEPTEMBER 29th

"Disc" reported that the Stones had been approached by Paragon Publicity Ltd. to appear at a special charity pop show, at Croydon Fairfield Halls, in aid of the British Olympics Appeal Fund, but had declined due to Mick's filming commitments, in "Performance". (The bathing scene featuring Mick, Anita and Michele Breton took two days to shoot, on a closed set!)

OCTOBER

Charlie produced six tracks (actually part of a continuous performance) for The People Band, at Olympic Studios. (The album was released on the Transatlantic label, in February 1970). Peter Whitehead's film "Tonite Let's All Make Love In London" (completed in 1967) was given a limited showing, in London. The 70 minute film featured the following Rolling Stones related content:- "Have You Seen Your Mother, Baby..." and "Lady

Mick as Turner, in "Performance"

Jane" (promos from the Albert Hall) with Mick being interviewed (see Sept.23rd 1966 entry), Keith at the premiere of "Cul de Sac" (see June 2nd 1966 entry) plus Andrew Oldham producing and being interviewed at a Twice As Much recording session. The soundtrack album, on the Instant label, (an Immediate offshoot) was released Friday, October 11th, featuring Mick and Andrew Oldham soundbites from the film and Chris Farlowe`s versions of "Out Of Time" and "Paint It Black".

THURSDAY OCTOBER 3rd

"The Daily Mail" announced The Stones had lost the battle with Decca over the "Beggar's Banquet" sleeve design (which had caused a three month delay in it's release). Mick: "I don`t find it at all offensive. Decca has put out a sleeve showing an atom bomb exploding ("The Atomic Tom Jones"). I find that more upsetting!"

FRIDAY OCTOBER 4th

Marianne, resting at a £105 per week mansion in Tuam, County Galway, announced she was expecting Mick's baby, but had no intention of marriage. "I don't want to be married to Mick. I don't want to be married at all." Mick: "I am absolutely delighted that Marianne and I are having a baby. We hope to have three more." (Mick visited her and Nicholas on his weekends off, from filming "Performance").

SATURDAY OCTOBER 12th

Mick made a guest appearance on David Frost's new LWT (London Weekend Television) programme "Frost On Saturday" (networked live across the ITV network 6:45-7:29 pm from Studio One in Wembley). Mick was interviewed by Frost which sparked off a lively "living in sin" debate with "morals campaigner", Mary Whitehouse (over the recent furore re: Mick's non-marriage to Marianne, despite her pregnancy. The Archbishop of Canterbury had called the couple's decision "very sad"). During her first point, she addressed Mick as "Michael", to which he dryly retorted "Call me Mick, dear!", thus gaining the first round! The "Should Mick Marry Marianne" debate even reached the pages of the music press, where "Disc" readers were polled for their opinions. The result, published one week later, was a majority "No".

Rehearsing and filming "Sympathy for the Devil", for "Frost on Saturday", November 29th

FRIDAY OCTOBER 25th

Mick was in the audience for Frank Zappa and the Mothers of Invention's concert at the Royal Albert Hall.

THURSDAY OCTOBER 31st

At the Stones office, in Mayfair, Tom Keylock gave Charlie a present of a horse, carved out of one solid piece of wood. "I've always wanted to buy something for Charlie" Tom said, "he's so difficult though. I mean things like L.P's and such don't mean anything...when I gave it to him, I've never seen anyone so knocked out!"

FRIDAY NOVEMBER 1st

After filming his final scenes for "Performance", Mick went to the

Stones office, where he was interviewed by Keith Altham, for the N.M.E. On the non-appearance of "Beggar's Banquet": "I've lost interest in that situation. It has been a complete waste of energy. We agreed to them using a different sleeve in the end and it still hasn't been realised yet....Now that I've finished on the film, we're going back into the recording studio to get a new single out by Christmas. I haven't written anything yet, but we'll do it the usual way by getting it together in the studio at the time."

NOVEMBER

Mick composed the Moog synthesiser soundtrack (at his Cheyne Walk home) to the film "Invocation Of My Demon Brother", written and directed by occultist, Kenneth Anger (released a year later, also featuring footage shot at the July 5th, 1969 Hyde Park concert). Mick's score was originally intended for Anger's aborted "Lucifer Rising" film, which was to feature the Stones, in acting roles.

SATURDAY NOVEMBER 9th

The group and Decca finally reached an agreement over the sleeve for the "Beggar's Banquet" album. (The artwork would now be in the style of an R.S.V.P "Invitation Card"). Mick: "It's been a complete waste of time". Mick, Keith and Brian went to Tiny Tim's concert at the Royal Albert Hall.

SUNDAY NOVEMBER 10th

Mick was interviewed on Radio 2's "Movie Go Round" about "Performance". The film, plagued by censorship hassles, did not go on general release in England until January 4th, 1971, where it received it`s official premiere at the Warner West End Cinema, London.

FRIDAY 15th - SUNDAY NOVEMBER 17th

Recording "You Can't Always Get What You Want" at Olympic Studios (working from 10 pm - 6:15 am, on the 17th). Producer Jimmy Miller played drums, Al Kooper; piano, organ and French horn overdubs, while Rocky Dijon added percussion.

SUNDAY NOVEMBER 17th

Mick was interviewed by John Peel on BBC Radio One's "Top Gear". During the programme (transmitted between 3pm-5pm), Mick revealed the Stones plans to undertake a major world tour.

TUESDAY NOVEMBER 19th

Marianne was admitted to a North London nursing home, from Cheyne Walk.

WEDNESDAY NOVEMBER 20th

The press announced that Marianne had lost the baby after five and a half months pregnancy. Mick: "Marianne has lost the baby, following pregnancy complications. She is all right, but we are both terribly upset."

THURSDAY NOVEMBER 21st

Brian bought Cotchford Farm, fifty miles south east of London, near Hartfield, Sussex, for the sum of £35,000. The house once belonged to A. A. Milne, the author of "Winnie the Pooh".

SATURDAY NOVEMBER 23rd

"Beggar's Banquet" was finally released in the U.S.A. (It's release in the U.K was held back to Friday, Dec 5th, to coincide with an elaborate press launch, planned by PR man, Les Perrin -see entry).

"Disc" reported: "Jethro Tull join Traffic and American acts Taj Mahal and Dr. John for the Rolling Stones hour long colour T.V. spectacular "The Rolling Stones Rock and Roll Circus", which starts production next month. Three independent T.V companies have already applied for

screening rights. The Stones will also use five-star acts from the world-famous 200-year old Sir Robert Fosset's Circus- clowns, jugglers, cowboys, a flying trapeze and a boxing kangaroo. It will be ready for screening by January 1". Stones P.R woman, Georgia "Jo" Bergman explained to an initially disbelieving Press Corp:-"Yes, it really is going to happen. The Stones wanted to get people into their movie. All the artists involved were responsible for getting it together. Nobody sold out. The Stones got down what they wanted to get down and it was all done inside of two weeks."

SUNDAY NOVEMBER 24th

Mick was interviewed by "One Plus One" co-producer, Iain Quarrier for the late-night BBC2 arts programme "Release", talking at great length about the film (clips of which were inserted into the finished programme). It was transmitted November 30th, between 10:15 -10:55pm and also included music from Octagon.

FRIDAY NOVEMBER 29th

The Stones rehearsed and then taped (with Mick's vocals live) "Sympathy For The Devil", at Studio One, Wembley, for the following night's "Frost On Saturday" programme, transmitted across the ITV network between 10:55 -

Les Perrin plants one on Brian, "Beggars Banquet" launch, December 5th

11:40 pm. "One Plus One", (starring The Rolling Stones, Anne Wiazewski, Iain Quarrier and Francoise Pascal) received it's world premiere at the National Film Theatre, London. (The film was not released in America until March 11th, 1970). Producer Quarrier, later changed the film's title to "Sympathy For The Devil" and re-edited the film (against Godard's wishes) to include longer sequences of the group (see June 4th-11th entry).

WEDNESDAY DECEMBER 4th

Mick and Marianne met Lord and Lady Montague, at the U.K premiere of the musical "Hair", at the Shaftesbury Theatre, London.

THURSDAY DECEMBER 5th

The group threw a £1,000 press launch for "Beggar's Banquet" in the Elizabethan Room at the Kensington Gore Hotel, London. The party took the form of a 16th-century style banquet, complete with "serving wenches", with low cut gowns, serving exotic dishes - a boar's head included - and roast beef, pouring mead into tankards Proceedings began when Mick, wearing a frock coat, starched but collar-less evening shirt, grey top hat and white plastic fork in his jacket buttonhole, advised the guests: "Get Drunk!!" As toasts were drunk, and the album blared forth, Mick announced: "I hope you've all had enough to eat and drink and I hope you've all enjoyed yourselves. But we didn't invite you here just to eat and drink, did we?!" With that, he opened one of the gold

confectionery boxes (given to each of the guests, with "Don't open until next Wednesday" printed on it) and pushed a plastic-foam custard meringue pie into the face of Brian, the cue for a mirthful custard pie fight to break out. No-one was spared, including guest of honour, Lord Harlech (President of the Board of British Film Censors and former British ambassador in Washington), much to the horror of the Decca executives present. "Send your clothes cleaning bills to us, dears" Mick gaily announced. Keith, who had been absent from the party (he claimed his driver had got lost!), arrived after the guests had gone, in time for the final photocall.(The others still had traces of custard about their faces). BBC, ITN and Movietone newscrews were on hand to cover the event.

FRIDAY DECEMBER 6th

The Stones and the Who rehearsed at the Marquee, in Wardour Street, for camera tests, during the first stages of the "Rock and Roll Circus" filming. Due to high-tech cameras, specially ordered from France, (which were able to simultaneously shoot film and videotape) having not arrived in the country, initial filming went no further, until the 10th.

SATURDAY DECEMBER 7th

A full page advert for the new album appeared in "Record Mirror", carrying the caption: "Just listen to the Beggar`s Banquet". Richard Goldstein, in "The New York Times" reviewed the album claiming that while The Beatles were "still searching - and it showed", the Stones had "found out where they were and were building".

SUNDAY DECEMBER 8th

The Stones recorded the soundtrack (which they would part-mime to) for the "Rock 'N' Roll Circus" television special, at Olympic Studios, with Jimmy Miller and Glyn Johns. (Orchestral arrangements were scored by Tony Visconti).

MONDAY DECEMBER 9th

"Rock and Roll Circus" cast rehearsals at the Londonderry House Hotel, Park Lane.

TUESDAY 10th - THURSDAY DECEMBER 12th

The Rolling Stones, with guests John Lennon, Yoko Ono, Marianne Faithfull, Eric Clapton, Mitch Mitchell, The Who (replacing Traffic, who had recently split), Jethro Tull (who had been chosen over recently formed Led Zeppelin), Taj Mahal (in place of Dr John), American model, Donyale Luna, French avant-garde violinist, Ivry Gitlis and classical pianist, Julius Katchen, all assembled at the Stonebridge Park studios of InterTel (VTR Services) in Wembley to tape "The Rolling Stones- Rock and Roll Circus". (Directed by Michael Lindsay-Hogg, filmed by Tony Richardson, produced by Sandford Lieberson and financed by the Stones themselves, to the tune of £50,000). The first day (10th) was spent with rehearsals (beginning at midday) and initial filming. Half a circus tent was draped around one end of the studio, with a circus ring that came apart in the centre. Sawdust was spread around the ring, while at the opposite end of the studio, an archway, covered with bare bulbs, like a sideshow,

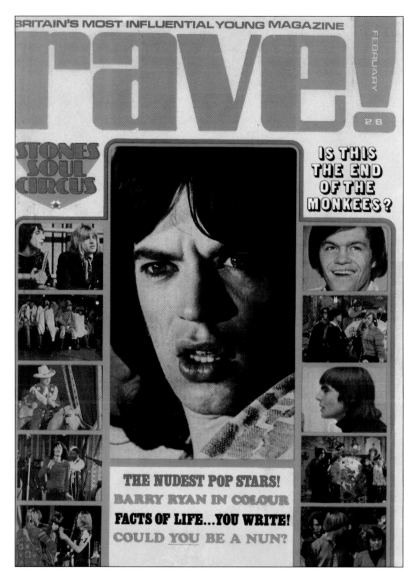

BRITAIN'S MOST INFLUENTIAL YOUNG MAGAZINE

rave!

FEBRUARY

2.6

STONES
SOUL
CIRCUS

IS THIS
THE END
OF THE
MONKEES?

THE NUDEST POP STARS!
BARRY RYAN IN COLOUR
FACTS OF LIFE...YOU WRITE!
COULD YOU BE A NUN?

Opposite page: "You've heard of Oxford Circus...", the Rolling Stones "Rock and Roll Circus" Above: Brian with Yoko Ono, John Lennon, and five year old Julian Lennon, at the rehearsals, December 10th

became the artistes entranceway. Outside, in the car-park, a mobile 4-track unit (manned by Jimmy Miller and Glyn Johns), was recording activities over the two day schedule, for a proposed charity soundtrack album (that, like the film, was eventually scrapped). There were some seventeen items to run through and by 5 o'clock, only three or four of the acts had been dealt with; Mick with a (heavily sedated) Bengal tiger, Mick and Keith in a knife-throwing act plus various circus performers. Anita Pallenburg was due to appear as a bearded lady, but was ill throughout the filming. (A boxing kangaroo was withdrawn after John and Yoko complained it was demeaning to animals.) While the cameras were being put into position, the special "one-off" supergroup, comprising John Lennon, Eric Clapton (guitars), Keith Richard (bass) and Mitch Mitchell (drums), dubbed "The Dirty Mac" (in true Lennon fashion!), jammed on '50's rock 'n' roll numbers, such as "Peggy Sue" and "Sweet Little Sixteen", with Mick joining in on occasional vocals (occasional, as he was still busy trying to organise last-minute proceedings). The Who rehearsed "A Quick One" (While He's Away)",

with Keith Moon dressed as a clown, complete with full face make-up. On the second full-filming day (11th), all were at the studio from noon, for an exhausting 18 hours. A specially-invited audience, (including some who had waited since 8am to be admitted), comprising 800 winners of an N.M.E. ticket draw were present to add atmosphere to the proceedings. They were each given a brightly coloured poncho and felt hat to wear and all were seated in stands, arranged in a horseshoe around the ring. (The day had been divided up into three separate two and a half hour filming sessions: morning-12:30 - 3pm, afternoon - 3:30-6pm and evening- 7 - 9:30pm, although complications made the filming drag on much longer.) At noon, Linsday-Hogg was in the viewing room watching the previous day's rushes. Brian told reporters: "If you had told me four years ago that we would have been involved in something like this, I would never have believed you, but everyone is really enjoying themselves. Someone asked John (Lennon) what kind of amp he wanted

and he just said "Oh one that plays!" The idea is that if everyone has fun, the people who watch will too!" Many celebrities had turned down invites to sit in the "Royal Box". These included Yul Brynner, Chuck Connors and Roger Moore. Brigitte Bardot politely declined the invitation of becoming ringmistress, due to contractual obligations. Mia Farrow had agreed to appear as a clown, but failed to show. Instead, she sent her friend, top fashion model, Donyale Luna, who appeared as the fire eater's assistant (and was wooed behind the scenes, by Brian). The show's main cast lined up in the circus ring for ten minutes for the benefit of the press cameras. John was dressed as a tumbler, Yoko (a witch), Eric Clapton wore a suit of many colours, while Mick became the ringmaster (with the other Stones dressed in military costumes). After a 15 minute technical hitch (while the artists waited in the entrance tunnel), filming proper was ready to commence. With Lindsay-Hogg giving the signal; lights, sound, action, the line-up parade (for the title sequence) was first to be filmed. The cast were lead out by acrobats, midgets and a cowboy on horseback (the latter an extra in the 1943 Mickey Rooney/Judy Garland film, "Girl Crazy"). Each musician was

playing an uncharacteristic wind instrument (e.g John Lennon - a trumpet, Keith Richard - a tuba, Pete Townshend - a saxophone, etc.). This scene had to be re-taken several times, a portent of the technical glitches that hampered the production throughout the day. Mick made his hearty introduction: "You've heard of Oxford Circus, you've heard of Piccadilly Circus and this is the Rolling Stones "Rock and Roll Circus" and we've got sights and sounds and marvels to delight your eyes and ears and you'll be able to see the very first one of these in a few moments" (which confirmed the original intention of selling the finished product to commercial television). Jethro Tull, originally due to do three numbers, were curtailed by time restrictions, to miming "A Song For Jeffrey", several times. Taj Mahal, due to work permit hassles, were the circus's best kept secret, being billed as "A,N Other" on the film

A fan's eye view of the Stones outside Olympic Studios 1968/9

clapperboards. They performed a live version of Homer Bank's "(Ain't That) A Lot Of Love". Bill, dressed in a clown's outfit, introduced a typical slapstick routine involving two clowns (who ran amongst the crowd disgorging buckets of confetti). As time dragged on between each act, (with lights being re-positioned and cameras re-loaded), a "warm-up" man told jokes over the P.A. in a vain attempt to keep the audience amused. Keith, dressed as a circus dandy (complete with monocle, top-hat and cigar) introduced fire-eater Danny Kimara and his assistant, Donyale Luna. (Stones session player, Rocky Dijon beat a bongo throughout their dramatic act). Charlie introduced a nervous Marianne Faithfull singing "Something Better" (the original choice of "Sister Morphine" was filmed but eventually vetoed, in mind of possible censorship problems), perched upon a divan, dressed in an aubergine gown. (Between each take, Mick stepped into the ring and crouched beside her, offering encouragement). Brian, wearing a top-hat, with devil's horns protruding from it, introduced classical pianist, Julius Katchen, from a balcony. A trapeze was set-up, with stainless-steel hoops and bars and a pair of aging acrobats dramatically ascended, going through their paces, whilst below them, Katchen, in full evening dress, performed a recital of Chopin and Brahms. At 8pm, there was a break for dinner in the backstage canteen, on the floor above the set. Off the set, Mick and John Lennon (the latter, eating brown rice with chopsticks, renamed himself Winston Legthigh for the occasion!), introduced the Dirty Mac supergroup, who assembled onstage, at approximately 10pm. While the crew set up, the band ran through "Yer Blues" (which had just been released as a track on The Beatles "White Album"). Yoko lay in a black bag at Lennon's feet, holding his hand between takes. After completing a particularly fiery version, the band launched into an improvised jam, featuring virtuoso violinist Ivry Gitlis (who was the first to record Stravinsky's and Berg's violin concertos) and Yoko, who emerged from the bag, to wail along (the jam later dubbed "Her Blues"). While the lights were being tested, at 11pm, The Who ran through several takes of "A Quick One (While He's Away)" (or "The Who Mini-Opera" as it read on the clapperboard). The band were on particularly fine form and pulled out all the stops on each successive version (Keith Moon poured water over his drums and flung a floor-tom, over his shoulder as a cue for the cameramen!). With the audience's excitement level heightened, the long wait involved with setting the Stones "T-shaped" stage up (complete with a catwalk for Mick to prance up and down on) soon brought everyone back down to earth. Further "link" scenes were shot (a clown scene was hastily improvised to keep the wearisome crowd entertained) and Ivry Gitlis returned to overdub a violin solo, onto his recording of Paganini's First Violin Concerto (taped earlier). By this time, it was past midnight, with still no sign of the Stones and the audience was fast depleting to catch last minute public transport. Finally, at 2am, the Stones plugged in (with Nicky Hopkins on piano and Rocky Dijon on percussion). The group warmed up with

"Route 66" and "Confessin' The Blues" (not filmed, as the cameras were being re-positioned), while studio technicians wheeled on several primitive strobe machines for the first filmed song "Jumping Jack Flash". The floor manager urged the audience not to look at them. "They will blind you!" he intoned dramatically. "Jumping Jack Flash" was run through three times, as was "Parachute Woman" which followed. Between songs, the band jammed old blues numbers, such as Elmore James' "Look On Yonder Wall" and Robert Johnson's "Walkin' Blues" and interminably discussed (with Lindsay-Hogg & Glyn Johns), whether or not another take was in order. "No Expectations" initially featured Mick playing an acoustic guitar (tuned for him by Keith), balanced on one knee, his leg resting on a chair. The final take featured Mick handing the guitar to Keith, while he concentrated solely on vocals. The group then premiered the newly-recorded "You Can't Always Get What You Want", each take building in intensity. By 4am, the filming still hadn't been completed and the idea of resuming work the next day was briefly considered. After one take to get the sound balance right and with the clock ticking towards five, the band delivered a scorching "Sympathy For The Devil" (with Mick on his knees, unpeeling his shirt to reveal tattooed devils' head's on his torso and biceps). The closing "Salt Of The Earth" sequence featured the Stones and guests sitting among the audience, wearing matching capes and hats. What little audience left were, by now, completely exhausted, so, unprompted, Pete Townshend, Keith Moon and Who roadie, Bob Pridden enlivened proceedings. (Townshend tied two large cushions to his head, like a Pope's diadem, dancing like a dervish amongst the fans, while Moon tied himself to people with a spare cape!) A shattered Mick briefly thanked the audience and bidded viewers "goodnight", over the opening notes of "Salt Of The Earth". (Mick and Keith sang a live vocal over the studio backing track, with everybody joining in on the last chorus, swaying from side-to-side, reading the words off a gigantic board.) As the last notes faded, the Stones, guests and audience waved a frantic farewell and 18 hours of filming were completed. At 6:30 am, buses (specially arranged by the Stones office) took the last diehard fans homeward.

With programmers of the London Weekend Television station showing an early interest in the production, the Stones (and Lindsay-Hogg) prepared a 54-minute black and white title-less cut (which still resides in the ITV archives), as intended for possible (monochrome) transmission early in 1969, featuring:-

Part One: Entrance of the cast and Mick's introduction/Comm. Insert/Mick's introduction to "A Song For Jeffrey"-Jethro Tull/Keith's introduction to Donyale Lunya & Danny Kimara's fire-eating act/Keith's introduction to "A Quick One (While He's Away)" (mini-opera) -The Who/Bill announcing comm. break. Part Two:-Donyale Luna with tiger/ "(Ain't That) A Lot Of Love"-Taj Mahal/Bill's introduction to the clowns/Charlie's introduction to "Something Better"-Marianne Faithfull. Part Three:-Brian's introduction to Julius Katchen/The trapeze artists/Mick and John Lennon's introduction to "Yer Blues"-The Dirty Mac/ "Her Blues" (featuring Ivry Gitlis & Yoko Ono). Part Four: "You Can't Always Get What You Want" (featuring Nicky Hopkins) and "Sympathy For The Devil" (featuring Nicky Hopkins and Rocky Dijon)/ Mick's farewell announcement and "The Salt Of The Earth" finale'. (The bulk of video footage shot was for monitoring purposes only and was later wiped, not only to preserve re-usable tape, but European commercial television stations still preferred film.)

The Stones (Jagger in particular) were still not happy with the finished result and made vague plans to re-shoot their segment (see June 21st 1969 entry). The first (related) footage of the event to appear was included in a German ORF television documentary on John Lennon ("A Piece Of His Mind" broadcast April, 1969), which an independent film crew had shot. This consisted of Lennon and Jagger, off the filmset, breaking into an accapella rendition of "Yer Blues" (Lennon removing Jagger's coat, striptease-style, while Yoko and Lennon's 5 year-old son, Julian looked on) and an excerpt from the "Yer Blues" / "Her Blues" jam. For a while, there was talk of releasing it as a feature film for theatre distribution, which amounted to nothing. Many reasons have been proffered as to the film's eventual non-appearance (the most common being The Who upstaging their hosts), but one factor that did influence the group's decision was the severance of ties with business manager, Allen Klein (in 1970). Klein did consider re-editing the footage, in a vain attempt to sell it to The Who as "The Who's Rock And Roll Circus". Pete Townshend evidently, had not forgotten the film and both he and Jagger dug out The Who's segment to view in 1977, when production work started on "The Kids Are Alright" documentary. (Bill Wyman later claimed that the footage in question, was never returned). Klein still owns the film and at the time of writing a finished version (with an accompanying CD soundtrack). (See also May 10th and June 21st, 1969 entries).

SATURDAY DECEMBER 14th
Mick appeared on BBC Radio One, being interviewed live on the programme "Scene And Heard". The short feature, where Mick spoke at great length about the filming of the "Rock 'N' Roll Circus" was transmitted between 6:32-7:30pm.

WEDNESDAY DECEMBER 18th
Mick, Keith, Anita and Marianne left Lisbon by ship, for a Christmas vacation in Rio de Janeiro, Brazil to find "their magicians". "We have become very interested in magic, and we are very serious about this trip", Keith told a "Sunday Express" reporter on December 8th. "We are hoping to see this magician who practices both white and black magic. He has a very long and difficult name which we cannot pronounce, we just call him "Banana" for short!" Brian and Suki also chose to spend their Yuletide in an exotic location, namely Ceylon, where they visited science fiction author, Arthur C Clarke ("2001:A Space Odyssey").

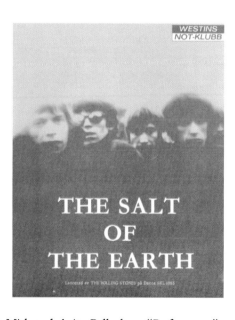

Left: Mick and Anita Pallenburg, "Performance".

BEGGAR'S BANQUET
THE ROLLING STONES

Ⓢ SKL 4955   Ⓜ LK 4955

DECCA

THE ROLLING STONES

SATURDAY JANUARY 4th

Brian, who was currently holidaying in Kandy, was furious after being refused accommodation at several hotels. They had accused him of being a "penniless beatnik". Whilst surrounded by reporters, he took a large roll of banknotes from his pocket, telling them: "I am not a beatnik, I work for my living. I have money and I do not wish to be treated as a second class citizen!"

MONDAY JANUARY 13th

At the Appeals Court, Brians appeal against conviction (see Sept 30th 1968 entry) was dismissed in his absence.

SATURDAY JANUARY 18th

"The Daily Sketch" reported that Mick and Keith "had been barred from an exclusive hotel for wearing "op art" pants and nothing else. They were asked to leave the Hotel Crillon in Lima, Peru, after ignoring the hotel manager's plea to change their clothes. The two members of the Stones were last night staying at the equally exclusive Hotel Boliviar".

SATURDAY FEBRUARY 8th

The N.M.E. reported that the group had denied plans for a world tour to start in Europe, mid-March (with The Flying Burrito Brothers as support) and continuing to America on March 21st. A Stones spokesman told the paper: "At this stage nothing is signed or even decided and no steps can be taken until Brian Jones returns from Ceylon. The confusion regarding The Flying Burrito's probably stems from the fact that one of them, ex-Byrd Gram Parsons, is a good friend of Keith Richard's and Keith may produce the group's next L.P. Undoubtedly, the Stones will play concerts this year, but absolutely nothing is finalised."

SUNDAY FEBRUARY 9th - SUNDAY MAY 4th

The group block-booked sessions at Olympic Studios, with Glyn Johns and Jimmy Miller, working on:-

"Toss The Coin"

"The Vulture"

"Old Glory"

"You Can't Always Get What You Want" (overdubbed to include 50 members of the London Bach Choir, as well as session choristers: Madelaine Bell, Doris Troy and actress, Nanette Newman. The arrangement was scored by Jack Nitzche on March 15th.). Brian Jones was conspicuous only through his absence at most of these sessions.

FRIDAY FEBRUARY 21st

Decca released the Marianne Faithfull single "Sister Morphine" (written by Marianne with Mick and Keith) backed by "Something Better" (produced by Mick and arranged by Jack Nitzsche - see July 5th - 24th, 1968 entries). The musicians on the sessions featured: Mick on acoustic guitar, Charlie on drums, Ry Cooder on guitar and Jack Nitzche on piano. It was withdrawn after 48 hours, due to the controversial A-side. An angry Marianne made Mick meet Sir Edward Lewis, to re-instate it, to no avail.

MONDAY FEBRUARY 24th

An interview with Mick in conversation with Chris Denning, was transmitted on BBC Radio One as part of the programme "Scene And Heard" (broadcast between 6:32 -7:30pm).

SATURDAY MARCH 22nd

The original "pencilled-in" date for a show at New York's Madison Square Garden, which would have marked the start of an aborted world tour through Asia and South America (culminating at the Royal Albert Hall in London).

MONDAY 5th and TUESDAY MAY 6th

Keith attended sessions at Olympic Studios (engineered by Glyn Johns), for Billy Preston's Apple album "That's The Way God Planned It", adding bass on two versions of the title track (released as a single June 27th). The sessions (featuring Eric Clapton, Ginger Baker, Klaus Voorman and singer Doris Troy), were produced by George Harrison.

WEDNESDAY MAY 7th

Recording continued at Olympic, with guests Nicky Hopkins and Ry Cooder, but due to a personality clash with Cooder, Keith stayed away from the sessions (not returning until June 8th). This infamous session produced the "Jamming With Edward" album (released January1972 on Rolling Stones Records):-

"The Boudoir Stomp"

"It Hurts Me Too"

"Edward's Thrump Up"

"Blow With Ry"

Tom Keylock and Stones accountant Fred Trowbridge escort Mick and Marianne from Marlborough Magistrates Court, May 29th

"Interlude a la El Hoppo" / "The Loveliest Night Of The Year"
"Highland Fling"

SATURDAY MAY 10th

The N.M.E reported that the Stones may launch their own "Pear" label next February, after the termination of their contract with Decca. Like The Beatles Apple label, the group would appear on the label which would be used to develop new talent. There would also be a connection between the two groups in the form of business manager, Allen Klein. No official statement could be obtained from the Stones office, although one spokesman commented: "It's extremely unlikely at the present time". The paper also reported that work had restarted on "The Rock and Roll Circus", after director, Michael Lindsay-Hogg had undergone a lengthy operation." He is now editing the film, but there is still extensive soundtracking to be completed. It is not yet possible to say when the finished show will be ready to offer to television companies." (Lindsay-Hogg was simultaneously editing The Beatles "Get Back" film, released a year later as "Let It Be". On January 5th, John Lennon had filmed his

surreal introduction to the Stones "Circus" set, at Twickenham Studios). "The group has been very busy recording and now has quite a number of tracks in the can, principally for an album, but a single will probably be chosen from one of the sessions".

FRIDAY MAY 16th

The sessions at Olympic continued:-

"Sister Morphine" (revised version featuring new lyrics, Ry Cooder on slide and Jack Nitszche on piano). N.B: final overdubs/mixing were completed at Olympic the following year.

"Love In Vain" (second version featuring Ry Cooder on mandolin)

"Let It Bleed" (Stu - piano)

"Midnight Rambler" (Brian-slide. Mick-harp)

"Monkey Man" (Nicky Hopkins-piano. Jimmy Miller-tambourine).

Brian's parents spent the weekend of the 16th-18th at Cotchford Farm (the last occasion they would see him).

WEDNESDAY MAY 21st

A photo session was held at St.Katherine's Dock, near Tower Bridge, continuing at photographer, Ethan Russell's studio, designed for the sleeve of the "Through The Past Darkly" album (see Sept.12th entry).

WEDNESDAY MAY 28th

Mick and Marianne were arrested in the evening at their home in Cheyne Walk, after a drugs squad raid, headed by Detective Sergeant Robin Constable.

THURSDAY MAY 29th

Mick, wearing a purple suit and violet shirt, appeared for a 20 second hearing at Marlborough Street Magistrates Court, where he and Marianne Faithfull were each remanded on bail, of £50 in their own recognisance until June 27th on a charge of possessing cannabis. The couple (who were charged under their full names of "Michael Philip Jagger" and "Marianne Evelyn Dunbar") were later smuggled out through a back entrance of the court.

FRIDAY MAY 30th - SUNDAY JUNE 15th

Olympic Studios (minus Brian), with Nicky Hopkins on piano:-
"Honky Tonk Women" (Jimmy Miller-cowbell)
"Jiving Sister Fanny"
"Gimme Shelter" (Nicky Hopkins-piano, Jimmy Miller-percussion)
"Country Honk" (with Nanette Newman on backing vocals)
"Live With Me" (first version)
"Loving Cup" (first version)
The sessions on May 30th and June 1st, recording "Honky Tonk Women", marked the debut of 21-year old guitarist, Mick Taylor, who had been recommended to Jagger, by Taylor's ex-employer, John Mayall.

JUNE

Mid-month, Brian began rehearsals, at Cotchford Farm for a proposed new group he was assembling. Alexis Korner, Micky Waller, John Mayall and Mitch Mitchell were among the musicians that came down to "blow". Ian Stewart declined the offer, telling Brian: "I've started one group with you and that's enough!"

WEDNESDAY JUNE 4th

"The Evening Standard" reported that 500 people in Glenrowan, near Melbourne, Australia had signed a petition in protest at the casting of Mick Jagger in the role of Australia's famous folk hero, Ned Kelly.

SATURDAY JUNE 7th

Mick was among the 150,000 audience at the free Hyde Park concert debut given by "supergroup" Blind Faith and "liked the idea of The Stones doing the same thing only bigger and better!" That morning, Keith and Anita were injured as their Mercedes swerved off the road near Keith's Redlands home in West Sussex. Anita, who was six months pregnant, broke her collar bone, and was rushed to St.Richard's Hospital in nearby Chichester, while Keith escaped unhurt. The car was a write-off.

SUNDAY JUNE 8th

At 7:15 pm, Mick, Keith and Charlie drove down to Cotchford Farm, after mixing "Honky Tonk Women" at Olympic. The final outcome of the meeting was Brian being asked to leave the group he had helped form. (Although there was a vague promise of the split being only temporary, for the sake of a U.S tour). He was offered a one-off payment of £100,000 to be followed by a yearly payment of £20,000, for as long as the Stones continued to exist. A hastily arranged press release quoted Mick: "Brian wants to play music which is more to his taste than playing ours...we've parted on the best of terms. Obviously, friendships like ours don't break up just like that." Brian put on a brave face: "The Rolling Stones music is not to my taste anymore, I want to play my own kind of music. Their music has progressed at a tangent to my own musical tastes...I no longer see eye to eye with the others over the discs we are cutting."

THURSDAY JUNE 12th - FRIDAY JULY 4th

The Stones commenced off and on afternoon rehearsals at the Beatles basement Apple studio, at 3 Savile Row (concurrent with recording at Olympic), for their intended return to live work, at Hyde Park. Numbers rehearsed included Otis Redding's "I've Been Loving You Too Long", which never made the final set-list. George Harrison visited on the afternoon of the 17th, but declined an offer to "jam".

FRIDAY JUNE 13th

At 2:30pm, the Stones held a press conference and photocall at London's Hyde Park to announce the new "Rolling Stone", Mick Taylor. Taylor told newshounds: "I was invited to do a session with the Rolling Stones (see May 30th entry). It puzzled me. I had never met Mick Jagger in my life and here he was phoning me. I went down and played on some tracks and thought little more about it. Then they asked me if I wanted to be a Stone? I was amazed. I said "I'd love to be a Stone", and that was that." Jagger: "He doesn't play anything like Brian. He's a blues player and wants to play rock 'n' roll, so that's okay". Taylor would remark, the following year: "I just assumed I was the best guitarist available at the time". (In fact other guitarists had reportedly been under consideration, including Eric Clapton and apparently, 22-year old ex-Jeff Beck Group bassist, Ronnie Wood, who was currently out-of-work.)

SATURDAY JUNE 14th

In the N.M.E, Mick was interviewed by Richard Green on the new recruit: "He's on one track of the album, but I don't know which album because they'll be one out in September and another before Xmas. We've got 17 songs up to now and we'll have to sort out which ones go on which album."

MONDAY JUNE 16th

The group recorded their first TV appearance with Mick Taylor, on "The David Frost Show", at Stonebridge House Studios, Wembley. After afternoon rehearsals, they videotaped, in colour, mimed performances of "Honky Tonk Women" and "You Can't Always Get What You Want", recorded by the Westinghouse Group ("Group W"), for transmission across the USA. An application from Blackhill Enterprises was submitted to The Ministry Of Building and Walks for permission to stage a concert in Hyde Park. (The go-ahead was received on June 20th.)

SATURDAY JUNE 21st

Mick was interviewed by Richard Green of the NME:-"The Rock and

Roll Circus" will probably be shown in the Autumn to coincide with the album. The editings not quite finished yet. It'll blow your mind, baby. TV is so appallingly bad, this is just what it needs. It's not hard to be good on TV, but this one is good. I guess in the autumn, we'll do another TV show, probably in America. I'd like to play in America again". An interview with Chris Welch, appeared in "Melody Maker", during which Mick dismissed the possibility of the group "going back to their roots" with a concert at Ken Colyer's Jazz Club and revealed he and Keith had written about 24 new songs. Mick also touched on the subject of the forthcoming Rome concerts (see June 25th & 26th entries). "We chose Rome for the concert because it is a very good visual thing, and the other reason which I haven't told anyone else, is I wasn't satisfied with The Rolling Stones part of the "Rock and Roll Circus" we made, and we want to do it again in the Colosseum, which was the first ever circus". Mick also spoke of the new LP, due out in September: "We wanted it out in July, but the moguls of the record industry say it's a bad month, because all the factories that make records are on holiday!".

WEDNESDAY JUNE 25th and THURSDAY JUNE 26th

The dates for two proposed "free" open-air concerts, at the Colosseum in Rome. The concerts had to be scrapped, due to insufficient time to make filming arrangements with the Italian R.A.I TV team.

FRIDAY JUNE 27th

Mick and Marianne's drug case was adjourned until September 29th, each on £50 bail, making them free to travel to Australia for their controversial roles in Tony Richardson's "Ned Kelly".

THURSDAY JUNE 30th

After a 4-8pm rehearsal at the Apple studio, the Stones returned to Olympic (with Jimmy Miller and Glyn Johns), for a midnight to 4:45am session, working on:-

"I Don't Know Why" (Stevie Wonder) (Two versions rehearsed/recorded).

THURSDAY JULY 3rd

Shortly after midnight, Brian Jones was found at the bottom of the swimming pool situated in the grounds of his Cotchford Farm home. His body was discovered by houseguest, 22-year old nurse Janet Lawson, who called an ambulance. 44 year old builder Frank Thorogood (who had been renovating Cotchford), pulled Brian from the pool, while Brian's 22-year old Swedish girlfriend, student Anna Wohlin, applied artificial respiration. However, Brian was dead by the time the doctor arrived. He was 27. The circumstances surrounding his death are still shrouded in mystery. The Stones were at Olympic Studios, listening to playbacks of "I Don't Know Why", when the call came through from Tom Keylock's wife to Ian Stewart just after 2 am. Bill had already left the session and was awoken at the Londonderry House Hotel, by a phone call from Charlie at 3 am, informing him of the news. Several hours later, with the morning papers headlines screaming the tragic news, the grief stricken group assembled at the BBC Lime Grove Studios to honour a "Top Of The Pops" booking, arriving for a 10 am

camera rehearsal. The group taped two different inserts for "Honky Tonk Women", for use while Mick was in Australia. The first was transmitted July 10th, BBC-1 7:31- 8:00 pm, with repeat showings in the editions broadcast July 17th and 31st (all BBC 1 7:30-8:00 pm). The second premiered in the August 7th edition and was repeated August 14th and 21st (all BBC 1 7:30 - 7:59 pm).For both performances and each subsequent repeat, the group were paid £183. 15 shillings. The group taped a third insert on December 12th (see entry). A recording session booked at Olympic was cancelled. Instead, Mick and Marianne went to a rowdy party thrown by future Stones business adviser, Prince Rupert Loewenstein, held in a marquee in the garden of his Kensington home. Live music was provided by Yes, Stalactites and Al Wynn. Distinguished guests included:- Princess Margaret, actors Peter Sellers and Peter Wyngarde, fashion designer Hardy Amies, Lord Harlech and Lord and Lady Tavistock.

FRIDAY JULY 4th

The group's fifteenth British single: "Honky Tonk Women" B/W "You Can't Always Get What You Want" was released, becoming their eighth

Below: Mick gives some last minute instructions regarding the Hyde Park show to secretary Jo Bergman

Above and opposite: Hyde Park, July 5th

U.K No.1. Mick scotched rumours that tomorrow's concert at the Park would be cancelled as a mark of respect for Brian. "He would of wanted it to go on...we will now do the concert for him. I hope people will understand that it's because of our love for him that we are still doing it!" "The Evening Standard" carried an interview with Mick by Ray Connolly, where he revealed the group "...will be playing tracks from our next album "Sticky Fingers", at tomorrow's Hyde Park concert" and that as well as America, the band would be touring Europe and the UK in September. In "Record Mirror", Mick Taylor dismissed reports that The Beatles would appear at tomorrow's Hyde Park Concert. (As it turned out, only Paul was present).

SATURDAY JULY 5th
The group performed a free concert before an estimated audience of 300,000 at London's Hyde Park, in the Cockpit Area. Running from 1pm-5pm, the event (swiftly designated as "a tribute to Brian Jones"), was promoted by Blackhill Enterprises (who had promoted free concerts by Pink Floyd and Blind Faith on the same soil). Support Acts (in order):- The Third Ear Band, King Crimson, Screw, Alexis Korner's New Church, Family and Battered Ornaments. Panic ensued, in the morning, when Mick awoke with a sore throat. A doctor, representing the insurance company behind "Ned Kelly", warned Mick that if he sang and strained (or lost) his voice, he could be liable for costs incurred in holding up the film production. At a press conference, held at 11am, Jagger, ITV/Granada (who were filming the day's events for a future television special, at the Stones request) and Blackhill Enterprises

assured all, that Mick's larynx was well enough to perform. Jagger: "Our doctor suggested the problem with my voice was a feedback over Brian". Jo Durden Smith, a Granada Television director, who had a successful Doors documentary "The Doors Are Open", to his credit, had already considered the options. "It was an extremely tense situation. We began to consider putting voice tracks through the sound system and just having him miming with the group". In total, six directors and camera units worked on the programme, filming 11 hours of footage including the sun rising over the park, the crowds streaming into the park (some having camped overnight), Tom Keylock advising a gang of fifty Hells Angels (security for the event!) on crowd control, a group of hippies meeting in the Kings Road at 10:30am enroute to the park and numerous shots within (and above) the vast crowd. The first act on the bill, The Third Ear Band, took the stage at 1pm, after MC Sam Cutler's opening announcements. A separate crew filmed Mick, Marianne and her son Nicholas, leaving 48 Cheyne Walk at 2:30pm, being driven to the Londonderry House Hotel, on Park Lane (the band's HQ before and after the show), to rendezvous with the rest of the group (and Allen Klein). Jagger also gave a pre-show interview (for Durden-Smith), discussing his expectations for the show. The cameras then followed the green World War Two army ambulance, delivering the group from the hotel to their backstage caravan, where a last minute rehearsal (with a very nervous Mick Taylor), took place, 15 minutes before showtime. Mick advised Sam Cutler to quieten the crowd in advance, as he intended a reading in memory of Brian, before the show would start. To a tumultuous reception, the group took the stage (designed by Chip Monck, featuring a massive "Beggars Banquet" backdrop) at 5:25 pm. After Jagger (wearing a white "dress", designed by "Mr. Fish") implored the crowd, in a none too subtle fashion, to quieten, he read from Shelley's "Adonais", as a tribute to his departed comrade. With the opening bars of the traditional blues, "I'm Yours And I'm Hers", Tom Keylock and other stagehands opened a number of cardboard boxes, releasing 2,000 white butterflies (obtained from a farm in Dorset, at a cost of £300) into the summer air. (Jagger:-"There was no reason, it just seemed right"). Unfortunately, this rather grand gesture fell flat, literally, as most plummeted from suffocation after having been confined for some hours. The cramped V.I.P enclosure (to the left of the stage) included Marianne and Nicholas, Allen Klein, Michael Cooper, Robert Fraser, Paul McCartney, Tony Hicks (of The Hollies), Donovan and singer/actress Marsha Hunt. The set-list continued (as follows):- "Jumping Jack Flash" / "I'm Free" / "Mercy, Mercy" / "Stray Cat Blues" / "Down Home Girl"/ "No Expectations" / "Love In Vain" / "Loving Cup" / "Honky Tonk Women" / "Midnight Rambler" / "Satisfaction" / "Street Fighting Man" and a 10-minutes plus "Sympathy For The Devil" (complete with African troupe). (The Granada crews continued to film the concert's aftermath, with the crowds drifting home). The first transmission of "The Stones In The Park", (co-directed by Durden-Smith & Leslie Woodhead and described by "The Guardian" as "a major event in English social history and a major documentary event for television") was Tuesday, September 2nd, only in certain ITV regions, between 10:30-11:29pm. The 53 minute programme (which took a month to edit) contained the following tracks (in part or whole) from the concert (in order of appearance):- "Midnight Rambler" / "Street Fighting Man" / "Satisfaction" / "I'm Free" (all interspersed or superimposed over pre-concert footage) / Eulogy For Brian/ "I'm Yours And I'm Hers" / "Jumping Jack Flash" / "Honky Tonk Women" / "Love In Vain" / "Sympathy For The Devil". (The show was one of the entrants chosen to represent ITV at the Monte Carlo Television Festival in February 1970). Television news cameras also filmed part of the concert from the left side of the stage. Despite the rustiness of the Stones set (it was their first full-length show in two years) and accusations of narcissism directed at Jagger (considering it was in Brian's memory) in the underground press, the event was deemed largely a success, thanks to the good behaviour of the crowd (who even disposed of their litter when dispersing), with only several arrests. Park keepers later assessed minor damage at little more than £100. Following the Hyde Park show, Mick, still dressed in his stage garb, dashed from the Londonderry Hotel to the nearby Royal Albert Hall, with Marsha Hunt, to catch the last night of the "Pop Proms '69" season, starring The Who and Chuck Berry.

SUNDAY JULY 6th

Mick taped an interview in the morning with Johnny Moran, for the BBC Radio One programme "Scene And Heard", broadcast 3:00-4:00 pm and

repeated two days later, between 7:45 - 8:45 pm. In the afternoon, he and Marianne flew out to Australia to begin filming their roles in Tony Richardson's "Ned Kelly", arriving in Sydney on the 7th.

TUESDAY JULY 8th

Staying on the 45th floor of the Chevron-Hilton, Marianne took an overdose of 150 Tuinols (sleeping tablets) and lapsed into a five-day coma. After Mick was unable to wake her, she was rushed to St. Vincent's Hospital, where a stomach-pumping operation saved her life. Her part in "Ned Kelly" was given to 19-year old Australian actress,

THE ROLLING STONES

You can't always get what you want
Honky Tonk Women

45 rpm   F12952

DECCA

Polly Ryrie. When she regained consciousness, a fretful Mick was by her bedside. "Don't worry...", she reassured him, "wild horses wouldn't drag me away..."

WEDNESDAY JULY 9th

The coroner investigating Brian's death, Dr Angus Sommerville, recorded a verdict of death by "misadventure, under the influence of alcohol and drugs". The press also reported that Bill Wyman had been granted a "decree nisi" in London's Divorce Court to end his marriage to Diane. (The proceedings inadvertently revealed his true age of 32!)

THURSDAY JULY 10th

Brian's funeral took place at St.Mary's Church, in his home town of Cheltenham. His body was carried in a bronze coffin, flown especially from New York. An additional 50 wreaths (including ones sent from Mick and Marianne and Keith and Anita) were carried in six hearses. The Rolling Stones Fan Club sent a wreath of roses in the shape of a dog. Canon Hugh Evan Hopkins, Rector of the Church where Brian once sang as a choirboy, read Brian's own epitaph: "Please don't judge me too harshly". Of The Stones, only Bill and Charlie attended the service. Other mourners included Brian's parents, his sister Barbara, Ian Stewart, Eric Easton, Tom Keylock and Suki Poitier. Linda Lawrence and her 5 year-old son Julian had flown in from LA, the previous day, to attend. Over 300 people (including intrusive press) gathered around the graveside, at the Priory Road Cemetery. Pete Townshend wrote and recorded an unreleased tribute at his Eel Pie Studios entitled: "A Normal Day For Brian, A Man Who Died Every Day". In New York, on NBC TV's "Johnny Carson Show", Jimi Hendrix dedicated "Lover Man" to Brian. George Harrison paid tribute in the July 12th edition of "Disc". News coverage of the funeral was broadcast in BBC and ITV evening bulletins. German NDR-TV's "Beat Club" screened a tribute, during Show 45, on August 2nd, consisting of black and white clips from Hyde Park, the funeral, and English fans largely indifferent reactions to his death.

FRIDAY JULY 11th

"Record Mirror" carried an interview with Mick Taylor. "There is enough material for two LP`s in the can, but I'm only on about four tracks", adding "...no recording has taken place since the single was made". The group had stopped recording for 10 weeks, awaiting Mick's return from Australia.

SUNDAY 13th - THURSDAY JULY 31st

Shooting "Ned Kelly" on location, at Bungendone, near Canberra.(Mick had his hair cropped and wore a false beard for the role.)

TUESDAY JULY 15th

During a break from filming, Mick was interviewed by Sydney radio station 2SM.

SUNDAY AUGUST 10th

Keith and Anita's first child, a son Marlon, was born at King`s College Hospital, London. The family moved into a 5-storey mansion, at No.3 Cheyne Walk, bought for £20,000.

Mick on the film set of "Ned Kelly" in Australia.

MONDAY AUGUST 18th

During an action scene for "Ned Kelly", Mick nearly lost his hand, when an ancient pistol misfired in his grip.

SUNDAY AUGUST 31st

Keith and Charlie flew to the Isle of Wight to watch Bob Dylan and The Band's bill-topping appearance at the 2nd Annual "Isle Of Wight Rock And Pop Festival". Amongst the star studded audience were Beatles, John, George and Ringo and Fleetwood Mac.

SEPTEMBER

The End album, "Introspection" (all tracks produced by Bill Wyman and engineered by Glyn Johns), was released by Decca.

FRIDAY SEPTEMBER 12th

"Through The Past Darkly (Big Hits Vol.2)" was released in a hexagonal sleeve (it's production overseen by Mick), with a touching tribute to Brian ("With this you see, remember me and bear me in your mind, Let all the world say what they may, Speak of me as you find"), inside the gatefold. Mick completed filming his role in "Ned Kelly". (The much-maligned film received it's world premiere in Glenrowan, near Melbourne on July 28th, 1970).

WEDNESDAY SEPTEMBER 17th

Bill and Charlie went to Olympic Studios for a Leon Russell session (co-produced by Denny Cordell and Leon Russell. Engineer: Glyn Johns). The sessions continued until the second week of October. Songs recorded (all written by Leon Russell) included:-

"Roll Away The Stone" (co-written by Greg Dempsey)

"Pisces Apple Lady"

"Hurtsome Body"

"Delta Lady"

"Shoot Out On The Plantation"

"I Put A Spell On You".

Russell also recorded "(Can't Seem To) Get A Line On You", an early version of "Shine A Light", featuring Mick on vocals and Ringo Starr on drums. (The Stones recorded "Shine A Light", a year later at Olympic, releasing it on 1972's "Exile On Main Street").

THURSDAY OCTOBER 16th

Mick and Marianne arrived home from a two-week holiday in Indonesia.

FRIDAY OCTOBER 17th

All five Stones left Heathrow for Los Angeles, in preparation for a 14 city, 18 concert, 22 day tour of the USA (their first since 1966). Travelling with the entourage was fashion designer, Ossie Clark, who designed Mick's dramatic stage costumes.

SATURDAY 18th - MONDAY OCTOBER 27th

Sessions at the Elektra and Warner Brothers Studios, Hollywood, with Jimmy Miller and Glyn Johns, (Bruce Botnick co-engineered) to complete and mix "Let It Bleed". These included:-
"Gimme Shelter" (final overdubs - Mick-harp and Merry Clayton - backing vocals)
"Country Honk" (final overdub - Byron Berline on fiddle, recorded in the studio's parking lot)
"Live With Me" (second version featuring Leon Russell and Nicky Hopkins on piano, Keith on bass and Bobby Keys making his debut on tenor saxophone)
"I Don`t Know The Reason Why" (Bobby Keys-sax)
"All Down The Line" (first acoustic versions)
"I`m Going Down" (two alternate versions).
While in L.A, Mick and Keith stayed at Stephen Stills mansion in Laurel Canyon, Bill and Astrid stayed with Mick and Rose Taylor at the Beverley

Flying to LA, October 17th.

Wilshire, while Charlie, Shirley and Seraphina stayed at a rented mansion, previously owned by the Du Pont family, overlooking Sunset Strip. The group used this as their West Coast HQ, shooting a photo session there for Terry O'Neill. After recording, the evenings were often spent visiting clubs along the Sunset Strip, mainly The Whiskey A Go-Go (where a special table was reserved for the entourage), to check out the evening's floorshow. On the 19th, the group went to dinner at the "Yamato-E" Japanese restaurant, before going to the Ash Grove club to see Taj Mahal support Arthur Crudup. During the evening of the 24th, a 33rd birthday party for Bill was thrown at the home of Stephen Stills. The guest of honour left early after feeling the effects of a particularly potent brand of "hash cookie", he had unwittingly sampled.

MONDAY OCTOBER 27th

The group gave a press conference in the Sans Souci room of the Beverly Wilshire hotel, to announce the tour. The conference was covered by all major radio & T.V stations, as well as film makers David and Albert Maysles, (whose credentials included a documentary on The Beatles 1964 American Tour, entitled "What's Happening!"), who had been hired to film the band on the road, for a proposed documentary (see Nov 27th entry).

TUESDAY OCTOBER 28th - SATURDAY NOVEMBER 1st

The group began rehearsals for their upcoming US tour, in the basement of Stephen Stills house. Songs rehearsed included:-Eddie Taylor's "Bad Boy" / "Street Fighting Man" / "Monkey Man" / "Sympathy For The Devil"

Within hours of tickets going on sale for the tour, all shows were a complete sell out. Extra dates in the form of an afternoon show at Madison Square Gardens, and a second at the Los Angeles Forum, were also completely sold out, in record time.

SUNDAY NOVEMBER 2nd

Back to the Warner Brothers Studios for the first of four days rehearsals (on the soundstage where the movie "They Shoot Horses, Don't They?" was shot). The first day included:-
"Carol" / "Sympathy For The Devil" / "Midnight Rambler" / "I'm Free" / "Stray Cat Blues" / "Little Queenie" / "Satisfaction" / "Honky Tonk Women" / "Street Fighting Man" / "Love In Vain" / "Prodigal Son".
The group rehearsed each song at least four times.

MONDAY NOVEMBER 3rd

The second day's rehearsal:-
"Jumping Jack Flash" / "Carol" / "Sympathy For The Devil" / "Stray Cat Blues" / "Midnight Rambler" / "Love In Vain" / "I'm Free" / "Let It Bleed" / "Satisfaction" / "Honky Tonk Women" / "Street Fighting Man".

TUESDAY NOVEMBER 4th

The third day's rehearsal:- "Jumping Jack Flash" / "Satisfaction" / "Honky Tonk Women" / "Street Fighting Man"

WEDNESDAY NOVEMBER 5th

The group spent a large part of the day rehearsing "Midnight Rambler".

FRIDAY NOVEMBER 7th

The Rolling Stones sixth US tour opened with a "warm-up" show at the State University, Fort Collins, Colorado (soundchecking before the show). Set List:-
"Jumping Jack Flash" / "Carol" / "Sympathy For The Devil" / "Stray Cat Blues" / "Midnight Rambler" / "Under My Thumb" / "Prodigal Son" / "Love In Vain" / "I'm Free" / "Little Queenie" / "Gimme Shelter" / "Satisfaction" / "Honky Tonk Women" / "Street Fighting Man". Supports on the tour consisted B.B King, Terry Reid and the Ike and Tina Turner Revue. (Chuck Berry, featured on some dates.)

SATURDAY NOVEMBER 8th

Inglewood Forum, Los Angeles. (Two sell-out shows. 18,000 at both.)
Due to a mix up in bookings, two top Ice Hockey teams agreed to play their match in the afternoon. Prior to the shows, the band jammed backstage with bluesman Booker White. The first 75 min set which started two hours late, due to the organisers miscalculating the time necessary to transform the arena from hockey to concert hall consisted of:-
Mick's intro "Has it really been 3 years?!" - "Jumping Jack Flash" / "Carol" / "Sympathy For The Devil" / "Stray Cat Blues"/ "Prodigal Son" / "Love In Vain" / "I`m Free" / "Midnight Rambler" / "Live With Me" / "Little Queenie" / "Satisfaction" / "Honky Tonk Women" / "Street Fighting Man".

For the second (added) show, which began at 3:30 in the early hours of November 9th (and finished at 5:15am!), the 105 min set varied to:-
"Jumping Jack Flash" / "Carol" / "Sympathy For The Devil" / "Stray Cat Blues" / "Prodigal Son" / "You Gotta Move" / "Love In Vain" / "I`m Free" / "Under My Thumb" / "Midnight Rambler" / "Live With Me"/ Mick's intro: "It's been 3 years and we're really having fun. If it's O.K, we'd like to play a little bit longer for you!" - "Little Queenie" / "Satisfaction" / "Honky Tonk Women" / "Street Fighting Man". (Stu played piano on "Carol" and "Little Queenie".)

The Stones also grossed $230,000, thus beating the previous best for a concert in Los Angeles, set by The Beatles at Dodger Stadium, in 1966. Experts predicted that the current US tour would gross the group more than £2,000,000 (with the group taking £700,000) which prompted Ralph Gleason of the "San Francisco Chronicle" to snipe: "Are the Rolling Stones really able to use all that money?...How much can the Rolling Stones take to England after the deduction of taxes? How much profit do the British manager, the American manager and the agency have to make?!"

SUNDAY NOVEMBER 9th

Coliseum, Alameda Co, Oakland. (Two shows.) The first set (due to a power failure after the opener, the acoustic songs were hastily brought forward):-
"Jumping Jack Flash" / "Prodigal Son" / "You Gotta Move" / "Carol" / "Sympathy For The Devil" / "Stray Cat Blues" / "Love In Vain" / "I'm Free" / "Under My Thumb" / "Midnight Rambler" / "Live With Me" / "Little Queenie" / "Satisfaction" / "Honky Tonk Women" / "Street Fighting Man".

The second show, as with the previous day, began in the early hours of November 10th, with set variations:-
"Jumping Jack Flash" / "Carol" / "Sympathy For The Devil" / "Stray Cat Blues" / "Prodigal Son" / "You Gotta Move" / "Love In Vain" / "I'm Free" / "Under My Thumb"/ "Midnight Rambler" / "Live With Me" / "Gimme Shelter" / "Little Queenie" / "Satisfaction" / "Honky Tonk Women" / "Street Fighting Man".

(Promoter Bill Graham recorded both shows. Selections from the late show were later transmitted on Radio KSAN, the alleged source for the infamous "Liver Than You'll Ever Be" bootleg). Back in England, the management of the Royal Albert Hall refused to accept the Stones booking for a major concert on their return from the States. The Stones office booked alternative venues at the Saville Theatre and the Lyceum for December.

MONDAY NOVEMBER 10th

Sports Arena, San Diego. Set-List:-
"Jumping Jack Flash" / "Carol" / "Sympathy For The Devil"/ "Stray Cat Blues" / "Prodigal Son" / "You Gotta Move" / "Love In Vain" / "I'm Free" / "Under My Thumb" / "Midnight Rambler" / "Live With Me" / "Little Queenie" / "Satisfaction" / "Honky Tonk Women" / "Street Fighting Man".

TUESDAY NOVEMBER 11th

Coliseum, Pheonix, Arizona. Set-List:-
"Jumping Jack Flash" / "Carol" / "Sympathy For The Devil" / "Stray Cat Blues" / "Prodigal Son" / "You Gotta Move" / "Love In Vain" / "Under My Thumb" / "Midnight Rambler" / "Live With Me" / "Gimme Shelter" / "Little Queenie".

THURSDAY NOVEMBER 13th

Moody Coliseum, Dallas, Texas. Set-List:-
"Jumping Jack Flash"/ "Carol" / "Sympathy For The Devil" / "Stray Cat Blues" / "You Gotta Move" / "Love In Vain" / "Under My Thumb" / "Midnight Rambler" / "Live With Me" / "Little Queenie" / "Satisfaction" / "Honky Tonk Women" / "Street Fighting Man".

FRIDAY NOVEMBER 14th

University Coliseum, Auburn. The set-list was identical to the Dallas concert the previous day.

SATURDAY NOVEMBER 15th

University of Illinois Assembly Hall, Champaign. (Two shows.) Both set-list's as per the previous day(s).

SUNDAY NOVEMBER 16th

International Amphitheatre, Chicago. Set-List:-
"Jumping Jack Flash" / "Carol" / "Sympathy For The Devil" / "Stray Cat Blues" / "Love In Vain" / "Prodigal Son" / "Under My Thumb" / "Midnight Rambler" / "Live With Me" / "Little Queenie" / "Satisfaction" / "Honky Tonk Women" / "Street Fighting Man".

TUESDAY NOVEMBER 18th

The Stones returned to Studio 50, in New York City, to tape their sixth (and last) appearance (the first with Mick Taylor) on the "Ed Sullivan Show". After extensive afternoon rehearsals, the group mimed (without an audience),with Mick's vocals live:- "Gimme Shelter" and "Love in Vain" ("from their new album, "Let It Bleed" as announced by Ed) in the first half of the show and "Honky Tonk Women", in the second. (The recorded show was first transmitted Sunday, November 23rd, 8:00 - 9:00pm EST).

WEDNESDAY NOVEMBER 19th

"Michael Kohlhaas - Der Rebell", a 1968, 95 minute film, directed by Volker Schlondorff, produced by Oceanic Film Production-Gina Productions, starring David Warner in the title role, Anna Karina as Elizabeth and Anita Pallenburg as Katrina, opened at the New Victoria Cinema, London. The plot concerned a man revenging injustices he has suffered, until it eventually destroys him. "The fate of a character who cares nothing for his own safety in his fight against power and authority." Keith had a cameo role in the film, as Nagel's man (for which he had to undergo a hair trim, his first in two years!).

THURSDAY NOVEMBER 20th

Inglewood Forum, Los Angeles.(Two shows.)

MONDAY NOVEMBER 24th

Olympia Stadium, Detroit. (Two shows.) Ist Show Set List:- "Jumping Jack Flash" / "Carol" / "Sympathy For The Devil" / "Stray Cat Blues" / "Love In Vain" / "Prodigal Son" / "You Gotta Move" / "Under My Thumb" / "Midnight Rambler" / "Live With Me" / "Little Queenie" / "Satisfaction" / "Honky Tonk Women" / "Street Fighting Man".

TUESDAY NOVEMBER 25th

Spectrum Sports Arena, Philadelphia. Set List:- "Jumping Jack Flash" / "Carol" / "Sympathy For The Devil" / "Stray Cat Blues" / "Love In Vain" / "Under My Thumb" / "Midnight Rambler" / "Live With Me" / "Little Queenie" / "Satisfaction" / "Honky Tonk Women" / "Street Fighting Man".

WEDNESDAY NOVEMBER 26th

The group gave a 3:30pm press conference at the Rainbow Grill, New York. During the conference, they announced they would be playing a free open-air concert in San Francisco after the tour ended, on December 6th, as a "Thank You" to their American fans (and, according to more cynical observers, to counteract bad publicity over high ticket prices- see Nov.8th entry). Civic Center, Baltimore (recorded by Glyn Johns-see Nov.27th entry). Set:- "Jumping Jack Flash" / "Carol" / "Sympathy For The Devil" / "Stray Cat Blues" / "Love In Vain" (which when re-mixed, was included on the "Get Yer Ya-Ya's Out" album)/"You Gotta Move" / "Under My Thumb" / "I'm Free" / "Midnight Rambler" / "Live With Me" / "Satisfaction" / "Honky Tonk Women".

THURSDAY NOVEMBER 27th

The group played the first of three sell-out shows at Madison Square Gardens, New York, all being filmed (including backstage scenes) by the Maysles Brothers (see Oct.18th-27th entry), as well as being recorded by Glyn Johns on the Wally Heider 16-track mobile recording studio for a live album, released the following September (after judicious editing and overdubbing) as "Get Yer Ya-Ya"s Out". The set-list:- "Jumping Jack Flash" / "Carol" / "Sympathy For The Devil" / "Stray Cat Blues" / "Love In Vain" / "Prodigal Son" / "You Gotta Move" / "Under My Thumb/ "I'm Free" / "Midnight Rambler" / "Live With Me" / "Little Queenie" / "Satisfaction" / "Honky Tonk Women" / "Street Fighting Man". Backstage visitors included Leonard Bernstein and "birthday boy" Jimi Hendrix, who was drawn into the inevitable jam (filmed by the Maysles but left on the cutting room floor).

FRIDAY NOVEMBER 28th

Two shows at M.S.G.. The afternoon show (with a reduced running time) featured:- "Jumping Jack Flash" / "Carol" / "Sympathy For The Devil" / "Stray Cat Blues" / "Love In Vain" / "Midnight Rambler" / "Live With Me" / "Little Queenie" / "Satisfaction" / "Honky Tonk Women". The evening set:- "Jumping Jack Flash" / "Carol" / "Sympathy For The Devil" / "Stray Cat Blues" / "Under My Thumb" / "I'm Free" / "Love In Vain" / "Midnight Rambler" / "Live With Me" / "Little Queenie" / "Satisfaction"/Honky Tonk Women"/"Street Fighting Man".
It was estimated that each of the four shows had grossed $100,000, with an estimated 55,000 attending.

SATURDAY NOVEMBER 29th

"Let It Bleed" was released in the USA (Dec. 5th in the U.K), certified gold, with advance orders of 400,000. The Gardens, Boston. (Two shows.) Afternoon set list:- "Jumping Jack Flash" / "Carol" / "Sympathy For The Devil" / "Stray Cat Blues" / "Love In Vain" / "Under My Thumb" / "Midnight Rambler" / "Live With Me" / "Little Queenie" / "Satisfaction" / "Honky Tonk Women" / "Street Fighting Man". Evening:- "Jumping Jack Flash" / "Carol" / "Sympathy For The Devil" / "Stray Cat Blues" / "Love In Vain" / "Prodigal Son" / "You Gotta Move" / "Under My Thumb" / "Midnight Rambler" / "live With Me" / "Little Queenie" / "Satisfaction" / "Honky Tonk Women" / "Street Fighting Man".

SUNDAY NOVEMBER 30th

Miami Pop Festival, held at the International Raceway, West Palm Beach. Set List:- "Jumping Jack Flash" / "Carol" / "Sympathy For The Devil" / "Stray Cat Blues" / "Love In Vain" / "Under My Thumb" / "Midnight Rambler" / "Gimme Shelter" / "Live With Me" / "Little Queenie" / "Satisfaction" / "Honky Tonk Women" / "Street Fighting Man".
The Stones did not arrive on stage until the early hours of December 1st, to an estimated audience close to 55,000. The right-wing John Birch Society failed in their attempts to stop the show, claiming that "...the

Right: Richard Nixon "greets" Mick and tour manager Sam Cutler at Detroit's Metro Airport, November 24th

Stones will corrupt the moral character of youth!"

MONDAY 1st - THURSDAY DECEMBER 4th

Whilst staying at the Colonnades Hotel at Palm Beach, an impromptu jam session, with Mick singing, accompanied by Keith on guitar, was filmed by the Maysles. The group flew to Alabama, checking into the Holiday Inn, for four days of recording at the Muscle Shoals Sound Studios, engineered by Jim Dickinson and Jimmy Johnson. During the sessions (filmed by the Maysles), the following were rehearsed and recorded:-

"You Gotta Move"

"Brown Sugar" (Stu - piano)

"Wild Horses" (Jim Dickinson - piano). Versions were reputedly taped with Joe Walsh (then of the James Gang) on slide guitar and Bernie Leadon and "Sneaky" Pete Kleinow, of the Flying Burrito Brothers, on tap piano and steel guitar, respectively. Keith later maintained he wrote the song's chorus, in the studio bathroom (see July 8th entry).

All received final overdubs and mixes at Olympic Studios the following year and were included on the "Sticky Fingers" album (April 1971).

SATURDAY DECEMBER 6th

The Stones ended their American tour with a notorious free open-air concert, before an estimated 200,000 - 500,000 fans at the Altamont Speedway Track in Livermore, 50 miles north of San Francisco (with all-star supports:-Santana, The Flying Burrito Brothers, Jefferson Airplane and Crosby, Stills, Nash & Young). The event was organised by Rock Scully, the manager of The Grateful Dead. Mick described the show as "a Xmas present to our American fans". The original desired venue for the show was Golden Gate Park, in San Francisco (but the application was turned down by city councillors). Then, after visiting various sites, Sear's Point Racetrack in San Francisco was given the nod but the owners backed down at the very last minute. There were conflicting reports as to the reason for the change of heart. The Stones claimed they refused to appear at the location following a dispute with the track's management regarding "filming rights", while the racetrack's owners claimed they backed down over the idea, fearing "possible trouble from such a potentially large crowd". At the eleventh hour, after an on-air radio appeal, the owner of the Altamont Speedway, Dick Carter, came to the rescue, offering his land in return for the free publicity. During the afternoon of Dec 5th, the Bay Area airwaves were flooded with previews for the event, advising concert goers of the change of venue. By nightfall, the sheer volume of attendees to the show caused traffic jams of up to twenty miles long and ten miles wide, in all directions. The Stones (and entourage) drove up from San Francisco to inspect the festival site, late that cold evening, mingling with fans, around their campfires, before returning to the Huntingdon Hotel. (Except for Keith, who stayed overnight in a backstage trailer). The disorganised event was a disaster from start to finish and an ugly atmosphere pervaded from the start when Jagger was punched in the mouth by a crazed "fan", as he arrived by helicopter at the festival site, during the afternoon. A local chapter of Hells Angels were hired as security guards after being recommended by Rock Scully, as being "no trouble", when policing the Dead's shows. (The Stones had found the English version of the Angels effective at Hyde Park (see July 5th entry) and agreed when payment was fixed at a large tanker of beer!) Unable to control the large crowd and crazed on beer (and the bad acid that was rife), the Angels resorted to violence, beating members of the crowd indiscriminately with billiard cues throughout the afternoon's music.(Marty Balin, of the Airplane, after witnessing one particularly brutal beating, tried to remonstrate with them and was knocked out cold, for his efforts.) As darkness fell (and the desert cold crept in), the crowd grew ever restless, as there was still no sign of the headliners, (the Stones had adopted a deliberate "keep 'em waiting, keep' em wanting!" policy throughout this whole tour) and the violence threatened to flare up again. (The reason for the delay, according to some insiders, was that Jagger wouldn't leave his backstage trailer, until it was dark enough for Chip Monck's lighting to illuminate his dramatic stage make-up. Another reason given was Bill Wyman's late arrival.) When the group finally arrived on stage, they found themselves hopelessly outnumbered by the amount of people (official or otherwise), on or around the platform and despite vain pleas to remove themselves, it remained this way throughout their set:- "Jumping Jack Flash" / "Carol" / "Sympathy For The Devil" (2 false starts with Jagger's limp efforts to halt the disturbances in the crowd) / Elmore James "The Sun Is Shining" / "Stray Cat Blues" / "Love In Vain" / "Under My Thumb", during which, 18 year-old Meredith Hunter, was stabbed to death near the front of the stage after a scuffle with several Angels (caught on film by one of the Maysles' crew). The Angel responsible claimed the youth pulled a gun (as seen in the film), but it was never found. / "Brown Sugar" / "Midnight Rambler"/ "Live With Me" / "Gimme Shelter" / "Little Queenie" / "Satisfaction" / "Honky Tonk

Women" and "Street Fighting Man". With the Hells Angels helping Mick throw rose petals into the crowd, the whole debacle came to an end. The group (and entourage) beat a hasty exit, piling into a waiting helicopter that ascended (with twice it's normal weight), from the site of an event that was to continue to haunt the band for years to come. The charitable concert was marred by further tragedies. Two fans, aged 22 years, were killed when a Plymouth convertible ran over them as they lay on the ground in the darkness and another "under the influence of drugs", drowned when he fell into an irrigation channel whilst being chased by police. A young girl, standing near the stage, had her ankle broken when she was in the path of an Angel's motor bike ploughing through the crowd. There were hundreds of incidents reported during the show, (including many "bad trips" and personal injuries) which kept the woefully inadequate number of 19 doctors and 6 psychiatrists occupied. While four deaths were reported, four had given birth! A spokeswoman for the Red Cross explained:-"The excitement apparently induced premature labour!" The Altamont footage, (including the stabbing), would later form the climactic finale to the Maysles and Charlotte Zwerin's documentary film "Gimme Shelter" (which also featured much of the Madison Square Gardens - see Nov. 27/28th entries and Muscle Shoals -see Dec.1st-4th entry footage). Due to the events that transpired, the Maysles Brothers (and the group) designated all proceeds from the film and subsequent TV coverage be donated to an orphanage for Vietnamese babies. The "Gimme Shelter" film received it's premiere exactly one year later on December 6th, 1970, at the Plaza Theatre, New York. Reviews of the film were uniformly positive (some implied that the Stones image and music had somehow caused the violence at Altamont). Liz Smith of "Cosmopolitan" gushed: "Absolutely devastating, it's overwhelming. I can't get it out of my mind. It is a wild experience". (Her review was later printed on the film poster).

SUNDAY DECEMBER 7th

The aftermath of Altamont was covered by local TV and radio stations, most notably KSAN in San Francisco, who featured talkback interviews with eye-witnesses to the unfolding events. These included Sonny Barger (head of the local Hells Angels chapter), who was less than complimentary about the English charges he had been guarding less than 24 hours earlier and promoter Rock Scully, (who had suggested the idea of the Angels' in the first place) absolving himself of all blame: "The Rolling Stones signed the contract. They've got what they paid for. Let it bleed, man!"

MONDAY DECEMBER 8th

Keith and Charlie flew back to Heathrow. Keith arrived to find himself in the middle of a Home Office wrangle involving Anita Pallenburg. Their ultimatum: "Marry or get out of England". (They had been holding her Italian passport since July, after turning her request down for a visa extension). Anita: "It's just like living in a police state". Bill and Mick Taylor stayed on in America, returning home on the 10th. Mick flew on

to Switzerland for business reasons, returning home on the 11th.

THURSDAY DECEMBER 11th

Mick returned to Heathrow Airport. While he had been on tour, Marianne had absconded to Rome with film producer, Mario Schifano and her son Nicholas.

FRIDAY DECEMBER 12th

A busy day for the Stones at the BBC with the recording of three shows (in colour) at the TV Centre, Wood Lane. (Mick dressed in the black jumpsuit and cape he'd worn throughout the USA tour). The group arrived at 2:30pm in Studio E for camera rehearsals, taping "Honky Tonk Women" for inclusion in "Top Of The Pops '69", the first of two parts looking back at the best selling records of the year. (Transmitted BBC1, December 25th, 2:15-2:59pm.) Later, at 8:00pm, still in Studio E, the group rehearsed and recorded, "Let It Bleed" for the first of two BBC TV "end of the '60's" celebratory programmes, entitled "Ten Years Of What?" (transmitted BBC2 December 28th, 7:25 - 9:50pm). The programme, introduced by DJ Jimmy Savile and BBC newsreader Robert Dougall, featured a wide-ranging, affectionate look back at the decade, with contributions from "round the world yachtsman", Sir Francis Chichester, author Malcolm Muggeridge, M.P. Enoch Powell, DJ John Peel, the actress Susan Hampshire and even The Archbishop of Canterbury. Amongst the items looked back on was an extract from episode 26 of the popular drama series "The Forsyth Saga", poems written by C. Day-Lewis and a report on the ground breaking heart transplant. The Stones segment (lasting a full 5 minutes 28 seconds) was featured alongside a studio performance by The Bonzo Dog Doo-Dah Band, while music from The Beatles and The Who, amongst others, was played over miscellaneous newsreel film (supplied by Visnews, CBC, NBC, The British Aircraft Corporation and The Royal Society of the Prevention of Cruelty to Birds!). "Satisfaction" was also played in this newsreel section of the programme. The second programme in this vein, "Pop Go The Sixties", was a BBC/ZDF TV co-production, also hosted by Jimmy Savile and (from Germany) Kifie Von Kalekheath. On the same set, the Stones performed "Gimme Shelter" (4 minutes 25 seconds) for the programme, also featuring:- The Bachelors, Kenny Ball and his Jazzmen, Cilla Black, Adam Faith, The Hollies, The Tremeloes, The Who, The Kinks, Lulu, Cliff Richard, The Shadows, Helen Shapiro, Sandie Shaw, The Ascot Brothers, Johnny Harris (and his orchestra) performing "Satisfaction" and The Breakaways. 8 seconds of "Satisfaction" and 7 seconds of "Get Off Of My Cloud" were used on the show's closing credits, broadcast between 10:40 - 11:49 pm, on Friday, December 19th. All three inserts taped featured Mick's vocals live over the original backing tracks (Merry Clayton's vocal, on "Gimme Shelter" being cut completely).

Left: Anita and 3 month old Marlon greet Keith at Heathrow, December 18th
Right: Mario Schifano, Marianne and Mick arrive at Marlborough Magistrates Court, December 18th

SUNDAY DECEMBER 14th

The group spent the afternoon in rehearsal at the Saville Theatre, for two concerts, at the venue (the first of four one hour shows over the week. An additional concert was added, due to the previous three being sell-outs). The shows, before almost 2,500 fans, began at 5:00 and 8:30pm, and were intended as another "Christmas present to their fans". The first show started 20 minutes late and according to reviews, fans applauded 'politely" and were allowed to dance in the aisles. The group performed a 55 minute reduced set (the acoustic songs were scrapped, due to a fault with Keith's guitar) in a show lasting approximately two and a half hours. It was decided that the guests on the bill would not be officially announced before the concerts had begun. They were: Shakin' Stevens and the Sunsets, a conjuror, David

Saville Theatre Xmas shows, December 14th.

fined £200 with £52 costs. Marianne was acquitted.)

SUNDAY DECEMBER 21st

The group performed two sell-out concerts (5:00 & 9:00pm) at the Lyceum, in the Strand. Upon entering the building, fans were covered with artificial snow from a huge bag hanging from the ceiling. Mr. Peter Smith, the General Manager of the Lyceum: "This is Christmas and we thought we'd give everyone a surprise, although this came earlier than anticipated." The queue of fans entering the building stretched nearly half a mile along the Strand. 2,100 tickets were sold for each of the performances. Dozens of policemen were on duty in the Strand and in the theatre. In nearby Burleigh Street, steel crash barriers were erected and the roads were closed off to traffic.

SATURDAY DECEMBER 27th

ITN newsreels of the Stones drug busts were included in an end-of-the-decade special, "A Child Of The Sixties" (ITV 10:10 to 11:40 pm), which examined the '60's through the eyes of 20-year old Oxford graduate, Gyles Brandneth, "whose knowledge and understanding of the world around him was shaped almost exclusively, by television".

Berglass and Mighty Baby. Set List (early show):-"Jumping Jack Flash" / "Carol" / "Sympathy For The Devil" / "Stray Cat Blues" / "Love In Vain" / "Under My Thumb" / "Midnight Rambler" / "Live With Me" / "Little Queenie" / "Satisfaction" / "Street Fighting Man".

MONDAY DECEMBER 15th

The group resumed work at Olympic Studios, with Jimmy Miller and Glyn Johns, on the following:-

"You Gotta Move" (aborted alternate version)

"Wild Horses" (various alternate mixes)

"Dead Flowers" (first version, with Stu on piano).

THURSDAY DECEMBER 18th

Mick and Marianne's cannabis case was adjourned to Monday, January 26th, 1970 at Marlborough Magistrates Court. (On this date, Mick was

Brian Jones 1942 - 1969

Tom Keylock escorts Brian's sister, Barbara and Suki Poitier away from St Mary's Church, Cheltenham, July 10th 1969

TOM KEYLOCK- A MINDERS DIARY.

"Tom Keylock was to be a key figure in the unfolding drama of life within the Stones" (Bill Wyman. 'Stone Alone').

"Stone by Stone"

MICK.

Mick is very hard to sum up or describe. I could read the others really well but never Mick. He was very deep and fucking clever!! No way was he an idiot like the media try, or at least tried to make him out. When he did "The David Frost Show", I had tried to talk him out of it, because Frost was made out to be this brilliant intellectual, very "eyebrow". I said "Mick, he's out to crucify you, make you look thick!" but Mick said 'No, no, don't worry. I've got it all sussed out". So he did the show and came out totally on top! As he got up and walked off, he winked at me, as if to say, "Told You So!". He was never a problem. He would always get lumbered with a lot of layabouts and hangers-on and he'd ask me "Tom, do us a favour and get rid of them but do it in a nice way", because he was always aware of his position. He knew he couldn't just tell them to "fuck off", so I'd say " 'Ere, excuse me, Mick, you're wanted in the studio" and he'd give it all this "Oh, how awkward, I never realised, Tom! You never told me!" He was the ultimate diplomat.

KEITH.

Keith I admired the most. He had a lot of bottle (courage). He didn't give a shit for nobody! I've always thought that if I'd had a son, I would have liked him to be like Keith. I don`t mean, pull the same strokes as Keith, just have his temperament and "bottle". He was a bit of a scatterbrain though, but a true family man. He may not think so, but I used to see him playing with my kids and his dogs, Ratbag and Bumbles, when we would holiday at Redlands and he showed his real side. Heart of gold and not nearly as hard as he'd like to think he is!

CHARLIE.

Charlie is exactly how the public have always perceived him. Very, very quiet. He never bothered anyone and wasn't bothered by anyone. He always spent a lot of time away by himself up in his room, mainly talking to Shirley on the phone. In those days, he hated touring, although I've since heard, he's now very keen on it. It's only taken 30 years for him to grow to like it!! That's very Charlie, doing things at his own pace. He never would ask me to do much of anything, always preferring to do it himself, drive himself to places, etc. I'd forget he was there most of the time, bless him! I'll always remember talking to Charlie, just after he'd bought the old bakery at Lewes. He'd confided in me that he and Shirley had been unsuccessfully trying for a baby. He was getting quite down about it. He'd been to the doctors about it. He was so frustrated. I told him not to worry, don't go having the idea about having a "bunk-up",

every frantic minute you get, with just the idea of getting Shirley pregnant in mind. I assured him that as soon as they stopped worrying themselves, stressing out, it would just happen and lo and behold, they had Seraphina. I really felt I'd become a father figure to them, giving them the benefit of my older years of experience or maybe it was because I ended up with four daughters of me own! That showed I was experienced in one thing at least!

BILL.

Bill was quiet like Charlie. He wasn't into the limelight thing of being seen at this club or that club, raving all night and getting drunk, like Brian was. His main interest, in fact, his only interest, outside music, as far as I could make out, was birds (girls). He got through hundreds! When he couldn't get out of a hotel, he'd tell me which ones he wanted and I'd have to sneak them in. That would piss the security off, every time. One bloke I remember said to me, "Do me a fucking favour and make up your mind. You're telling us to keep them out and all the time you're pulling them in!!"

BRIAN.

Brian was something else, a really complicated couple of blokes. He really didn't give a shit about nothing or anyone and yet he was very soft and helpless. He couldn't punch his way out of a paper bag but then again, he was fucking vicious! He went through something completely different. I never could work out what he was up to, because he was a born liar. He would lie to Keith, to Mick, to everyone. He would say something to Keith and Keith would say "Hold it, I never said that!" or "I never did that!" and Brian would lie to his face and say "Yes you did. What the fuck are you on about?!" He could tell you one thing, convince you it was true and then tell someone else the complete opposite. You could not trust him, especially with drugs on more than one occasion. I've had to practically strip search him and he'd still manage to get out of his bonce (head). I'm sorry to say that as much as I liked him, he was a fuckin' born liar!!

1965

DIARY OF A MINDER - TOM KEYLOCK
September 2nd, 1965

My first encounter with those 'orrible Rolling Stones came via a sub-contracted job from another car hire firm, "Clays Car Hire". They were a chauffeurs outfit to the entertainment world, run by the late Frank Payne.

Apparently, no one at Clays would take the account, so Frank passed it over to my firm. He made it sound like he was doing me a personal favour. He said it was an account job, in the name of Andrew Oldham and he was too busy to take it on any more. He didn't mention anything about all his drivers not wanting it!

I turned up at Ivor Court, that's where his (Oldhams) office was then and I was shown through to his office by a secretary and there's this young bloke, wearing dark glasses, sitting behind a desk with all these phones on it. (Probably only one of them worked though, thinking back. He was all show, Oldham!)

He took one look at me and waved me outside, saying "They're not here yet", sort of off-hand like. That was a bad start right away. Oldham was very toffy nosed (stuck up), always talking down to people and I don't like that. I've never talked down to anyone and I expect the same courtesy, so he got my back up straight away.

I didn't know who he meant when he said "They're not here yet", so I waited outside with the secretary, who kept on looking up nervously and smiling, saying "Oh, they'll be here in a minute" and "They're always late". That went on for what seemed forever, until I was just about to leave. I thought "I'm getting screwed around here, I'm off!". That's when she gets all animated, "They're here, they're here!". I remember being very sarcastic and going "Hooray, Hooray!!"

Then I saw them. I thought "Who the fuck are this dodgy looking lot?!" Oldham came bounding out of his office, saying (to no one in particular) "This is the driver", pointing at me and saying "This is the 'Rolling Stones. Take us to Wembley. We're late!" I remember thinking it funny that they all filed into the car, one at a time, through the same door, single file. "That's odd!", I thought. I'd find out later what that was all about. That was when I got my first proper look at them. They were very small, immaculately dressed, with a lot of hair. That was how I would have summed them up, if I'd had to give a description. When all that stuff came out later, about them being dirty smelly layabouts, it was rubbish. They were spotless. Mind you, they got a bit dodgy looking in later years, I must admit!

As soon as we pulled away, they started fucking around. Brian was the first to start. They had the control in the back, that operated the windows and the dividing shutter between the front and back (it was an Austin Princess limo). So he's got that and he's making them all go up and down. I had him down as the ring leader. He was the cockiest one, trying to get a reaction straight off. I wasn't having any of that so I pulled up sharp and spun round and shouted in my best Cockney, "Oy, do me a favour, knock it off! This is my car and it cost me a lot of money, now leave it out!"

They were all sitting there, looking at me in silence. I don't think they were used to anyone having a go back at them. Then Brian piped up, "Alright". That was all he said, so we pull away again and the little bastard had to do it one more time, didn't he?! They all sat there smoking, until you couldn't see them anymore in the mirror, just hear them laughing and swearing. I thought "What have I got involved with here?!"

READY STEADY GO!
September 2nd, 1965

When we got to the studios in Wembley, the place was under siege. There were hundreds of screaming girls, in the road. We were swept through the middle of them, with them banging on the roof and windows. Its a miracle that I never crushed one, because I wasn't prepared for this sort of carry on. We pulled up round the back, where there was a little car park inside the complex and I opened the door and they piled out single file again, amidst the cigarette smoke and screams. It was quite weird. The next thing, this proper jobsworth comes tearing out of his cabin, waving his clipboard, shouting "You can't leave your car here, sir. You must move it outside!" This was met with a resounding "Fuck off! I'm leaving it here!" "No, no its the directors parking space" he replies, getting very hot and bothered. "I don't care its staying here, I'm not putting it outside with that lot" I informed him, pointing at the screamers. Then the director, Michael Lindsay-Hogg, pulls right up behind us and he's shouting about having it towed away. I found out after, that he had come especially to see the Stones, which if I'd known, I'd have said it was their car and I could have left it there, but no, like an idiot, I park it outside. After the show I went to get the car and it was fucked! The kids had scratched "I love Mick", "I love Brian", all over the paintwork. That was the final straw. I stormed back into the studio in order to give Oldham a mouthful, when as quick as a flash, he's spotted the problem and he's got his chequebook out, saying "Send me the bill for your car". That took the wind out of my sails, good and proper! I'd been wearing my uniform up till then, but just then looking at the wreck of a car, it didn't seem appropriate so I threw the hat and coat in the boot (trunk), slammed the lid, loosened me tie and lit up a fag (cigarette). That's when Mick said "I think we're gonna like you". "Oh yeah?!" I replied. "Well, I don't know if I'm gonna like you lot, do I?!"

Looking at my car, it was obvious why no one at Clays had wanted the Stones account. I was already into Oldham for a new spray job, but because he'd offered to pay, it didn't seem so bad after all. What more damage could there be done?! Oldham was true to his word and he did pay up. I didn't get another job with the band for a few weeks, except once, when Keith asked if I would take him shopping. He wanted to go up the West End of London to buy some clobber (clothes). I'd got a call from Oldhams office, saying would I pick up Keith Richards at so and so address. Now I never knew yet, which Stone was which, so I went and bought that album, the one that has a picture of each member on the back and tells you what their favourite colour is etc, etc. So I've got this on the floor next to me, and as I'm getting closer to Keith, I'm looking at the picture thinking "Brian, No", "Charlie, No"... "Ah yes Keith!"

BRITISH TOUR -
Liverpool Empire. October 15th, 1965

I was in two minds about doing a whole tour with the Stones, but I had a young family at the time, a Car Hire company and a mortgage. So weighing it up was easy, it was obvious I needed the money. There was a little bit of excitement involved I'll admit, but if I was honest, I must say I did it for the money. Looking back, I realise it was the beginning of the most exciting period of my life. Back then there was, and this is true, a thing called a Sunday ruling. We got a memo at the Liverpool Empire that stipulated that Mr Jagger, lead singer with the pop group, The Rolling Stones, can perform tonight by singing, only he must not move. The officials collared me thinking that because I was obviously older, I had some sort of sway over the group, an authority figure. Now I had seen the group perform by now, so I knew this ruling just wasn't going to go down too well with Mick, so I acted dumb and asked what they meant. This little guy informs me that Mick must not move on the stage or make any suggestive moves or do anything that he considered went against the Sunday ruling. I thought the best course of action was to call their bluff. "Well" I said, "I can't imagine Mr Jagger, what little I know of him of course, being able to keep still while performing, so I suggest you cancel the show, but I'll tell you one thing, I wouldn't like to be in your shoes when you do". With that, I led him out on to the stage and from behind the curtain, the screams were deafening. Thousands of kids screaming their lungs out and stamping their feet, chanting "We Want The Stones, We Want The Stones". I looked at this little bloke and said "Go on then, tell them you're cancelling the show, they'll understand about the Sunday ruling, after they rip the place to shreds!!"
I left him there and went to tell the lads in the dressing room, just in case he did it. Mick went mad yelling "You're fucking joking", Keith and Brian were laughing like drains, while Bill and Charlie didn't seem bothered either way. Mick was really mad. "Sort it out Tom, for fuck's sake!" I went back to the official and he's still standing there, as white as a sheet, looking at his watch. "Well mate, they're already half an hour

late, what are you going to do?!"
The Sunday ruling was conveniently forgotten, the band went on and the place went mad. I'll never forget that night. It's the first time I'd experienced such volume and mayhem. The Stones had, through no fault of their own, pushed the kids patience to the limit. I'm sure that was the beginning of their reputation for being late. They were learning fast, all the tricks of working an audience. The following morning I went to get them all up, starting with Charlie, as he was the one who was the easiest to manage in most things. I went into his room and he was still fast asleep. I went to give him a shake and noticed his wardrobe door move. I went over to it and opened it to find two young girls inside. They had been there all night, watching Charlie sleep through the crack in the door. They hadn't touched him, or spoken to him, they just wanted to watch him sleep! "How did you get in here?" I asked. "We ain't telling you", they said, "cos then you'll stop us!" When I told Charlie, he laughed and said "That's fucking creepy!" I can guarantee that was the only time I ever found a bird (girl) in Charlie's room. He never went in for pulling (picking up women) on the road, he was so straight and in love with Shirley. He just wasn't bothered.

Sydney February 19th, 1966

1966

May 25th, 1966 - MEETING DYLAN.

The first time I remember the Stones meeting up with Dylan was at Dolly's club, in Mayfair. I was in fact, minding Dylan on this tour, the one that was made into a documentary ("Eat The Document"). I was asked to do it, while the Stones weren't working. I say the Stones, but it was only Keith and Brian and Paul McCartney, who came down. Everyone was there to watch some band or other, but mostly to have a drink. It was like a meeting place for a lot of musicians at the time. Anyway, Brian and Keith got totally pissed (drunk) and suddenly, Keith takes offense at Dylan's song "Like A Rolling Stone" and accuses Dylan of taking the piss (making them look like idiots). Brian joins in and wants to thump him and the whole scene starts to get ugly. Now, Dylan is totally uptight and wants to leave and get back to the Mayfair Hotel, where he's staying. He wasn't in any fit state anyway, not that he could punch his way out of a paper bag, he's that small! Keith is saying "Come on you, out of the way!", but I said "Look, when I work for you, I do the same for you. Right now, I'm looking after him. You'll have to come through me!!". So with that, I grab Dylan and drag him out and throw him into my big Austin Princess and scream off, much to my relief. Then I look in the rear view mirror and right behind me are Keith and Brian, in Brian's Rolls-Royce. Brian's driving, pissed out of his head! I get to the hotel and get Dylan in, when I see Brian trying to get the Rolls up onto the pavement and through the revolving doors!!

October 7th, 1966 Colston Hall, Bristol

That was a crazy night. Ike and Tina Turner were on the bill and Ike accused Tina of giving Mick the eye. He went berserk backstage and in their dressing room, smashing the place to bits! We were all next door, listening in stunned silence. Keith was saying "We should do something" and Brian was going "Nah, fuck em they're married, its got nothing to do with us" and I suppose there was some truth to that. Then Ike's burst in, looking for Mick and we're like "Hey, calm down there's nothing going on, man, no way!". Mick, thank god, wasn't there. We managed to calm Ike down and I took him and got him a drink which was another bad idea. Ike didn't mix well with booze. After I left him, I went to find Mick and warn him to lay off the flirting with Tina, because Ike's a nutter. Well I found him alright. In fact, I found him and Tina under the stage, going at it good and proper! I actually tripped over them, in the dark and Mick turned round saying "Who the fucks there, who's that?!" I flew out of there sharpish, thinking "How fucking lucky he was with me disturbing him, instead of Ike!" I missed a lot of that

tour, because I had one of my regular clients over. According to my diary, it was probably Shirley Maclaine. I would always drop anything if at all possible for Shirley, she's a lovely lady. I sent one of my drivers to cover for me, George Cauldfield. George was a good bloke, but after two days he rings me up and threatens to quit there and then. "I'd rather do a fucking funeral than do this" he said, "I'm leaving!". I was back for the last show at Southampton and managed to convince George to stay on with the firm, by giving him the day off with pay, before driving down to see the boys. The first one I see is Brian leaning at the bar with these group of girls, fag (cigarette) in his mouth, cocky little bastard. "Hey Tom, its great to see you back, that other bloke was a bit funny, wasn't he?". "No Brian, e' ain't funny, e's bleeding sane!" I replied.

Recording Studios 1966

Tom Jones was in the studio next door recording "The Green Green Grass of Home". I was in there with Mick when we came up with the idea of getting a lawn mower full up with grass and putting it in his studio for a laugh. Mick wasn't up for it but Brian was, so we went looking for this lawn mower which was just about the most ridiculous idea ever, seeing as there wasn't even so much as a blade of grass nearby for miles, let alone something to mow it with, but this never stopped Brian! He never did get it together. In fact he never even came back!. That night, Bill asked me where Brian was, "Looking for a lawn mower" I replied. No one questioned Brian's logic!

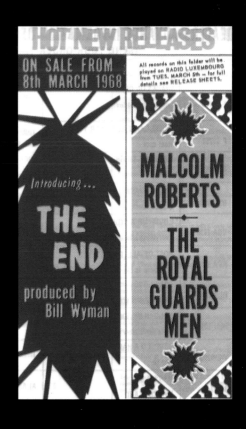

1967

THE ROAD TO MARRAKESH
February 25th/26th, 1967

I drove Keith's Bentley across to France alone, while Brian and Anita, Keith and some bird (girl) called Debbie Dixon flew over. Debbie was going out with a friend of the band, a director named Donald Cammell, although I think she had ideas of making up a cosy little foursome with Keith. Fuck me, how wrong could she be!

We were all to meet at the Georges V hotel in Paris, then drive down to Tangier and meet up with Mick, Marianne, Micheal Cooper and Christopher Gibbs. Simple! That trip was a nightmare! I booked all the rooms and dumped the luggage in them. Anita must have had more clothes with her than Dorothy Perkins (clothes store), bleeding feather boas, hats, the lot! I always hated carrying her bags, fucking dozens of em! The trip reminds me, excuse me digressing, but it brings something to mind that happened, the first night we spent in Paris, at a jazz club run by Tubby Hayes. During the course of the night, everyone got well pissed (drunk) and stoned. Tubby, for a laugh, asks me for all our passports. He then proceeds to stamp each one with his Green Club symbol, "Tubby Hayes Famous Jazz Club", bang right in the middle of everyone's passports. I forgot all about it for years. I'd been in and out of the country since then like a yo yo and then one day, "Excuse me sir", the customs bloke grabs me by the shoulder. "Can you explain the irregular stamp on your passport?" "Yes, its Tubby Hayes, a club in Paris", I tell him. "Well you're not supposed to do that, sir, that's defacing Her Royal Majesty's passport and it's against the law." "Well, I didn't do it" I protested, "Tubby did it!"

That was it! I'm carted off into a room and I'm given a fucking lecture, while my luggage is inspected, the whole bit. I've often wondered if any of the others ever got pulled (stopped). That would have made me laugh because they wouldn't have had the faintest idea where that stamp came from! The first bit of aggravation started the next day, when we were checking out of the Georges V. I went to sort out the bill. I was going to pay using Keith's Diners Club card, because they never seemed to have any cash on them and I was fucked if I was going to pay! The hotel manager comes out and informs me, "Sorry Sir, we don't accept Diners Club." "That's OK", I says, "I'll be back in a minute." I went to Keith's room, got his cheque book out of his bag and returned to the front desk. I said to the manager "Could you work it out in English?" "Certainly sir" he replies. So I get the bill and in those days, you could only take fifteen pounds out of England at a time and the bill was about five times that, plus I couldn't be fucked about getting Keith to sign it, so

I signed it myself "Keith Richard", handed it back and rushed back to the rooms to get everyone out quick. I told Keith what was happening and said "Come on out lively! I think we're going to get a pull." Just then the phone rang and its the concierge asking for me to come back down. "Fuck it, he's sussed it", I tell Keith and he's saying "Sort them out, we'll get in the car!" Keith and Brian were very close at this point and game for anything, so they got their bags and go heading for the car, while I report back to the front desk. "This is no good!" says the manager. He's going mad, holding Keith's cheque up. "This no good, you not only forge cheque, you forge signature!" "Well send the bill to Allen Klein", I said, "He'll pay it in American money."

"No, no, no, no, we can't do that. You have no account here. I call the police!" With that, he's straight on the blower (phone). Its now getting out of hand, because they have now seen Keith and Brian throwing the bags into the car, with Anita's feathers going everywhere. "Wait!, wait!" the manager's shouting. So I manage to calm him down by saying I'll pay the bill in dollars myself. "Very good, sir" says the manager and he puts the phone down. So I pull out a different cheque book, grab Keith out of the car and say " 'Ere, sign this". Keith signs it and I give it to the manager who recognises that it's Keith whose signed it, with his own name and begrudgingly storms off.

I turns to Keith and says "We'd better go now, get in the fucking car!". We hit the gas and "Whoosh", we're off, just as the manager and half the staff come running out of the hotel, yelling at us to stop! "Now what's up with him?" Brian asks. Keith is killing himself laughing. "Tom just palmed him off with a Lloyds Bank Regent Street cheque, written out in dollars!!"

February 27th, 1967

The journey to Toulouse. It was like Cliff Richard's "Summer Holiday". It was coming up to Brian's birthday and he was in a great mood, intent on celebrating in style. He was smoking a lot of hash and drinking heavily in the back of the car, during the journey, until he came over really ill, with what I put down to an asthma attack, combined with too much dope and booze. I mean it doesn't take Einstein to realise if you've got a bad asthma problem, you don't smoke your fucking head off in a confined space, in the back of a bleedin car!

We took him to a hospital near Toulouse, the Centre Hospitalier D' Albi in Tarn and they admitted him straight away, he looked that bad. I found the rest of us a hotel nearby and booked us in (this one took Diners Club!), called the office in London and told them our position, then went back to see how he was.

The doctor said he wanted to keep him in for a few days, so I thought "Well that's the end of the trip". But Brian called us in and in true heroic style, told us to carry on in the morning without him, saying he would catch up with us later.

he insisted until Keith agreed. I didn't want to leave him there because I was mainly there to look after him and it was his birthday after all. But Keith was paying and we were all in his car, so it was settled.

28th February, 1967

The next unexpected change of plan comes courtesy of Debbie Dixon, who the following morning, informs me she's going home four days into the trip. This is later explained away by the sight of Keith and Anita, emerging together, ever so coyly into the hotel reception. "Oy, oy" I thought, "this is getting worse!" We checked out and I rang the hospital and left a message telling Brian we would be in touch that night from our next stop, which was Valencia. Now this is a typical example of Brian. In the one breath he's told us to go on without him and in the next, I find out he's rung the office in London and told them we've fucked off and left him! So now there's only Keith and Anita left in the back. We head out

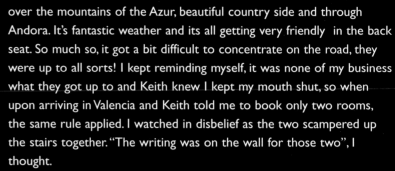

over the mountains of the Azur, beautiful country side and through Andora. It's fantastic weather and its all getting very friendly in the back seat. So much so, it got a bit difficult to concentrate on the road, they were up to all sorts! I kept reminding myself, it was none of my business what they got up to and Keith knew I kept my mouth shut, so when upon arriving in Valencia and Keith told me to book only two rooms, the same rule applied. I watched in disbelief as the two scampered up the stairs together. "The writing was on the wall for those two", I thought.

Fully expecting to see no more of Keith that night I settled in at the hotel bar and ordered the first of what I considered a well deserved drink. A couple of hours later and about half a bottle of whiskey later, suitably refreshed and ready for bed, I was pissed off to see Keith and Anita heading over to my perch.

"Lets go out Tom, know any clubs?". Keith had an insatiable appetite for everything. Anyone else would have been content to have an early night, so to speak, with Anita but with Keith, its never enough. He's always moving on to the next thing. I dragged myself away from the bar and reluctantly got back in the car, followed by Keith and Anita, giggling like a couple of naughty school kids. I managed to find a club cum bar, thankfully not too far from the hotel. We got a table and I managed to keep one eye open and sink a few more whiskeys, while Keith and Anita drank, smoked, smooched and generally larked about, looking blissfully happy with themselves.

Then came the time to leave. The bill came to me and Keith gave me his Diners Card and left without giving his signature, so I signed it "Keith Richards" again.

I began to leave, when the manager comes back and asks "Which one of you is Keith Richards?" "He is" I reply, pointing over to Keith. "Could you sign this again, please", the manager asks, pushing the bill back at me. I in turn give it to Keith and tell him to sign it. Now the manager is well and truly aggravated having seen us both sign the same name. "You wait here" he says. The next thing I know, the police are all over us, demanding our passports. "Passportee, passportee" " I haven't got them", I innocently replies," I left them at the hotel". Now Keith's getting annoyed and he's yelling at me, saying "Go and get the the fucking things!"

The police didn't speak much English, so it was obvious they were going to take us in and worry about it all later.

We were taken to the police station and interrogated for fucking hours, them speaking hardly any English and me speaking no Spanish. Anita turned out to be a right bitch, she was fluent in about a dozen languages and she could have got it sorted out a lot quicker but she didn't do a thing! Eventually, I was escorted back to the hotel at

daybreak and was allowed to get the passports. We settled the bill and were released. Keith continued giving me a bollocking for not carrying the fucking things, saying it was all my fault, never mind the fact Anita hadn't said a bleeding word!

We got back to the hotel and there was a telegram from Brian, telling Anita to go back to the hospital for him, as he was being discharged soon. I gave it to Anita and she screwed it up.

Brian, assuming we simply hadn't received it, sent another telegram, this time to the office in London, saying he felt much better and could they book him on the first available flight to Tangier. He signed off by saying he would recuperate fully in the sun. We drove down to Marbella, where we booked in, for a few nights, at this hotel, which was a bit of a regular haunt for the Stones and their ever-widening circle of beautiful people and hangers-on, so we always got well looked after; best food, best service and the most discreet staff, always ready to turn a blind eye, if you know what I mean! All in all, it was the perfect setting for the blossoming, risky love affair that I`d been witnessing in my rear view mirror, to cement itself.

March 5th, 1967.

Anita, in all her wisdom, had decided to return to Toulouse for Brian. I'd greeted the news with a familiar, shrugged acceptance and said nothing, for nothing remained beyond Anita! Both she and Keith sat silently in the back, lost in thought, staring blankly out of the windows, throughout the journey to the airport. I wanted to ask what was going on but the eerie silence told me, I'd be better off saying nothing. We saw her off and I turned to Keith hoping for an explanation. "She'll be back" was all he said and with that, he strolled purposely back to the Bentley. Keith made for miserable company for the remainder of the journey through Gibraltar and North Africa, so I was more than glad when we finally hit Tangier. Mick, Christopher Gibbs, Michael Cooper and Brion Gyson had already checked in at the El Minzah and were sitting by the pool, looking very relaxed. Keith went over to join them, while I checked us both in. I noticed that Brian was booked in a room with Anita while Keith only had a single room reservation. "This was worse than a fucking "Carry On" film, I thought.

March 14th/15th, 1967.

The first I knew of Brian's arrival in Marrakesh was the sound of his voice coming from the room along the corridor. He was screaming at Anita. He obviously knew something had gone on between her and Keith, but not to what extent. I knew he would want to grill me for what I knew, so I decided to make myself scarce. After all, Anita was the sort of bird who'd fill in the gaps for him. She enjoyed rubbing people's noses in the shit and what she didn't tell him, she'd leave to his imagination. I decided to take some holiday snaps, in order to take some of the tension out of the air. The atmosphere was so bad and anyway,

Cecil Beaton, the royal smudger (photographer), was in the hotel, taking pictures of the band. He might have needed a couple of pointers! Brian started drinking heavily, his mood getting more and more morose. It was getting late now and he was getting himself into a right state. I sat in a dark corner of the bar, out of sight, so I could keep an eye on him but he somehow managed to slip out, without me seeing him. I was still mean`t to be looking after him, so I dragged myself away from the bar and began patrolling the streets, looking for him. I soon tired of that and figured he`d make his way back eventually, and he might even have calmed down a bit, so I went back to the bar to wait. Well, he found his way back, alright, but he certainly wasn't calm. He was completely off his crust (head), staggering through the lobby, sandwiched between these two dodgy looking Berber whores, the ones that have those peculiar blue tattoo's all over them, the type made up of thousands of little blue dots. Horrible! Brian was fascinated by the tattoo's. They tattooed every part of their bodies, if you know what I mean and they don`t come cheap, those two cost Brian a fortune! They were holding Brian up and heading for Anita's room. I followed them up the stairs, trying to point out the error of his plan, but he wasn't having any of it! All hell broke loose, when they reached the room. Brian had the idea that he was going to get Anita to perform with these two birds. Anita naturally declined the offer and Brian smashed the room to bits. Anita grabbed her clothes and legged it to Keith's room, leaving Brian with these women, in amongst the wreckage. It was very symbolic! Looking at Brian, I thought "That's yer lot, mate! You`ve really blown it this time!" That moment was the beginning of the end for him and you know what, I think he knew it too!

March 16th, 1967.

This was the start of Brian's deliberate exclusion from the band. Nothing was said, but you could feel it. Every one was uncomfortable around Brian, terrible atmosphere, much, much worse than before, uptight. Keith had arranged for he and Anita to scarper (escape) and a plan was hatched for Brion Gyson to take him up the Atlas Mountains to where that tribe of Arabs played pipes and what not. Brian wanted to record them. I think he had already done a bit with them and he was anxious to go again. It's always been said that I got him out of the way, in order to work for Keith, swap loyalties, that sort of thing, but that`s not how it happened. Sure, I got on with Keith, probably the best out of them all, but I didn't manoeuvre myself into Keith's life at Brian's expense. I really cared for the boy but he really had gone too far. I was told to get him out of the way, by Keith. So I made up a story about a plane load of "News Of The World" reporters landing in Marrakesh, in order to persecute the band with more lies. I told this to Gyson and said bring him back at six. Gyson took him off and got him completely stoned with these nutters he knew, the Mejdouri Brothers! He was hardly looking out for his welfare either. No sooner had he gone, Keith and Anita were parking the car up. I asked Keith "What about when he gets back?!" "Fuck' im!" was his reply. "We're leaving the bastard here and you're driving!" So that was that! I drove the getaway car. We motored to Tangiers where we stopped for the night and got the ferry the following morning. Brian had, evidently, gone back to the hotel and found that everyone, including Mick, had checked out. That must have really hurt. I heard later that Gyson had to call a doctor in order to give him a (needle) jab, so he would sleep. He was in such a state, Gyson thought Brian would kill himself. Well, Brian had all these problems for sure, but then, didn't we all and some of mine were about to start. I'd bought a big block of hash off of a dealer called Achmed, in Tangiers, thinking it would last us on the journey home, if we was careful, but I hadn't bargained on Anita's antics! She started showing off to all the Arabs, waving her feather boas about, playing up to them, turning what was already the most conspicuous looking vehicle, travelling on the ferry, into a fucking sideshow! The Arabs are a funny lot and word soon gets around and there she was, actually drawing a fucking crowd. It was only a matter of time before the old bill (police) would get wind of us! Sure enough, I spotted these two plain-clothes coppers, lurking in the crowd. I could tell them a mile off, I just knew it! I turned to Keith and said "Listen, that's Old Bill over there and I'm holding the gear! I'm gonna dump it!" "No,no,no!", Anita pipes up, "don`t dump it!" I told her "Leave off, I'm not getting my collar felt (searched) for drugs! That`s all I need, to wind up in a nick (prison) out here!" While we were having our whispered argument, I hadn't noticed that the two suspect coppers were almost on top of us. "Quick, head for the car!" I said under my breath. That's when it became obvious they were police because they followed right after us. I couldn't get the fucking hash out of my pocket quick enough to drop it, before we had reached the car, so with Keith and Anita blocking the coppers view. I pushed the button that opened the petrol cap automatically and chucked it in and slammed it shut, with about a second to spare! I was fumbling with my keys, just as they walked to the front of the car. I put the keys back in my pocket and mumbled something about "Getting it later". Just what later meant, I'm fucked if I knew! I turned on my heels and walked away from the car. Keith and Anita had kept on walking. "Fucking hell, thanks Keith! "I thought,"did they see me or not!" They never said a word. They walked around the car and I slipped out of sight. The second we docked, we were in the car and heading for the "off" ramp. For a minute, I thought we'd got off before them and then I hear, "Pull over here! " They appeared out of nowhere, as soon as the bleedin' wheels hit dry land. We were the only car pulled over. The luggage was dragged out of the boot and it's contents were literally dumped on the floor. Our clothes were strewn everywhere. "Search them!" one of the bastards said to the other. He began to go through the clothes, picking them up as if they were diseased and throwing them on the ground, then barks at me to pick them all up! To which I replied "You fuckin' pick' em up, I ain't!" Now Keith's giving it the "Hold on, Tom, 'ole boy! They're only doing their job!", because he thinks I've dumped the hash and I'm shitting meself! Then the nightmare got worse! They took the car into a garage and drove it over a pit so they could give it a right going over. "That was it!", I thought, "I've fuckin' had it now!" I was already making a mental note of what nick life (prison) would be like! Keith was just standing

around, looking very much the harassed "Rock Star", so I thought I'd unload a bit of the worry on him. I sidled up to him and whispered in his ear that I hadn't managed to dump the gear and walked away. That's when his tone changed completely towards his interrogators. He's calling them fuckin' this and fuckin' that! All I could do was stand and watch, with me arms folded, leaning against the petrol tank of the car. Eventually, they figured they had searched the car sufficiently and we were frog-marched into separate rooms and I was strip-searched. Then as quickly as we had been hauled in, we were bundled out of these rooms and basically told to fuck off! We drove for about 15 minutes and stopped. Then Keith says "Well,we got out of that one, so you must have managed to dump it in the end. How did you do it, when we were completely fuckin` surrounded?!" "I haven't!" I replied. "What?!" Keith cried. I sprung the petrol cap and said " 'Ere we are!" Keith's face was a picture but it didn't teach him anything. All he said was "Fuckin' Groovy!!", grabbed the dope and rolled a joint!

April 5th, 1967. ARRIVAL IN BOLOGNA.
Brian turned up at the airport, tripping out of his brain. "Are you carrying?" I asked. "No,no,no" he said. I took him into the toilets and searched him. He was clean. "Where is it?" I asked, knowing he'd scored somewhere. "I've taken it man" was all he said. It turns out he'd taken 6 leapers in one hit. He was flying for 3 days. He did Milan and Rome, without even knowing he had done them!

April 6th, 1967. ROME WITH THE MOVE.
The Birmingham band, The Move, were on the bill for Rome. They had a violent stage act at the time, very destructive. Carl Wayne, the lead singer, was known for smashing up equipment and stage props like TV sets with a fireman's axe. They were definitely a big name and we got wind that they were out to upstage the Stones, who didn't use gimmicks. That wasn't the main worry, though. What worried me more was the riot police. The police in Rome classed four people standing on a street corner as a riot and didn't hold the English in very high regard at the best of times, let alone a bunch of long-haired musicians. I went to The Move's dressing room and told them "Right, you lot!! No fucking

about!! The Italians are dodgy and would love a reason to lock the lot of us up, so if you've got any tricks planned, fucking forget about it!!" It turns out The Move had set up flash bombs, and smoke bombs everywhere and were going to let them off at the end of their set, filling the stadium with smoke and scaring the horses to death. It would have definitely started a riot, because the Stones wouldn't have been able to play in the smoke. The Stones were well pissed off when they heard and wanted to sort The Move out. I hate to think what would have happened if I'd let them at each other, not that Brian would have noticed anything, he was still flying from the leapers. He went on stage and was shouting at Stu that his amp was broken. Good 'ole Stu strolled over to his amp, looked at it and said "You cunt, you never had it switched on!!"

WARSAW APRIL 13th, 1967.

We were staying at the Orbis-Europejski hotel, a right craphole but apparently the best that Warsaw had to offer. The Stones were booked for two concerts, both at the state-run Opera House, "Sala Kongresowej". They only did them out of curiosity, they certainly weren't making much, a grand, all in. Amazingly enough, two English kids came up to me, at the hotel, both from Hampstead. Their father turned out to be a Polish Jew and they were doing a year's schooling there. They both wanted tickets for the gig. It turns out that all the tickets had been given to the Communist workers under some scheme, where if they worked enough overtime, they got a ticket for their kids. There were strict instructions that the kids were forbidden to scream, stand up or shout, they could clap only! It was shocking. I took an interpreter (who we'll call Stig, as I can't remember his name) and went to the guy who was in charge, only it wasn't a guy who was in charge, it was a bird (girl), a great, big bird. I'm not kidding, she was like Arnold Schwarzenegger, fucking huge! "I want two tickets' I told Stig and he rattled off my demand. She barked back something which was obviously "no", but we went through the charade anyway. "I'm sorry, sir, you can't have them" Stig informs me. "Well, I fucking want them, tell her!" I tell Stig, "and what's more, tell her if I don't get them, the band don't go on!" which was a massive bluff, seeing as I had no authority to say such a thing. This was relayed to the monster woman and she wasn't amused. She starts shouting at Stig, telling him I can't do such a thing, to which I'm trying to shout louder, "You just watch me do it!!" She glared at me, nostrils flaring! For a minute, it was a fucking, frightening sight and then she stuffed two tickets in Stig's hand and stomped off down the corridor, like a big buffalo, snorting!

No one, including me, had told the band of the no dancing ruling, until they were actually on stage. I remember Mick sidling over to me, in the wings and saying "What's all this?!" He couldn't believe he wasn't getting a reaction. The audience was deadly silent. It was the kids outside, the real fans, who couldn't get in, that they should have been playing to.

We'd brought several boxes of Stones singles with us, with the intention of giving them away as radio competition prizes,etc. Now bearing in mind, a single in England at that time, came to about half a crown, but in Poland, it would fetch a month's wages! So I collared my new Polish mate, Stig and told him to get in the car and drive, while I grabbed these boxes of records. With Stig behind the wheel and me in the back, we drove out along the perimeter of the Square, outside the venue. I wound the windows down and started to frisbee these records out into the crowd. It went brilliantly. The kids were going absolutely berserk, grabbing at the discs and rushing the guards, trampling the barriers down. Stig stopped the car and we ran into the hotel. It was fucking mayhem, but at least the kids came away with something. Later, I was approached by a Polish reporter who had rung my room and had asked to see me in person. He said he had a proposition for me. Well, this got my natural curiosity going, so I went down to see him. I met him in the bar, naturally, and asked him what he wanted. He told me he wanted an exclusive interview with Mick, to which I told him "No way!" Now what's your proposition?!" He told me that when I went round throwing the records to the kids, the Polish authorities had set up a machine gun, high up on the front of the Opera House and had it trained on the crowd. They were loading it up and preparing to fire, just as we ran out of records. I didn't believe him at first, but then he produced two rolls of film from his pocket and

explained the photos were useless to him as he could never get them published in Poland and even if he did, he would most likely get done in (killed) for his effort! He told me he could make more money (and live a lot longer) if he got an interview with Mick, plus I could have the film. I grabbed the film and told him to follow me. I pulled Les Perrin (Stones PR man) to one side and repeated this guy's story. Les was sceptical but with his keen sense of what the pictures would be worth to Fleet Street, he agreed to gamble. Mick happily did the interview while Les and I imagined how our front-page exclusive would look back home. The only problem was getting the film out of Poland. I didn't fancy being accused of some sort of subversive behaviour, or sampling Polish prison food either. So I grabbed hold of Don Short, who was over there with us doing a feature for the "Daily Mirror" and said "Oy Don, here's a good story for ya! All you got to do is smuggle it out of here and I'll split the money with you!" Now, Don obviously wasn't made of serious Fleet Street stuff because he didn't want to know. He was all; "No,no,no,not me,no way!! I've got my feature, fuck that stuff!!" Well, I thought that's not the spirit, so when the plane was delayed, the first chance I got, I put the film into his raincoat pocket! We boarded the plane under strict scrutiny and miraculously the plane took off without us being searched. Once we were airborne, I called over to Don, " 'Ere Don, where's your raincoat?!!" "Up there" he said, pointing to the rack above his head. I got up and walked over to it and pulled the film out of the pocket. He went completely off his head! Later in England, we got the films developed and as promised, there were the machine guns, pointing at the kids and more alarmingly, at me!! I never did get them to Fleet Street because within hours of returning them to the Stones office, they mysteriously vanished.

AFTERMATH OF REDLANDS BUST. 1967

The whole of 1967 seemed like one long wait in between court appearances. Morale was at an all-time low and the music the group were making seemed half finished. The Beatles had forged ahead with their studio work, leaving The Stones looking a bit short of ideas. It was a very worrying time and I began to fear there was a very real chance of at least one of the boys, if not two, going down (to prison) for a long time and I think they thought so too. It was during this period, that I was down at Redlands, looking after Keith, while he was out on bail. Anita was away in Rome, filming "Barbarella" and he spent the whole time, moping around and ringing her up constantly. I said " 'Ere Keith, I'm fed up with sitting around here, looking at your miserable face! Why don't we fuck off to Rome?!" "Don't take the piss, Tom! You know they won't let me out of the country!" Keith said. "I've had a brainwave" I told him. "Ring Anita and tell her to send a telegram over from Roger adim (the director) saying you're wanted over there to write the film score and you have to watch the rushes." "But I'm not!" was Keith's half-hearted reply. "No one bloody knows that!!" I had to explain. I rung up Michael Havers, his lawyer and fed him what I'd cooked up, stressing the point that, by not letting Keith go, it was, in fact, losing Keith his livelihood and in view of the possibility of Keith facing a fucking big fine, "at best", the situation needed sorting out. "That's an interesting point, Tom. I'll see what I can do" was his response. We waited and waited and eventually, Havers got us into the High Court, where they miraculously agreed, providing I coughed up ten grand bail and on the condition, I went with him and guarantee personally that I'd deliver him back to face the music, on court day. We got the office to post bail and I drove Keith and Peter Howard, another of his solicitors, to the airport. "See ya in Rome!" Now I'd already broken the rules by not accompanying him on the plane, as Howard quite rightly pointed out, but he agreed to overlook it if I promised to take him with me, in the Bentley. Apparently, he'd never been to Rome. We all met up on the film set, where we were given a V.I.P tour and were invited to a special after-shoot party, organised by Jane Fonda, Vadim's missus (wife) at the time. Everyone had to bring

something to the party, so I told Keith I'd make a big hash cookie, as our contribution. I drove to a food store and bought a few boxes of cake and chocolate mix and took it back to the hotel. I followed the instructions, as best I could but it looked horrible. I'd already scored the stash, upon arrival, from one of the many contacts I'd sorted out across Europe, so I had all my ingredients and amazingly enough, when it was finally ready, it looked half-decent. I triumphantly presented my cake at the party, where Keith and Anita and a few of the cast and crew greedily tucked in. I had successfully managed to steer Peter Howard away from my concoction. It wouldn't have done to have had Keith represented by a stoned solicitor, as interesting as it sounds. Keith came up to me, at the party later and started complaining the cake wasn't having any effect. I was most put out seeing as I'd put the whole of the gear in the mix at once! I thought I must have been done and that wasn't on, when BANG! everyone was in outer space, I mean, they were gone! The actor, John Phillip-Law, who played the part of the blind angel, said to me

later "I didn't need those wings, Tom, I was flying for days without them!!" He wasn't joking. If you watch that film now, you can see how much he was out of it!

BRIAN PALASTANGA. 1967

Palastanga was the guy that took over driving Brian around, after I'd gone to work for Keith pretty much full-time. I was responsible, in a way, for the hiring of the drivers/bodyguards and I didn't always pick them well and I think he was one of those oversights on my part. I got a frantic call from Brian one day, saying I had to come round to his flat right away, it was urgent! I asked him where Palastanga was and he said "It's him I want to talk about!" I raced around there and both he and Suki were in a right state. I asked him what the problem was. "I've had my cameras nicked!" (stolen), Brian told me. "Suki said she'd left them on the window ledge and now they've vanished. They were both full of film and I have to have those films back, Tom!", Brian was pleading. I didn't like to ask what the film was of but knowing Brian, I could hazard a guess and judging by Suki's blushing, I think I had it right! It was obvious, they both suspected Palastanga, who according to Brian, was never around when he was needed anyway, but I couldn't simply go and accuse him. I left it a couple of days and then went down Palastanga's local (pub) "The Compasses", one Sunday lunch time, to see a mutual friend of our's, Elfie Boots, who was a regular drinker there. Sure enough, Elfie was there, sitting at the bar. Before I could even ask him anything, he calls me over and says, " 'Ere, that Palastanga's been a bit flash, ain't 'e?!" It turned out he'd been driving himself around in Brian's Roller (Rolls-Royce), lording it up and at the same time, he's been trying to unload (sell) a couple of cameras. Now that's too much of a coincidence, I thought, so I got on the phone and rang Palastanga and invited him down for a drink. He pulled up in Brian's Roller, just as Elfie had said and came in. I grabbed hold of him and said, "I'll ask you a question and I'll ask it only once, where are the two cameras that you were trying to knock out (sell) in here?!" He made all the usual protests of innocence, so I called Elfie over and confronted them both. "Did he (Palastanga) try and sell two cameras in 'ere?!" "Yeah, two choice (good) ones, they were!" said Elfie. Well, that was all I needed. My patience ran out and I punched Palastanga straight in the mouth, knocking all his front teeth out. I took the car keys and informed him he was now sacked.

PICKING BRIAN UP FROM PRISON.
October 31st, 1967

I went to pick Brian up from Wormwood Scrubs. What a name for a prison! It's a horrible place, a real house of horrors, I got depressed just sitting in there for an hour. Eventually, I saw Brian being escorted across the yard. He had the biggest two coppers I'd seen in my life, manacled to him either side, tugging him along. He was only a little bloke, Brian, to start with, but with those two monkeys towering over him, he seemed to visibly shrink even more. He looked a very sorry sight. He was dressed in what he called "his court suit", a dark grey pinstripe three-piece suit. He'd been told by his lawyers, to smarten himself up and to be honest, at the beginning of his court appearances, he looked very confident and together. But he went downhill fast, as it dragged on and on, they really broke him down. He looked dog-rough.

He had gone through a lot of changes, so much so, he didn't even look like Brian anymore. He looked like someone completely different. It was frightening to see the change in him. There was this picture that I had stolen of Brian being arrested outside his flat and it showed the size of these coppers that were sent to nab (arrest) him. They definitely sent the biggest they could get to physically intimidate him. They did such a good job of breaking his spirit, that when he said he'd thought about killing himself, I really believed him. His eyes had no life in them and this was all on top of Anita leaving him for Keith. Boy, he was in a bad way. That day, he walked up to me and said, "I'm really glad to see you, Tom. Can we get out of here, please?!" No-one else had bothered to see if he was O.K. I felt desperately sorry for him that day.

1968/9

BRIAN AND JIMI
January 26th 1968

Jimi invited Brian down to the studio, where the Experience were recording, to play on a track. They just wanted to jam with him initially and see how it sounded because Jimi and Brian got on great together, which I think got up Mick and Keith's nose a bit, which Brian was happy about. Anyway, Brian calls me and says "Can you pick me up and drive me down there?" I got round to him and I'm expecting him to come out with a guitar but he's standing there with this bloody great Indian sitar and all manner of other Eastern contraptions. Apparently, Jimi and Noel had heard him play this thing and wanted him to jam with the band because they were so impressed with his ability. He was really into it at the time, you see he wasn't off his crust, all of the time. They played until about five in the morning. There's meant to be this tape knocking around but I haven't heard it. Noel would probably know more. The funny thing was I took both Jimi and Brian back to Jimi's flat, so they could smoke a joint or two or three and the stuff they played together on two acoustics... Made yer hair curl! Brilliant!!

ROCK 'N' ROLL CIRCUS. 1968/69

Everyone knows the classic Jagger excuse about the film not being shown because he thought his performance wasn't up to scratch. Well, that's all bollocks (rubbish), they played great. It's got more to do with international wranglings, than anything else, but having said that, there was some genuine concern over things. Brian wasn't really pulling his weight, but for whatever reason, someone wasn't entirely happy with the finished product and it was suggested they re-shoot their section. They wanted a new location and I, merely thinking out loud, suggested the Colosseum, in Rome. "That's round, like a circus ring", I reasoned.

Mick loved the idea and I was duly dispatched to fix it up. I met up with Klein's nephew, Ronnie Schneider and worked out a deal, where I flew to Rome, greased the right palms to arrange a date for early the next year (1969). It all went like clockwork and was all set to go, until Michael Lindsay-Hogg, the director, threw a spanner in the works. "I don't fly, it's in my contract!" he told me. "Come on", I said,"I'll hold your hand!" There's nothing to it.", but it was no good, he was adamant he wouldn't fly anywhere. So that idea was dropped, which was a great shame, it would have made a brilliant spectacle and one they should still consider. Mind you, imagine the damage those fucking amps would do. They'd probably make the whole thing collapse! So that exotic location went out the window and the stinking old Marquee, on Wardour Street, was picked as an alternative. Talk about fucking "chalk and cheese!! The first attempt at a re-shoot was shot by Lion T.V and featured both the Stones and the Who. We filmed one day's worth, just prior to Christmas (1968), but it went into cans, just like the rest of it. I've never seen any of it since.

July 5th 1969 HYDE PARK.

When Brian died, everyone thought the Stones would automatically cancel the Hyde Park show. Even in the office, the word was the show couldn't possibly go ahead, but I knew Mick would never blow it out. He had turned the whole thing into a come back sort of thing and even something like Brian dying, wasn't gonna ruin his day. That' s when he had the idea of making it a tribute to Brian, or was it Charlie who said it?! Anyway, it got Mick off the hook! They rehearsed in the Beatles Apple basement studio in Savile Row. I never did see a Beatle around the joint, which I thought was odd, at the time, so there was no jamming going on, which I'd hoped for, but there you go! One Stones myth, if you can call it that, was they were driven through the park, in an armoured van. It was in fact, an old army ambulance painted green! Every Stones book I've ever read always says an armoured van.Rubbish! The guy from Blackhill, Sam Cutler, got it from an old props place we used. It was a right old flimsy thing! Another thing that's always stuck in my mind was that there was only one copper assigned to the gig. One

copper on a bike, assigned to police 200,000 people! We were so amazed, we filmed him and you can see him in the finished film. We had the Hell's Angels too, but they were a fucking joke. They weren't real Angels, not like the Americans have. These were Micky Mouse Angels. I didn't even see their motorbikes. They must have all come up on the bus. Altamont had real angels, we had ton-up Teddy Boys from Penge!. The Stones were very nervous. They hadn't played in front of a crowd for over a year and this crowd was huge, so there wasn't much hell-raising going on, at the Londonderry Hotel. The stage had this huge blown-up picture, from "Beggars Banquet", of Brian pissed out of his head, in the background. I didn't notice it until I walked onstage with the band. It made me laugh. It wasn't the best picture to remember him by, but funnily enough, that's how I remember him and there he was, looking down at the stage, pissed and laughing at the others. He was right, too, because they sounded awful, I'm afraid! The amazing thing after the gig was the park being left spotless! We gave out hundreds of black bin bags and asked the crowd to put all their rubbish in them and amazingly, they did! Driving back from the hotel, I saw this huge pile of bin bags in the centre of the park. I thought the whole day went really well, considering Brian had just died and the band were cut up about it, despite what anyone might say. A lot of people found it came as no surprise, but I think secretly, every one thought Brian would go on like that forever. Others have said he was getting himself together at the end, but that's bollocks. He honestly didn't have a chance, he was too far gone. I saw him at the end and he wasn't getting any better. He was invited to Hyde Park and I told him so, but all he said was "Fuck 'em. I bet I'm the only one who has to pay!" The whole thing with the poem and the butterflies was because I don't think Mick was capable of expressing his feelings about what had happened. So it was an easy way of saying something profound and to use someone else's words to do it. Quite clever. Bollocks, but clever!! Here again, the Stones myth machine said the band let those poor butterflies, suffocate in the heat, inside these boxes and when they were opened, most of them were dead. It was really because one of the Hell's Angels fell over pissed and crushed a box full!

KLEIN AND KEYLOCK. 1969

Every story concerning Allen Klein is legendary but I only ever dealt with him directly once. Keith had his heart set on a house in London. Cheyne Walk, in Chelsea to be exact. Mick already had one there, so now Keith wants one! Anyway, he needed 25 grand for a deposit, which was a fucking lot of money back then. It's still a lot now, but imagine that, in the '60s and for just a deposit! Keith had sent dozens of telexes to Klein, in New York, who was ignoring them because he didn't want to free up funds. He couldn't be reached and wouldn't return any of Keith's calls. Keith was getting really pissed off because some Labour M.P had put in a bid for the same house, which made matters worse, in Keith's

eyes. He had a great mistrust of any politician and Labour were stinging everyone, at the time, with these tax policies, so this was now personal. Keith started in on me, "Fucking get it together, Tom, sort this shit out!!" "I can't do anything if Klein ignores every telex and phone call we make, can I?!!" Keith hit the roof, "Get your fuckin' arse over there and get it sorted, Tom. I don't care how, just sort it!!" Weighing up the situation, I realised I had no other choice but to go over to see Klein personally. I arrived in New York, a little worse for wear and marched straight in to his offices. I was pissed off by now too, and I wanted him to know it. I leaned menacingly over the desk of his personal assistant, who was very surprised to see me. "What are you doing here?!" she kept saying. "I want some money for Keith!" "But Mr. Klein is out!" "That's bullshit!!" I roared. Klein had a security system fitted, with a button under the assistant's desk, that she had to press in order to reach his inner sanctum. I leaned over, found the button and pressed it. The door clicked open, I vaulted over her desk and I bolted towards it! Bingo, I was in, face-to-face, with Klein. I could hear his assistant flapping around outside: "Stop, Mr Keylock!!, you can't…"etc, etc, as the door clicked shut behind me. I thought to myself, I can!! I explained to Klein about Keith and told him, as patiently as I could, that I wasn't leaving until I got his money. "I'm going to sit here, opposite you, day and night, listening to every call you make until you give me it!!" This stand-off lasted about an hour, until he gave in and handed over the money. I got a cab straight to the airport and was back in London an hour before Keith would've lost the house, as it turns out!

AFTER THOUGHT

That was one of the last things I did for Keith or any of the Stones. I was tired and needed a break, or so I thought. What I realised later, was that I needed a complete change. I had to get my personal life in order. I had spent practically every day living with the band and had neglected my own family. I'd missed my eldest daughters grow up and we were expecting my youngest, Alison. I was determined I wouldn't make the same mistake with her childhood.

A friend of mine in New York had made me an offer to work on some film projects and I decided to go to the States, to see if it was viable. As it turned out, I was offered the job as producer on the music film, 'Supershow', which starred, amongst others Buddy Guy, Colosseum, Eric Clapton and Led Zeppelin, in one of their earliest film appearances. It seemed like a sensible job, so I rang Keith and said "I'm off, I've had enough. I need to do something for myself." I don't think he ever forgave me, in a funny way. A little while later, he rang me in New York and asked if I would come back, and I told him I couldn't. I think he took that as a personal slight, me dropping him. But it was the right job for me, and I've still got a great family around me, which I doubt would have been the case if I'd have stayed with the Stones!

Keith and Charlie at the 2nd Annual Isle of Wight Pop Festival with (top) Michael Cooper and Robert Fraser, and (bottom) Tony King. August 16th 1969

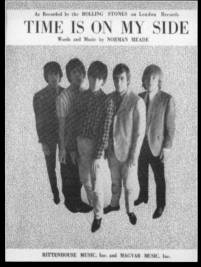

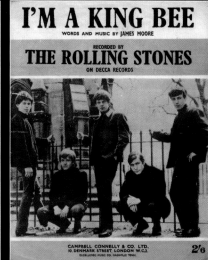

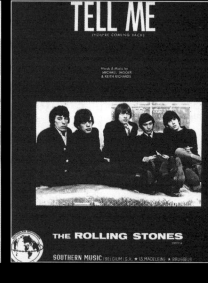

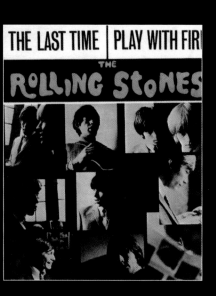

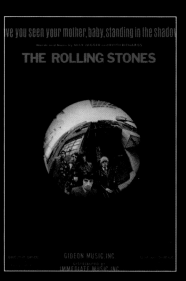

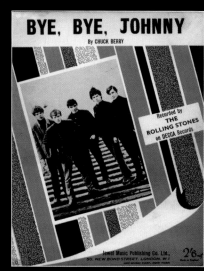

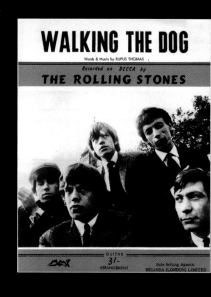

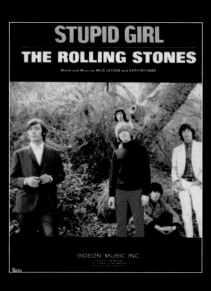

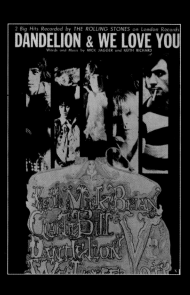

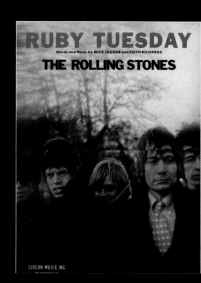

ODEON, CHELTENHAM

General Manager - E. A. GISLINGHAM
Tel. 24081

6.30 THURS., 10th SEPT. 8.45

For One
Day Only

ON THE STAGE
(In place of the usual film performance)

For One
Day Only

ROBERT STIGWOOD ASSOCIATES LTD PRESENTS—

The Sensational ROLLING STONES

INEZ and CHARLIE FOXX

MIKE BERRY and The Innocents

SIMON SCOTT with The LE ROYS

your Compere
DON SPENCER

The MOJOS

SEATS

Stalls 10/6 8/6 7/6

Circle 10/6 8/6 6/6

To The Box Office, Odeon, Cheltenham (Advance booking from Mon., Aug. 24th at 10.30 a.m.) The Rolling Stones
Please forward_____ _____ Seats at _____ for the 6.30/8.45 performance on Thursday, 10th September
          I enclose stamped addressed envelope and P.O./Cheque value_____
NAME _____
ADDRESS _____

Hastings Print—— Company, Portland Place, Hastings. Telephone Hastings 2450.

Above: A rare handbill for a show in Brian's hometown, 1964.

WORLD'S POP STARS IN COLOUR COLOUR COLOUR

Fabulous

11 KING SIZE FULL COLOUR PIN-UPS
MERSEYS STONES APPLEJACKS
PLUS NEW FACES

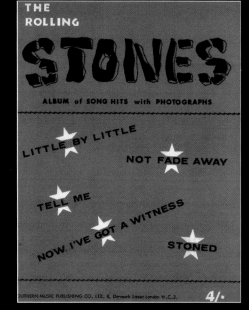

THE ROLLING STONES

ALBUM of SONG HITS with PHOTOGRAPHS

LITTLE BY LITTLE

NOT FADE AWAY

TELL ME

NOW, I'VE GOT A WITNESS

STONED

SOUTHERN MUSIC PUBLISHING CO. LTD. 8, Denmark Street London W.C.2.

4/-

WORLD'S POP STARS IN COLOUR COLOUR COLOUR

Fabulous
AT HOME
KING SIZE FULL COLOUR PIN-UPS OF
BILL WYMAN ● SPENCER DAVIS GROUP ● JOHN LENNON
PLUS ●●● ROBERT VAUGHN ● JULIE FELIX ● P. J. PROBY
●●● 1st RYAN BROS GIANT PIC—THIS WEEK BARRY
ALSO EXCLUSIVE COLOUR OF MARIANNE & HER BABY 4 READERS MUST WIN VISIT TO SMALL FACES' HOME

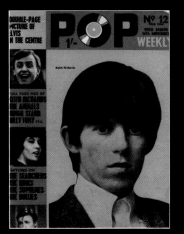

POP WEEKLY
No. 12

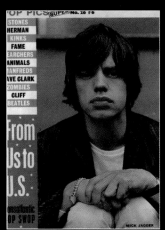

STONES
HERMAN
KINKS
FAME
SEARCHERS
ANIMALS
MANFREDS
DAVE CLARK
ZOMBIES
CLIFF
BEATLES

From Us to U.S.

MICK JAGGER

Valentine POP '67 SPECIAL

DISCS
TV
FILMS

HOW TO SELL YOUR SONG

BEAT INSTRUMENTAL

MONTHLY 2/6   APR No.

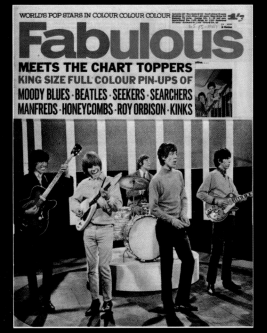

WORLD'S POP STARS IN COLOUR COLOUR COLOUR

Fabulous
MEETS THE CHART TOPPERS
KING SIZE FULL COLOUR PIN-UPS OF
MOODY BLUES · BEATLES · SEEKERS · SEARCHERS
MANFREDS · HONEYCOMBS · ROY ORBISON · KINKS

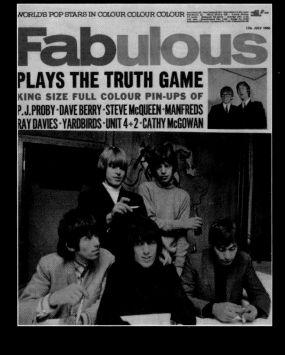

WORLD'S POP STARS IN COLOUR COLOUR COLOUR

Fabulous
PLAYS THE TRUTH GAME
KING SIZE FULL COLOUR PIN-UPS OF
P. J. PROBY · DAVE BERRY · STEVE McQUEEN · MANFREDS
RAY DAVIES · YARDBIRDS · UNIT 4+2 · CATHY McGOWAN

WORLD'S POP STARS IN COLOUR COLOUR COLOUR

Fabulous
ON A SUMMER SPREE
11 KING SIZE FULL COLOUR PIN-UPS
HOLLIES STONES MOJOS HAYLEY ETC

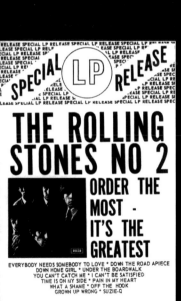

BRIAN JONES

MICK

BILL WYMAN

CHARLIE WATTS

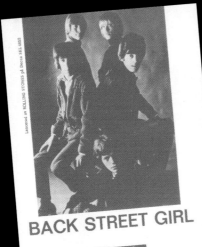

BACK STREET GIRL

WESTINS
NOT-KLUBB

WESTINS
NOT-KLUBB

PLEASE GO HOME

SCHLAGERKLUBBEN

**COOL CALM
AND COLLECTED**

PAINT IT, BLACK

RECORDED BY THE ROLLING STONES ON DECCA

MIRAGE MUSIC LTD.

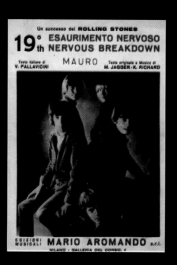

Un successo dei ROLLING STONES

**19º ESAURIMENTO NERVOSO
th NERVOUS BREAKDOWN**

Testo italiano di
V. PALLAVICINI

MAURO

Testo originale e Musica di
M. JAGGER - K. RICHARD

MARIO AROMANDO s.r.l.
MILANO - GALLERIA DEL CORSO, 4

pop FOTO
bee gees

GRATIS

SHOES

John Smith presents

The Rolling Stones

Little Red Rooster

Words and Music by
WILLIE DIXON

Recorded by
THE
ROLLING STONES
on DECCA Records

Jewel Music Publishing Co., Ltd.

2/6

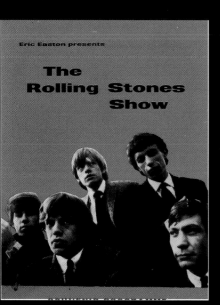

Eric Easton presents

The Rolling Stones Show

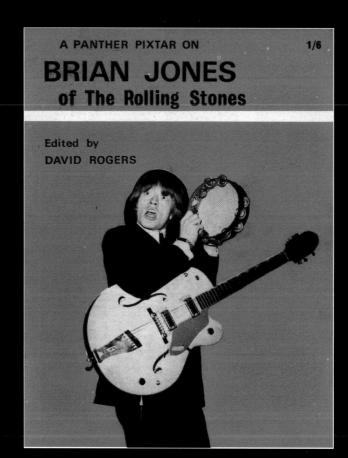

A PANTHER PIXTAR ON   1/6

BRIAN JONES
of The Rolling Stones

Edited by
DAVID ROGERS

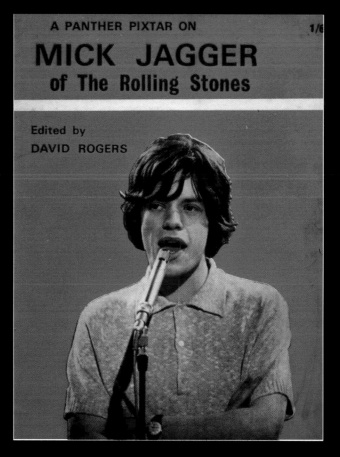

A PANTHER PIXTAR ON   1/6

MICK JAGGER
of The Rolling Stones

Edited by
DAVID ROGERS

YOU BETTER MOVE ON
WORDS AND MUSIC BY ARTHUR ALEXANDER

RECORDED BY
THE ROLLING STONES
ON DECCA RECORD D F E 8560

DOMINION MUSIC CO. LTD.

Get Your Kicks On
"ROUTE 66!..."
by BOB TROUP

RECORDED BY
THE ROLLING STONES on DECCA

EDWIN H. MORRIS & CO., LTD.

STREET FIGHTING MAN

Recorded by THE ROLLING STONES on Decca F 12952

WESTINS
NOT-KLUBB

NOT FADE AWAY
By CHARLES HARDIN & NORMAN PETTY

Recorded on DECCA F11845 by
THE ROLLING STONES

SOUTHERN MUSIC PUBLISHING CO., LTD., 8, Denmark Street, London, W.C.2.   2/6

THE ROLLING STONES DISCOGRAPHY 1963 - 1969.
U.K SINGLES
"Come On"/ "I Want To Be Loved", June 7th 1963. Decca F11675.
"Poison Ivy"/ "Fortune Teller", August 28th 1963. Decca F11742.(Release cancelled).
"I Wanna Be Your Man"/ "Stoned", November 1st 1963. Decca F11764.(Initial copies had B-side mis-spelt as "Stones").
"Not Fade Away"/ "Little By Little", February 21st 1964. Decca F11845.
"It's All Over Now"/ "Good Times,Bad Times", June 26th 1964. Decca F11934.
"Little Red Rooster"/ "Off The Hook", November 13th 1964. Decca F12014.
"The Last Time"/ "Play With Fire", February 26th 1965. Decca F12104.
"(I Can't Get No) Satisfaction"/ "The Under Assistant West Coast Promotion Man", July 1965.Decca F12220 - release cancelled.
"(I Can't Get No) Satisfaction"/ "The Spider And The Fly", August 20th 1965. Decca F12220.
"Get Off Of My Cloud"/ "The Singer Not The Song", October 22nd 1965. Decca F12263.
"19th Nervous Breakdown"/ "As Tears Go By", February 4th 1966. Decca F12331.
"Paint It,Black"/ "Long Long While", May 13th 1966. Decca F12395.
"Have You Seen Your Mother,Baby,Standing In The Shadow?"/ "Who's Driving Your Plane?", September 23rd 1966. Decca F12497.
"Let's Spend The Night Together"/ "Ruby Tuesday", January 13th 1967. Decca F12456.
"We Love You"/ "Dandelion", August 18th 1967. Decca F12654.
"Jumpin' Jack Flash"/ "Child Of The Moon", May 25th 1968. Decca F12782.
"Honky Tonk Women"/ "You Can't Always Get What You Want", July 4th 1969. Decca F12952.

U.K E.P's
"THE ROLLING STONES", January 17th 1964.Decca DFE 8560.
A:"Bye Bye Johnny"/ "Money"
B:"You Better Move On"/ "Poison Ivy".
"FIVE BY FIVE", August 14th 1964.Decca DFE 8590.
A:"If You Need Me"/ "Empty Heart"/ "2120 South Michigan Avenue"
B:"Confessin' The Blues"/ "Around And Around".
"GOT LIVE IF YOU WANT IT!", June 11th 1965.Decca DFE 8620.
A:"We Want The Stones"/ "Everybody Needs Somebody To Love" - "Pain In My Heart"/ "Route 66"
B:"I'm Movin' On"/ "I'm Alright".

U.K ALBUM'S
"THE ROLLING STONES", April 26th 1964. Decca LK 4605 (mono).
A:"Route 66"/ "I Just Wanna Make Love To You"/ "Honest I Do"/ "I Need You Baby*"/ "Now I've Got A Witness (Like Uncle Phil And Uncle Gene)"/ "Little By Little"
B:"I'm A King Bee"/ "Carol"/ "Tell Me+"/ "Can I Get A Witness"/ "You Can Make It If You Try"/ "Walking The Dog".
N.B:First pressings listed * as "Mona" and featured a 2:52 version of + ,which was hastily withdrawn.
"THE ROLLING STONES NO.2", January 15th 1965.Decca LK 4661 (mono).
A:"Everybody Needs Somebody To Love"/ "Down Home Girl"/ "You Can't Catch Me"/ "What A Shame"/ "Grown Up Wrong".
B:"Down The Road Apiece"/ "Under The Boardwalk"/ "I Can't Be Satisfied"/ "Pain In My Heart"/ "Off The Hook"/ "Susie Q".
N.B:First pressings had Andrew Oldham's potentially offending sleeve note included:"This is the Stones new disc within.Cast deep in your pockets for loot to buy this disc of groovies and fancy words.If you don't have the bread,see that blind man, knock him on the head,steal his wallet and lo and behold, you have the loot, if you put in the boot, good, another one sold!".
"OUT OF OUR HEADS", September 24th 1965. Decca LK 4733 (mono).SKL 4733 (stereo).
A:"She Said Yeah"/ "Mercy Mercy"/ "Hitch Hike"/ "That's How Strong My Love Is"/ "Good Times"/ "Gotta Get Away"
B: "Talkin' 'Bout You"/ "Cry To Me"/ "Oh Baby (We Got A Good Thing Goin')"/ "Heart Of Stone"/ "The Under Assistant West Coast Promotion Man"/ "I'm Free".
"AFTERMATH", April 15th 1966. Decca LK 4786 (mono).SKL 4786 (stereo).
A:"Mother's Little Helper"/ "Stupid Girl"/ "Lady Jane"/ "Under My Thumb"/ "Doncha Bother Me"/ "Goin'Home"
B:"Flight 505"/ "High And Dry"/ "Out Of Time"/ "It's Not Easy"/ "I Am Waiting"/ "Take It Or Leave It"/ "Think"/ "What To Do".
"BIG HITS (HIGH TIDE AND GREEN GRASS)",November 4th 1966. Decca TXL 101 (mono).TXS 101 (stereo).
A:"Have You Seen Your Mother,Baby,Standing In The Shadow?"/ "Paint It Black"/ "It's All Over Now"/ "The Last Time"/ "Heart Of Stone"/ "Not Fade Away"/ "Come On"
B:"(I Can't Get No) Satisfaction"/ "Get Off Of My Cloud"/ "As Tears Go By"/ "19th Nervous Breakdown"/ "Lady Jane"/ "Time Is On My Side"/ "Little Red Rooster".
"BETWEEN THE BUTTONS", January 20th 1967. Decca LK 4852 (mono).SKL

4852 (stereo).
A:"Yesterday's Papers"/ "My Obsession"/ "Back Street Girl"/ "Connection"/ "She Smiled Sweetly"/ "Cool Calm And Collected"
B:"All Sold Out"/ "Please Go Home"/ "Who's Been Sleeping Here"/ "Complicated"/ "Miss Amanda Jones"/ "Something Happened To Me Yesterday".
"THEIR SATANIC MAJESTIES REQUEST", December 8th 1967. Decca TXL 103 (mono).TXS 103 (stereo).
A:"Sing This All Together"/ "Citadel"/ "In Another Land"/ "2000 Man"/ "Sing This All Together (See What Happens)"
B:"She's A Rainbow"/ "The Lantern"/ "Gomper"/ "2000 Light Years From Home"/ "On With The Show".
"BEGGARS BANQUET", December 5th 1968. Decca LK 4955 (mono).SKL 4955 (stereo).
A;"Sympathy For The Devil"/ "No Expectations"/ "Dear Doctor"/ "Parachute Woman"/ "Jigsaw Puzzle"
B:"Street Fighting Man"/ "Prodigal Son"/ "Stray Cat Blues"/ "Factory Girl"/ "Salt Of The Earth".
"THROUGH THE PAST DARKLY (BIG HITS VOL.2)", September 12th 1969.Decca Lk 5019 (mono).SKL 5019 (stereo).
A:"Jumping Jack Flash"/ "Mother's Little Helper"/ "2000 Light Years From Home"/ "Let's Spend The Night Together"/ "You Better Move On"/ "We Love You"
B:"Street Fighting Man"/ "She's A Rainbow"/ "Ruby Tuesday"/ "Dandelion"/ "Sittin' On A Fence"/ "Honky Tonk Women".
"THE PROMOTIONAL ALBUM", November 28th 1969. Decca RSM 1 (stereo) (UK). London RSD 1 (USA).
A:"Route 66"/ "Walking The Dog"/ "Around And Around"/ "Everybody Needs Somebody To Love"/ "Off The Hook"/ "Susie Q"/ "I'm Free"
B:"She Said Yeah"/ "Under My Thumb"/ "Stupid Girl"/ "2000 Man"/ "Sympathy For The Devil"/ "Prodigal Son"/ "Love In Vain".
N.B Limited release of 200 copies, distributed to radio stations.
"LET IT BLEED", December 5th 1969. Decca LK 5025 (mono).SKL 5025 (stereo).
A:"Gimme Shelter"/ "Love In Vain"/ "Country Honk"/ "Live With Me"/ "Let It Bleed"
B:"Midnight Rambler"/ "You Got The Silver"/ "Monkey Man"/ "You Can't Always Get What You Want".

U.S SINGLES
"I Wanna Be Your Man" / "Come On", January 1964. (release cancelled).
"Not Fade Away" / "Stoned",February 1964. (release cancelled).
"Not Fade Away" / "I Wanna Be Your Man", March 7th 1964. London 9657.
"Tell Me" / "I Just Wanna Make Love To You", June 6th 1964. London 9682.
"It's All Over Now" / "Good Times, Bad Times", July 25th 1964. London 9687.
"Time Is On My Side" / "Congratulations", September 26th 1964. London 9708.
"Heart Of Stone" / "What A Shame", December 19th 1964. London 9725.
"The Last Time" / "Play With Fire", March 13th 1965. London 9741.
"(I Can't Get No) Satisfaction" / "The Under Assistant West Coast Promotion Man", May 29th 1965. London 9766.
"Get Off Of My Cloud" / "I'm Free", September 25th 1965. London 9792.
"As Tears Go By" / "Gotta Get Away", December 18th 1965. London 9808.
"19th Nervous Breakdown" / "Sad Day", February 12th 1966. London 9823.
"Paint It Black" / "Stupid Girl", May 7th 1966. London 901.
"Mother's Little Helper" / "Lady Jane", July 2nd 1966. London 902.
"Have You Seen Your Mother,Baby,Standing In The Shadow?" / "Who's Driving Your Plane?", September 24th 1966. London 903.
"Ruby Tuesday" / "Let's Spend The Night Together", January 14th 1967. London 904.
"We Love You"/ "Dandelion", September 2nd 1967. London 905.
"In Another Land" (a 2:48 edit, credited to "Bill Wyman")/ "The Lantern", November 25th 1967. London 907.
"She's A Rainbow"/ "2000 Light Years From Home", December 9th 1967. London 906.
"Jumpin' Jack Flash" / "Child Of The Moon", June 1st 1968. London 908.
"Street Fighting Man"/ "No Expectations", August 31st 1968. London 909.
"Honky Tonk Women"/ "You Can't Always Get What You Want", July 5th 1969. London 910.

U.S ALBUMS
"ENGLAND'S NEWEST HITMAKERS-THE ROLLING STONES", May 30th 1964. London LL 3375 (mono). PS 375 (stereo).
A:"Not Fade Away"/ "Route 66"/ "I Just Wanna Make Love To You"/ "Honest I Do"/ "Now I've Got A Witness (Like Uncle Phil And Uncle Gene)"/ "Little By Little"
B:"I'm A King Bee"/ "Carol"/ "Tell Me"/ "Can I Get A Witness"/ "You Can Make It If You Try"/ "Walking The Dog".
"12 X 5", October 17th 1964.London LL 3402 (mono). PS 402 (stereo).
A:"Around And Around"/ "Confessin' The Blues"/ "Empty Heart"/ "Time Is On My Side"/ "Good Times,Bad Times"/ "It's All Over Now"
B:"2120 South Michigan Avenue"/ "Under The Boardwalk"/ "Congratulations"/ "Grown Up Wrong"/ "If You Need Me"/ "Susie Q".
"THE ROLLING STONES NOW!", February 13th 1965. London LL 3420 (mono).PS 420 (stereo).

A:"Everybody Needs Somebody To Love*"/ "Down Home Girl"/ "You Can't Catch Me"/ "Heart Of Stone"/ "What A Shame"/ "Mona (I Need You Baby)"
B:"Down The Road Apiece"/ "Off The Hook"/ "Pain In My Heart"/ "Oh Baby (We Got A Good Thing Goin')"/"
"Little Red Rooster"/ "Surprise,Surprise".
N.B:* was a studio run-through, issued by mistake.
"OUT OF OUR HEADS", July 31st 1965. London LL 3429 (mono). PS 429 (stereo).
A:"Mercy Mercy"/ "Hitch Hike"/ "The Last Time"/ "That's How Strong My Love Is"/ "Good Times"/ "I'm Alright"
B:"(I Can't Get No) Satisfaction"/ "Cry To Me"/ "The Under Assistant West Coast Promotion Man"/ "Play With Fire"/ "The Spider And The Fly"/ "One More Try".
"DECEMBER'S CHILDREN (AND EVERYBODY'S)", December 4th 1965. London LL 3451 (mono).PS 451 (stereo).
A:"She Said Yeah"/ "Talkin' 'Bout You"/ "You Better Move On"/ "Look What You've Done"/ "The Singer Not The Song"/ "Route 66"
B:"Get Off Of My Cloud"/ "I'm Free"/ "As Tears Go By"/ "Gotta Get Away"/ "Blue Turns To GreY"/ "I'm Moving On".
"BIG HITS (HIGH TIDE AND GREEN GRASS)", March 26th 1966. London NP 1 (mono).NPS 1 (stereo).
A:"(I Can't Get No) Satisfaction"/ "The Last Time"/ "As Tears Go By"/ "Time Is On My Side"/ "It's All Over Now"/ "Tell Me"
B:"19th Nervous Breakdown"/ "Heart Of Stone"/ "Get Off Of My Cloud"/ "Not Fade Away"/ "Good Times,Bad Times"/ "Play With Fire"
"AFTERMATH", July 2nd 1966. London LL 3476 (mono).PS 476 (stereo).
A:"Paint It Black"/ "Stupid Girl"/ "Lady Jane"/ "Under My Thumb"/ "Doncha Bother Me"/ "Think"
B:"Flight 505"/ "High And Dry"/ "It's Not Easy"/ "I Am Waiting"/ "Goin' Home".
"GOT LIVE IF YOU WANT IT!", December 10th 1966. London LL 3493 (mono).PS 493 (stereo).
A:"Under My Thumb"/ "Get Off Of My Cloud"/ "Lady Jane"/ "Not Fade Away"/ "I've Been Loving You Too Long"/ "Fortune Teller"
B:"The Last Time"/ "19th Nervous Breakdown"/ "Time Is On My Side"/ "I'm Alright"/ "Have You Seen Your Mother,Baby,Standing In The Shadow?" / "(I Can't Get No) Satisfaction".
"BETWEEN THE BUTTONS", February 11th 1967. London LL 3499 (mono).PS 499 (stereo).
A:"Let's Spend The Night Together"/ "Yesterday's Papers"/ "Ruby Tuesday"/ "Connection"/ "She Smiled Sweetly"/ "Cool,Calm And Collected".
B:"All Sold Out"/ "My Obsession"/ "Who's Been Sleeping Here"/ "Complicated"/ "Miss Amanda Jones"/ "Something Happened To Me Yesterday".
"FLOWERS", July 15th 1967. London LL 3509 (mono). PS 509 (stereo).
A:"Ruby Tuesday"/ "Have You Seen Your Mother,Baby,Standing In The Shadow?"/ "Let's Spend The Night Together"/ "Lady Jane"/ "Out Of Time" (edited)/ "My Girl"
B:"Back Street Girl"/ "Please Go Home"/ "Mother's Little Helper"/ "Take It Or Leave It"/ "Ride On Baby"/ "Sittin' On A Fence".
"THEIR SATANIC MAJESTIES REQUEST", November 25th 1967. London NP 2 (mono).NPS 2 (stereo).
-Tracks as per U.K release-.
"BEGGARS BANQUET", November 23rd 1968. London PS 539 (stereo).
-Tracks as per U.K release-.
"THROUGH THE PAST DARKLY (BIG HITS VOL.2)", September 13th 1969. London NPS 3 (stereo).
A:"Paint It Black" / "Ruby Tuesday" / "She's A Rainbow"/ "Jumping Jack Flash"/ "Mother's Little Helper"/ "Let's Spend The Night Together"
B:"Honky Tonk Women"/ "Dandelion"/ "2000 Light Years From Home"/ "Have You Seen Your Mother, Baby, Standing In The Shadow?" / "Street Fighting Man".
"LET IT BLEED", November 29th 1969. London NPS 4 (stereo).
-Tracks as per U.K release-.

IMPORTANT COMPILATIONS 1963 - 1969
"THANK YOUR LUCKY STARS Vol.Two", September 27th 1963. Decca LK 4554 (mono) - features "Come On".
"READY STEADY GO!", January 10th 1964. Decca LK 4577 (mono) - features "Come On" and "I Wanna Be Your Man".
"SATURDAY CLUB", February 7th 1964. Decca LK 4583 (mono) - features "Poison Ivy" and "Fortune Teller" (originally scheduled for release as Decca 45 F11742).
"FOURTEEN", May 21st 1965. Decca LK 4695 (mono) - features "Surprise Surprise".
"BLUES ANYTIME Vol. One", October 1968. Immediate IMLP 014 (mono). The first in a series of British blues compilations, featuring artists loosely affiliated to Immediate Records. The sleeve notes list an ad-hoc line-up, consisting:- Eric Clapton and Jimmy Page (guitars), Mick Jagger (harp), Ian Stewart (piano), Bill Wyman (bass) and Chris Winters (drums), performing on the tracks (credited to Clapton/Page):- "Snake Drive", "Tribute To Elmore" and "West Coast Idea". Of the three, judging by the aural evidence, only the latter appears to have any alleged Stones connection, hence it's non-inclusion in the book's main chronology.

PHOTOGRAPHIC ACKNOWLEDGMENTS

Pages 3, 32, 42-44, 69, 72, 75-76, 82, 118-119, 128, 133, 143, 168, 196, 213 - David Wedgbury.

Pages 7, 12, 35, 53, 54, 56, 73, 78, 131, 136-137, 164, 172, 189, 205 (Andrew Sacks), 206 (Joe Sia), 215, (top & middle) 240, Tony Gale/Pictorial Press.

Pages 5, 13 - Rex Features.

Pages 30, 68, 135 (top), 160, 168, 183, 202 - Syndication International.

Pages 31, 36, 52, 64, 83, 98-99 (Glenn A. Baker), 121, 130, 139, 156-157, 198, 201, 218 (Glenn A. Baker) - Redfern's.

Pages 38, 80, 103, 105 - Marc Sharratt.

Pages 41, 57, 178, 208 - Associated Newspapers Ltd.

Page 45 - Roz Fleetwood.

Pages 46-50, 58, 65-66, 89, 148 - Peter Stuart.

Pages 59-61 - Dawn Malloy.

Pages 62, 91 (left), 92, 125 (top), 146 (top), 152, 154, 155 (left), 158, 160, 162 (bottom), 165, 170 (top right), 174 (top), 179, 182, 185 (right), 194, 212 - Press Association Ltd.

Page 70 - Julian Allison.

Page 84 - Dave Hogan.

Page 85 - West Australian Newspapers Ltd.

Pages 87, 106-107, 129, 141-142, 144, 146 (bottom), 147, 149, 155 (right), 162 (top left), 171, 197, 211, 214, 215 (bottom), 217, 219, 221-230 - Tom Keylock.

Pages 90, 114 - Barrie Wentzell.

Pages 95, 112 - Dezo Hoffman.

Pages 96 (top), 135 (bottom) - The Scotsman Publications Ltd.

Page 96 (bottom) - James Murchison.

Page 127 - Topham Picture Point.

Page 151 - United Press International (U.K) Ltd.

Page 153 - Piotr Kaczkowski.

Page 170 (bottom) - Kathy Etchingham.

Page 173 - Douglas McKenzie.

Page 174 (bottom) - Cupid Productions Ltd.

Pages 184, 186-187 - Doug McLauchlan.

Pages 199 (bottom), 210 - S.K.R Photos International.

Page 199 (top) - Alec Byrne Photography.

Page 209 - Central Press Photos Ltd.

Page 231 - Ted Tuksa.

To be Continued